STRETCHING
TURBO C

D. Tolbert

KENT PORTER

STRETCHING TURBO C

BRADY
New York

BRADY

Simon & Schuster, Inc.
Gulf + Western Building
One Gulf + Western Plaza
New York, NY 10023

DISTRIBUTED BY PRENTICE HALL TRADE

Manufactured in the United States of America

1 2 3 4 5 6 7 8 9 10

Library of Congress Cataloging-in-Publication Data
Porter, Kent.
    Stretching Turbo C / Kent Porter.
        p.   cm.

    Bibliography: p.
    Includes index.
    1. C (Computer program language)   2. Turbo C (Computer program)
I. Title.
QA76.73.C15P675   1989
005.26 — dc19   88–38997
    ISBN 0–13–852781–4   CIP

CONTENTS

PREFACE

This is a book for programmers who already write in C and who want to know more about how to use DOS in general and Turbo C in particular. If you're new to C, you need an introductory book right now and this one later.

This book proceeds from the assumption that you're fairly fluent in C, and that if you haven't worked with Turbo C before, you're intelligent enough to read the manuals and figure out how to work the product. Therefore, we don't discuss the Turbo C programming environment at all, and we spend very little ink and paper explaining basic concepts of the language. Nor do we restate what's in the Turbo C manuals; you can read them at no additional cost, since they come with the product. This book is not surrogate documentation for a pirated copy of Turbo C. Rather, it interacts with and complements the official documentation.

Software manuals tell how to use the product—which buttons to push, how to compile, what features and built-in capabilities are available—but not what to do with it. They assume that you know intuitively how to apply the product and all its goodies to your software projects.

But probably you don't. That's where guys like me make a living with books like this one. A software product manual is like the owner's guide for a radial-arm saw; it tells you how to use the saw, but not how to build a house. If you want to build a house, you have to buy another book that tells how to apply the saw. This book tells how to apply the software in building applications. In its turn, it assumes that you have the basic language skills analogous to carpentry skills, such as driving nails and dropping a plumb line and reading blueprints.

Someone once asked me what I was writing, and I said, "I'm writing a book that takes people competent in basic C to a fairly advanced level." I stand by that as the objective for this book, and I hope the book does that for you. It was never my intention to discuss every detail and pimple of Turbo C, every function and option and bug and data structure and #include file and possible usage. Instead, the thrust throughout has been to give you insights into the application of this remarkably supple C language implementation to the problems that confront programmers as they develop advanced software, especially for DOS-based machines.

That being the case, I have deliberately skirted around some of the obscure corners of C as implemented in the Borland product. Nowhere in this book (except here) will you find a mention of **ssignal()/gsignal()**, **ioctl()**, **setjmp()/longjmp()**, and other such oddities. That's not to say they're unimportant;

perhaps they are for your application. If so, maybe you need yet another book to show you how to use them, or maybe the in-depth treatment of the subjects covered here will give you the broadened insights to apply topics not specifically discussed to your needs.

The benefit of a book like this is that it not only provides specific techniques and tools, but that it increases your understanding of the language as a whole and stimulates your imagination. A book that purports to cover every application of every feature of Turbo C or any other language is either a superficial restatement of the documentation, or else so ambitious as to be unaffordable, and probably unwritable as well. The emphasis has instead been on providing workable solutions to common programming issues.

So what does the book cover? Here's a sampling:

- Part I furnishes programming techniques for working with disks, files, directories and subdirectories, volume labels, and random-access files up to the level of indexing and cross-referencing records.
- Part II deals with the user interface, working from the lowest level of the ROM BIOS through windowing and display management to the keyboard. Much of this part is devoted to developing menus and pop-up/pull-down windows, and software tools and skeleton programs that you can adapt to your needs.
- Part III delves into computer graphics: natural coordinate systems, business charts, 2D objects, and complex curves.
- Part IV looks inward at methods for managing data dynamically with linked lists, queues, stacks, binary trees, and irregular data structures.
- Part V is a grab-bag of sophisticated systems programming techniques: analyzing .EXE files, using DOS environment variables, managing parent and child processes such as exiting to and returning from DOS within a Turbo C program, interrupt-handling, and using EMS.

So that's what this book covers. Before we get on with it, there is an additional and perhaps sticky point that deserves mention.

This first has to do with affiliation. It's no secret; I used to write articles for Borland's now-discontinued *TURBO TECHNIX* magazine, and I'm a computer journalist working inside the relatively small town of the personal computer industry. As such I know some people who work at Borland, which is a 30-minute drive from where I sit writing these words. Some of them I count among my friends, as well as being professional associates. During the writing of this book, Borland furnished me with a free copy of Turbo C and official access to the folks responsible for it. For that I'm grateful.

But as a professional journalist, I am in no way beholden to Borland beyond acknowledging their support. My job is to be fair and objective, and that's all. They understand that, I understand that, and you should as well.

This book was published by a company that has no affiliation whatsoever with Borland. In no way does it represent an endorsement or promotion of Turbo C either by the Brady Books division of Simon and Schuster, or by me, or by *Dr. Dobb's Journal,* of which I am the Senior Technical Editor. Instead, it is an aid to understanding how to use Turbo C.

I can only hope that you learn as much from reading and using this book as I learned from writing it.

Happy programming.

K.P.

ACKNOWLEDGMENTS

In particular I want to thank Jeff Duntemann and Ron Copeland for being my tireless cheering section. Others who contributed to this project (whether they know it or not) are Janice Mandel, Joe Esposito, Julie Fallowfield, Herb Gellis, Kent Dahlgren, Neil Rubenking, Michael Abrash, Tyler Sperry, Ray Duncan, Al Stevens, Laura McKenna, and Eloise Engle Paananen. There are lots of others besides. Thanks to you all.

Chapters 4, 7, 14, and 20 are based in part on articles originally published in Borland's *TURBO TECHNIX* magazine.

Trademarked Products Cited in the Text:

Name	Owner
Turbo C	Borland International
Turbo Pascal	Borland International
IBM	International Business Machines
MS-DOS	Microsoft
PC-DOS	IBM
Lotus 1-2-3	Lotus Development Corp.
dBASE	Ashton-Tate
PS/2	IBM
UNIX	AT&T
OS/MVS	IBM
XTREE	Executive Systems, Inc.
CP/M	Digital Research
Norton Utilities	Peter Norton Computing
Norton Guides	Peter Norton Computing
Microsoft Windows	Microsoft
Framework	Ashton-Tate
Paradox	Ansa (div of Borland Int'l)
Reflex	Borland International
pfs	Software Publishing

Limits of Liability and Disclaimer of Warranty

The author and publisher of this book have used their best efforts in preparing this book and the programs contained in it. These efforts include the development, research, and testing of the theories and programs to determine their effectiveness. The author and publisher make no warranty of any kind, expressed or implied, with regard to these programs or the documentation contained in this book. The author and publisher shall not be liable in any event for incidental or consequential damages in connection with, or arising out of, the furnishing, performance, or use of these programs.

PART I

All About Disks in Turbo C

When you were a neophyte programmer, you no doubt learned to read and write sequential files. Maybe you also learned to work with random files (or *direct* files, as they're sometimes called), which let you jump around without regard to sequence. Many programmers, having mastered these two basic methods of file access, mistakenly assume that they have learned everything they'll ever need to know about disks and files.

After all, it's easy to take the disk system for granted. Quietly and reliably, it stores your data and coughs it back up on demand, which is exactly what one expects of a storage medium. So what else is there to say?

Plenty, and the next few chapters will explore disks and files in some depth. Why? Because a thorough knowledge of the subject will make you a much more savvy programmer capable of writing highly sophisticated software.

The chapters of Part I delve into the "secret" information kept in disk areas normally out of the sight of programs, manipulate the volume label, and produce directory listings, among other useful tricks. They also cover the various options Turbo C offers for file I/O, and develop strategies for indexing random files so that you can instantly go directly to the record you want.

Caveat: Some of the operations discussed here are armed and dangerous, capable of doing grievous injury to a disk until you've perfected them. Never use a hard disk or a floppy that you care about for testing. Instead, draw from your used-floppy pool, so that you don't lose anything of value if something goes wrong.

When you finish with this section of the book, you'll have a thorough understanding of the disk system and how to exploit its capabilities in Turbo C to write high-powered software.

CHAPTER 1

EXPLORING THE DISK

T he meat of this chapter has to do with getting the disk to reveal information about itself and its contents. The Turbo C libraries come with a number of functions for making inquiries of the disk. Where Turbo C has no built-in function for a particular inquiry operation, we'll create our own using calls to DOS.

For the sake of completeness, and in case it's something you don't know, we'll begin by discussing how a disk works and how DOS organizes it. If you're comfortable with your understanding of disks, you can skip a few pages to the discussion of inquiring about the disk's characteristics.

Diskology 101: How a Disk Works

There are two basic kinds of disk technology at work in today's personal computers, called *floppy* and *hard* (or fixed) disks. A third technology, *microfloppies*, is beginning to take hold with the advent of IBM's PS/2 machines. While the physical media differ, the principles of operation and organization are the same for all three, and also for variants such as Bernoulli Boxes and other removable disk cartridge products.

A disk rotates at some fixed rate of speed, ranging from around 300 RPM for a floppy up to several thousand RPM for high-capacity hard disks. A movable device called the *head* writes data on the disk in the form of tiny magnetic spots. This occurs as the surface passes under the head. The spots are of reversed polarity, so that a spot with a negative charge might represent a 0 bit, and one with a positive charge, a 1 bit. Later, the head retrieves data by sensing the charges as they pass, constructing bytes from them, and sending the information to the computer.

Naturally, the head doesn't write data wherever it feels like it. It follows rigid rules regarding the placement of data. The DOS FORMAT utility establishes the rules when it prepares the disk for use, subdividing the entire writable surface into manageable units.

The unit first in importance is the *track*. Tracks are concentric circles of data, and each has a number. The lowest-numbered track (0) is closest to the outside of the disk. Each track is further subdivided into several units called *sectors*, which are numbered starting from 1 (not 0). A sector holds a fixed number of bytes, usually 512. A normal 5¼" diskette has nine sectors per track, or 4,608 bytes in each complete circuit of the disk. Since the diskette holds 360K (368,640 bytes) of data, simple math reveals that there are 80 tracks. Higher-capacity media have both more tracks and more sectors per track.

The FORMAT utility creates sectors by writing a uniquely identifiable *control block* at the start of each one. These control blocks are not accessible to programs, but instead are for the use of the disk controller in locating a specific address. The control block indicates the sector number and other information. For example, it tells whether the sector is usable, and, if in use, it includes linkage pointers to the adjacent sectors belonging to its occupant. Because files do not necessarily occupy contiguous sectors, the pointers give DOS a means for chaining through the file in logical sequence. Thus, the sector control blocks effect a linked list on the disk.

The sectors are set up in an interleaved fashion. That is, the logical sector structure is different from the physical sequence. If the interleave factor is 2, for example, the following might be the correspondence of physical to logical sectors:

Physical	Logical
1	1
2	21
3	2
4	22
5	3
etc.	etc.

The effect is that there is one physical sector between each pair of logical sectors. The reason is to give the disk controller time to perform any necessary calculations and operations (e.g., sending the most recently read sector to the computer) between actual disk I/Os. It does these things while a sector of no interest is passing under the head, and completes them in time to watch for the next logical sector.

A disk has two sides, of course, and DOS uses both. When it writes a large file, it fills the track on surface 0, continues in the same track on surface 1 until it's full, then moves to the next track and resumes writing on surface 0. This goes on for as long as there are data. A new file always begins at the 0th byte of its first sector. If the file is not an even multiple of 512 bytes—few are—the unused remainder of the last sector is filled with hex character 1A (ASCII 26, or ÷EZ from the keyboard), which DOS recognizes as an end-of-file marker.

From this, you can see that DOS has an addressing scheme for finding data on the disk. The address consists of three elements: track number, surface (or head) number, and sector number. Given those three elements, DOS can locate any 512-byte chunk of data on the disk, regardless of the disk's capacity, and direct the head to it. *Random file access,* which we discuss in Chapter 6, further narrows the selection down to the specific starting byte of a data record within that 512-byte sector.

This addressing information must, of course, be stored somewhere, so that DOS can later recall where it put a file and go there to fetch it. That's what the disk directory does. DOS reserves part of the disk to serve as a directory. For each file, it creates a 32-byte structure containing the file name, its date and time stamps, its attribute (normal, hidden, read-only, etc.), and its disk address, among other things. When you open a file, you tell DOS to find the directory entry for that file and prepare to read or write at its first sector address or some offset thereof, which it can calculate based on the addressing information in the directory entry.

Another level of control is also required in managing the disk. This level concerns itself with keeping track of disk space that is both occupied and available for assignment to new data. DOS maintains a structure on the disk called the File Allocation Table, or FAT, for this purpose. Each time DOS needs a place to put more data, it refers to the FAT to determine where it can put it.

To avoid becoming unwieldy in size, the FAT doesn't keep track of individual sectors. Instead it deals in units of storage space called clusters. A cluster is some power of two sectors. The following table shows common cluster sizes for IBM-class machines:

Disk	Power of 2	Sectors/ cluster	Cluster size
Floppy	1	2	1,024
AT hard disk	2	4	2,048
XT hard disk	3	8	4,096

There are some inefficiencies inherent in this scheme. For example, if you write a file of 2,047 bytes to an AT hard disk, you'll take one cluster, or 2,048 bytes. However, if the file is 2,049 bytes—one more than the cluster size—DOS allocates two clusters, or 4,096 bytes, to it. That's a lot of wasted space for one lousy byte. Because files are of random lengths, on average you waste one-half of a cluster for every file no matter what the cluster size. This is a particularly acute problem with the XT, which on average wastes 2K on every file it puts into a hard disk. No doubt that's why the cluster size dropped with the later AT machines.

DOS reserves track 0 on every disk for its own use; user data are never written in this track. Track 0, head 0, sector 0 contains a record called the *boot sector,* which we'll discuss in detail later in this chapter. This is followed by the FAT, which is in turn followed by the root directory of the disk. If the disk is bootable—i.e., you can start the computer by inserting it into drive A:; or if it's a hard disk containing the operating system—DOS also owns track 1, where it stores the programs necessary to get the machine up and running.

The directory of a bootable disk must have the two hidden system entries for IBMBIO.COM and IBMDOS.COM (or a clone manufacturer's equivalents) as its first two entries. These files contain the essence of the operating system. You cannot boot the computer from a disk that doesn't have these mandatory directory entries in the requisite place. That explains why you can't install DOS with the SYS utility on a diskette that already contains other files. SYS responds that there isn't enough space; in fact, the first two directory entries are already committed, so the error message lies.

The DOS routines that control disk allocation always assign the lowest available cluster to new data. After extended use, this can lead to disk fragmentation, in which hunks of files get splattered all over the place in a crazy-quilt pattern that causes degradation of disk performance because the head spends so much time jumping from track to track. Hard disks are especially prone to this problem. Here's an example of how fragmentation occurs:

1. You write FILE.A, which occupies clusters 1 and 2.
2. You write FILE.B, which DOS places in cluster 3.
3. You erase FILE.A, freeing its clusters.
4. You append data to the end of FILE.B. When it goes beyond the end of cluster 3, DOS assigns the now-free cluster 1 to it.
5. You create FILE.C. The first part goes into cluster 2, which is free, but since FILE.A occupies the third cluster, the rest of FILE.C goes into cluster 4.

The problem is caused by erasing FILE.A and opening a hole in the Swiss cheese. Later, FILE.B's sequence is cluster 3, then cluster 1, while FILE.C's is cluster 2 followed by cluster 4. There are only two files on the disk, but both are fragmented and the head has to jump around to chain through them.

This situation is inevitable in DOS, and there's not much you can do about it except to buy a disk-optimization program that reshuffles files so that they occupy consecutive clusters. We raise the point here only because it's a fact of life, and so that you'll realize that your perception of slowing disk performance is factual and not subjective.

Now that we've laid out the basic organization of disks, let's see how your Turbo C programs can put it to use.

Inquiring About the Disk's Characteristics

Software operates in the blind. That is, it can't look at the computer or read the manual to find out what sort of machine it's dealing with, but instead must grope around to learn about its environment. Potentially, it then adjusts its behavior accordingly.

An operating system, be it DOS, UNIX, OS/MVS, or whatever, is primarily a manipulator of control blocks. In C parlance, a control block is analogous to a structure: a predefined sequence of data elements describing something. Therefore, in interfacing with DOS, much of our concern is to define structures reflecting the operating system control blocks, fill them in, and work on them.

The rest of this chapter deals with disk inquiry functions and their applications.

Identifying the Disk Type

Perhaps the simplest inquiry we can make of a disk is to ask it to identify itself. Turbo C furnishes the function **getdisk()**, which passes the question along and returns the answer as a digit in which **0** = A, **1** = B, and so on. This number indicates the default disk, that is, the one whose letter name appears as a prompt on the screen, and to which all disk I/Os are directed unless otherwise specified.

Note that DOS and Turbo C as well suffer from a degree of inconsistency in numeric drive indicators. Sometimes **0** means the A drive, and other times it means the default drive while A is indicated by **1**. When a numeric drive indicator is required, always look up the function specifications to see which scheme to use.

If a disk operation takes the **0** = default mode and you want to perform the operation on the default disk, just pass it **0** for the drive. Easy. However, if it needs a specific drive indicator and you don't know which is the default, you can use **getdisk()** instead of a literal digit as the drive parameter. This solves the problem neatly. That's what **getdisk()** is for.

Getting Disk Information

Software can't blithely assume anything, especially considering the wide variety of disk hardware now on the market. Turbo C furnishes the built-in function **getfat()**, which fills in a predefined structure with the most important information about a disk.

The structure used by **getfat()** is defined in Turbo C's include file DOS.H. Its format is:

```
struct fatinfo {
    char fi_sclus;                          /* sectors per cluster */
    char fi_fatid;                          /* FAT ID byte */
    int  fi_nclus;                          /* number of clusters */
    int  fi_bysec;                          /* bytes per sector */
```

A call to **getfat()** fills in this structure so that you can later pull out its fields.
There are two versions of the function: **getfat()** lets you specify a drive, while **getfatd()** refers only to the default drive (the one that is currently active). When you call **getfat()**, you have to pass a drive argument whose values are as follows:

Drive	Argument
Default	0
A:	1
B:	2
C:	3, etc.

The second argument in **getfat()** and the only one for **getfatd()** is a pointer to a variable of type **struct fatinfo**. You might declare this variable as

    struct fatinfo diskinfo;

and call the routines with

    getfat (driveno, &diskinfo);

or

    getfatd (&diskinfo);

depending on which drive you want to query.
So what do you do with this information when you have it? There are a couple of possibilities.

Computing the Disk Size

You can calculate the amount of total storage space on the disk. The formula is

    Sectors/cluster * Number of sectors * Bytes/sector

given from the structure by the expression

    disksize = (long) diskinfo.fi_sclus *
        diskinfo.finclus * diskinfo.fi_bysec;

Since the result of this calculation is inevitably a number greater than the capacity of an integer (32,767), the variable disksize must be a long and the result of the calculation is thus cast as such.

Program 1.1 demonstrates this discussion, taking the default drive as the test case.

Program 1.1 **Computing the Default Disk's Capacity**

```
/* DISKSIZE.C: Computes size of default disk */

#include <dos.h>

void main ()
{
struct fatinfo diskinfo;
long           disksize;

    getfatd (&diskinfo);                        /* get disk info */
    puts ("Information about default drive:");
    printf ("\n  Sectors per cluster  %5u",
        diskinfo.fi_sclus);
    printf ("\n  Number of clusters   %5u",
        diskinfo.fi_nclus);
    printf ("\n  Bytes per sector     %5u",
        diskinfo.fi_bysec);
    disksize = (long) diskinfo.fi_sclus * diskinfo.fi_nclus
        * diskinfo.fi_bysec;
    printf ("\n\n  Disk capacity is %lu", disksize);
}
```

Building Appropriate Buffer Sizes

Your software can optimize disk performance by reading and writing buffers that exactly correspond to the disk cluster size. Calculate the cluster size as

Sectors per cluster * Bytes per sector

or, using the **diskinfo** structure, as

buffsize = diskinfo.fi_sclus * diskinfo.fi_bysec;

Since no sane version of DOS uses a cluster size greater than 32,767 bytes, the buffsize variable can safely be declared as an integer in C.

It might not be easy to use this information to your advantage, but it can be done. For example, if your program writes one byte at a time to a disk file, you could declare a heap node of buffsize bytes and continually add bytes to it, checking each time for buffer overflow. When the buffer is full, write it to disk, fill it with 0x1A (end-of-file characters), and start again at the beginning. Although this entails some buffer-management overhead, it will usually result in improved disk performance.

Determining Free Space Left on the Disk

Often it's not enough simply to know the total capacity of a disk; you need to find out how much of that capacity is available. For this, Turbo C furnishes the function **getdfree()**, which fills in a structure with:

Field	Information
df__avail	Available clusters
df__total	Total clusters
df__bsec	Bytes per sector
df__sclus	Sectors per cluster

This structure is defined in DOS.H as **struct dfree**. You might allocate a variable of this type with

    struct dfree dskinf;

To call **getdfree()**, pass a drive designator (where default = **0**, A = **1**, etc.) and the address of the structured variable. For example, if you're interested in drive B:, call the function with

    getdfree (2, &dskinf);

You can use the same equations described above in Computing the Disk Size to calculate bytes of free and occupied space.

One excellent application of this function is in giving your software the smarts to recognize in advance that it's going to run out of disk space during a file save. If you have data in lists, trees, or arrays, and you want to write it to disk, it's easy to calculate the number of bytes: Just multiply node size by number of items. Compare the result with the free space. If less than, it's safe to write, and if greater than, ask the user to mount a new floppy or whatever is appropriate. This simple precaution prevents the disgrace and outright harm of having the program terminate abnormally via DOS's critical error handler, thus losing all the data.

If you want to make your program really smart, you can carry this idea a step farther, recognizing when a hard disk is about to run out of space and diverting the data to a floppy. The next section covers how to get the disk to bare its soul.

Reading the Boot Sector

When FORMAT prepares a disk, it writes a special record called the *boot sector*, located at track 0, head 0, sector 1. This record—that is, structure in C terms—contains fundamental information about the disk that is not available anywhere else, and also a short bootstrap program that loads the operating system.

The boot sector is not a file, and consequently we have to go to some lengths to read it. The means is interrupt 25h, absolute disk read. This is an obscure and seldom-used interrupt, since it bypasses all of DOS's file management to fetch one or more specified sectors directly.

Before we get into that, though, let's see what's in the boot sector. The structure defined in Program 1.2 shows the contents, which are exhaustive as regards the physical disk.

Program 1.2 **Contents of the Disk Boot Sector**

```
/* BOOTSEC.H: Header file describing DOS boot sector      */
/*      (track 0, head 0, sector 1) on any formatted disk */
/* ------------------------------------------------------ */
typedef struct {
  unsigned char signature;       /* E9h or EBh if formatted */
  unsigned      skip;                      /* no value */
  char          oem [8];                /* OEM identifier */
  unsigned      byPerSec;   /* start of BPB: bytes/sector */
  char          secPerClus;        /* sectors per cluster */
  unsigned      resSecs;            /* reserved sectors */
  char          nFats;      /* # of FATs retained on disk */
  unsigned      nRootEnts;      /* # of root dir entries */
  unsigned      totSec;        /* # of sectors in volume */
  unsigned char mediaDescr;     /* media descriptor byte */
  unsigned      secPerFat;           /* sectors per FAT */
  unsigned      secPerTrack;       /* sectors per track */
  unsigned      nHeads;     /* # of heads (surfaces) */
  unsigned      nHidden;         /* # of hidden sectors */
  char          loader [482];    /* bootstrap loader area */
} BOOTSEC;
```

The signature byte tells whether or not the disk is formatted. This byte, which must be either 0E9h or 0EBh, is actually a jump instruction to the bootstrap loader farther down in the boot sector. Anything else and the disk is either unformatted or else formatted for an operating system other than DOS; in both cases, the contents of the rest of the boot sector one is probably useless.

The OEM identifier shows the computer manufacturer and DOS version used to format the disk. This is a normal null-terminated string.

Some of the following information is accessible through **getfat()** and **getdfree()** discussed above; this is where they get it. Other information, such as the number of reserved sectors, FATs, and heads, is used by the disk device driver to calculate addresses.

The media descriptor byte tells what kind of disk this is. Its values map to media types as follows:

Value	Medium
0F8h	Hard disk
0F9h	5¼' floppy, DS, 15 sectors
0FCh	5¼' floppy, SS, 9 sectors
0FDh	5¼' floppy, DS, 9 sectors
0FEh	5¼' floppy, SS, 8 sectors
0FFh	5¼' floppy, DS, 8 sectors

There's nothing you can learn about the disk from the **loader[]** field. It's merely a machine-language program for starting the computer, followed by some error messages. This program is always present in the boot sector, even if the disk is not bootable (that's if IBMBIO.COM and IBMDOS.COM are not the first two files in the root directory). Its only function on an unbootable disk is to display the nonsystem disk message if you attempt to start the system from it.

The Turbo C library contains the function **absread()**, which performs an absolute disk read. That is, it bypasses all of DOS' normal disk- and file-management routines, positions the read/write head at a specific sector, and reads n sectors into a memory buffer. You can use it to fetch the boot sector with

```
absread (drive, 1, 0, &buffer);
```

where:

drive is an integer (0 = drive A, 1 = B, and so on.).

1 is the number of sectors to read.

0 is the starting logical sector (logical sectors are all the sectors of the disk sequentially numbered starting at 0).

&buffer is the offset address of the buffer that will receive the results read from disk (must be a multiple of 512 bytes corresponding to the number of sectors read: 512 * 1 in this case, mapped to a structure of type BOOTSEC defined in Program 1.2).

As an example, consider the following code fragment.

```
void main ()
{
BOOTSEC boot;
int     disk;

    disk = 'C' — 'A';
    absread (disk, 1, 0, &boot);
    . . . .
```

This code reads the boot sector from drive C into a BOOTSEC structure. Thereafter, you can refer to boot sector fields as **boot.signature, boot.nHeads,** and so on. For example, the number of clusters on the disk can be calculated as

nClus = boot.totSec boot.byPerSec;

Program 1.3 contains the program DISKPARM.C, which lists the disk parameters in the boot sector of any disk. Note how it computes the disk drive number. The function **getch()** gets a keystroke from the keyboard without echoing it. The **toupper()** macro converts it to uppercase, and the expression subtracts the ASCII value of 'A' from the result. Thus, if you type either lowercase b or uppercase B, the disk variable is assigned the numeric value 1, which corresponds to the B drive indicator.

It's easy to adapt this utility for inclusion in your own programs as a function that will reveal hidden information about the disk.

Program 1.3 **Utility to List Any Disk's Boot Sector**

```
/* DISKPARM.C: Shows contents of disk boot sector */

#include <stdio.h>
#include <string.h>
#include <dos.h>
#include <bootsec.h>
#include <ctype.h>
#include <conio.h>

void main ()
{
BOOTSEC  boot;
char     disk;

   puts ("\nWhich disk do you want to see?");
   disk = toupper (getch ()) - 'A';
   absread (disk, 1, 0, &boot);
   printf ("\n\nBoot sector for drive %c:\n", disk + 'A');
   printf ("\n  Signature                   %02X",
                   (unsigned char) boot.signature);
   printf ("\n  OEM                         %s",
           boot.oem);
   printf ("\n  Bytes per sector            %d",
           boot.byPerSec);
   printf ("\n  Sectors per cluster         %d",
           boot.secPerClus);
   printf ("\n  Number of reserved sectors  %d",
           boot.resSecs);
   printf ("\n  Number of FATs              %d",
           boot.nFats);
   printf ("\n  Number of root entries      %d",
           boot.nRootEnts);
```

Program 1.3 **(continued)**

```
    printf ("\n   Total number of sectors         %u",
            boot.totSec);
    printf ("\n   Media descriptor                %02X",
            (unsigned char) boot.mediaDescr);
    printf ("\n   Sectors per FAT                 %d",
            boot.secPerFat);
    printf ("\n   Sectors per track               %d",
            boot.secPerTrack);
    printf ("\n   Number of drive heads           %d",
            boot.nHeads);
    printf ("\n   Number of hidden sectors        %u",
            boot.nHidden);
}
```

Now that we've seen how to acquire general information about a disk, let's narrow the field of inquiry down to a more specific level. The next chapter deals with directories and how to read and manipulate them in Turbo C.

CHAPTER 2

Directory Assistance

t's essential for software operating on MS-DOS machines to navigate among directories, which are an essential feature of the DOS landscape. Turbo C provides a comprehensive set of tools for writing programs that do so easily and efficiently, and the purpose of this chapter is to familiarize you with them.

The Turbo C functions provide a number of directory-related services, among them creating, changing, and deleting subdirectories, exploding and combining pathnames, moving files between directories, searching paths, and renaming files. We'll examine these operations with examples, combining them in various practical applications.

Before we begin, let's clear up one potentially confusing bit of terminology: the term *path*. A *subdirectory* is a child of a higher-level directory, which might in turn be the child of another yet higher. The highest-level directory on the disk is the *root*, designated in DOS notation by a single backslash; for example, **C:** indicates the root directory of the C drive. The entire sequence of directories that must be traversed to reach the current subdirectory is the *path* (or *pathname*). In the recommended Turbo C setup, **INCLUDE** is a child of TURBOC, whose parent is the root. Thus, on drive C the path to INCLUDE is

    C:\TURBOC\INCLUDE

Thus, a subdirectory is an entity such as **INCLUDE**, while the path is a description of the route to it.

Determining the Current Directory _____

Chapter 1 discussed the **getdisk()** function, which tells a program which disk drive is the current default. Turbo C also furnishes a pair of analogous functions, **getcwd()** and **getcurdir()**, for determining the currently active directory. While both functions do roughly the same thing—furnish a string containing the current directory path—they vary somewhat in their implementation and functionality.

The **cwd** in **getcwd()** stands for "current working directory." The **#include** file DIR.H specifies the **getcwd()** function prototype as

```
char *getcwd (char *buf, int n);
```

where **buf** is a pointer to a buffer that will receive the pathname and **n** is the maximum allowable length including the null terminator. The function loads ***buf** with the pathname, including the drive designator (letter plus colon). Since DOS allows pathnames up to 65 characters long and the drive information and null terminator are another three characters, the highest sensible value for the **n** parameter is 68.

The function returns the address of the character string. Normally this is the same as **buf**, and you can treat the call as if to a void function, that is, disregard the returned value, as in

```
getcwd (&dir, 68);
```

However, you can pass NULL as the **buf** argument. In that case, **getcwd()** allocates an object of n characters on the heap, loads the pathname into it, and returns a pointer to the object, for example,

```
cwd = getcwd (NULL, 68);
```

This is useful if you only need to retain the pathname briefly or if you're short on data space, since it doesn't use any memory in the program's working area (except for the two to four bytes for the **cwd** pointer). Thus, you can free the space later with

```
free (cwd)
```

The **getcwd()** function only returns the pathname to the current directory on the default drive, hence the term *working* (since any open/close activity affects this directory).

In contrast, **getcurdir()** returns the current subdirectory on any drive attached to the system, whether that drive is active or not. For example, you might start execution from the C drive and later switch to A for some activity. At any time, you can issue **getcurdir()** to inquire about the current directory on either A or C.

The **#include** file DIR.H specifies the **getcurdir()** prototype as

```
int getcurdir (int drive, char *direc);
```

where **drive** is a numeric drive designator (0 = default, 1 = A, and so on), and **direc** is a pointer to a character array large enough to hold any directory

//BradyLine

You rely on Brady's bestselling computer books for up-to-date information about high technology. Now turn to BradyLine for the details behind the titles.

Find out what new trends in technology spark Brady's authors and editors. Read about what they're working on, and predicting, for the future. Get to know the authors through interviews and profiles, and get to know each other through your questions and comments.

BradyLine keeps you ahead of the trends with the stories behind the latest computer developments. Informative previews of forthcoming books and excerpts from new titles keep you apprised of what's going on in the fields that interest you most.

- Peter Norton on operating systems
- Jim Seymour on business productivity
- Jerry Daniels, Mary Jane Mara, Robert Eckhardt, and Cynthia Harriman on Macintosh development, productivity, and connectivity

Get the Spark. Get BradyLine.

Published quarterly, beginning with the Summer 1988 issue. Free exclusively to our customers. Just fill out and mail this card to begin your subscription.

Name _____

Address _____

City _____ State _____ Zip _____

Name of Book Purchased _____

Date of Purchase _____

Where was this book purchased?   *(circle one)*

Retail Store   Computer Store   Mail Order

F
R
E
E

Mail this card for your free subscription to BradyLine

Brady Books
One Gulf+Western Plaza
New York, NY 10023

path. The path does NOT include the drive but does have a null terminator; DIR.H thoughtfully furnishes the constant **MAXDIR** as the maximum allowable length for this path. Thus you can declare a string as

    char path [MAXDIR];

and get the current directory for drive A with

    getcurdir (1, path);

The string declaration guarantees that the fetched pathname will never overrun other data.

This function lacks the **NULL** option of **getcwd()**. You must always pass it a valid address. It returns **0** if successful and −1 otherwise. An example of an unsuccessful call is in passing a disk drive that doesn't exist. The call also fails if you request the current directory for a floppy drive, and either the door is open or the drive is empty.

To summarize, use **getcurdir()** to get the current directory from any drive, and **getcwd()** to find the full current working directory pathname for the default drive.

One of the most useful applications of these functions is in jotting down where you are in the subdirectory structure before you change directories and/or drives (which we discuss next). Later, you can use the path fetched by **getcurdir()** or **getcwd()** to restore the system to its original state; it would be rude indeed to quit and leave the user off in some strange corner of the disk known only to your program. Another use is in noting the location of a file found by **searchpath()**, discussed later in this chapter.

Manipulating Directories _____

As a DOS user, you're no doubt well acquainted with the DOS commands **CHDIR, MKDIR,** and **RMDIR** (alias **CD, MD,** and **RD**), which change, make, and remove directories, respectively. Turbo C has exactly equivalent functions going by the unsurprising names **chdir()**, **mkdir()**, and **rmdir()**.

Since these are such familiar DOS operations, they don't require much explanation. The same rules and effects apply. For example, **chdir()** switches from the current directory to a different one on the same drive, and all subsequent operations occur in the new directory. If you specify a different drive in the path given to **chdir()**, the directory becomes active on that drive, but the drive itself does not become the default (the same occurs under similar circumstances with the command-level CHDIR in DOS, in case you didn't realize that; try it). The **rmdir()** function cannot remove the current working directory, nor can it remove a subdirectory that still contains files, nor can it delete the root, just as in

DOS's **RMDIR.** All three functions signal success by returning **0** and failure with a −1 returned value.

As mentioned earlier, it's inconsiderate to change directories unless you provide a means for restoring the current one. Use **getcwd()** or **getcurdir()** to note the current directory before rampaging off to a far corner of the disk system. The next section, dealing with searching for a specific file, shows an example.

Searching for a File

Many DOS users, especially those with hard disks, set up complex directory structures and, through the PATH command in their AUTOEXEC.BAT file, furnish one or more paths to be searched for specific files.

For example, to avoid cluttering the root directory, it's prudent to place all DOS utility programs into a subdirectory, typically called \DOS or \SYSTEM or some such. Other utilities might go into a child directory under \DOS called \UTILS. Thus, for system utilities, the path is \DOS\UTILS. When a specific command is typed at the keyboard, DOS first looks in the root. If it can't find the program there, it goes to \DOS. The search ends there when the program is found; otherwise, it continues on to \DOS\UTILS.

A user can further confound this process by setting up a secondary line of inquiry when the first fails to produce the program being sought. This is indicated by a semicolon in the PATH string, followed by the next search path. For example, you might put all your favorite applications into a root-parented subdirectory called \MYFAVES. You can then specify the following path in the AUTOEXEC.BAT file:

```
PATH \DOS\UTILS;\MYFAVES
```

Now DOS, failing to find the sought file in the path \DOS\UTILS, returns to the root and tries a different path in \MYFAVES.

This PATH command sets an environmental string reading

```
PATH=\DOS\UTILS;\MYFAVES
```

We'll discuss environmental strings in detail in Chapter 23. For now, it's important only to know that system-level specifications for lines of inquiry in finding a file exist, and that they are accessible.

DOS uses search paths only for finding executable files (.COM and .EXE in that order). Turbo C's **searchpath()** uses the same PATH= environmental string, but goes one better over DOS in that it can seek any file—executable or data — along the same path. This has important implications if you're writing software that needs access to specific DOS files whose location might be anywhere along the search path. An example is in spawning a process; that is, executing another program under the control of yours.

Perhaps your program needs to format a diskette before writing data to it. Instead of attempting the herculean task of writing your own version of FORMAT, you could simply execute FORMAT.COM as a spawned task. We'll talk about spawning tasks in Chapter 28. Our concern right now is in locating a copy of FORMAT.COM, for which we can use Turbo C's **searchpath()** function.

The **#include** file DIR.H contains the function prototype, which is

```
char *searchpath (char *filename);
```

The **filename** argument is a literal string or a pointer to a string containing the name of the file being sought. The function returns the address of a string (on the heap) into which is loaded the full path to the file. When the function fails to find the **filename,** it returns **NULL.**

Let's say you declare the resulting path as

```
char  *filepath;
```

indicating that you expect to be given a completed pathname as a pointer. Now you can look for FORMAT.COM with

```
filepath = searchpath ("FORMAT.COM");
```

Here's what happens. The function first looks in the current directory for FORMAT.COM. Failing to find it, **searchpath()** fetches the PATH= environmental string built by AUTOEXEC.BAT or a more recent PATH command (the most recent prevails). It looks in the root, then pursues each path until it either finds a copy of FORMAT.COM or exhausts all possibilities.

Say **searchpath()** finds FORMAT.COM in subdirectory \DOS. The returned string filepath then reads

```
\DOS\FORMAT.COM
```

This is usually enough information to open a data file or spawn an executable program.

Using this example, you could print out the complete path to the file with the following code fragment:

```
filepath = searchpath ("FORMAT.COM");
printf ("Path to FORMAT.COM is %s", filepath);
```

which outputs the string above in the variable field.

In some cases, you might want to isolate the path from the filename itself, and perhaps further process this information. For that you can use the functions described next.

Manipulating Path Components

Turbo C furnishes the two offsetting functions fnsplit() and fnmerge(), which respectively break down and combine the elements of a path. Continuing the example begun above, you could use fnsplit() to determine the drive and subdirectory path where FORMAT.COM resides. You might then change the filename components (name and extension) to get at other files in the same subdirectory. We'll illustrate this in the directory listing program developed later in the chapter.

These functions complement each other. That is, the output from fnsplit() is four separate strings representing the drive, directory path, filename, and extension for a specific file. You can feed the strings back into fnmerge() and end up with exactly the same full pathname that was the original input to fnsplit().

There isn't much purpose in that, of course. The idea behind the two is that you use fnsplit() to break out the components, do something to one or more, then recombine them with fnmerge(), which produces a new full path to the desired file. Or you can use them separately. You might use searchpath() with FORMAT.COM to determine where the DOS utilities are stashed, then isolate the directory path. Later, to run CHKDSK, you recombine the directory path with the new filename (CHKDSK.COM) using fnmerge() and voila! You have direct access to the desired program without the overhead of another searchpath() call.

The #nclude file DIR.H specifies maximum lengths for each of the null-terminated text elements used by fnsplit() and fnmerge(), which are as follows:

Constant	Value	Meaning
MAXPATH	80	Length of entire path
MAXDRIVE	3	Drive including colon
MAXDIR	66	Directory path, including backslashes
MAXFILE	9	Filename before extension
MAXEXT	5	Extension including preceding period

The prototype for function fnsplit() is

```
int fnsplit (char *path, char *drive, char *dir, char *name, char *ext);
```

In this case, *path is a pointer to the pathname to be exploded into its component parts. The other arguments are pointers to where the results of the explosion go. As an example, suppose we've used searchpath() as described above to get the path to FORMAT.COM, loading the string filepath with

    \DOS\FORMAT.COM

and we've already declared the variables

    char drive [MAXDRIVE], dir [MAXDIR],
    name [MAXFILE], ext [MAXEXT];
    int flags;

The function call

    flags = fnsplit (filepath, drive, dir, name, ext);

produces the following null-terminated results:

    drive = null (indicating default drive)
    dir = \DOS\
    name = FORMAT
    ext = .COM

(The returned value flag is discussed later.)
    We want to replace FORMAT with CHKDSK, so we execute the standard C statement

    strcpy (name, "CHKDSK");

which places CHKDSK into the name string.
    Now we can recombine the complete pathname using fnmerge(). The prototype's arguments are the same as for fnsplit(), with the call being

    fnmerge (filepath, drive, dir, name, ext)

This is exactly assymetrical from the fnsplit() call. Here the filepath argument is the destination, while the other arguments contain the values to be imploded. The resulting filepath argument is

    \DOS\CHKDSK.COM

Note that, since the drive parameter is a null string, fnmerge() ignores it entirely, thus creating a path suitable for the default drive.
    Now let's discuss the flags returned by fnsplit(). The flags are bits indicating components present in the fields exploded by the function. The high-order byte is all zeros. The low-order byte takes the form in Figure 2.1.

Figure 2.1 **Meanings of Bits Set in Flags Returned by fnsplit() Function**

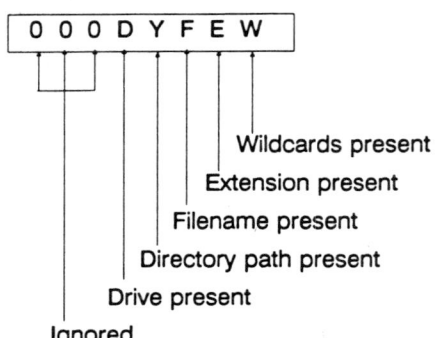

You can use these flag bits to determine the components placed in the specified fields. The **#include** file DIR.H defines bitwise constants for this purpose as follows:

Constant	Value	Meaning
DRIVE	10h	Drive present
DIRECTORY	08h	Directory path present
FILENAME	04h	Filename present
EXTENSION	02h	Extension present
WILDCARDS	01h	Wildcards present*

*Wildcards are * and ? characters, which allow searches for a range of files. Under DOS conventions, any number of characters are substituted for * and any one character replaces the ? character.

In the context of the current example, the following returns **FALSE** since no drive is specified:

    flags & DRIVE;

Similarly, the following returns **TRUE** since a directory path is present:

    flags & DIRECTORY;

You can use such tests to find out which components **fnsplit()** exploded from the full pathname.

Listing a Directory

Did you ever wonder how systems such as Lotus 1-2-3, dBASE III, and Turbo C itself produce directory listings from within the software? You're about to find out, using the Turbo C functions **findfirst()** and **findnext()**. In the process, we'll tie together much of the preceding discussion of other Turbo C directory-manipulation tools.

The findfirst() and findnext() functions are C translations of DOS interrupt 21h, functions 4Eh and 4Fh. They search a directory for entries matching a specification. Each time a match is found, the search stops and the function fills in a structure from which you can fetch the file information.

Findfirst() locates the first directory block satisfying the specification. Thereafter, call findnext() repeatedly to locate additional matches. Findnext() always resumes the search immediately after the point where it left off last time, so that you don't get duplicate file entries. Both functions return **0** on success and **−1** when either there's an error in the search specification or no further matching entries exist in the directory.

The Turbo C **#include** file DIR.H defines **struct ffblk**, which represents the structure of the DOS file entry block. This structure contains six fields, of which five are useful to programs. Chapter 3 delves into the interpretation of these fields; for now, we'll concentrate on the process of searching directories, and use only the filename field **ff_name[]** from the structure.

Let's say you declare a pointer to the structured variable as

```
struct ffblk *file;
```

and allocate heap space for the structure with

```
file = (struct ffblk*) malloc (sizeof (struct ffblk));
```

Thereafter, upon successful return from findfirst() and findnext(), you can refer to the filename as

```
file->ff_name;
```

The directory search process must always begin with a call to findfirst(). In addition to performing the first search operation, this function sets up the specifications in the **ffblk** structure for subsequent use by findnext().

There are two elements in the specification: a name mask and an attribute mask. We say *mask* because these elements typically include wildcards leading to the discovery of several matching file entries. The wildcards in the name field are as you might expect: asterisk (*) to mean any number and combination of characters, and question mark (?) to indicate any single character. Thus the wildcard to find all files having the extension .BAT is *.BAT, while the wildcard to find all files having the form PAYROLL plus one character plus any extension is PAYROLL?.*.

The attribute describes characteristics of a file: hidden, read-only, normal, and so on. The next chapter discusses file attributes at length. In searching a directory, we can set up a wildcard attribute that will find all matching file entries regardless of their characteristics. This is the hex byte **0FFh** (all bits turned on).

The prototype for **findfirst()** is

```
int findfirst (char *spec, struct ffblk *found, int attr);
```

To find the first entry in the current directory having the extension .C, you can issue the call

```
result = findfirst ("*.C", file, 0×FF);
```

where **result** is an integer variable and **file** is a pointer to the allocated space as described earlier.

If **findfirst()** returns **0** to signal success, you can list **file->ff_name**, then begin a loop that repeatedly calls **findnext()** and lists subsequent filenames until **findnext()** returns −1. The call to **findnext()** is

```
result = findnext (file);
```

in accordance with the prototype

```
int findnext (struct ffblk *found);
```

Caution: The **findfirst()/findnext()** functions alter the disk transfer address (DTA), a global pointer maintained by DOS for performing file operations. This isn't a problem if your program is like the demo in Program 2.1, performing no disk operations other than the directory search. When searches and other disk operations are mixed, use the Turbo C functions **getdta()** and **setdta()** to fetch and restore the old DTA before and after each search call. Example:

```
while (result ==0) {
   oldDTA = getdta();
   result = findnext (file);
   setdta (oldDTA);
   if (result == 0) . . .;

}
```

Failure to restore the DTA may result in erratic program behavior, and you won't have a clue as to why.

Now let's write a program that lists all the .COM files in the root directory of the default disk. The equivalent **DIR** command at the DOS prompt level (**DIR \ *.COM**) is less powerful than this program will be, because it does not list the hidden system files IBMBIO.COM and IBMDOS.COM or their equivalents in other MS-DOS implementations. Since we will search with the wildcard attribute **OFFh**, our program will list *all* .COM files regardless of their attributes.

The program (ROOTCOM.C in Program 2.1) uses several of the directory operations discussed in this chapter: DTA functions, **chdir()**, **getcurdir()**, and **findfirst()/findnext()**. Note that the **chdir()** call to switch to the root directory needs a double backslash. This is because backslash is a special lead-in character in C, normally indicating a nonprinting control sequence. To output a literal backslash, you have to code two of them in sequence.

The **getdta()** and **setdta()** calls are superfluous in this example, since the program performs no disk operations other than searching the directory. They are here merely to illustrate their use in a typical situation; they'd be essential if this program were a portion of a larger one that did file operations elsewhere.

The program uses **getcurdir()** to jot down the current directory on entry. It then switches to the root to do its job. Just before quitting, it calls **chdir(oldpath)** to restore the old directory, so that the user isn't left stranded in the root. This is "courteous programming."

The rest of the program should be self-explanatory in the context of this chapter's contents.

Program 2.1 **Searching and Listing a Directory**

```
/* ROOTCOM.C: List .COM files in root dir of default drive. */
/*   If disk is bootable, shows the hidden system files,     */
/*   which normally don't appear from the DIR command.       */
/* --------------------------------------------------------- */

#include <dir.h>
#include <dos.h>
#include <stdio.h>
#include <alloc.h>

void main ()
{
struct ffblk *file;                   /* file block pointer */
char far     *oldDTA;          /* old disk transfer address */
char         *oldpath;        /* directory where we are now */
int          result;          /* success code from searches */

/*  Note where we are on entry */
   oldDTA = getdta ();                           /* save DTA */
   oldpath = malloc (MAXDIR);              /* space for path */
   getcurdir (0, oldpath);                 /* now get the path */

/* Begin search */
   chdir ("\\");                            /* switch to root */
   file = malloc (sizeof (struct ffblk));
```

Program 2.1 (continued)

```
   puts ("\nListing of .COM files in root directory:");
   result = findfirst ("*.COM", file, 0xFF);   /* find first */

/* Continue search until all .COM files found */
   while (result == 0) {
     puts file->ff_name);                       /* list entry */
     result = findnext (file);                  /* get next match */
   }
   puts ("\n-- End of list\n");

/* Restore status and quit */
   setdta (oldDTA);                                    /* DTA */
   chdir (oldpath);                               /* old path */
}
```

To become more comfortable with these directory operations, experiment with the program. You might modify it so that it goes to the \TURBOC\INCLUDE directory and lists all .H files, or to your Lotus directory to show all .WK? files, or whatever else strikes your fancy. Chapter 3 develops a generalized subdirectory listing utility that builds on this program.

Now that you're familiar with directory operations, let's see how to find out and interpret information specific to individual files.

CHAPTER **3**

FINDING OUT MORE ABOUT FILES

D OS stores a number of items of information about files in their directory entries. This information is accessible to Turbo C programs in a couple of ways. The subject of this chapter is how to get at file information and how to interpret it.

Before getting into details, let's discuss how DOS classifies disk files.

About File Attributes

DOS 2.0 and higher has six different classifications for disk files. These classifications—or *attributes* as they are more properly called—affect permissible operations on files. Additionally, DOS uses the attribute descriptor to flag files that have been modified since the last backup with a characteristic officially called *archive* but more commonly referred to as the *dirty bit*.

The file directory block carries an eight-bit attribute byte whose bit meanings are as follows:

Bit	Meaning
00h	Normal read/write file*
01h	Read-only
02h	Hidden file (not listed by DIR)
04h	System file (ditto, owned by DOS)
08h	Volume label
10h	Subdirectory
20h	Archive ("dirty")*

* An attribute of 20h means a normal file eligible for backup due to modification since last backup.

These bit settings are sometimes ORed together in various combinations. For example, 03h indicates a read-only hidden file (combination of 01h and 02h), while 24h means a system file that has been modified since its last backup.

The volume label (08h) is a special directory entry that we'll discuss in the next chapter. It looks like a file, but it isn't one and can't be treated as such.

DOS uses the file attribute to control permissible operations on files. For example, you can delete only normal files (attribute 00h or 20h) with the ERASE alias DEL command. Similarly, DIR is blind to hidden and system files, and treats the volume label and subdirectory entries in special ways.

The read-only attribute places a file in a middling position between hidden and normal. When marked read-only, the file entry shows up when you type DIR and you can open it from a program for input, but not for output. You cannot erase a read-only file; it must first be changed to normal. Thus, read-only status is an effective way to prevent accidental erasure of important data. If you must write to such a file, have your application change its status, write the data, then change its attribute back to read-only.

In effect, DOS uses the attribute to support a somewhat defensive stance concerning file access. This is justified inasmuch as files that are other than "normal" are entitled to special protection. Otherwise why flag them as such?

Consequently, DOS surrenders information about the attribute somewhat reluctantly, and in ordinary file I/O doesn't even admit to the existence of non-normal files.

Let's say, for example, that you want to ascertain if the diskette in drive A is bootable. The presence of IBMBIO.COM, a hidden system file, indicates that it is, and its absence means it's not. You can find out if any normal file is present by attempting to open it with **fopen()** or **open()**, but that doesn't work with a hidden/system file; DOS returns an error code as if the special file didn't exist, even though it does. One way to find out if IBMBIO.COM is on the diskette is to call **findfirst()** as described in Chapter 2, specifying the filename as a literal and passing the wildcard attribute 0FFh. If the operation is successful (**0** returned), the diskette is bootable.

An easier method for determining the attributes of a specific file is to use the Turbo C function **__chmod()** defined in **#include** file sys\stat.h. This function has two options, one to inquire about a file's attributes, another to change them (discussed next). To inquire about the attributes of A:SOME.FIL, code the call

```
attrib = __chmod ("'A:SOME.FIL", 0);
```

The **0** option indicates an inquiry, and **__chmod()** thus returns the attribute byte to **attrib**. This function is capable of finding hidden and otherwise non-visible files.

The Turbo C **#include** file DIR.H provides mask constants for the attribute bits, which are as follows:

Bits	Constant	Meaning
01h	FA_RDONLY	Read-only
02h	FA_HIDDEN	Hidden
04h	FA_SYSTEM	System
08h	FA_LABEL	Volume label
10h	FA_DIREC	Subdirectory
20h	FA_ARCHIVE	Archivable

You can AND these masks with the returned attribute byte to interpret the file's attribute(s). For example,

```
if (attrib & FA_HIDDEN) {
  /* the file is hidden */
} else {
  /* it's not; maybe check others */
}
```

Note that the constants don't define a normal file with attributes 00h or 20h. You can identify a normal file with the following test:

```
if (!attrib | (attrib & FA_ARCHIVE)) {
  /* file is normal read/write */
} else {
  /* it's not */
}
```

Changing a File's Attribute

When you identify a non-normal file and you want to open it for ordinary I/O, you must first change its attributes to normal read/write. Note: You can open a read-only file for input using normal calls, but if you want to write to a read-only, system, and/or hidden file, call _chmod() with option 1. For example, to convert A:ROFILE.DAT to a normal file, code the call as

```
_chmod ("A:ROFILE.DAT", 1, FA BL_ARCHIVE);
```

Note that, with option **1**, _chmod() takes one more argument—the new attribute—than with option **0** described earlier.

This procedure conditions the file so that you can process it normally, but it's eligible for backup. After you close the file, it's usually advisable to restore it to its former protected status using the same procedure. This suggests that you save the old attribute byte before making the change, as in the following fragment:

```
oldAttr = __chmod ("A:ROFILE.DAT", 0);          /* get old attr */
__chmod ("A:ROFILE.DAT", 1, FA__ARCHIVE);       /* make normal */
                                                /* update the file */
...
__chmod ("A:ROFILE.DAT", 1, oldAttr);           /* back to old attr*/
```

You can also use __chmod() to place a newly written file under DOS' protection. After close, set the desired attribute.

File Date and Time

DOS writes a time-stamp into the directory block each time you (or any program that accesses it) modifies a file. A modification is any operation except read-only, and includes creating, rewriting, appending, and replacing records. The time-stamp has two parts: date and time of day. At the same time that it updates the time-stamp, DOS sets the dirty bit (20h) in the attribute byte.

The time-stamp is accessible from Turbo C in a couple of ways. One, fetched from the ffblk structure loaded by findfirst()/findnext(), requires interpretation. The other can be plucked directly with a minimum of interpretation from a structure initialized by a call to the Turbo C function getftime().

Raw Time-Stamps

The ffblk structure loaded by findfirst()/findnext() represents exactly the raw format of time-stamps maintained by DOS in the directory entry. The fields ff__ftime and ff__fdate are 16-bit integers zoned into bit fields.

Figure 3.1 **File Time-Stamp Format**

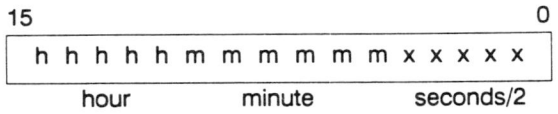

The time-of-day stamp reflects the approximate time the file was last closed after a change (or created if new). The time is approximate in that its seconds field is actually the time-of-day seconds divided by 2; for example, 14 in this field means that the file was closed 28 or 29 seconds after the minute. Because one seldom cares about such hair-splitting as the exact second of file closure, this is "good enough." Figure 3.1 illustrates the format of the file time-stamp.

Extracting the fields from this integral value involves some shifting and ANDing to mask out unwanted bits. The following are C expressions that retrieve the values:

```
hour = file->ff_ftime >>11;
min = ff->ftime >>5) & 0×3F;
sec = (file->ff_ftime & 0×1f) * 2;
```

The "H" field in Figure 3.1 becomes 0 at midnight and advances to 23 at 11:00 P.M., thus keeping military time. Routines to print out the file time have to adjust for this; the subdirectory listing utility later in this chapter (Program 3.2) shows how. File time- and date-stamp formats are different from the system clock formats, although derived from them within the innards of DOS. You should be aware that the system clock is slightly inaccurate, gaining a bit less than one-half second per hour. It adjusts for this discrepancy by pausing 9.65 seconds before rolling over to the next day. This is not a problem (except in benchmark tests!) if all events are measured within the context of the system clock.

Figure 3.2 **File Date-Stamp Format**

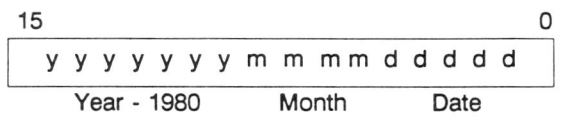

The raw file date-stamp is similar to the time-of-day stamp, but has a different format shown in Figure 3.2. In this case, the seven high-order bits contain a number in the range 0–119, which must be added to 1980 to obtain the calendar year. The month and date fields correspond exactly to real-world calendars. Therefore, the expressions to derive the field values are:

```
year = (file->ff_fdate >> 9) ×1980;
month = (file->ff_fdate >> 5) & 0×0F;
date = file->ff_fdate & 0×1F;
```

All of this isn't terribly difficult, but it places the burden of interpreting the file time-stamps on the programmer (you). Under certain circumstances, it's easier to obtain the file time- and date-stamps from a call to the Turbo C function **getftime()**, which we cover next.

Interpreted Time-Stamps

Obtaining the file date and time is easier when the file has been opened with a call to either **open()** or **_open()**, thus associating it with a handle (we'll discuss the distinctions between file FCB and handle functions in Chapter 5). When an open file is associated with a handle, you can issue a call to the Turbo C function **getftime()**, which fills in a predefined bitfield structure with the requisite information.

The Turbo C **#include** file IO.H defines **struct ftime**, shown in page 184 of the *Turbo C 2.0 Reference Guide* (the manual suggests that it's in DOS.H, but it's not). This structure gives all the time-stamp information from the two-second increment to the year (less 1980). Say the file was opened with

```
handle = open (filepath, access);
```

(see pp. 257–259 of the *Turbo C 2.0 Reference Guide*) and you have made the declaration

```
struct ftime fstamp;
```

After the call

```
getftime (handle, &fstamp);
```

you can extract members from the **fstamp** variable, which **getftime()** has filled in. For example:

```
hour = fstamp.ft_hour;
year = fstamp.ft_year + 1980;
```

This is easier than deciphering the raw fields in the **ffblk** structure furnished by **findfirst()/findnext()**, but the down side is that the file must first have been opened with a handle function, entailing disk overhead.

Incidentally, the **getftime()** function has a corresponding **setftime()** that you can use to set the file date and time to something other than what DOS would normally provide. To use this function, fill in a variable bound to **struct ftime** and issue the call using an open handle. It's difficult to conceive of a need for this function, which overrides DOS, except in deliberately falsifying the file's time stamps.

Tradeoffs

When you're creating a directory listing, it's cheaper in terms of overhead to interpret the raw time-stamps via the shift-and-mask expressions given above. The findfirst()/findnext() functions load file information from disk automatically; that's what they do, and all *you* have to do is interpret that information. Computed operations are almost always faster than disk operations, supported by the established fact that any CPU spends more time on average waiting for the disk to do its thing than it does performing actual work.

On the other hand, if a file is already open using one of the handle functions (open(), _open(), creat(), _creat(), creatnew(), creattemp(), or dup() in Turbo C), its time-stamp information is present in memory. Therefore the CPU spends little time fetching it and filling in the ftime structure. There is essentially no overhead in retrieving information about open files.

Consequently:

1. If a file is not open and you just want to inquire about it, use findfirst() or findnext() as appropriate and interpret the stamps.
2. If a file is open, ask getftime() to interpret the stamps for you, then retrieve them from the filled-in variable bound to struc ftime.

Of course, there's other information you might want to determine about a given file. Let's investigate the possibilities further.

File Size

Chapter 1 discussed how DOS allocates file space in clusters comprised of some multiple of the sector size. Since DOS assigns file space in these increments, it stands to reason that any given file's actual length is less than—or at most equal to—the space allocated to it. A file's size cannot be greater than its allocated space, but it might be as much as 4,095 bytes less, depending on the cluster size.

As with time-stamps, the method for determining file size depends on whether the file block was fetched from the directory with findfirst()/findnext(), or the file is open and associated with a handle. In both cases, the size is expressed in bytes, and since files can potentially be quite large, this quantity is of necessity a long integer.

The ffblk structure filled in by findfirst()/findnext() contains the long field ff_fsize. Thus you can print it directly using a statement such as

```
printf ("\nFilesize %lu", file.ff_fsize);
```

The format specification **%lu** indicates an unsigned long integer.

For a file that is already open, you can obtain the size using the Turbo C function **filelength()**, the prototype of which is specified in IO.H as

```
long filelength (int handle);
```

In other words, **filelength()** returns a long integer giving the length in bytes of the file associated with the handle.

Demonstration

Program 3.1 lists FILETIME.C, which illustrates the discussion up to this point. The program uses **findfirst()** to locate the first version of itself in the default directory, which might be a .C, a .OBJ, a .BAK, or a .EXE file. When it finds it, it lists the time- and date-stamps and size of the file from the **ffblk** structure. Next it opens the same file and calls **getftime()** to obtain the same information using the handle. This shows how you can get the same information by two different means depending on whether you're searching the directory or dealing with an open file.

In the **han_report()** function, note that it's necessary to extract the year and seconds fields and adjust them to real-world values outside the **ftime** structure. That's because these are bitfields the same size as those in the actual time- and date-stamps (Figures 3.1 and 3.2), which are not large enough to accommodate the full values.

Program 3.1 **Getting Time-Stamps by Different Means**

```
/* FILETIME.C: Demonstrates two methods for getting the   */
/*    time, date, and size of a file, depending on status */
/* ------------------------------------------------------- */

/* INCLUDES FOR TURBO C PROTOTYPES AND STRUCTURES */
#include <dos.h>
#include <dir.h>
#include <mem.h>
#include <fcntl.h>
#include <io.h>
#include <stdio.h>

/* LOCAL FUNCTION PROTOTYPES */
void dir_report (struct ffblk *file);
void han_report (int han);
/* ------------------------- */
void main ()
```

Program 3.1 **(continued)**

```c
{
struct ffblk file;
int         handle;

/* Report file information from findfirst() */
   if (findfirst ("filetime.*", &file, 0xff) == 0) {
      puts ("File info obtained from findfirst() function:");
      dir_report (&file);

/* Report same information from getftime() */
      handle = open (file.ff_name, O_RDONLY);  /* open file */
      han_report (handle);                     /* report info */
      close (handle);                          /* close the file */
   }
} /* ------------------------ */
void dir_report (struct ffblk *file)
{                     /* print file info from directory block */
int  hour, min, sec, year, mo, date;

   printf ("\nFile = %s", file->ff_name);     /* print name */
   hour = file->ff_ftime >> 11;               /* compute hour */
   min  = (file->ff_ftime >> 5) & 0x3F;       /* minutes */
   sec  = (file->ff_ftime & 0x1F) * 2;        /* seconds */
   printf
         ("\nTime-of-day stamp is %.2d:%.2d:%d (military time)",
      hour, min, sec);                        /* print date info */
   year = (file->ff_fdate >> 9) + 1980;       /* compute year */
   mo   = (file->ff_fdate >> 5) & 0x0F;       /* month */
   date = file->ff_fdate & 0x1F;              /* date*/
   printf ("\nDate stamp is %.2d/%.2d/%d",
            mo, date, year);                  /* print date stamp */
   printf ("\nFile size is %lu", file->ff_fsize);  /* size */
} /* ---------------------- */
void han_report (int handle)
{                     /* print file info for open file */
struct ftime opened;
int          year, sec;

   puts
         ("\n\n\nInfo for same file from handle functions:");
   getftime (handle, &opened);
   year = opened.ft_year + 1980;             /* get correct year */
   sec = opened.ft_tsec * 2;                 /* and seconds */
   printf
         ("\nTime-of-day stamp is %.2d:%.2d:%d (military time)",
      opened.ft_hour, opened.ft_min, sec);
   printf ("\nDate stamp is %.2d/%.2d/%d",    /* file date */
      opened.ft_month, opened.ft_day, year);
   printf ("\nFile size is %lu",
         filelength (handle));                /* size */
} /* ---------------------- */
```

An Alternative to the DOS DIR Command

Probably the most-used command in DOS' repertoire is **DIR,** which lists the files in a directory. As venerable and useful as it is, there are a couple of shortcomings in this command.

First, it doesn't let you know if there are hidden and system files in the directory. This is a problem when you're attempting to remove a directory from the disk. You issue the command

DEL *.*

which ostensibly deletes all the files, but in fact doesn't touch those that are out of sight. Later you issue the **RMDIR** command and DOS mysteriously refuses to cooperate. The only way to find out why (that there are still files in the directory) is to use a DOS shell such as XTREE to inspect the directory for invisible contents. DOS itself won't tell you, and it contains no command for changing the survivors' attributes.

The second problem with **DIR** is that it doesn't tell you how much space the directory's contents occupy. This becomes an issue when you plan to back up the directory; how many diskettes do you need to have ready? The only way to figure it out is manually: Round each file's byte count to the next-higher cluster size and add them up. This is the kind of job we invented computers to do for us, yet DOS itself doesn't.

It was to overcome these disappointments that we decided to write the SUB.C program in Program 3.2. It's an improved version of DOS's **DIR** command in that it shows:

- All files and their attributes, plus time-stamps
- The number of bytes in each file and the space in K allocated to it as a function of cluster size
- Number of files in the directory, total bytes, and total space taken by all files in K
- Free space remaining on the disk

This program ties together many of the elements covered from Chapter 1 onward. Its general flow is:

- Get and remember the current directory.
- Find out what directory to search.
- List the specified contents of the target directory.
- Show summary information.
- Restore the original directory.
- Quit.

The details of these operations are broken down into 13 local functions. One—function **error()**—deals with error-handling. The others are implementations and/or expansions of material we've already covered.

One merits additional discussion. Function **ftime()** converts the file's time-of-day stamp into civilian time. Briefly, it computes the military hour by extracting the five-bit hours field (see Figure 3.1). If the hour is less than 1—i.e. it's between midnight and 1:00 A.M.—it assigns 12 to the civilian hour. Otherwise, if the military hour is between 1300 and 2400, it subtracts 12 to derive civilian time, setting it via the ternary operator in C. The military hour is used to determine whether to indicate A.M. or P.M. on the output. This kind of convoluted logic is necessary to reconcile the discrepancy between the military time kept internally by the computer (in which one minute before midnight is 23:59 but one minute after is 0:01) and civilian time, where one minute after midnight is 12:01 A.M.

If you type the unadorned command

```
SUB
```

the program lists the entire contents of the current directory. You can also include command-line arguments. For example, to list all the .WKS files in your Lotus subdirectory, you can type

```
SUB \LOTUS\*.WKS
```

The program is "considerate" in that it always returns to the original directory before ending. You can also use it to list the contents of directories on other drives.

It's not perfect as it stands, and we make no apologies. There are certain shortcomings in Turbo C's **fnsplit()** function that cause it to return invalid results for a path that is, in fact, valid, thus causing the program to end with an error. For example, if you're in the \TURBOC directory and you want to list files in its child subdirectory INCLUDE, **fnsplit()** isn't smart enough to figure out the command

```
SUB INCLUDE
```

Instead, you have to type

```
SUB \TURBOC\INCLUDE
```

Similarly, when in a subdirectory, the command

```
SUB \*.BAT
```

(which specifies all the .BAT files in the root) results in early termination with an invalid path message. There is no workaround for this; the only thing you can do is type

**SUB **

which lists everything in the root. It's possible to fix these problems with some creative programming, and we encourage you to do so. We chose not to in the interests of space and publishing costs; the program is already over 200 lines long, and it will probably take half again as many lines to endow it with the smarts to deal with these minor problems. The purpose here is to furnish a reasonably complete, functional program that illustrates the discussion.

Take on its refinement as your own project, and make it even more useful than it is.

Program 3.2 **A Subdirectory Listing Utility**

```
/* SUB.C: Lists any subdirectory per command line argument.  */
/*      Anything left out of the argument becomes a wildcard. */
/* ----------------------------------------------------------- */
/* INCLUDES */
#include <stdio.h>
#include <dir.h>
#include <errno.h>
#include <dos.h>

/* CONSTANTS */
#define   MAXLINES  21                    /* entries per screen */

/* GLOBALS */
char            path [MAXPATH],         /* pathname for search */
                drive [MAXDRIVE],              /* drive */
                dir [MAXDIR],              /* subdirectory */
                name [MAXFILE],              /* file name */
                ext [MAXEXT],              /* extension */
                olddir [MAXDIR],       /* current directory */
                mask [MAXFILE+MAXEXT];    /* dir search mask */
int             disk;                      /* current drive */
struct ffblk    file;               /* file directory block */
struct fatinfo  fat;                /* file alloc table info */

/* LOCAL FUNCTION PROTOTYPES */
void splitUp ( char *argstr );
void addDrive ( char *argstr );
void dfltArg ( char *arg, char *curr );
void error ( char *msg );
void pmerge ( char *pn, char *dr, char *sub );
void fmerge ( char *mk, char *nm, char *xt );
void listdir ( void );
void showfree ( int disk );
void heading ( void );
```

Program 3.2 **(continued)**

```c
void fdate ( int d );
void ftime ( int t );
void fattr ( char a );
long fsize ( long sz );

void main (int argc, char *argv[])
{
/* FIND OUT WHERE WE ARE */
  disk = getdisk();                         /* get current disk */
  getcwd ( olddir, MAXDIR );                /* and directory */

/* FIND OUT DRIVE AND DIR WE WANT TO SEARCH */
  if ( argc == 1 )                  /* list whole current dir */
    dfltArg ( path, olddir );               /* with default arg */
  else                             /* get command line arg */
    strcpy ( path, argv[1] );
  splitUp ( path );                     /* break down search arg */

/* GO TO TARGET DIRECTORY AND LIST IT */
  pmerge ( path, drive, dir);          /* build directory path */
  fmerge ( mask, name, ext );            /* build search mask */

  if ( chdir ( path ) == -1 ) {     /* switch to search path */
    chdir ( olddir );
    error ( "SUB" );                         /* path not found */
  }
  getfat ( disk+1, &fat );                /* get disk info */
  listdir ();                          /* list subdirectory */
  showfree ( disk+1 );              /* show free space remaining */
  chdir ( olddir );                  /* restore original path */
} /* ----------------------- */

void  dfltArg (char *dflt, char *curr)
{                                       /* set default argument */
int    p;

  strcpy ( dflt, curr );                    /* copy current dir */
  p = strlen ( dflt );                  /* find end of pathname */
  strcpy ( &dflt[p], "\\*.*" );              /* add wildcards */
} /* ----------------------- */

void splitUp (char *args)
{                         /* parse search arg and complete it */
int    flag;

  addDrive (args);    /* make sure there's a drive designator */
  flag = fnsplit (args, drive, dir, name, ext);
  if (!(flag & EXTENSION)) {        /* if no extension found, */
    dfltArg (args, args);                          /* add it */
    fnsplit (args, drive, dir, name, ext);  /* and try again */
  }
} /* ----------------------- */
```

Program 3.2 (continued)

```c
void   addDrive (char *path)              /* add drive desig to path */
{
char    temp [MAXPATH];                   /* temporary string */
int     p = 0;

   if ( path [1] != ':' ) {
      strcpy ( temp, path );
      path [p++] = disk + 65;            /* convert to A, B, etc. */
      path [p++] = ':';                  /* insert colon */
      if (temp [0] != '\\')
         path [p++] = '\\';              /* and backslash */
      strcpy (&path [p], temp);          /* restore the rest */
   }
} /* ---------------------- */

void   error (char *msg)                  /* bomb off on error */
{
   perror ( msg );                        /* display DOS error message */
   exit ( 1 );                            /* quit */
} /* ---------------------- */

void   pmerge (char *pth, char *dr, char *sub)  /* make path */
{
int    p;

   fnmerge (pth, dr, sub, NULL, NULL);    /* recombine path */
   p = strlen ( pth ) - 1;
   if ( p > 1 && pth [p] == '\\' )
      pth [p] = '\0';                      /* remove slash at end */
} /* ---------------------- */

void   fmerge (char *mk, char *nm, char *xt)   /* make mask */
{
   fnmerge ( mk, NULL, NULL, nm, xt );
} /* ---------------------- */

void  heading (void)                       /* print report heading */
{
   printf ( "\n\nDirectory listing for %s", path );
   printf ( "\nName                Date        Time" );
   printf ( "       Attrib      Bytes      Size" );
} /* ---------------------- */

void  listdir (void)            /* list subdir per search criteria */
{
int    line = MAXLINES, thru, nfiles = 0;
long   k = 0L, b = 0L;

   heading ();
   thru = findfirst (mask, &file, 0xFF);   /* find first match */
   while ( !thru ) {
      nfiles++;                            /* count files */
```

Program 3.2 **(continued)**

```
      printf ( "\n%-20s", file.ff_name );       /* print filename */
      fdate ( file.ff_fdate );                      /* file date */
      ftime ( file.ff_ftime );                      /* file time */
      fattr ( file.ff_attrib );              /* file attributes */
      k += fsize ( file.ff_fsize );               /* file size */
      b += file.ff_fsize;                        /* total bytes */
      if ( !line-- ) {                            /* count line */
        printf ( "\nPress any key for more..." );
        getch ();
        heading ();
        line = MAXLINES;
      }
      thru = findnext ( &file );              /* get next file */
    }
    if ( nfiles == 0 )
      puts ("\nFile not found");
    else
      printf ("\n%d files, total bytes = %lu, total space = %luK",
          nfiles, b, k );
} /* ---------------------- */

void  showfree (int disk)          /* show free space on disk */
{
struct dfree  drive;
unsigned long avail;

    getdfree ( disk, &drive );
    avail = (unsigned long) drive.df_avail * drive.df_bsec *
          drive.df_sclus;
    printf ("\nFree space on drive %c = %lu\n\n",
          disk + 'A' - 1, avail);
} /* ---------------------- */

void  fdate (int d)                          /* show file date */
{
    printf ( "%02d/", (d & 0x01E0) >> 5 );          /* month */
    printf ( "%02d/", d & 0x001F );                  /* date */
    printf ( "%02d  ", (( d >> 9 ) & 0x007F ) + 80 ); /* year */
} /* ---------------------- */

void  ftime (int t)                          /* show file time */
{
int   mh, h;

  mh = ( t >> 11 ) & 0x001F;                  /* compute hour */
  if ( mh < 1 ) h = 12;
  else
    h = ( mh >= 12 ) ? mh - 12 : mh;          /* civilian time */
  printf ( "%2d:", h );                              /* hour */
  printf ( "%02d", ( t & 0x07E0 ) >> 5 );          /* minute */
  cputs ( ( mh >= 12 ) ? "p    " : "a    " );     /* am or pm */
} /* ---------------------- */
```

Program 3.2 **(continued)**

```
void   fattr (char a)                      /* show file attributes */
{
char    bit = 0x20;
char    attr[] = "ADLSHR";
int     i;

  for ( i = 0; i < 6; i++ ) {
    putchar ( (a & bit) ? attr[i] : '.' );   /* attrib or dot */
    bit >>= 1;                               /* shift to next bit */
  }
  cputs ( "     " );
} /* --------------------- */

long   fsize (long sz)                          /* show file size */
{                    /* return space in K actually occupied by file */
long    gran, clus;

  printf ( "%9lu   ", sz );                       /* show bytes */
  clus = fat.fi_bysec * fat.fi_sclus; /* clust size in bytes */
  gran = sz / clus;                              /* full clusters */
  if ( sz % clus ) gran++;               /* bump for partial cluster */
  gran *= clus / 1024;                   /* space in K taken by file */
  printf ( "%4luK", gran );                          /* show it */
  return ( gran );
} /* --------------------- */
```

Now that we've covered the directory manipulations of normal and protected files, let's consider a special kind of directory entry: the volume label.

CHAPTER 4

Volume Labels

This chapter discusses a special kind of directory entry called the volume label, and furnishes a "bulletproof" method for manipulating the volume label on any disk.

Of all the many features and conveniences DOS offers, probably none is as neglected as the volume label. It's not hard to see why; DOS works just as well with disks that don't have one as with those that do. In fact, DOS doesn't even do anything with the label except display it (or a message saying there isn't one) when you list the directory, and there are no DOS calls to manipulate the label. So why bother with it?

Labels can be useful for a number of things. One example is detecting when a diskette has been switched while files are still open. Another is in safeguarding sensitive information by refusing to write to a disk that lacks the right label. Here we examine some uses for labels and show how to read, write, and change them from within Turbo C programs.

First let's pin down what a label is, and how it's stored on disk. There's nothing magical about a label. It's simply a special entry in the disk's root directory. All file entries in DOS 2.0 and higher carry a byte describing the file's attributes (normal, hidden, read-only, and so on). A label is an entry with an attribute byte whose value is 08H. No space is allocated to the entry. It's much like a file that was created and then closed without any data being written to it. The only space a label occupies, then, is the 32 bytes taken by each directory entry.

This explains why a label is limited to 11 characters. In the directory, DOS reserves 11 bytes for a file name, with the name itself being left-justified in the first eight bytes and the extension left-justified within the last three. DOS ignores this convention when storing and retrieving a label, instead left-justifying the label in the complete 11-character field and padding to the right with spaces to fill unused positions. You can have up to eleven characters in a label because that's how many bytes there are in a directory entry.

The attribute byte governs how DOS treats each entry. When you list the directory, you only see normal and read-only files. The **DIR** command skips over those with other attributes. That's why IOMBIO.COM, IBMDOS.COM, and other hidden and system files don't show up in the listing. Neither does the label, except in a special message at the top.

Most of the DOS file-management routines and all of them in Turbo C except for findfirst() and findnext() don't deal with files having unusual attributes. You have to work at it when fooling with the label, and writing a label should be considered armed and dangerous inasmuch as it can potentially maim the directory. Later we'll deal with safe methods for manipulating labels from within Turbo C programs.

Meanwhile, let's consider some uses for labels.

What Are They Good For?

The mainframe world has been using volume labels for years. No doubt that's where the idea came from when Microsoft set out to create DOS. They're particularly useful for identifying removable media such as disk packs and floppies, but they can also serve to distinguish among fixed media such as multiple hard disks. In short, a label answers the question, "Who are you?"

There are several reasons you might want to ask this of a disk. One is in determining whether a diskette has been switched in the drive before writing to an open file. I have horror stories, and probably most other PC "power users" do as well, about switching disks to save multiple copies of a file being edited. Later you discover that the disks are corrupted beyond redemption. If every diskette had a unique label and the program checked the label before writing, this wouldn't happen. Later we'll discuss the problem of unlabeled disks (which are indistinguishable from one another) and what to do about them in this context.

Another application for labels is in protecting sensitive data. Software, by and large, is naive about this. It cheerfully writes anything on any disk. An electronic prowler can thus bring up an application, save the company's most intimate secrets on any old disk, and take them away to be analyzed. Making a program label-sensitive isn't a cureall for industrial espionage, but it can help. Develop a sensible, harmless-looking labeling system for floppies containing sensitive data, keep those floppies locked up, and make the program that reads and writes them check labels. If a program balks at writing to the intruder's diskette because it has the wrong label, he or she won't have a clue as to why. This is especially so since it never occurs to anyone using micros that disk labels might be important.

You can also effect a form of copy protection for your software using labels. It works like this: The first time the program runs, it checks the disk label. If there is no label, it creates one. In either case, it modifies itself by initializing a label field within the code space, then saves its own image to disk. Thereafter, each time the program starts, it checks the actual label against the one it expects. If they don't match, the program aborts.

No doubt there are other uses for labels as well. Our purpose here is not to present an exhaustive list, but to give you some ideas about how to put this unappreciated DOS feature to work protecting your disks, data, and software.

What to Do About Unlabeled Disks

One unlabeled disk looks the same as the next, and since few DOS users bother to label floppies, this makes it impossible to detect if diskettes have been swapped in the drive. Consequently, if your program is going to check for switched diskettes before writing to an open file, it must first determine the label of the diskette from which it initially read the data. When no label exists, it must create one that has a good chance of being unique.

Suggestion: Make a string out of the system time and label the diskette with it. By going down to the level of hundredths of a second, there is virtually no chance that any two diskettes will ever be assigned the same label.

Having so tagged the diskette, the program can then check the current label against the "read-from" label before performing a write. If they're not the same, tell the user to put the correct disk back in the drive. This is a sensible way to avoid the accidental corruption of diskettes.

DOS Is Finicky

There are rules about labels, and DOS brooks no argument about them. If you violate the rules, DOS refuses to write out the label, but it doesn't explain why. Its only response is to return **0FFh** in the AL register, meaning that the operation was unsuccessful.

Because a label is a kind of filename, you can only use characters that are valid within the name of any DOS file. The DOS manual spells them out; in general they're any printable character, less the wildcard characters ? and *. The 11-byte field must be padded with trailing spaces.

These restrictions pose a special problem for C programs, since C always terminates a string with an ASCII zero (the \0 character) and leaves garbage after it. Consequently, after loading the label into the file control block and before asking DOS to put it on the disk, you have to replace the null terminator and any other garbage in the 11-byte field with spaces. The **pad()** function in the program in Program 4.1 furnishes this service.

A label can only have a meaningful existence in the root directory. Theoretically it's possible to copy one to a subdirectory, but DOS would never notice it and your software would have to go to extraordinary lengths to find it. It's been reported here and there that DOS has bugs with regard to labels, which can cause it to garble directories, lose files, and even render the disk useless.

For these reasons, it's advisable to limit a disk to one label properly placed in the root where it belongs. Manipulate the label using the "safe" procedures outlined next and shown in the VOLUME.C program in Program 4.1. While this program closely parellels DOS's LABEL utility, its structures and functions illustrate how to manipulate volume labels from within any Turbo C program.

Program 4.1 **Program for Manipulating Disk Labels**

```
/* VOLUME.C: Reads and writes volume label */

/* INCLUDES */
#include <stdio.h>
#include <dos.h>
#include <string.h>
#include <ctype.h>
#include <conio.h>

/* CONSTANTS */
#define PROMPT "\nLabel is limited to 11 characters:"
#define BEEP  7
#ifndef TRUE
#define TRUE   1
#define FALSE 0
#endif

/* LOCAL FUNCTION PROTOTYPES */
char  gotlabel (void);
void  change (void);
void  addlabel (void);
void  pad (char name[]);

/* GLOBALS */
union REGS  reg;                                /* register set */
struct {            /* simulated xfcb loaded by DOS fcn 11h */
  char      skip1[8];              /* space to old label */
  char      oldlabel[11];                    /* old label */
  char      skip2[5];              /* space to new label */
  char      newlabel[11];                    /* new label */
  char      skip3[29];    /* to make struct 64 bytes long */
} dta;
struct xfcb fcbx = {{0xFF}, /* init xfcb for label search */
                    {"\0\0\0\0\0"},         /* reserved zeros */
                    {FA_LABEL},      /* set label attribute */
                   };
/* ------------------------- */

void main ()
{
char    exists;

/* INITIALIZE */
  setdta (MK_FP (_DS, (unsigned) & dta));
  puts ("\nGet volume label from which drive?");
```

Program 4.1 **(continued)**

```c
    fcbx.xfcb_fcb.fcb_drive =                   /* get drive */
          toupper (getch ()) - '@';
    strcpy (fcbx.xfcb_fcb.fcb_name,
          "???????????");                       /* set wildcard */

/* PROCESS */
  if (exists = gotlabel ())
    printf ("\nLabel of drive %c is %.11s",
          fcbx.xfcb_fcb.fcb_drive + '@', dta.oldlabel);
  else
    printf ("\nDrive %c has no label",
          fcbx.xfcb_fcb.fcb_drive + '@');
  puts ("\n\nDo you want to write a new label? (y/n)");
  if (toupper (getch ()) == 'Y')
    if (exists)
      change ();
    else
      addlabel ();
} /* --------------------- */

char  gotlabel (void)                /* read label from disk */
                          /* returns TRUE if found, else FALSE */
{
  reg.x.dx = (unsigned) &fcbx;            /* point DX to fcbx */
  reg.h.ah = 0x11;             /* DOS fcn: search for first */
  intdos (&reg, &reg);                          /* call DOS */
  if (!reg.h.al)                  /* AL = 0 when successful */
    return (TRUE);
  else              /* non-zero AL means no label found */
    return (FALSE);
} /* --------------------- */

void  change (void)                  /* change disk label */
{                           /* same DOS call as renaming file */
  puts (PROMPT);
  scanf ("%11s", dta.newlabel);          /* ignore > 11 chars */
  pad (dta.newlabel);               /* pad with trailing spaces */
  reg.x.dx = (unsigned) &dta;          /* point to dta buffer */
  reg.h.ah = 0x17;                  /* DOS fcn: rename file */
  intdos (&reg, &reg);                          /* call DOS */
  if (!reg.h.al)                  /* AL = 0 when successful */
    printf ("\n\nLabel successfully changed to %.11s",
          dta.newlabel);
  else {
    puts ("\n\nUnsuccessful! Disk may be damaged");
    putchar (BEEP);
  }
} /* --------------------- */

void  addlabel (void)           /* label an unlabeled disk */
{                           /* same DOS call as creating new file */
  puts (PROMPT);
```

Program 4.1 **(continued)**

```
    scanf ("%11s", fcbx.xfcb_fcb.fcb_name); /* get 11 chars */
    pad (fcbx.xfcb_fcb.fcb_name);      /* pad w/trailing spcs */
    reg.x.dx = (unsigned) &fcbx;          /* use xfcb for this */
    reg.h.ah = 0x16;                  /* DOS fcn: create file */
    intdos (&reg, &reg);                          /* call DOS */
    if (!reg.h.al)                 /* AL = 0 when successful */
      printf ("\n\nDisk is now labeled %.11s",
              fcbx.xfcb_fcb.fcb_name);
    else {
      puts ("\n\nUnsuccessful! Root directory may be full");
      putchar (BEEP);
    }
} /* ----------------------- */


void  pad (char name[])
                       /* pad filename with trailing spaces */
{               /* DOS chokes on C null terminator in filename */
int    p;

    if (strlen (name) < 11)
      for (p = strlen (name); p < 11; p++)
        name[p] = ' ';
} /* ----------------------- */
```

Operating on Disk Labels

DOS provides two sets of functions for operating on files. One set came into existence with DOS 2.x and uses an integer called the *handle* to identify a given open file; the handle routines accomodate tree-structured directories. The other set of file-handling functions are holdovers from DOS 1.x, which in turn were inherited from CP/M. It is these low-level functions, specifically 11h, 16h, and 17h under interrupt 21h, that must be used to operate on labels. These functions only work on the root directory, which explains why a label is meaningless anywhere else.

The low-level functions use a structure called a file control block (FCB) instead of a handle. There are two types of FCBs, the standard format and a stretched version called the extended FCB, or XFCB. The extended format is an ordinary FCB preceded by an eight-byte header containing, among other things, an attribute byte. DOS functions 11h, 16h, and 17h recognize which FCB format they're dealing with by checking the first byte; it's always 0FFh in an XFCB.

You have to use an XFCB when working with a label, since attribute byte 08h is a necessary part of the label format. Turbo C furnishes definitions of the FCB and XFCB in **#include** file DOS.H, and the Turbo C function **find-first()** discussed in Chapter 2 can be used to read a label. However, Turbo C furnishes no function to change a label. Because these are risky operations that require careful control, it's best to use the Turbo C **intdos()** function with appropriate register setups.

Reading a Label

To read a label, use DOS function 11h. This function refers to an initialized XFCB to find out what you want to look for in the root directory. If it finds a match, it writes the corresponding XFCB to a separate 64-byte buffer called the DTA, for disk transfer address, and returns 0 in register AL to indicate success. If there is no match (no label in this case), function 11h returns **0FFh** and the DTA is unchanged. Following a successful read, you can fetch the label from offset 08h of the DTA.

Thus, before looking for the label, you have to do some setup. The first thing is to develop the DTA structure. For reasons we'll discuss later in connection with changing a label, this is not merely a copy of the XFCB definition given in dos.h. An entry under GLOBALS in the heading of Program 4.1 defines the structured variable dta.

Next you need to initialize a copy of the XFCB format as shown in the declaration of **struct xfcb fcbx** in the program. The variable **fcbx** thus has its first byte set to 0FFh to identify an XFCB to DOS, the reserved prefix field set to zeros, and the attribute byte set to 08h for a label (constant FA__LABEL is defined in DOS.H). Now you can begin execution.

The first executable step is to tell DOS where the DTA is. Do this by passing a far pointer to the Trubo C **setdta()** function, indicating the segment and offset of the structured variable. Next put the disk drive indicator into the **fcb__drive** field of structured variable fcbx. Finally, fill the filename and extension fields of fcbx with the wildcard character (?), which tells function 11h to return whatever name it finds in association with a label entry.

Now you can actually search for the label. Function **gotlabel()** in the program performs this task. Put the offset of fcbx into register DX, function 11h into AH, and call DOS with **intdos()**. If register AL contains **0FFh** on return, DOS did not find a label, and a 0 in AL means that it loaded the label's XFCB into the DTA.

Based on a simple test of register AL, then, you can either fetch the label name from .oldlabel, or determine that the disk is unlabeled. What you do from that point is application-dependent; VOLUME.C reports the outcome and asks if you want to write a new label. It proceeds based on the reply to the query and on whether or not the disk is already labeled. A less interactive program might act according to different decision rules, simply storing the label if one exists and writing one if it doesn't, without asking the user's permission or preference.

Changing an Existing Label _____

If you want to change an existing label to something else, proceed as though renaming a file using DOS function 17h. Turbo C has no equivalent that provides the necessary level of control for labels.

DOS function 17h requires deliberate corruption of the XFCB in the DTA. Write the new label starting six bytes after the end of the old label (field **newlabel** in the structure), and pad the remainder of the field with spaces. Because the DTA's attribute and **oldlabel** fields are already set (by function 11h), no other change to the DTA is required.

The **change()** function in the listing shows what to do next. Load the offset to the variable into register DX, DOS function 17h into AH, and call **intdos()**.

On return, register AL contains the result. It's **0** if successful, and potentially a catastrophe if **0FFh**. Any time this call is unsuccessful, immediately inspect the involved disk for damage to the FAT and root directory.

There are three probable causes for failure: You're trying to change a label that doesn't exist, your program set up the newname field in the DTA incorrectly, or your copy of DOS is corrupted. In the first two cases, DOS simply refuses to process the request and never goes to the disk, so damage is unlikely.

Labeling an Unlabeled Disk _____

Never assume that a disk is unlabeled. Instead, check first for the existence of a label by attempting to read it. If you get **0FFh** back in register AL, you know for certain that the disk is unlabeled. The reasons for this are twofold. DOS may suffer a nervous breakdown over having two labels in the same directory, and even if it doesn't, it will only recognize the first one it finds and ignore the second.

DOS function 16h creates a new file, and that's the function you use to write a label. In changing the label as discussed above, you use the DTA; to write a new label, instead use the same XFCB structure you set up for the search with function 11h. As the listing for function **addlabel()** shows, copy the label into the filename field at offset 08h (**field fcbx.xfcb__fcb.fcb__name** in the program). Although this field is officially eight bytes long, followed by another three for the extension, C will let you copy up to the full 11 characters into the name field. Don't forget to pad the unused bytes with trailing spaces, lest DOS choke on the invalid null terminator. Nothing else needs to be done to prepare the XFCB.

Write the label into the root directory by placing the offset of the structured fcbx variable into register DX, DOS function 16h into register AH, and issuing **indos()**.

On return, DOS returns **0** in register AL for a successful save and **0FFh** if unsuccessful. Failure usually occurs for one of two reasons: an improperly developed XFCB, or a full directory.

While at first glance labels don't seem to have much purpose, in fact they can be used creatively by sophisticated programs as a tool for protecting disks, data, and even software. Because DOS furnishes no specific calls for operating on labels, it's necessary to develop one's own. Writing labels to disk can be perilous unless you apply common sense and a bit of care, and then it's quite a simple and safe operation. The methods furnished here provide useful and reliable techniques for taking advantage of this ignored feature of DOS.

Having covered a broad spectrum of disk and directory manipulation, let's move on to file-handling in Turbo C.

CHAPTER 5

Seventy-One Things
to Do With a File

I f ever a subject begged for clarification, it's file-handling in Turbo C. The language provides 71 functions—plus several variants thereupon—for manipulating files. Some are general functions, others rely on a file handle, and still others deal with streams, requiring a special file descriptor structure. While this much flexibility provides for tremendous power in file operations, it's bewildering. This chapter and the next attempt to sort the mess of functions into something comprehensible.

For a complete, annotated listing of Turbo C file control functions, see Appendix B. This chapter illustrates practical uses for many of them, but not all; its thrust is to give an overview of the possibilities.

Handles and Streams

The Turbo C documentation uses two terms with reference to files, but it doesn't explain what they mean. Let's do it here. The terms are *handle* and *stream*.

A *handle* is an identifier (an integer) that DOS assigns to input/output entities to keep track of them. It is, in effect, a reference number. If DOS assigns the handle 6 to file XYZ.DAT when it's opened, you specify handle 6 in subsequent file operations and DOS knows which open file you want to work on. About 20 of the 71 file functions in Turbo C use handles.

DOS predefines five handles, assigning them (whether actually used in a program or not) to logical devices that function as virtual files. They are as follows:

Handle	Purpose	DOS Device	C stream
0	Standard input	CON	stdin
1	Standard output	CON	stdout
2	Standard error	CON	stderr
3	Auxiliary	AUX	stdaux
4	List	PRN	stdprn

The CON device is a catch-all name for the keyboard and display, AUX generally means a serial port, and PRN stands for the printer. DOS automatically opens these five I/O files for any program in execution.

For each predefined handle, there is a corresponding standard C stream that is generally more useful. You can use the stream names as "file variables," and it's not necessary to issue a **fopen()** before referring to them. For example, to write to the printer, simply code a statement such as

```
fprintf (stdprn, "\n%s", "This is printed output");
```

Because DOS predefines the five handles 0–4, the first numeric handle it assigns to a program's file is 5, and so on upward. You'll probably never need to know the actual value of a given handle; open functions return it to a variable, and you pass that variable as an argument to other handle functions.

A *stream* is any source or destination for data that moves serially, that is, byte by byte. For example, when you read data from a disk file, the data arrive in a stream of bytes and get stored in memory or processed sequentially in some other fashion. Similarly, if you write a string of characters to a file, you are sending a stream of data. The source and destination for these operations are thus stream files.

By this definition, the keyboard, printer, and display screen can also be stream files, and so can an auxiliary device such as a serial port. The concept of a stream file is therefore not limited to data on disk; any device that sends and/or receives data sequentially can be a stream.

While a handle can and often does represent a stream, Turbo C differentiates between handle functions and stream functions. A handle function returns or requires the DOS-assigned handle. On the other hand, a stream function utilizes a data structure known as the FILE object, and returns or requires a pointer to that structure in lieu of a handle.

The FILE object is defined in STDIO.H with a **typedef**. A program using any of the nearly 30 stream functions—that is, virtually any program that does file operations—should thus **#include** <**stdio.h**> at the top to make the FILE structure available.

Files themselves are represented as pointers to FILE structures. For example, if you want to read from a disk file and write to the printer, you can declare the requisite pointers as

```
FILE *diskFile, *lst;
```

The **fopen()** function and its variants **fdopen()** and **freopen()** return pointers to static FILE structures when successful. Thus the call

```
diskFile = fopen ("INPUT.FIL", "r");
```

assigns to diskFile a pointer to the structure associated with INPUT.FIL. All subsequent stream operations on this file require the pointer. For example, to close the file later:

```
fclose (diskFile);
```

Some of the handle and stream functions are parallel. Examples are **read()/ fread()**, **write()/fwrite()**, **eof()/feof()**, **close()/fclose()**, and **tell()/ftell()**. In these cases and others, the **f** prefix indicates a stream function. However, an **f** prefix is not a dead giveaway: **fstat()** is a handle function, and **fnsplit()** is neither but instead a general utility function. Many of the functions are unique to one or the other file-identification methods. For example, the file time and date can only be accessed via a handle function, while formatted text output to a file can only be accomplished via a stream function.

You can open a file with either a handle or a stream function: **open()** and **fopen()**, respectively. This would seem to pose a dilemma; if some operations are only possible with handles and others only with stream functions, which way should you open the file if you want to do some of both?

Fortunately, Turbo C furnishes a bridge function to solve this problem. This is **fileno()**, which returns the handle associated with a stream. Use it as follows:

```
FILE *infil;                        /* declare stream pointer */
int    strhan;                      /* handle for stream file */
{
    infil = fopen ("SOME.FIL", "r");
    strhan = fileno (infil);
    . . .
}
```

Now you can pass the **strhan** variable to functions requiring a handle; both **infil** and **strhan** identify the same file.

The **fdopen()** function provides a bridge in the opposite direction: associating a stream with an open handle. However, it's more complicated to use. Unless you know in advance that all operations you'll want to perform on a file are through handle functions, here's a general rule:

- Open files as streams with **fopen()**.
- Before calling the first handle function (if any), use **fileno()** to get the handle for the stream.

Now let's classify some groups of file operations and see how to use this wealth of functions.

Operations on Unopened Files _____

Although most file operations occur on files that are opened—that is, made accessible to the program via an internal communications link—there are a few that we can perform on unopened files. We discussed one in Chapter 2 in connection with the **searchpath()** function, which determines the location of a named file along the chain of directories specified by the DOS PATH command. Four others, which we'll cover here, are determining the accessibility of a file, changing its read/write permission, renaming, and erasing.

A common technique in C is to open a file within an **if()** statement and check the value returned by **open()** or **fopen()** to find out if the operation was successful. Example:

```
if ((fpp = fopen ("SOME.FIL", "r")) !=NULL)
   /* process the file */
else
   /* file was not opened */
```

This method, though widely used, has a couple of drawbacks. First, the **fopen()** statement itself is intuitive only because it so often appears in programs. Try translating it into a concise statement in plain English sometime. The second drawback is that it often leads to difficult program logic; the **else** condition might appear a page or more after the open, where it's hard to find.

An easier way is to check first for the existence of a file and its access permission. If the file doesn't exist or perhaps is read-only when you intend to write to it, you can deal with the problem up front and not as the **otherwise** case in a failed open.

The Turbo C **access()** function lets you check the accessibility of an unopened file. As a fringe benefit, you can also use it to see if a specified directory exists. The call is made as follows:

```
retval = access (filepath, accmode);
```

where:

- **filepath** is a pointer to the character string containing the path to the file or directory.
- **accmode** is a bit pattern described below.
- **retval** is an integer, which receives **0** or **−1** from the function.

The **accmode** bit patterns correspond to the access permission you're inquiring about. Those valid in DOS are:

Pattern	Meaning
06	Read and write permission
04	Read permission
02	Write permission
00	Existence

The *Turbo C Reference Manual* also shows 01, execute permission, but this has no meaning in DOS and is merely carried over for compatibility with Unix; if a file is visible in the directory (that is, not hidden) and you inquire about permission 01, **access()** replies that it is executable even if it's a data file.

Suppose you want to see if the existing DATA.FIL can be written to. The call

```
retval = access ("DATA.FIL", 2);
```

returns **0** to retval, indicating that it's a normal read/write file. You can proceed with the open and write operations.

But let's say that the file has a read-only attribute, meaning that DOS won't let you write to it. In that case, **access()** returns **−1** to indicate that the requested permission is invalid for the file. You might handle this situation as follows:

```
if (access ("DATA.FIL", 2) == −1) {
    puts ("File is read-only");
    exit (1);
}
```

The program quits when DATA.FIL cannot be written to, and otherwise it falls through the condition to normal file operations following the closing curly brace.

A more elegant way to deal with this might be to change the mode of the file to read/write using the **chmod()** function, a close relative of **__chmod()** discussed in Chapter 3. To do this, **#include <sys\stat.h>** and issue the statement

```
chmod ("DATA.FIL", S__IWRITE);
```

Under DOS, write permission implies read permission, so a file set to **S__IWRITE** becomes **read/write**. If your program might be ported to Unix, however, code the second argument as **S__IREADIS__IWRITE**, since Unix supports write-only files.

To check for the existence of a file or directory, pass permission pattern 0 as an argument to **access()**. The function returns **0** when the path exists and **−1** when it does not.

The return value **−1** can have more than one meaning. You always get **−1** when the file or directory doesn't exist; you can also get **−1** when the requested permission is invalid for the file. Turbo C provides a means for interpreting −1.

The **#include** file errno.h contains the declaration for the global system variable errno, as well as a number of constants indicating various error conditions. If you **#include** errno.h in your program, you can check errno for a value indicating what −1 means when returned by **access()**. There are three possible errno values from this function:

errno == EZERO   No error
errno == ENOENT   No such file or path
errno == EACCES   Permission denied

The **unlink()** function deletes a file. It is equivalent to the DOS commands **DEL** and **ERASE,** and takes the form

    retval = unlink (filename);

The returned values are the same as for **access()**, and so are the possible settings of errno. Usually it's no big deal if **unlink()** fails—the worst that can happen is that the file continues to exist—so you can safely ignore the returned value in most cases.

The last operation on unopened files that we'll discuss is renaming. It takes the form

    retval = rename (oldname, newname);

Assignment of **0** to retval indicates success, and −1 means failure. On −1, errno can have any of three possible values, which are:

errno == ENOENT   No such file
errno == EACCES   Permission denied
errno == ENOTSAM   Not on same disk

The last error might raise your eyebrows. That's because **rename()** is more powerful than it seems on the surface. Not only can it rename a file, but it can also move that file from one directory to another. For example, say that you want to remove SOME.FIL from the \APPLIC directory and place it in \BACKUP, retaining the same filename. The statement to do this is

    retval = rename (\APPLIC\SOME.DAT,
                \BACKUP\SOME.DAT);

Afterwards, SOME.DAT no longer appears in the \APPLIC directory. Note that the physical file does not move; instead, its directory entry is relocated into \BACKUP. This is a much more efficient way to shuffle files among directories than doing copies and deletes.

Opening Files

Turbo C furnishes eight functions for opening files, and a whole bunch of options besides. Most of the time you'll use only one or two of them—**fopen()** and **open()**—but you should be aware of the others and their options. In general, the other open functions are specialized, and the options provide for a high degree of control over the subsequent status of the file.

There are four file-creation functions: **creat()**, **_creat()**, **creatnew()**, and **creattemp()**. We'll discuss the latter in the next section, which involves temporary files.

The sibling functions **creat()** and **_creat()** make a new file, or erase an existing file's contents and prepare it to receive entirely new data. These functions fail when attempting to open existing files marked read-only.

The **creat()** function opens or creates a normal read/write file in text mode (unless the global variable **_fmode** is set to **O_BINARY**). In Turbo C, a text mode file undergoes translation of new-line information: in memory, a new line, represented by the character \n, is a single line feed (LF), but when written to disk, this is translated into a carriage return/line feed (CRLF) sequence. The opposite translation occurs when reading from disk. The call to **creat()** is

```
newhandle = creat ("DATA.FIL", access);
```

where **access** is one of the following constants defined in SYS\STAT.H:

Access constant	Meaning
S_IWRITE	Write access
S_IREAD	Read-only access
S_IWRITE|S_IREAD	Normal read/write access

Note that write access only (**S_IWRITE**) is equivalent to read/write access (**S_IWRITE | S_IREAD**), since in DOS, permission to write implies permission to read. Thus the first and third entries achieve the same file access status.

The **creat()** function does nothing with this access information until the file is closed. At that time, it sets the attribute byte according to the access argument.

The **_creat()** function always opens a file in binary mode (unless the global variable **_fmode** is set to **O_TEXT**). In binary mode, no translation is performed on new line information (more on this in the next chapter). The call to **_creat** is slightly different from its sibling's:

```
newhandle = _creat ("DATA.FIL", attribute);
```

In this case, the **attribute** argument can be any of the file attributes defined in DOS.H and discussed in Chapter 3: hidden, system, read-only, and so on.

Both **creat()** and **__creat()** will clobber an existing file's contents unless the file is marked read-only. The **creatnew()** function safeguards against this; **creatnew()** fails if the file already exists, thus preventing the program from accidentally wiping out data. Otherwise it's the same as **__creat()**.

The **fopen()** and **open()** functions have much in common. The chief difference is that **fopen()** is a stream function, and **open()** returns a file handle. But while they are otherwise parallel functions, the details of their options differ.
differ.

The usual way to open a file is to declare a pointer to a static FILE structure as

FILE *fp;

and then open it with

fp = fopen (filename, access);

where **filename** is the path and name of the file, and **access** is one of the following strings surrounded by double quotes:

Access type	Meaning
"r"	Read from file sequentially
"w"	Begin sequential writing at start of file[1]
"a"	Begin sequential writing at end of file (append)
"r+"	Read and write file[2]
"w+"	Same as "r+"
"a+"	Same as "r+" except file pointer is positioned at end of file

[1] The "w" access mode erases an existing file's contents upon opening it, so that new data start at the beginning. If the file does not exist when opened for writing, creates it.

[2] The plus-sign modifiers indicate update (read/write) modes, while their absence indicates one-way file operations.

The **fopen()** function returns a **NULL** pointer if the open attempt was unsuccessful. An example of an unsuccessful attempt is when you try to open a nonexistent file in access mode "r" (read). As mentioned earlier, you can open a file and test for success in the same (nonintuitive) statement with

if ((fp = fopen (filepath, "r")) != NULL) { . . .

An alternative way to open a file is with the handle functions **open()** and **__open()**. The second—**__open()** with the preceding underscore—takes advantage of DOS 3.x capabilities, but it potentially cannot be ported to other C implementations. For more information on **__open()**, see pages 256–257 in the *Turbo C 2.0 Reference Guide*.

The **open()** function returns a handle when successful, or −1 when it's not. You can specify a number of access options, which are defined in FCNTL.H. The most common are equivalent to those for **fopen()**:

Option	Equivalent to	Meaning
O__RDONLY	"r"	Read only
O__WRONLY	"w"	Write only
O__RDWR	"r+"	Read/write

Less common access options relevant to DOS systems are:

Option	Meaning
O__APPEND	Equivalent to fopen( ) "a"
O__CREAT	Create new file and set attribute byte per the optional permissions argument*
O__TRUNC	Erase file contents
O__BINARY	Explicitly open in binary mode (no newline translation)
O__TEXT	Explicitly open in text mode

*Permission arguments are the same as for creat( ) above, and are defined in SYS\STAT.H.

As mentioned earlier in this chapter, it's generally advisable to open files as streams using **fopen()**. If you need to get the file handle, you can do so with the **fileno()** function, passing the stream pointer as an argument.

The **freopen()** function is useful for replacing one stream with another. It saves the step of closing a stream before associating its pointer with the next file. When you issue **freopen()**, the buffer for the currently open stream is flushed, the file is closed, and the replacement file is opened. This function is handy for switching I/O from one stream to another.

The program REOPEN.C in Program 5.1 illustrates **freopen()**, and also moving between stream and handle I/O. The program opens DISK.FIL as a stream and writes some text to it using the stream function **fprintf()**. It then repoints the stream to the printer, where it writes the same text. Next, it reopens the disk file in append mode, gets its handle, and writes the text again, this time using the handle function **write()**. After you run the program, type **DISK.FIL**; it will contain the same message twice, and the text will also appear as a printout.

Program 5.1 **Reopening a File and Switching Between Stream and Handle Operations**

```
/* REOPEN.C: Demos freopen(), mixed stream and handle
            I/O to same file */

#include <stdio.h>

main ()
{
FILE    *out;
int     handle;
char    buf[] = "\nNow is the time for all good men",
        fil[] = "DISK.FIL";

   out = fopen (fil, "w");                    /* open disk file */
   fprintf (out, "%s", buf);                  /* write as stream */
   out = freopen ("PRN", "w", out); /* reopen for printer */
   fprintf (out, "%s", buf);                  /* write as stream */
   out = freopen ("disk.fil", "a", out);   /* reopen disk */
   handle = fileno (out);                     /* get handle */
   printf ("\nHandle is %d", handle);         /* show handle */
   write (handle, buf, sizeof (buf));      /* write w/handle */
   fclose (out);                              /* close stream */
}
```

Working with Temporary Files

Complex programs, especially those that work with large amounts of data, occasionally need a place to stash results as they work. Compilers are a good example, and so are sort utilities, editors that work on more than one file at a time, and other challenging applications. They write interim results for temporary safekeeping, and later return to reclaim them for further processing. That's what temporary files are about.

Because a temporary file exists only for the duration of the program run, there's no reason for the programmer or user even to know its name. The program itself can assign a unique name, create the file, use it, and later erase it with **unlink()** during clean-up at the end of the job.

The **creattemp()** function exists for this purpose. Pass **creattemp()** a string containing the path to the directory where you want the file to reside (terminated with a backslash) and the file's attribute, and the function automatically assigns a unique filename and opens the file for output.

The path must be a string variable with enough extra room to contain an eight-character filename plus a null terminator. For example, say you want to create a temporary file in the \TURBOC directory. The path specification is \TURBOC\ which occupies eight characters. Therefore the variable must have at least 17 character positions; eight for the path, eight for the filename, and one for the null terminator. You might declare this as

```
char path[17] = "\\TURBOC\\";
```

Note that double backslashes are necessary to convince the compiler that you really mean literal backslashes; each generates a single \ character in the resulting string. After initializing the path, either through a declaration as shown here or with a call to **strcpy()**, create the file with

```
handle = creattemp (path, 0);
```

The **0** argument indicates a normal read/write file. You can also specify special file attributes defined in DOS.H, such as **FA_HIDDEN** for a hidden file. Usually, because the file exists only for the duration of program execution, there is no reason to give it anything but an ordinary attribute.

The **creattemp()** function loads the assigned filename into the eight characters following the end of the path. The filename, if you look at it, appears bizarre. It reads something like 162E135F. The name is built up from the system time using hex notation, so 16 is the hour (2200, or 10 P.M.), 2E is the minute (46 minutes after the hour), and the rest derives from the system timer ticks, which occur 18.2 times per second. Thus, there is virtually no chance that two temporary files—no matter when created — will ever have conflicting names.

creattemp() is a handle function that places the new file into sequential output mode. Thus all output to the temporary file must be done using **write()**, which is a handle operation. When everything has been written to the file, close it with **close(handle)**. You can reopen it for input later on as either a stream or a handle file. Courtesy dictates that, when the temporary file is no longer needed, you dispose of it by closing, then unlinking. For the reopen and **unlink()** operations, pass the path completed by the original call to **creattemp()**, as in

```
unlink (path);
```

Generating Other Unique Filenames

Closely related to temporary files is the occasional need to obtain a more conventional filename that is easier to understand and remember than hex gibberish based on the system clock. For example, you might want to create some semipermanent files that pass from one program to another, as in a general ledger system that receives files from the subsystems devoted to payables, receivable, payroll, and inventory. Or maybe you're simply tired of dreaming up filenames and you want the system to do it for you.

You can ask Turbo C to generate a unique filename with the **mktemp()** function. To use **mktemp()**, pass as an argument a string variable containing six "X" characters. The function scans the current directory and formulates a unique filename that does not conflict with any existing name. It replaces the "X" template with this new name, which follows the sequence AA.AAA, AA.AAB, AA.AAC, . . . ,ZZ.ZZZ.

Note that, though the function scans the directory to prevent conflict, it doesn't actually create a file with the new name. Thus, if you want to reserve the name before generating another, you must create a file by that name before calling **mktemp()** again. If you don't, **mktemp()** will repeatedly return the same name.

The program TEMP.C in Program 5.2 illustrates **mktemp()** and **creattemp()** in action. It reports the first available unique name found by **mktemp()** and the path (in the TURBOC directory) to the unique file opened by **creattemp()**. The AA.* filename returned by **mktemp()** does not actually become a file, but the one that **creattemp()** makes does. Thus, **unlink()** deletes the temporary file before the program ends.

Program 5.2 **Creating Unique Filenames**

```
/* TEMP.C: Shows temporary filenames from mktemp() and
           creattemp() */

#include <dir.h>
#include <io.h>

main ()
{
char    name1[] = "XXXXXX", name2[80] = "\\TURBOC\\";
int     handle;

   mktemp (name1);
   printf ("\nName generated by mktemp:  %s", name1);
   handle = creattemp (name2, 0);
   printf ("\nFile created by creattemp: %s", name2);
   close (handle);
   unlink (name2);
}
```

Sequential Operations on Files

There are two ways to perform I/O on open files: sequential and random. The latter is also called direct file I/O and, occasionally in C literature, update mode. The next chapter discusses random file operations, while here we concentrate on sequential mode.

Sequential I/O proceeds exactly as its name suggests: in chronological order. As a program processes data, it writes results to the file. Each time, the file grows because new information is added to its end. Later, other code reads the file in precisely the same order as it was written.

Sequential processing has been with us for as long as computers have had external storage media. It's useful, time-honored, and proven, but not very flexible. If you want the 325th record in a sequential file, you have to read through 324 unwanted records to get to it. Sequential processing is thus inefficient for retrieving specific records (if you want to do that, see Chapter 6). However, it's still the best method for automatically processing batches of related information, usually with a loop smart enough to handle all possible conditions in the data.

Computer applications abound with batch processing requirements: business sytems (payroll, billing), utilities such as compilers and text-printers, even some seemingly interactive programs such as editors (which read text from a file into the heap, let the user modify it, and then write the changed text back out, always maintaining the logical sequence of the characters). The standard devices—keyboard, display, printer, and so on—are purely sequential "files" in that operations involving them cannot be otherwise.

Unlike BASIC and some other languages, C makes little distinction between sequential and random I/O. The same functions are used for both, the primary difference being that in random I/O, additional instructions move the file pointer to affect where the I/O occurs. In the absence of such functions (**fseek()**/**lseek()** et al., discussed in the next chapter), the file pointer automatically advances to the next position as data are written or read. Thus, sequential I/O occurs by default in C.

Turbo C's libraries are rich with file I/O functions, which we can categorize as follows:

Character input:	fgetc(), fgets(), getc(), getw(), ungetc()
Character output:	fputc(), fputs(), putc(), putw()
Record input:	fread(), read()
Record output:	fwrite(), write()
Formatted input:	fscanf(), vfscanf()
Formatted output:	fprintf(), vfprintf()
Block input:	randbrd()
Block output:	randbwr()

An important aspect of sequential operations is detecting the end-of-file (EOF) condition during reads. Turbo C furnishes two functions for this purpose: **eof()** and **feof()**. The first is for files being operated on with handles, the second for streams. Both work the same way, returning FALSE (0) each time the file is read until the end of the file is reached, at which time they return TRUE (nonzero). In DOS text mode, EOF is signaled by the **Ctrl-Z** character (ASCII 26) embedded in text; in binary mode, by having exhausted the byte count indicated by the file size. The following code fragment opens and prints a stream text file until EOF:

```
if ((fp = fopen (file, "r")) != NULL)
   while (!feof (file))
      printf ("%c", fgetc (file));
```

Now suppose we're reading and processing a binary-image file in sequential mode, involving a buffer called image:

```
if ((handle = open (file, O_BINARY)) != −1)
   while (!eof (handle))
      if (read (handle, image, sizeof (image)))
         process (image);
```

In both cases, the EOF test says, in effect, "while not end-of-file do the following . . . " The while loop terminates when EOF is reached, and never executes if the file cannot be opened.

When you reach EOF (or even if you don't), you can go back to the start of a sequential disk file by issuing a **rewind()**. This stream function repositions the file pointer to the very first element. It gets its name and its spirit from operations on magnetic tape reels in the mainframe world. A call to **rewind()** automatically clears the EOF indicator returned by **feof()**.

Detecting and Handling File Errors _____

Most file-handling functions in C return a value indicating success (a positive non-zero) or failure (0 or −1). For example, **fread()/fwrite()** return the number of items processed, **read()/write()** return the number of bytes handled, **fopen()** returns a pointer, **open()** a handle, and so on. In general, stream functions return an effective 0 (including NULL) on failure, and handle functions return −1 since 0 is a valid handle.

This gives you a convenient method to test whether or not an operation was successful. Since 0 is a logical FALSE, you can perform a direct Boolean test on stream operations, as in

```
if (fread (buffer, 32, 2, stream))
   /* process the buffer contents */
```

No comparison is necessary; the test fails if fread() returns 0, and otherwise the operation was successful. A comparison *is* necessary with handle functions because −1 indicates failure. The handle equivalent of the test above is

```
if (read (handle, buffer, 64) != −1)
   /* process the buffer contents */
```

With streams, there's another way to detect an error: with the **ferror()** function. This function is TRUE (nonzero) when an error has occurred and FALSE when not. Maybe this seems backwards, but it makes sense in the context of its usage:

```
if (ferror (stream))
   /* an error has occurred */
else
   /* no error */
```

An error on input is most commonly EOF; on output, out of disk space. Other errors can occur as well, but they're much less common.

When an error on a stream has been detected, the error indicator stays on until you explicitly clear it. There are two ways of doing so. The **rewind()** function discussed above clears the EOF condition so that **feof()** again returns FALSE. The **clearerr()** function clears both the EOF condition and the stream's general error flag. Until you have cleared the error **flag(s)s**, further I/O to the stream will not work. Of course, if you issue **clearerr()** and retry the same failed operation, chances are good that you'll again encounter the error.

In that case, you might want to use a retry counter to keep the program from locking up in a loop; abort the job after a preset number of retries, or do something heroic like instructing the user to insert a fresh floppy in drive A so that data aren't lost due to a full disk. The circumstances of your application will dictate what sort of recovery is appropriate.

Closing Files

Some programmers tend to be lazy about closing files. After all, they reason, the compiler automatically inserts code to close any files that are still open when the program terminates. That's true, but it's sloppy programming. It's not like picking up your own mess on the theory that if you don't, somebody else will.

Good programming practice dictates that if you open a file, you have the responsibility to close it.

There are four file closure functions, two for handles and two for streams. The handle functions are almost identical both in appearance and operation: **close(handle)** and **_close(handle)**. The difference is in how they treat text files. The first, without a leading underscore, writes a **Ctrl-Z** character (1Ah) at the end of a text file, whereas **_close()** does not. Why does this matter? Because **Ctrl-Z** serves as an EOF marker in text files. Therefore, use **close()** with text files and **_close()** with binary files.

The normal way to detach a stream from the program is with **fclose(stream)**. To close all open streams, as at program termination, issue **closeall()**, which takes no arguments. The **closeall()** function closes all streams except the console. There is no equivalent group close function for handle files; you have to close them individually.

This chapter has toured many of the 71 Turbo C functions associated with file handling and briefly reviewed sequential I/O, with which you are no doubt familiar. Now let's move on to a more complex and flexible way of managing data: random files.

CHAPTER **6**

DATA MANAGEMENT WITH RANDOM-ACCESS FILES

This chapter continues the discussion of Turbo C file management begun in the last chapter, but it's a great deal more specific. Here we turn to random-access files and the construction of sophisticated, flexible databases that can deliver real power to your applications.

There is nothing special about a random-access file. Random files can be processed sequentially, and vice-versa. The only hard-and-fast rule concerning files that will be processed randomly is that their elements (records) must have a fixed length. That's not necessarily true of pure sequential files, although it often is.

Because of this fixed-length requirement, it's convenient to think of a random file as consisting of many instances of a given data structure. Each instance is a record. You define the structure, then read and write it as often as necessary, always on a boundary that is an integral multiple of the structure size.

Note that we said "read *and* write." Random access is bidirectional, allowing you to jump around in the file, reading a record here, writing another there. To update a record, you go to it, read it into memory, make the necessary changes, and then write it back into the same location.

Thus, random access lets you go directly to the record you need, jumping forward or backward over intervening records without having to read them as you must in sequential access. This makes any record in a random-access file instantly available to the program.

The problem with random access is in determining the location of a specific record. If the file contains records on 500 people, how do we know which one has information about Susan Brown? Fortunately, there are solutions to this problem, and later in the chapter we'll develop methods for indexing random files.

Text Versus Binary Mode

Turbo C supports two basic ways of treating file contents. In text mode, the default, a newline character (written \n in C notation) is represented in program memory by the line feed character 0Ah, but externally by two characters: carriage return and line feed (0Dh 0Ah). When a stream or handle I/O function operates in text mode, it performs the newline translation. Writing to a file, it expands newlines into the two-character sequence, and when reading from a file, the opposite.

Binary mode doesn't perform this translation. If it reads CR/LF, both characters appear internally; when it outputs a newline, the receiving device gets only the one character.

The newline translation mode is often important in random access, where record length and adherence to field boundaries within the structure are critical. If a random record containing a newline is written in text mode, one byte is automatically added and everything to the right of it in the record shifts one byte, disrupting the field alignment, causing numerics to become disastrously wrong, and potentially clobbering the first byte of the next record. Thus, random files should always be opened in binary mode.

The default mode—text or binary—is specified by the global variable __fmode, which is defined in FCNTL.H. The header file initializes __fmode as O__TEXT. You can override this default by making the assignment

    __fmode = O__BINARY;

and any subsequent opens (fopen(), open(), creat(), etc.) will be in binary mode.

However, it might not always be desirable to make files globally binary. If a program uses a couple of random files and several ordinary text files including output to the printer, you don't want to lose newline translation for them all. In that event, you can override the default text mode for the random files, forcing only them to be binary.

The way to do this with a stream is to append the character **b** to the file mode argument for **fopen()**. For example, to open DATA.SET for random access in binary mode, write

    stream = fopen ("DATA.SET", "r+b");

The equivalent handle open is even more explicit:

    handle = open ("DATA.SET", O__BINARY);

Similarly, you can coerce a file into text mode with the **t** suffix in **fopen()** and O__TEXT with the handle open. If you set __**fmode to** O__BINARY, the text file open must do this, or else newline translation will not be in effect.

File Pointers

Just as variables in memory have pointers to indicate their locations, so do records in files. A file pointer is a long (32-bit) integer giving the offset of the element as a byte count relative to the start of the file. That is, if a file contains 32-byte records, the first is at 0, the second at 32, the third at 64, and so on, and the file pointer must be set to the proper value—an integral multiple of 32 bytes in this case—for the I/O to occur correctly. Because a file is not segmented like memory in DOS machines but instead one continuous address space of indeterminate size, the file pointer must be a long. Otherwise no file could ever contain more than 64K bytes.

When a file I/O occurs, the file pointer automatically advances by as many bytes as were read or written. That is, if the file pointer is set at 64 and a 32-byte I/O occurs, the file pointer afterwards has advanced to 96.

Ugly things happen if the file pointer gets out of sync with the record size. Say the record size is 100 bytes and you're stepping through the file a record at a time. The pointer should always be either 0 or some multiple of 100. But for some reason, perhaps you read only six bytes from one of the records. The pointer will then advance to 506, let's say, instead of a multiple of 100. Thereafter, if you keep adding 100 to the pointer for each record processed, it will always be off by six bytes. This means that on a read, you'll miss the first six bytes of the current record but get six from the next. In other words, the pointer will have lost its ability to locate records, and what you'll see in the structure fields is garbage.

For this reason, random-access programs manage the file pointer carefully, ensuring that it always maintains integrity with respect to record boundaries. The best rule when dealing with fixed-length record files is always to read and write entire records, and never portions.

Controlling the File Pointer

Two fundamental routines allow software to read and set the file pointer. As you might expect, there are variants for stream and handle files:

Stream	Handle	Effect
ftell()	tell()	Read file pointer
fseek()	lseek()	Set pointer

These functions are only meaningful for disk files. If a file is actually a device—for example, the keyboard—the concept of a pointer to a location within it is irrelevant, just as random access itself is.

If there's any doubt, you can determine if the file is a physical device with the function **isatty()**. Pass the file handle as an argument, and **isatty()** returns **TRUE** if the file is a device and **FALSE** if not. Supposing that the file was opened as a stream, you can instead pass **fileno()** as an argument, as in

```
if (isatty) (fileno (stream))
   /* stream is a device */
else
   /* it's a disk file */
```

Of course, there's seldom much doubt; it's hard to think of a situation in which a particular file might be a sequential stream associated with a device under some circumstances and a random disk file under others.

In discussing pointers, we often refer to "moving" them. Of course a software pointer doesn't physically move, since it's a static variable located at some fixed memory address. Rather, to "move" a pointer is to change its value, so that it indicates a new position in the object pointed to (a file in this case).

The "tell" routines are the only means of getting the current file pointer setting. The pointer automatically advances during read and write operations, so the "seek" routines don't have an exclusive right to control the pointer. Their purpose is to jump elsewhere in the file, as when you want to go directly from the eighty-fourth record to the eleventh.

Most programming languages use a numbering system to indicate the relative positions of records within a file, so that the first record is #0, the second is #1, and so on. C does not. Instead, it uses the actual byte offset from the start of the file, expressed as a long. The tell functions return a long, and the seek functions take a long argument.

At first glance this might seem a drawback, having to deal with byte offsets rather than relative record numbers, but in fact it's an advantage. It avoids the overly strict "typing" of random-access files that sometimes hinders Pascal programmers, while at the same time losing none of the advantages of random access. With C, you can write a header record that describes the file—its field names, data types, number of records, and so on—and begin the random-access data above the header. That's exactly how systems such as dBASE and Reflex treat files, and why they're written in C rather than the similar but more restrictive Pascal.

If you're more comfortable with relative record numbers, it's easy to translate between them and byte offsets. For a file containing only random records (no header record), derive the byte offset from the record number with

```
offset = (long) recno * sizeof (record);
```

and the record number from the byte offset with

```
recno = (int) offset / sizeof (record);
```

In this case, the lowest record number must be zero.

If you have a header record, you have to factor its size into the translation.

```
offset = (long) (recno * sizeof (record)) + sizeof (header);
```

Going the other way,

```
recno = (int) (offset - sizeof (header)) / sizeof (record);
```

The "tell" functions are very simple. Pass the stream or handle variable as the argument, assigning the result to a long variable:

```
longOffset = ftell (stream);
```

or

```
longOffset = tell (handle);
```

The "seek" are a little more complicated, because you have to provide, in addition to the file variable, a long offset and an origin indicator. The origin indicator answers the question "offset relative to what?" or, as given in the *Turbo C Reference Manual,* "from where?" There are three origin indicators defined in STDIO.H, which are used in both **fseek()** and **lseek()**.

Indicator	Meaning
SEEK_SET	Byte offset from start of file
SEEK_CUR	Byte offset from current position
SEEK_END	Byte offset from end of file

Thus, to move the stream file pointer to absolute offset 1042 (relative to the start of the file), code

```
fseek (stream, 1042L, SEEK_SET);
```

The same thing in a handle file is

```
lseek (handle, 1042L, SEEK_SET);
```

Note that the **L** suffix is required after a literal offset to coerce the value to a long. You can also write the cast

   (long) 1042

to accomplish the same thing, but the **L** suffix is more concise.

The "tell" functions return a positive long on success and -1L on failure. The only conceivable failure is passing an invalid file variable (bad value or file is a device), since in a true disk file the pointer must always be pointing somewhere.

The "seek" functions also return values that you can check for error. On success, a seek returns the byte offset of the new file position, and on failure, -1L. A seek failure occurs if you attempt to move the pointer to a location beyond the end of the file or to a negative offset (conceptually in front of the file's first byte).

Now let's put these ideas to work in a couple of scenarios that we can build upon.

Scenario 1: Deriving the Key from the Data

This scenario provides a simple working example of interactive random access. It also presents one possible solution to the problem of determining which record contains the information you want.

Here's the situation. Suppose you work for a wholesaler who sells 1,000 different parts. Each item is identified by a part number, which ranges from 1,000 through 1,999. The company has a warehouse where it stores these items in any of 26 bays lettered A through Z. Your boss has given you the assignment of writing a program that, by part number, tells how many of the particular item are in stock and which bay they're in, and also allows clerks to adjust the inventory on hand as items are sold and restocked.

After studying the requirements, you decide that the system needs to keep three items of information for each part: the part number, the quantity on hand, and the bay where it's stored. Thus, the record structure is

```
struct {
  unsigned partno, onhand;
  char     bay;
} PARTREC;
```

You need a file that reasonably approximates reality in order to test the application during development. This is easy to create; use the loop counter for the part number, a random number for the quantity on hand, and cycle through the alphabet for the bay. Program 6.1, MKINV.C, does this as it creates a test inventory file in sequential mode. Run it so that you'll have some data for the random access program developed later.

Program 6.1 **Program to Create a Test File for the Inventory System**

```
/* MKINV.C: Creates test file for inventory system */

#include <stdio.h>
#include <stdlib.h>

typedef struct {
  unsigned  partno, onhand;
  char      bay;
} PARTREC;

void main ()
{
PARTREC    item;
FILE       *stream;
unsigned   n;
char       bay = 'A';

  if ((stream = fopen ("TEST.INV", "wb")) != 0) {
    for (n = 1000; n < 2000; n++) {
      item.partno = n;
      item.onhand = rand ();
      bay = (bay == 'Z') ? 'A' : ++bay;
      item.bay = bay;
      fwrite (&item, sizeof (item), 1, stream);
    }
    fclose (stream);
  } else
    puts ("Cannot create file");
}
```

The system for determining random-access record locations is quite simple. The part numbers run from 1,000 through 1,999, and the file is sorted in that order. Therefore record #0 is for part 1,000, record #1 for part 1,001, and so on. You can compute a record's byte offset, then, as follows:

record number + part number - 1000;

record offset + record number * sizeof (record);

For example, if the part number is 1,500, then it's at record 500, which is at byte offset 2,500 in the file (since the record length is five bytes).

This neatly solves the problem of locating a specific record based on a key value. Any time that some data element is serialized this way, you can use it as a locator key. Examples are customer, employee, and invoice numbers. If there are gaps in the sequence, write blank records as placeholders in the file. Those record slots will then be available when the keys are used, and the file positioning mechanism will remain intact.

The INVENTRY.C program in Program 6.2 implements this scheme for locating records. Having opened the file successfully, the program enters an apparently endless loop (**do while (1 == 1)**); the exit occurs when the user types a part number less than 1,000.

The **main**() function consists chiefly of this loop. It gets the part number from the user, fetches the record after computing its offset from the part number, and displays the record contents. If the user wants to do an update, a brief dialog ensues in function **update**() and the changed record is written back to the file. The message **No such part number** appears when the user has typed a number greater than 1,999; this is because the **fseek**() in **gotrecord**() fails, causing the function to return FALSE to main().

Note that file positioning with **fseek**() occurs immediately before the **fread**() in **gotrecord**() and the **fwrite**() in **update**(). That way you can be sure that the pointer is correctly positioned for the I/O. It's necessary to reposition the pointer back to the record's beginning before the **fwrite**() since the preceding **fread**() advanced it by five bytes.

The program never uses **ftell**() to determine where the pointer is. It doesn't need to. The controlling variable is offset, which in turn is derived from the part number. The offset variable only changes in direct response to a keyboard command to fetch a specific record. Consequently you always know where you are in the file, making it unnecessary to query the file pointer to find out. This is an example of the "careful" pointer management mentioned earlier.

Run the program and play with it. Study it, too. Though simple, it's quite powerful and clearly illustrates the quantum leap in capability that random access brings to software.

Program 6.2 **Random Access in Inventory Management**

```
/* INVENTRY.C: Parts inventory retrieval/update          */
/* This program processes TEST.INV in random-access mode, */
/*     allowing user to pull the record for any item by   */
/*     part number and, if needed, update stock on hand   */
/* ------------------------------------------------------- */

/* INCLUDES */
#include <stdio.h>
#include <ctype.h>
#include <stdlib.h>
#include <conio.h>
#include <process.h>

/* DEFINES */
```

Program 6.2 **(continued)**

```c
#ifndef TRUE
#define FALSE 0
#define TRUE  !FALSE
#endif
typedef struct {
  unsigned  partno, onhand;
  char      bay;
} PARTREC;

/* LOCAL FUNCTION PROTOTYPES */
int  gotrecord (FILE*, long, PARTREC*);
void showrecord (PARTREC);
int  updating (void);
void update (FILE*, long, PARTREC*);

/* ------------ BEGIN HERE ------------ */

void main ()
{
int     part;
char    input [6];
long    offset;
PARTREC item;
FILE    *f;

  if ((f = fopen ("TEST.INV", "r+b")) != NULL)
    do {
      printf ("\nPart number? (0-999 to quit) ");
      gets (input);                 /* get part # as string */
      part = (unsigned) atoi (input);   /* convert to nbr */
      offset = (long) (part - 1000) * sizeof (item);
      if (offset < 0L) {            /* if quitting then */
        fclose (f);                 /* close file and */
        exit (0);                        /* exit */
      }
      if (gotrecord (f, offset, &item)) {   /* if fetched */
        showrecord (item);             /* display record */
        if (updating ())            /* if update requested */
          update (f, offset, &item);          /* do it */
      } else
        puts ("\nNo such part number");
    } while (1 == 1);               /* loop until user quits */
  else
    puts ("Cannot open inventory file. Job ended.");
} /* ------------ LOCAL FUNCTIONS FOLLOW ---------------- */

int gotrecord (FILE *file, long position, PARTREC *record)
{             /* fetch record from indicated file position */
int  success = FALSE;

  if (fseek (file, position, SEEK_SET) != -1L)
    if (fread (record, sizeof (*record), 1, file))
      success = TRUE;
```

Program 6.2 **(continued)**

```
   return (success);
} /* ----------------------- */

void showrecord (PARTREC record)          /* display record */
{
   puts ("\n------------------------------");
   printf ("        PART NUMBER %u", record.partno);
   printf ("\nQuantity on hand   %u", record.onhand);
   printf ("\nStored in bay      %c", record.bay);
} /* ----------------------- */

int updating (void)          /* see if user wants to update */
{
char    reply;

   printf ("\n\nDo you want to update stock? (Y/N) ");
   reply = toupper (getche ());
   return ((reply == 'Y') ? TRUE : FALSE);
} /* ----------------------- */

void update (FILE *file, long position, PARTREC *record)
{                    /* update qty on hand if user wants to */
char    input [6];

   printf ("\nNew quantity on hand? ");
   gets (input);
   record->onhand = (unsigned) atoi (input);
   fseek (file, position, SEEK_SET);
   fwrite (record, sizeof (*record), 1, file);
} /* ----------------------- */
```

Scenario 2: Indexing Random Files

The first scenario showed how record locations can be derived from sequential data elements serving as the key. Now let's consider the case—occurring far more often—in which there is nothing about the data that lends itself to a relatively gap-free series of keys.

Examples of such data abound: people's names, Social Security numbers, manufacturers' part numbers, models of automobiles, equipment serial numbers, event time- and date-stamps, brand names, and so on. In all cases, we can introduce order by alphabetizing or otherwise sorting, but the result can never be inherently serial in the same sense that integers follow a predictable sequence. For example, these Social Security numbers are in order:

132–91–7425
219–27–0778
223–01–6981

However, there's no way we can manipulate them mathematically to compute 0, 1, 2, the offsets of the records containing them. Thus, we need some other method for locating the relevant record in a random-access file.

This brings us to indexing. Like the index for this book, a random file's index provides a means for quickly looking up a key and finding out where it is.

An index entry is a simple structure consisting of two basic fields: the key, and the related record's byte offset. Given an argument (a sought key), you search the list until you find a match, then use the offset to reach into the file and grab the record. Shortly we'll implement an index.

First, though, let's set the scenario. The Personnel Department wants a company-wide locator system giving, for each employee, the first and last name, Social Security number, department, and extension. In order to locate someone, they want to type in the person's last name. The program will then locate the record and show the other information. If it's not the right person (there might be two or more with the same last name), the user can signal the computer to continue the search.

The record structure for the file is as follows:

```
typedef struct {
   char last[12],
        first[10],
        ssn[12];
        dept[6],
        ext[5];
} LOCREC;
```

No such file exists, so it's first necessary to create it with a data entry program. MKLOCATR.C in Program 6.3 accepts information about employees and saves it in LOCATOR.FIL, which has fixed record lengths based on the LOCREC structure. Note that, although written in sequential mode, we will later process this file with random access.

Run the program and type in a dozen or so entries. This will give you something to experiment with in the next program, and also we'll use this file later in the chapter.

Program 6.3 Sequential Data Entry for Random Access Later

```
/* MKLOCATR.C: Data entry to build file for locator syst  */
/*    Data need not be in any particular order             */
/* -------------------------------------------------------- */

/* INCLUDES */
#include <stdio.h>
#include <string.h>

/* DEFINES */
```

Program 6.3 **(continued)**

```c
typedef struct {
  char   last[12], first[10], ssn[12], dept[6], ext[5];
} LOCREC;
#define FILENAME "LOCATOR.FIL"

void main ()
{
FILE    *loc;
LOCREC empl;
int     count = 0;

  if ((loc = fopen (FILENAME, "w+b")) != NULL) {
    putw (0, loc);          /* dummy rec count in file header */
    do {
      printf ("\nEmployee last name ");
      gets (empl.last);
      if (strlen (empl.last)) {
        printf ("  First name       ");
        gets (empl.first);
        printf ("  Social Sec #     ");
        gets (empl.ssn);
        printf ("  Department       ");
        gets (empl.dept);
        printf ("  Extension        ");
        gets (empl.ext);
        fwrite (&empl, sizeof (empl), 1, loc);
        ++count;                           /* count this record */
      }
    } while (strlen (empl.last));
    fseek (loc, 0L, SEEK_SET);            /* to start of file */
    putw (count, loc);      /* write record count in header */
    fclose (loc);
  } else
    puts ("Cannot open new locator file");
}
```

Because the resulting LOCATOR.FIL produced by this program will be indexed, it's not necessary to follow any particular order when keying the data. If the names are alphabetized that's fine, but it doesn't matter and yields no speed advantage in accessing records.

The data file now exists. The next step is to create an index. Sophisticated systems such as dBASE create and maintain the index automatically, adding, changing, and deleting index items as the contents of the indexed file change. For the sake of illustration, and to keep the sample programs from getting too long, we'll do it separately here. Once you're thoroughly familiar with the concepts, you can incorporate index management into your own applications.

Before we build the index, there's one thing you should note about LOCATOR.FIL. It has a header record consisting of a single integer giving the number of data records in the file. The count variable in Program 6.3 keeps track of how many are entered. At the start of the program, a dummy value is written to LOCATOR.FIL to serve as a placeholder. Data records thus begin at offset 2. Just before closing the file, the MKLOCATR program seeks the header record and writes the count to it. Usually header records are more complicated than this, but in this case it's all we need, and it does demonstrate how you can keep control information in a file.

We can use the record count in constructing the index, and also in processing the indexed data file later. The index creation is quite simple. Open the data file and create a new file that will become the index: LOCATOR.NDX is an appropriate name, since its first part associates it with LOCATOR.FIL and the suffix suggests an index.

From the source file's header, you can fetch the record count and use that as a loop counter. Note that, since the first data record is numbered 0, the count will be 99 if there are 100 records. Therefore, the file processing loop continues based on the condition

    rec <= nrecs;

which is the second clause of a for() statement.

The loop itself first gets the offset for the current record using **ftell()**, then reads the record from the source file. This sequence is necessary since **fread()** advances the file pointer, so that after the read it points to the next record. The last name field is plucked from the data record, and then the program writes the name and offset to the index file. The loop repeats until all records have been read, and then the program closes the files and ends. The process is very quick, taking no more than a few seconds even for large files.

The MKLOCNDX.C program in Program 6.4 implements these steps to create the index file. Run it, and then we'll use the two files to demonstrate indexed direct access.

Program 6.4 **Creating the Index for a Random File**

```
/* MKLOCNDX.C: Builds random-access index for LOCATOR.FIL */

/* INCLUDES */
#include <stdio.h>
#include <string.h>

/* DEFINES */
#define LOCATOR   "LOCATOR.FIL"
#define INDEX     "LOCATOR.NDX"
typedef struct {
  char  last[12], first[10], ssn[12], dept[6], ext[5];
} LOCREC;

typedef struct {
```

Program 6.4 **(continued)**

```
   char    name[12];
   long    offset;
} NDXREC;

void main ()
{
int     nrecs, rec;
FILE    *loc, *ndx;
LOCREC  empl;
NDXREC  index;

   if ((loc = fopen (LOCATOR, "rb")) != NULL) {
     nrecs = getw (loc);                  /* read file header */
     ndx = fopen (INDEX, "wb");           /* create index file */
     for (rec = 0; rec <= nrecs; rec++) {
       index.offset = ftell (loc);        /* get file offset */
       fread (&empl, sizeof (empl), 1, loc);    /* get rec */
       strcpy (index.name, empl.last);    /* name to index */
       fwrite (&index, sizeof(index), 1, ndx); /* write it */
     }
     fcloseall ();                        /* close both files */
   } else
     puts ("Cannot open locator file");
}
```

The resulting index file has fixed-length records, each containing the last name and offset for a particular record in the data file. This is advantageous because we can place the entire index file on the heap as a table with a single entry point (the head) and search it rapidly.

The standard **calloc()** function is available specifically for this purpose. **calloc()** says, in effect, to allocate dynamic space for n elements of m bytes each. Here, n is the record count from the data file's header, plus one, and m is the size of an index record. The NDXREC structure is 16 bytes, so if there are 100 records, **calloc()** gets 1,600 bytes for the index table.

It's necessary, of course, to know the address of the first element in the table, which is assigned to a pointer of type NDXREC. Say we've declared the following pointers:

NDXREC *list, *start;

Since **calloc()** returns a pointer to the allocated space, we can make the necessary assignment with

list = (NDXREC*) calloc (++nrecs, sizeof (NDXREC));

The list variable now points to the start of the table space. We can load the table by opening the index file and executing

```
fread (list, sizeof (NDXREC), nrecs, indexFile);
```

The index is now loaded and ready to do business.

The value of the list pointer is sacred and should never be changed, lest the program lose track of where the table begins. That's what the second pointer (start) is for: a working variable that we can use to indicate elements within the table.

Because the start pointer is bound to the NDXREC type, an interesting thing happens if we increment or otherwise perform arithmetic on it. Say we issue the statement

```
start = list;
```

The start pointer now points to the beginning of the table. But let's say we want to start searching the table at the second entry. We can advance the pointer with

```
++start;
```

The effect is to move the pointer to the next element. This is a logical increment; mathematically the pointer's value increases by **sizeof(objectPointedTo)**. The compiler does this automatically, relieving us of the burden of detailed pointer arithmetic.

To search the list, get the argument (a person's last name), and run through the index table comparing with the key. When a match is found, use the associated offset field to perform a seek in the data file, then read the data record.

You'll recall that duplicate last names are possible. Consequently, after displaying the fetched record, it's necessary to ask the user if it's the one he or she wants. If so, the search is completed. If not, however, advance the index pointer indicating the matching entry by one and resume the search.

The search concludes on one of two conditions: the desired data record is found, or the end of the list is encountered. The second case indicates that the desired record is not in the data file.

The LOCATOR.C program in Program 6.5 translates this discussion into action. The **main()** function performs all the necessary actions, farming out details to other functions. The program repeats until the user enters a blank line in response to the request for an employee's last name.

Program 6.5 **Implementing an Indexed File**

```c
/* LOCATE.C: Looks up employees in LOCATOR.FIL using   */
/*       random access index                           */
/* --------------------------------------------------- */
/* INCLUDES */
#include <stdio.h>
#include <string.h>
#include <alloc.h>
#include <stdlib.h>
#include <conio.h>
#include <ctype.h>

/* DEFINES */
#ifndef TRUE
#define FALSE 0
#define TRUE !FALSE
#endif
#define FILENAME   "LOCATOR.FIL"
#define INDEX      "LOCATOR.NDX"
typedef struct {
  char  last[12], first[10], ssn[12], dept[6], ext[5];
} LOCREC;                               /* file record format */
typedef struct {
  char  name[12];
  long  offset;
} NDXREC;                               /* index record format */

/* LOCAL FUNCTION PROTOTYPES */
NDXREC *getIndex (int);
void get (char*);
NDXREC *search (NDXREC*, char*, NDXREC*);
void fetch (FILE*, NDXREC*, LOCREC*);
int  display (LOCREC*);
/* -------------- BEGIN HERE ------------ */

void main ()
{
FILE      *loc;
char      key[12];
LOCREC    empl;
NDXREC    *head, *start, *matching, *tail;
int       located, nrecs;

  if ((loc = fopen (FILENAME, "r+b")) != NULL) {
    nrecs = getw (loc) + 1;             /* read file header */
    head = getIndex (nrecs);   /* get index, set head ptr */
    tail = head + nrecs;                /* set tail ptr */
    do {
      start = head;
      matching = NULL;
      get (key);
      if (strlen (key) > 1) {
```

```
        do {
          if ((matching = search (start, key,
                                  tail)) != NULL) {
            fetch (loc, matching, &empl);
            located = display (&empl);
            if (located) {                       /* halt search */
              matching = NULL;
              break;
            } else                              /* resume search */
              start = ++matching;   /* at next index entry */
          }
        } while (matching != NULL);
        if (!located)
          if (matching == NULL)
            puts ("\nNo match");
      }
    } while (strlen (key) > 1);
    fclose (loc);
  } else
    puts ("Cannot open locator file");
} /* ----------------------- */

NDXREC *getIndex (int recs)          /* load index on heap */
{
FILE    *index;
NDXREC *head;

  index = fopen (INDEX, "rb");
  head = (NDXREC*) calloc (recs, sizeof (NDXREC));
  fread (head, sizeof (NDXREC), recs, index);
  fclose (index);
  return (head);
} /* ----------------------- */

void get (char *key)             /* get search arg from user */
{
  printf ("\n\nLast name? ");
  gets (key);
} /* ----------------------- */

NDXREC *search (NDXREC *table, char *key, NDXREC *end)
{          /* search list for key, return pointer to match */
NDXREC  *next;

  next = table;
  while (next != end)
    if (strcmp (key, next->name) == 0)
      break;
    else
      ++next;
  return ((next == end) ? NULL : next);
} /* ----------------------- */
```

Program 6.5 **(continued)**

```
void fetch (FILE *random, NDXREC *matched, LOCREC *buffer)
{                   /* fetch matched record from random file */
   fseek (random, matched->offset, SEEK_SET);
   fread (buffer, sizeof (*buffer), 1, random); /* get rec */
} /* ---------------------- */

int display (LOCREC *empl)    /* display employee data and */
{                             /* return TRUE if the one sought */

   printf ("\nEmployee last name   %s", empl->last);
   printf ("\n   First name        %s", empl->first);
   printf ("\n   Soc Sec number    %s", empl->ssn);
   printf ("\n   Department        %s", empl->dept);
   printf ("\n   Extension         %s", empl->ext);
   printf ("\n\nIs this the one you want? (Y/N) ");
   return ((toupper (getche()) == 'Y') ? TRUE : FALSE);
} /* ---------------------- */
```

Relational Databases

As user's information requirements have become more complex, it has become necessary to develop more sophisticated ways of accommodating them. One such technique is through the use of relational databases.

A database is simply a collection of information; it's fair to call any given file a database. Usually, though, the term implies a collection of related items spread across several files. One file might contain employee names and Social Security numbers, another the addresses of those employees, still another their salary information, and so on. Taken as a whole, these files comprise a personnel database.

While it might seem on first impression that maintaining several separate files is more trouble than maintaining one that holds all the information, in fact there are a number of advantages that make splitting up the information worthwhile.

One of the most important advantages is in eliminating redundant data. Not only does this reduce disk space requirements, but it also does away with the need to make sure all instances of a given item are updated. For example, Jane Doe gets married and becomes Jane Smith. If all files are monolithic (contain everything needed for an application system), we have to update files containing Jane's employment records, salary information, pension plan, profit sharing, expense account, and so on. Some clerk will spend half the day scrounging through files to get all these updates done, and will probably miss at least one. When separate files contain distinct, nonredundant information, only one file needs updating to rename Jane Doe as Jane Smith.

Another major advantage follows from the first. Since each file comprising a database contains only one or a few closely related items, we can combine files in a mix-and-match fashion to get exactly the information we want, without having to filter out masses of data we don't. Thus, the use of separate files allows many applications to share classes of information.

The only thing we need to link files together this way is some common element, a thread that ties Bill Johnson's name, which might be record #251 in FILE.A, to his salary, which is record #87 in FILE.B, to his address, record #194 in FILE.C, and so on.

There are a couple of ways to approach this problem. One is called a hierarchical database, which employs an elaborate system of pointers. The master file record for Bill Johnson might contain his name and Social Security number, plus pointers to all his other records in all the files of the database. Furthermore, in order to hold down the number of master file accesses, records in the lower-level files might also contain pointers to records in other files.

This approach is often used in mainframe databases, where it works well because there's a professional staff to look after it. The problem with hierarchical databases is complexity: The pointer structure is so bewildering that it requires vigilant maintenance and the judgment to recognize when it needs to be rebuilt.

An easier solution, and one that works best in small computers, is to cross-relate files. Here, every file is set up for random access and has an index. For two files to be relationally joined, they must contain one data element in common, which is the indexed item for the related-to file.

An example illustrates how it works. Say we want to expand the locator system to include the employee's current salary. The salary file contains, of course, the salary, plus it must have one unique identifier that also occurs in the locator file. The Social Security number is a good candidate, since no two people share the same number.

A quick one-time program can pull these two items from the payroll file and write them into a new file. (Later, in order to reap the benefits of cross-relating, you'll also have to modify the payroll system to refer to the new salary file, which then becomes the sole repository of salary information.)

When the salary file exists, use a program such as that in Program 6.4 to make its index. All the information elements are now in place, and it remains only to modify the locator program for relational operation.

Here are the steps to perform a relational lookup for Bill Johnson:

1. Read the locator index onto the heap.
2. Read the salary index onto the heap.
3. Look up Bill Johnson's name and fetch his locator record as in Program 6.5.

4. Using the Social Security number from his locator record as the search argument, find the matching entry in the salary index.
5. Use the associated file pointer to seek his related record in the salary file.
6. Fetch it and display the results.

Similar steps apply to the payroll system, or any other program that needs to find out Bill's salary. All any system requires is his Social Security number, and it can then locate any information about Bill in any file.

This concludes our discussion of disks and files in Turbo C. It has been chiefly a look inward, from the program level toward the internal hardware and software aspects of data storage. The next part of the book looks outward toward the external world of the user interface.

PART II

The User Interface

The term *user interface* is so shopworn the computer industry should come up with something else. Regrettably, no one has, and we can't think of a name to nominate as its replacement either. Apparently we're stuck with it. No doubt the term owes its durability to its sweeping breadth.

The user interface encompasses all that the person using the system sees and touches: the keyboard, the display, the printer, and everything that happens to them. And that's the stuff of the next several chapters, including Part III. It's the longest part of the book because it's the most challenging and important part of programming, whether in Turbo C or any other language.

A program might do wonderful things internally, but if it doesn't look good, doesn't produce readable output, isn't intuitive or at least reasonably simple to operate, the folks using it won't be impressed. In fact, they won't even like it. They might use it, but they'll grumble.

In a wonderful book entitled *The Network Revolution: Confessions of a Computer Scientist* (AC/DC, Berkeley, CA, 1984), author Jacques Vallee pokes a lot of good fun at us computer types and how we seemingly go out of our way to make life difficult for the less technologically endowed, but his point is clear. It is our responsibility to remove the barriers between the common sense of the thinking animal at the keyboard and the slavish, often idiotic tool at his or her fingertips. That's what a good user interface does.

It's not easy to write a program with a good user interface. Often such programs devote more lines of code to controlling the screen than to doing "real" work like calculations and data manipulation.

So our goal in this part of the book is to ease your task as a programmer. We'll examine the issues and the methods, and

 then, whenever practicable, we'll develop libraries of routines that you can use in your programs, thus reducing the burdens of writing friendly software. After all, if your job is to make life easier for users, shouldn't that job be made easier for you, too?

So that's what the next dozen chapters are about.

CHAPTER 7

BASIC INPUT/ OUTPUT SYSTEM

Paradoxically, our voyage to the most visible part of software begins at the deepest bowels of the machine: the ROM BIOS (pronounced like two words, "rom BY-oss").

If you're unfamiliar with hardware, perhaps we should explain that a ROM is a read-only memory device with software instructions electronically "burned" into it, so that the instructions don't disappear when power is removed. A ROM and the machine language it contains are sometimes collectively called "firmware" since they occupy a middle ground between pure hardware and software. When a program is burned into a ROM and the ROM is plugged into a socket, the program becomes a permanent part of the machine.

In this case, the program is the BIOS, or Basic Input/Output System. The term describes only part of what the ROM BIOS actually does, but it is descriptive of the portion accessible to programmers. The ROM BIOS actually has two broad missions to perform:

1. It takes control of the machine when power is first applied. It's the ROM BIOS that makes you wait while it checks memory, exercises the processor to make sure it's functioning properly, inventories the attachments, and performs other initialization. After that, it supervises the loading of DOS and hands control to the operating system. In addition, the ROM BIOS supervises the warm boot (or restart) that occurs when you "three-key" the machine by simultaneously pressing **Ctrl, Alt,** and **Del.**
2. The ROM BIOS furnishes a number of DOS-like system subroutines that programs can call to perform input/output, determine the status of various devices, alter the video mode, and do other fundamental tasks at the machine level.

The start-up routines in the ROM BIOS cannot be readily called by programs, nor should they be. No doubt that's why those who designed it chose to ignore this important task when they gave it a name.

The ROM BIOS services that you can call from Turbo C programs break down into five categories as follows:

Interrupt	Purpose
1 0 h	Video services: 20 functions for controlling the display
1 3 h	Floppy disk services: six functions
1 4 h	Serial port services: four functions
1 6 h	Keyboard services: three functions
1 7 h	Printer services: three functions

Our purpose here is to discuss the ROM BIOS in general and some of its particulars with respect to programming in Turbo C. Thus, we'll talk about some specific calls in the appropriate places in later chapters, and some we won't cover at all. For a detailed description of the ROM BIOS, see Peter Norton's *Inside the IBM PC* (New York: Brady Books, 1986), and for exhaustive information about the ROM BIOS function calls, Ray Duncan's *Advanced MS-DOS* (Redmond, WA: Microsoft Press, 1986). Many other programmers' guides to the PC and clones also give the ROM BIOS extensive coverage.

Calling ROM BIOS Services from Turbo C

During power-up, the ROM BIOS installs pointers to its service routines in the system interrupt vector table in lowest memory. The interrupts are those listed above.

Any program that calls a ROM BIOS service, then, must execute the appropriate software interrupt. Because each service routine performs more than one function, it's necessary to pass a function code in register AH to specify the action you want. Often the functions require further information in other registers, which are effectively parameters. Moreover, some ROM BIOS calls return information in one or more registers, while others return nothing.

As a result, it's not practical to have a single generalized routine for calling any ROM BIOS function from C. Instead, you have to set up a unique calling sequence for each function.

In order to attain compatibility with a number of other C packages (Lattice, Microsoft, Aztec, and so on), Turbo C offers a bewildering array of alternatives for generating software interrupts. We'll discuss them in Chapter 26, which deals specifically with interrupts and handlers. Until then, we'll use a single method for generating interrupts to DOS and the ROM BIOS, which is Turbo C's int86() function.

This function has the prototype

```
int int86(int intNum,union REGS *inreg,
                    union REGS *outreg);
```

The REGS union is defined in DOS.H and covers all the byte registers AH through DL, all the word registers AX through DX, plus SI, DI, and the flags. For example, you might declare a variable as

union **REGS** reg;

and then assign a value to word register BX with

reg.x.bx = value;

and another value to byte register AH with

reg.h.ah = byteval;

The .x. infix represents a word register, and .h. a byte register, corresponding to the structures that comprise the REGS union.

Because the ROM BIOS often returns values in registers, it's advisable to declare two instances of the REGS union, for input to the call and output from it. In the examples in this book, the declarations are

union **REGS** inreg, outreg;

As an example of a ROM BIOS call, let's use interrupt 10h (video services), function 3 to determine information about the cursor in video page 0. The call requires function code 3 in register AH and the page number in BH. It returns the following information:

Register	Information
C H	Scan line for top of cursor
C L	Scan line for bottom of cursor
D H	Row (Y) of current cursor position
D L	Column (X) of cursor position

Set up the call, make it, and extract the returned information like this:

```
inreg.h.ah = 3;                          /* bios 10h function */
inreg.h.bh = 0;                          /* video page 0 */
int86 (0×10, &inreg, &outreg);           /* call */
curTop = outreg.h.ch;                    /* cursor top */
curBott = outreg.h.cl;                   /* and bottom */
y = outreg.h.dh;                         /* current row */
x = outreg.h.dl;                         /* and column */
```

The calls that return one or more values in registers are inquiry functions. Those that return nothing are control functions, such as positioning the cursor, writing to the display, or changing video mode. In the latter case, it's necessary only to set up the parameter registers and issue the interrupt; however, you must still pass two pointers to a REGS union. If they're the same, as in

    int86 (0×10, &reg, &reg);

that's acceptable and no conflict occurs.

The ROM BIOS Data Area

Since the ROM BIOS responds to inquiries, it's natural to suppose that it stores information about its status somewhere. And indeed it does. It owns a piece of memory called the ROM BIOS data area.

A ROM is a read-only memory, so the ROM BIOS cannot write temporary information into its own address space. Consequently, part of main memory is set aside in the IBM PC and compatibles to serve as a place where the ROM BIOS can keep its control and status information. This is a fixed block consisting of 132 bytes beginning at segment 40h. Because many commercial software packages refer directly to the ROM BIOS data area, IBM has publicly committed that it will keep this block intact for the foreseeable future.

Therefore it's safe to build programs that read the ROM BIOS data area. It is not safe to *write* to it, however, except in a very few cases that we'll discuss in due time. Be warned that indiscriminate tinkering with the contents is hazardous to the health of your computer and can potentially make real smoke.

Most of the BIOS data fields are unsigned bytes or integers, each of which has a unique meaning based on its position. Two of them are further broken down so that certain individual or grouped bits have a significance of their own. We can describe them in terms of Turbo C bit field structures.

A bit field structure is simply a way of subdividing a 16-bit word and giving each subdivision an identifier, so that it can be referred to as a variable. The smallest field is one bit, the largest 16. Assignment of the fields, which are unsigned, proceeds to the left from bit 0. If the fields don't take the entire word, the leftover bits are unused and unnamed, but the object itself still occupies one word of storage. Similarly, if the total number of bits for all fields exceeds 16, the compiler packs as much as it can into one word and sticks the rest into a second word, but without splitting a given field between the two. Both bit field structures in the BIOS data area occupy exactly 16 bits.

The first two typedefs in BIOSAREA.H (Program 7.1) show how to define a bit field structure. The only difference between this and a normal structure definition is the size specification following the field identifier; for example, **nLPT** consists of two bits, while **nu13** is a one-bit field. Sum the sizes and you'll find they come to 16.

Incidentally, there's nothing "official" about the field names in Program 7.1; they're of our choosing. Note that, in order to refer to members of the BIOSDATA structure, your program must initialize a pointer to its absolute address in memory (paragraph 40h). Example:

BIOSDATA far *bios = MK__FP (0×0040, 0);

Since we were just looking at the EQFLAGS structure, let's talk about what it contains.

Program 7.1 **Defining the ROM BIOS Data Area Contents**

```
/* biosarea.h: ROM BIOS data area at 0x0040:0 in memory */

#ifndef byte
#define byte    unsigned char        /* define byte as a type */
#endif

/* BIT FIELDS USED IN ROM BIOS DATA AREA */
typedef struct {
  unsigned  hasFloppies : 1,  /* 1 = system has floppy drives */
            nu1 : 1,                            /* not used */
            mbRAM : 2,        /* motherboard RAM size (obsolete) */
            initVideo : 2,               /* initial video mode */
            nDisks : 2,                /* nbr of floppy drives */
            nu8 : 1,                            /* not used */
            nSerialPorts : 3, /* nbr of serial ports attached */
            gamePort : 1,            /* 1 = game port attached */
            nu13 : 1,                           /* not used */
            nLPT : 2;               /* number of printers */
} EQFLAGS;          /* this is the equipment flags structure */

typedef struct {
  unsigned  riteShiftDown : 1,    /* 1 = right shift key down */
            leftShiftDown : 1,     /* 1 = left shift key down */
            ctrlShiftDown : 1,   /* 1 = ctrl-shift combo down */
            altShiftDown : 1,     /* 1 = alt-shift combo down */
            scrollLockOn : 1,      /* 1 = scroll lock mode on */
            numLockOn : 1,            /* 1 = num lock mode on */
            capsLockOn : 1,          /* 1 = caps lock mode on */
            insOn : 1,                   /* 1 = ins mode on */
            unused : 3,                      /* spare bits */
            ctrlNumLockOn : 1,    /* 1 = ctrl-NumLock mode on */
            scrollLockDown : 1,    /* 1 = scroll lock key down */
            numLockDown : 1,          /* 1 = num lock key down */
            capsLockDown : 1,        /* 1 = caps lock key down */
            insDown : 1;               /* 1 = ins key down */
} KBDFLAGS;          /* this is the keyboard flags structure */

typedef struct {
  unsigned  serialPortAddr[4];
  unsigned  parallelPortAddr[4];
```

Program 7.1 **(continued)**

```
    EQFLAGS       eqptFlags;
    byte          mfgrTestFlags;
    unsigned      mainMem;
    unsigned      expRAM;
    KBDFLAGS      kbdStat;
    byte          keypad;
    unsigned      kbdBuffHead;
    unsigned      kbdBuffTail;
    char          kbdBuff[32];
    byte          seekStat;
    byte          motorStat;
    byte          motorCnt;
    byte          diskErr;
    byte          NECStatus[7];
    byte          videoMode;
    unsigned      scrnWidth;
    unsigned      vidBuffSz;
    unsigned      vidBuffOfs;
    byte          cursPos[8][2];
    byte          cursBottom;
    byte          cursTop;
    byte          activeDispPage;
    unsigned      activeDispPort;
    byte          CRTModeReg;
    byte          palette;
    unsigned      dataEdgeTimeCount;
    unsigned      CRCReg;
    char          lastInputValue;
    unsigned      tick;
    int           hour;
    byte          timerOverflow;
    byte          brkStat;
    unsigned      resetFlag;
    long          hardDiskStat;
    byte          parallelTimeout[4];
    byte          serialTimeout[4];
    unsigned      kbdBuffOfs;
    unsigned      kbdBuffEnd;
} BIOSDATA;
```

The Equipment Flags

The third field in the BIOS data area is called the equipment flags, and it's brimming with information about the system configuration. Most of its bit fields are self-explanatory, either by their identifier names or from the comments, but a couple are not.

The initVideo field purports to describe the video mode that was in effect when the system first powered up, giving a clue as to which display adapter is present. The reliability of this field has eroded with the introduction of more advanced adapters such as Hercules, EGA, and VGA. Since it's a two-bit field, it can only convey four possible values, which are as follows:

Value	Meaning
0	Undefined
1	80 × 25 color
2	40 × 25 color
3	80 × 25 monochrome

Some CGA boards come up as undefined, as does the EGA. Except that when the EGA is working with a monochrome monitor, it comes up in mode 3. The Hercules card has an initial video mode of 1 and so does the MDS Genius full-page monitor, even though both are monochrome. Bottom line: this bit field is unreliable. You have to look elsewhere to identify the signature of the adapter, which we'll discuss presently.

The mbRAM field is another one that's obsolete, since it's based on early models of the PC. It used to indicate the motherboard RAM size, which went in 16K steps up to a maximum of 64K. Nowadays, with much more RAM on the motherboard, this field has become meaningless.

There are two related bit fields among the equipment flags that yield information about the attached floppy drives. The hasFloppies field is a Boolean; if **0**, the machine is driveless, and otherwise you can look at nDisks to find out how many drives there are. The number of floppy drives is one more than the contents of the nDisks field. That is, if nDisks is **0**, there's one drive, and if it's **3**, there are four.

Knowing how many diskette drives there are can make your programs smart. For example, if a drive malfunctions, you can instruct the user to mount a diskette in another drive if one exists.

The Keyboard Flags

The other bit field structure in the BIOS data area is the one called kbdStat, described by the KBDFLAGS structure. This structure gives the status of various nonprinting, mode-setting keys such as **Caps Lock** and **Insert**. The "down" fields show if the related key is currently being pressed, while the "on" fields indicate if the specified mode is in effect. A "Yes" is signified by a 1-bit.

This is one part of the ROM BIOS data area that you can safely modify. For instance, set **Caps Lock** on to make sure the user is entering case-sensitive data in uppercase. Or switch **Num Lock** on and tell the user to enter numerics via the keypad. Be sure to undo such sneaky mode settings later.

Video Information

A glance at the BIOSDATA structure in Program 7.1 reveals that it contains more than anyone would ever want to know about the system. Such things as the manufacturer's test flags, the disk drive motor status and rotation count, and the data edge timer count have an extremely high yawn factor. At the other end of the who-cares spectrum are such things as cursor and video information, which are in the middle of the structure.

The videoMode field identifies which mode is currently in effect, using the following values:

Value	Mode
00h	40 × 25 B&W text, color adapter
01h	40 × 25 color text
02h	80 × 25 B&W text, color adapter
03h	80 × 25 color text
04h	320 × 200 four-color graphics (CGA)
05h	320 × 200 four-color graphics, color burst off (CGA)
06h	640 × 200 monochrome graphics (CGA)
07h	80 × 25 monochrome (MDA or EGA with mono display)
08h	160 × 200 16-color graphics (PCjr)
09h	320 × 200 16-color graphics (PCjr)
0Ah	640 × 200 four-color graphics (PCjr)
0Dh	320 × 200 16-color graphics (EGA)
0Eh	640 × 200 16-color graphics (EGA)
0Fh	640 × 350 monochrome graphics (EGA)
10h	640 × 350 four- or 16-color graphics (EGA)

You can infer the screen width from the video mode, but the scrnWidth field tells you directly. It's always 40 or 80 columns with standard monitor/adapter configurations.

The ROM BIOS keeps track of separate cursor positions on each of the (up to) eight video pages possible with color adapters. The activeDispPage field indicates which page is currently visible. It also furnishes an index into the **cursPos** array, which gives cursor position information. Ordinarily, page 0 is active, and **cursPos[0][0]** and **cursPos[0][1]** contain the cursor column and row, respectively.

You can safely modify these array fields to control the cursor position. Change the two elements and the cursor moves instantly to its new location. You can similarly detect or change the cursor position on inactive pages, as when building a display image behind the scenes.

When you want to switch to a new page, don't write directly to the active-DispPage field. Instead, call ROM BIOS interrupt 10h, function 5. This is because the vidBuffOfs field, which identifies the memory location of the video buffer, must change simultaneously. It's easier and safer to let BIOS handle this juggling act.

The cursTop and cursBottom fields identify the shape of the cursor, which applies to all pages. The cursor is a block shape that partially or completely fills a character cell, and it's composed of scan lines with **0** at the top. The bottom scan line is **12** in monochrome (video mode 7) and **7** for all other modes. The default underscore cursor is the lowest two scan lines.

By writing to these fields, you can change the cursor shape. For example, when Insert mode goes into effect, you might set cursTop to **0** to form a full-cell block cursor. Restore the default shape (assuming you haven't changed the lower scan line) by subtracting one from cursBottom and storing the result in cursTop.

You can also hide the cursor by setting bit 5 of cursTop (logical OR with 20h). The cursor still has a position and behaves normally, but it isn't visible as an object on the display. Make it visible again by ANDing with 1Fh. A handy algorithm for toggling the cursor on and off is:

```
if (bios->cursTop & 0×20 != 0)
    bios->cursTop |= 0×1F;                              /* toggle on */
else
    bios->cursTop &= 0×20;                              /* toggle off*/
```

Each time this code is executed, it switches the cursor to its opposite state of visibility.

The palette field discloses which of the two four-color palette sets is selected for the CGA in a graphics mode. In any other mode, this field contains garbage. Also, writing to it has no effect. To change palettes, call ROM BIOS interrupt 10h, function 0Bh.

Keeping the Time

The two fields called hour and tick contain the values maintained by the ROM BIOS time-of-day clock. The hour field ranges from 0–23, keeping military time, while the tick field is an increment count. Each increment is $5/91$ of a second; stated another way, each second 18.2 ticks occur. At first glance this ridiculous interval seems like one that only a committee would come up with, but it becomes sensible when you realize that, at that rate, 65,536 ticks work out to 3,600 seconds, or one hour. Since a 16-bit object can represent a maximum of 65,536 values, the interval has a sensible basis.

When the count rolls over from its terminal value (FFFFh) to zero, a new hour begins and the hour field is incremented by the carry.

The dogged precision of computers produces a slight error in the interval, amounting to about 9.65 seconds in a 24-hour period. Consequently, as midnight draws nigh, the ROM BIOS clock appears to halt for that period in order to resynchronize itself with the real world.

Transcending the ROM BIOS

There are a couple of other interesting memory locations that are outside the ROM BIOS data area. Though not controlled by the ROM BIOS, they yield related hardware information.

The first of these is the EGA equipment byte, located three bytes beyond the end of the BIOS structure (at 0040h:0087h). The EGA board has its own ROM BIOS that, during power-up, notifies the world that it exists by writing data to this byte. If there's no EGA, the byte is 0, and otherwise, it's nonzero to signify an active EGA. Thus, testing this byte is a quick way to determine if the computer is EGA-equipped. Note that 0 is FALSE and nonzero TRUE, so you can use the construct

```
if (ega)
   /* EGA is present */
else
   /* it's not */
```

If you want to know more about the EGA configuration, test bit 1 (AND with 02h). The bit is on when the EGA is connected to a monochrome monitor and off when it has a color display.

The other location of interest is at F000h:FFFEh, which contains the machine ID. This can be important if your program needs a specific hardware platform in order to run. For example, you might have some assembly code requiring an 80286. You can check the machine ID and gracefully decline to execute on anything smaller than an AT.

Here are the machine IDs for IBM PCs:

ID	Model
FFh	Standard PC
FEh	XT
FDh	PCjr
FCh	AT, XT286, PS/2–50, PS/2–60
FAh	PS/2–30
F9h	PC Convertible
F8h	PS/2–80

Some early Compaq portables have a machine ID of 00h, but in general, compatibles carry the same machine ID as the model they clone.

Putting it to Work

We've talked about the ROM BIOS data area. Now let's do something with it, both to demonstrate that in fact it works and to develop a handy utility.

The program is called HARDWARE.C, and it's shown in Program 7.2. This program #includes BIOSAREA.H and uses many of the ROM BIOS fields to profile the system configuration. It reports on the following aspects of the hardware:

Machine type

Memory

Disk drives

Display

Ports

BIOSAREA.H doesn't define the two external locations we discussed earlier, so the program declares them itself. Both are far pointers to unsigned characters, which are initialized by MK_FP at creation. Why far pointers? Because the EGA and machine ID bytes are outside the program's data segment, so it takes 32 bits to find them.

Note how the program sifts through several pieces of evidence to discern the signature of the video adapter. The method given here isn't 100 percent reliable, but it should be accurate most of the time. (Note: The Turbo C graphics library discussed in Part III has an alternative method for identifying the video adapter.)

Program 7.2 **Utility to List the Hardware Configuration**

```
/* HARDWARE.C: Shows the system hardware configuration */

/* INCLUDES */
#include <stdio.h>
#include <dos.h>
#include <conio.h>
#include "biosarea.h"

void main ()
{
unsigned n, far *ega = MK_FP (0x0040, 0x0087);
unsigned char far *machineID = MK_FP (0xF000, 0xFFFE);
BIOSDATA far *bios = MK_FP (0x0000, 0x0400);
```

Program 7.2 **(continued)**

```c
clrscr();
puts ("SYSTEM HARDWARE CONFIGURATION");

printf ("±nMachine type                        %02X ",
        *machineID);
switch (*machineID) {
  case 0xFF: puts (" (PC)"); break;
  case 0xFE: puts (" (PC/XT)"); break;
  case 0xFD: puts (" (PCjr)"); break;
  case 0xFC: puts (" (PC/AT)"); break;
  case 0xF9: puts (" (PC Convertible)"); break;
  default:   puts (" (Unknown)");
}

printf ("±nMain memory size in K               %u±n±n",
        bios->mainMem);

puts ("Disk drives:");
if (!bios->eqptFlags.hasFloppies)
  n = 0;
else
  n = bios->eqptFlags.nDisks + 1;
printf ("  Number of diskette drives           %u±n", n);
printf ("  Hard disk installed                 %s±n±n",
        (bios->hardDiskStat == 0L) ? "No" : "Yes");

puts ("Display:");
printf ("  Initial video mode                  %u",
        bios->eqptFlags.initVideo);
switch (bios->eqptFlags.initVideo) {
  case 0: puts (" (Undefined)"); break;
  case 1: puts (" (80 x 25 color)"); break;
  case 2: puts (" (40 x 25 color)"); break;
  case 3: puts (" (80 x 25 monochrome)"); break;
}
printf ("  Current video mode                  %u",
        bios->videoMode);
switch (bios->videoMode) {
  case 0: puts (" (40 x 25 B&W text, color adapter)"); break;
  case 1: puts (" (40 x 25 color text)"); break;
  case 2: puts (" (80 x 25 B&W text, color adapter)"); break;
  case 3: puts (" (80 x 25 color text)"); break;
  case 7: if (*ega != 0)
            puts (" (EGA 80 x 25 B&W text mode)");
          else
            puts (" (Monochrome 80 x 25 text)");
          break;
  default:puts (" (Graphics mode)");
}
printf ("  Video buffer size in bytes          %u±n",
        bios->vidBuffSz);
```

Program 7.2 **(continued)**

```
printf ("  Active display page                    %u±n",
        bios->activeDispPage);
printf ("  Video adapter port address             %04Xh±n",
        bios->activeDispPort);
printf ("  Adapter type                           ");
if (*ega != 0)
  puts ("EGA");
else
  if ((bios->videoMode == 7) && (bios->vidBuffSz > 4096))
    puts ("Hercules");
  else
    if (bios->videoMode == 7)
      puts ("Monochrome");
    else
      if (bios->videoMode == 3)
        puts ("CGA");
      else
        if (bios->videoMode == 2)
          puts ("Compaq");
        else puts ("Unknown");

puts ("±nPorts:");
printf ("  Number of serial ports                 %u±n",
        bios->eqptFlags.nSerialPorts);
printf ("  Number of parallel ports               %u±n",
        bios->eqptFlags.nLPT);
printf ("  Game port attached                     %s±n",
        (bios->eqptFlags.gamePort) ? "Yes" : "No");
}
```

The ROM BIOS, though at the deepest accessible level of the machine, controls the highest level, which is the system's interaction with the outside world. Thus, in managing an effective user interface, our software lives at a middle level while manipulating the extremes. We'll see how in the chapters that follow.

CHAPTER 8

MANAGING THE TEXT SCREEN

Most of the interaction between the computer and its user is accomplished by means of text. The computer asks questions and the user types answers, or vice versa. Even when graphics are the product of computer activity, they usually result from extended periods of text exchange.

Therefore it can safely be said that text screens are the single most important aspect of the user interface. The user forms his or her impression of how "good" the program is from the appearance of text displays. Running time and even accuracy of results (within reason) are of lesser importance than understandable instructions, help panels, and the general accessibility of the program to human beings.

To a great extent, the "goodness" of the user interface is a matter of artistic judgment combined with the tools to make it happen. This is not a book about art, so we won't presume to tell you how to design your user interface. Instead we'll concentrate on the tools. They are the stuff of this chapter.

Video Control Functions Built into Turbo C

Turbo C comes with over 20 built-in functions for manipulating text screens. CONIO.H gives their prototypes and also defines some constants and a data structure. This library provides a fairly complete tool set, and serves as the basis for the enhancements developed later in this chapter and in the next.

The general intent of the CONIO.H functions is direct manipulation of the video memory. The functions bypass the ROM BIOS (which is used by traditional functions such as printf()), and thus they produce much faster screen writes. You can override direct screen access and force the CONIO.H functions to go through the ROM BIOS by resetting a global variable:

```
directvideo = 0;
```

The only time it makes sense to do this is when your software runs on a PC that isn't IBM compatible.

The CONIO.H functions of chief interest are as follows:

Text output:

cprintf()	Counterpart to **printf()**.
cputs()	String output.

Windowing:

window()	Define subset of screen as display.

Screen manipulation:

clrscr()	Clear current window.
clreol()	Clear to end of line.
delline()	Delete line at cursor, close from below.
gotoxy()	Reposition cursor.
insline()	Insert blank line at cursor.
movetext()	Copy text elsewhere on screen.

Screen save/restore:

gettext()	Copy screen image to memory.
puttext()	Copy memory image to screen.

Display control:

highvideo()	Turn on high-intensity text.
lowvideo()	Turn on low-intensity text.
normvideo()	Restore original text intensity.
textattr()	Set character attributes.
textbackground()	Set background attribute.
textcolor()	Set foreground attribute
textmode()	Set display to a mode.

Inquiry:

gettextinfo()	Determine status of current window.
wherex()	Get current cursor column.
wherey()	Get current cursor row.

Many of these functions are so intuitive that they need little explanation. For example, **gotoxy()** places the text cursor in a window whose upper left coordinates are {1, 1}. Program 8.1 illustrates text screen manipulation using 10 of them.

Program 8.1 **Manipulating Text with the CONIO.H Functions**

```c
/* SCRNIO.C: CONIO.H screen management functions */

#include <conio.h>

void main ()
{
int    row, col;

  clrscr ();                                    /* clear screen */
  highvideo ();                         /* high-intensity to follow */
  gotoxy (31, 1);                       /* center following text */
  cputs ("SCREEN MANAGEMENT");
  normvideo ();                         /* restore regular intensity */

  for (col = 1; col < 80; col += 40)    /* write some text */
    for (row = 3; row < 11; row++) {
      gotoxy (col, row);
      cprintf ("This begins at row %2d, column %2d",
             row, col);
    }

  gotoxy (1, 12);
  cputs ("Press any key to copy part of top to bottom...");
  getch ();                             /* wait for signal */
  movetext (1, 3, 39, 10, 1, 14);                /* copy */

  gotoxy (1, 12);
  clreol ();                            /* clear old prompt */
  cputs ("Press any key to insert a blank line...");
  getch ();                             /* wait */
  insline ();                           /* insert */

  gotoxy (1, 13);                       /* clear old prompt */
  clreol ();
  gotoxy (1, 12);                       /* write new prompt */
  cputs ("Press any key to delete this line...");
  getch ();
  delline ();

  gotoxy (1, 12);
  clreol ();                            /* clear old prompt */

  gotoxy (1, 25);
  cputs ("Press any key to end...");
  getch ();
  clrscr ();
}
```

The purposes and operation of some of the other functions, however, are less obvious than those in Program 8.1. The next several sections of this chapter deal with them.

Text Attributes

The display area on a normal video monitor consists of 25 rows by 80 columns, for a total of 2,000 cells (character positions). For each cell there are two bytes of information. The first (on even addresses) is the ASCII code for the character to be displayed at that position. Its companion is on the following odd address and indicates the character's display attributes.

The attribute byte is a bit-zoned value conveying the foreground and background colors of the cell, the intensity of the character image, and two special effects: blinking and underlined. The format of this byte is:

7	6 5 4	3	2 1 0
BLINK	Background	Intensity	Foreground

Turbo C's **textcolor()** function controls the foreground field (bits 0–3). The **highvideo()/lowvideo()/normvideo()** functions affect only bit 3; **highvideo()** turns it on, producing intense characters, and the other two turn it off. The **textbackground()** function controls bits 4–6. There is no specific function for bit 7. However, CONIO.H furnishes the constant BLINK, which has the value 0×80. To make red text blink, issue the call

    textcolor (RED | BLINK);

The OR operation sets the bit.

While the attribute bytes for monochrome and color adapters are identical, they have somewhat different effects, depending on the video monitor's capabilities. A monochrome monitor can only display a limited subset of attributes:

Normal video (light on dark)

Intense normal video (bright on dark)

Reverse video (dark on light)

Underlined character

Blinking character

Light-on-light or vice versa

You can turn on underlining on a monochrome monitor with

    textcolor (1);

and turn it off with

    textcolor (7);

Underlining is not available with a color monitor attached to a CGA, EGA, or VGA (you can't drive a color display with the MDA). Instead, the monochrome underline attribute produces a blue foreground, which is color 1. Otherwise, the zoning of the attribute byte is the same for both monochrome and color devices.

Bit 3 drives a basic color to its high-intensity counterpart. For example, when bit 3 is on, brown becomes yellow and gray becomes white. There are thus 8 possible background colors, and 16 for the foreground. Their values are:

Value	Basic	Value	Intense
0	Black	8	Dark gray
1	Blue	9	Light blue
2	Green	10	Light green
3	Cyan	11	Light cyan
4	Red	12	Light red
5	Magenta	13	Light magenta
6	Brown	14	Yellow
7	Light gray	15	White

CONIO.H furnishes the color names as constants (all caps, no spaces). Thus, to set the background to blue and the foreground text to light cyan, the calls are

    textbackground (BLUE);
    textcolor (LIGHTCYAN);

The combination of **textcolor()**, **textbackground()**, and video functions, along with constants in CONIO.H, gives you complete control over the appearance of text appearing on the display.

Windowing

A window is a portion of the text display that functions as though it were a complete screen. That is, the upper-left corner has text coordinates {1, 1}, the text wraps to the next line when it reaches the right border, and the contents scroll upward as new lines are added at the bottom. If the program issues a clrscr(), only the active window is cleared without affecting any area outside its boundaries.

Turbo C's default window is the whole display, which is typically 80 columns by 25 rows. But let's say you want to set aside the lower-right quadrant of the screen as an individual window. To do this, issue the statement

```
window (41, 13, 80, 25);
```

Now all text I/O occurs only in the lower-right quadrant. The statement

```
gotoxy (1, 1);
```

places the cursor in column 41, row 13 of the overall screen, and all areas outside the window are unreachable. In effect, the window becomes a self-contained virtual display.

The window remains in effect until the program either ends or issues another window() statement. For example, to restore full-screen operation, write

```
window (1, 1, 80, 25);
```

Similarly, to switch to another window occupying the space shown in Figure 8.1, the statement is

```
window (20, 6, 50, 18);
```

Note that the window() statement works in the coordinate space of the screen as a whole, and not of the current window.

Later, Program 8.2 will show an example of windowing.

Figure 8.1 **Selecting an Area Within the Display**

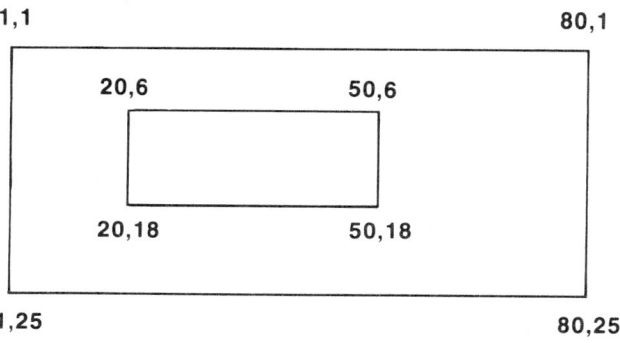

Saving and Restoring the Screen

User interfaces often need to overlay a portion of the screen, then restore it later to its previous appearance. You'll see examples of this in the next chapter in connection with pop-up windows and pull-down menus, as well as in Program 8.2 below.

While it seems almost magical to make an object vanish, restoring the information it previously covered, in fact the operation is quite simple. You copy part or all of the video buffer into program memory, then alter the screen. Later, you restore the display by copying the saved information back into the video buffer. Turbo C's **gettext()** and **puttext()** functions accomplish this; the first copies from the video buffer, and the second to it.

Because each character cell occupies two bytes, the memory space for storing a screen image has to have twice as many bytes as the number of characters in the saved area. For example, let's say you're saving the entire screen. The screen's area is 80 × 25 = 2,000 characters, so the memory requirement for storing it is 4,000 bytes. Similarly, if you're saving an area 20 columns by 5 rows, the storage requirement is 20 × 5 × 2 = 200 bytes.

This leads to a general algorithm for calculating the amount of storage space for any area whose coordinate boundaries are known:

$$space = (50 - 20 + 1) * (18 - 6 + 1) * 2$$
$$= 31 * 13 * 2$$
$$= 806 \text{ bytes}$$

A Demonstration

Now let's put this discussion of windowing and screen save/restore to work. Program 8.2 is a program called WINDEMO.C. This program writes some background text, then prompts you to press any key. For each of the first three keypresses it requests, it creates a new window somewhere on the display and fills the window with nonsense text in a different color. The program then requests three more keypresses, each time removing the most recent window and restoring the underlying screen.

As the program fills each window, note that the text wraps to the next line when it reaches the edge of the window, and that the contents of the window scroll without affecting the rest of the display. Note, too, that the third window overlaps the second. When the third window is removed, the overlaid part of the second comes back into view, and when the second goes away, the original text reappears. Thus a portion of the screen is actually buried under two layers, but it eventually gets uncovered as we strip away windows.

Program 8.2 **Windowing and Screen Save/Restore**

```c
/* WINDEMO.C: Shows windowing, screen save/restore */

#include <conio.h>

/* DEFINE TYPES */
typedef struct {                          /* window descriptor */
  int      l, t, r, b;
  char     image [800];
} WINDESCR;

/* GLOBAL WINDOW DESCRIPTORS */
WINDESCR w [] = {
  { 10, 10, 20, 20 },
  { 40,  5, 70, 15 },
  { 22, 12, 55, 17 }
};

/* LOCAL FUNCTION PROTOTYPES */
void prompt (char*);
int  space (int, int, int, int);
void fillwin (int);

/* ------------------------------------------------------- */

void main ()
{
int  n;

  clrscr ();                             /* clear the screen */
  textcolor (BROWN);
  for (n = 1; n < 23; n++) {  /* write some backgrnd text */
    gotoxy (n, n);
    cprintf ("This is at row %d, column %d", n, n);
  }

  for (n = 0; n < 3; n++) {       /* loop for three windows */
    prompt ("Press any key for next window");
    gettext (w[n].l, w[n].t, w[n].r,         /* save area */
             w[n].b, w[n].image);
    window (w[n].l, w[n].t,                  /* set window */
            w[n].r, w[n].b);
    fillwin (n);                            /* fill window */
  }

  for (n = 2; n >= 0; n--){         /* step back, erasing */
    prompt ("Press any key to erase last window");
    puttext (w[n].l, w[n].t, w[n].r,          /* restore */
             w[n].b, w[n].image);
  }

  prompt ("Press any key to quit");
```

Program 8.2 **(continued)**

```
  clrscr();
} /* ----------------------- */
void prompt (char *mssg)

   /* Write prompt message at bottom of scrn and wait */

{
  window (1, 1, 80, 25);          /* window is whole screen */
  gotoxy (1, 24);                     /* go to prompt line */
  clreol ();                              /* clear line */
  textcolor (WHITE);
  cputs (mssg);                          /* write message */
  getch ();                        /* hold until key pressed */
} /* ----------------------- */

void fillwin (int number)

   /* Fill active window with text */

{
int  i, c;

  clrscr ();                        /* clear active window */
  textcolor (number + 1);           /* blue, green, cyan */
  for (i = 0; i < 10; i++)                  /* ten times */
    for (c = 33; c < 127; c++)          /* print all chars */
      cprintf ("%c", c);
} /* ----------------------- */
```

The array of window descriptors (w[ ] at the top of the listing) allows the program to handle the whole process with a pair of loops in **main()**. The first loop builds the windows. The second steps backward, removing windows in LIFO (last in, first out) order.

It's important when unstacking windows to proceed in reverse order of creation; create 0, 1, 2, then remove 2, 1, 0 (or whatever number of windows you have). If you try some different order, the display may end up cluttered with unwanted garbage.

Inquiring About the Text Display

The library furnishes a function called **gettextinfo()** that returns all the information you need to know about the current state of the text display. This is useful when a screen-affecting function gets control and has to find out about the video status, lest it disrupt something it shouldn't.

Gettextinfo() fills in a structure called **text_info**, which is defined in CONIO.H. Declare a variable instance of this structure, then pass it as an argument to the function. When the function returns, the structured variable contains the video state information.

The program TEXTINFO.C in Program 8.3 illustrates this.

Program 8.3 **Inquiring About the Video State**

```
/* TEXTINFO.C: Reports the state of the text display */

#include <conio.h>

void main ()
{
struct text_info display;

    clrscr ();                              /* clear the screen */
    textcolor (YELLOW);
    gettextinfo (&display);                         /* inquire */
    cputs ("VIDEO STATUS:\n");              /* report results */
    textcolor (BROWN);
    cprintf ("\r\nLeft side of window            %2d",
            display.winleft);
    cprintf ("\r\nTop of window                  %2d",
            display.wintop);
    cprintf ("\r\nRight side of window           %2d",
            display.winright);
    cprintf ("\r\nBottom of window               %2d",
            display.winbottom);
    cprintf ("\r\nCurrent text attribute         %2d",
            display.attribute);
    cprintf ("\r\nNormal text attribute          %2d",
            display.normattr);
    cprintf ("\r\nCurrent video mode             %2d",
            display.currmode);
    cprintf ("\r\nNumber of rows on screen       %2d",
            display.screenheight);
    cprintf ("\r\nNumber of columns              %2d",
            display.screenwidth);
    cprintf ("\r\nCursor column position         %2d",
            display.curx);
    cprintf ("\r\nCursor row position            %2d",
            display.cury);
}
```

If you just want to determine the current cursor position, call **wherex()** and **wherey()**, which return the column and row respectively within the active window. You can also use these functions in calls to other functions, such as **gotoxy()**. For example, to move the cursor back to the start of the current line, write

```
gotoxy (1, wherey());
```

Now that we've covered the basics of text displays using the CONIO.H functions, let's begin building toward more advanced applications.

Drawing Text Boxes

Boxes around distinct areas of the screen add a professional touch to text displays. They visually fence off the things that you want the user to view separately: menus, pop-ups, dialog boxes, error messages, and the like.

Machines in the IBM PC class furnish graphics characters for drawing boxes. All such characters are in the extended ASCII set, with values in the range 128–255. There are three kinds of box-drawing characters: single-score, double-score, and conjunctions of the other two types (for example, a single line joining a double at right angles, two doubles crossing, and so on). Here we'll concentrate on simple boxes that use all of one type and form rectangles without interior lines. You might wish to expand this basic box-drawing capability into more sophisticated realms.

It takes six kinds of text characters to construct a simple box: horizontal, vertical, and corners. All of these text graphics characters pass through the center of the cells they occupy, and are thus equidistant from their neighbors both vertically and horizontally. Their ASCII values are as follows:

	Single	Double
Horizontal	196	205
Vertical	179	186
Upper left	218	201
Upper right	191	187
Lower right	217	188
Lower left	192	200

Figure 8.2 depicts the arrangement of ASCII values to construct a double-score box.

Figure 8.2 **Arrangement of Values for a Double Box**

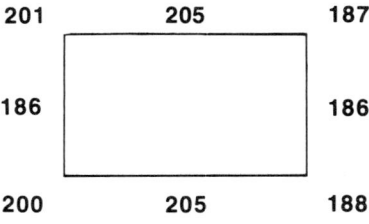

In coordinate geometry—the organizing principle of a computer screen—a rectangle is customarily described in terms of two sets of coordinates: the upper-left and lower-right corners, giving the X (column) and Y (row) of each. A box-drawing function can easily deal with this scheme, since any two opposing corners yield the coordinates for all four corners. For example, if the top-left is at {8, 3} and the lower-right at {24, 18}, then the lower-left is at {8, 18}, which is derived from the left side and the bottom.

There is one further assumption behind a box-drawing routine, which is that it might be called upon to draw any of *three* kinds of borders: none, single, or double. If none is specified, the routine should do nothing except return, and otherwise it should draw the box around the specified area.

The box-drawing function in Program 8.4 implements this. It's a generalized routine that calls on others in CONIO.H to do its job. Save it in TEXTBOX.C, and compile it to an .OBJ file for linking later to routines that use it.

Program 8.4 **Function to Draw Text Boxes**

```
/* TEXTBOX.C: Routine to draw boxes in text mode       */
/* The style argument determines the type of box drawn: */
/*          0 = no box                                  */
/*          1 = single-scored                           */
/*          2 = double-scored                           */
/* ---------------------------------------------------- */

#include <conio.h>

void textbox (int left, int top, int right,
              int bottom, int style)
{
register r, c;
static bord [][6] = {                    /* border characters */
        { 196, 179, 218, 191, 217, 192 },
        { 205, 186, 201, 187, 188, 200 }
};

  if (style == 0) return;                       /* no action */
  --style;                            /* index to border set */

  /* Draw horizontals */
  for (c = left + 1; c < right; c++) {
    gotoxy (c, top);                                /* top */
    cprintf ("%c", bord [style][0]);
    gotoxy (c, bottom);                          /* bottom */
    cprintf ("%c", bord [style][0]);
  }

  /* Draw verticals */
  for (r = top + 1; r < bottom; r++) {
    gotoxy (left, r);                              /* left */
```

Program 8.4 (continued)

```
  cprintf ("%c", bord [style][1]);
  gotoxy (right, r);                              /* right */
    cprintf ("%c", bord [style][1]);
  }

  /* Set corners */
  gotoxy (left, top);       cprintf ("%c", bord [style][2]);
  gotoxy (right, top);      cprintf ("%c", bord [style][3]);
  gotoxy (right, bottom);   cprintf ("%c", bord [style][4]);
  gotoxy (left, bottom);    cprintf ("%c", bord [style][5]);
} /* ----------------------- */
```

Note the two-dimensional static array (**bord**). The index to the correct character set (single or double score) is the **style** argument; if style is **0**, no border is drawn and the function simply returns. Otherwise, **style 1** means single-score and **style 2**, double. The function decrements **style** when not zero, so that **1** becomes **0** and accesses the first set of elements for single scoring, and **2** becomes **1** to access the second set.

The function constructs the box in this sequence:

1. Write horizontals across the top and bottom.
2. Write verticals down both sides.
3. Set the corners with their requisite characters.

You'll also need a header file to prototype the routine in TEXTBOX.C. It's TEXTBOX.H, which appears in Program 8.5.

Program 8.5 Header File for TEXTBOX.C

```
/* textbox.h: Prototype for textbox.obj module */

void textbox (int left, int top, int right,
              int bottom, int style);
```

Outlining a Window with a Text Box

Here's a procedure for drawing a text box around a window:

1. Determine the boundaries of the window.
2. Capture the defined area with **gettext()** if you intend to restore it later.
3. Define a window, set the foreground and background attributes, and issue a **clrscr()** to fill in the background color.
4. Draw the text box at the boundaries of the window.

5. Define another window one unit inside the first one. For example, if the original window is at {5, 10} and {15, 20}, the inner window is at {6, 9} and {16, 19}.

The window defined in step 3 serves no purpose except to contain the outline of the box. The second one in step 5 is the "real" text window. By shrinking the window after the box is drawn, you avoid the potential problem of oversized text wiping out the right and bottom borders.

The program in Program 8.6 puts this procedure to work. TBOX.C draws a box around the entire screen (except for the last two lines, which are the command prompt area), then sets the main window just inside the box. After writing some background text, it asks you to press any key to see the pop-up window. The window appears when you press a key and the program prompts for another keypress to make it go away. This restores the underlying text. A third keypress ends the program.

The **main()** function generally follows the steps outlined above, operating on the assumption that the initial video state inherits a full screen. The **makewindow()** function is an implementation of the steps with a few embellishments. Note the use of **gettextinfo()** in both **main()** and **makewindow()**; it captures the video state at entry so that exit processing can restore the adapter to its proper condition.

Program 8.6 Implementing Boxed Windows

```
/* TBOX.C: Outlining windows with text boxes */

#include <conio.h>
#include "textbox.h"

/* Constants */
#define  MAINFORE  YELLOW
#define  MAINBACK  BROWN
#define  MSSGFORE  BLACK
#define  BOXFORE   WHITE
#define  BOXBACK   RED

/* Globals */
char  save [156];

/* LOCAL FUNCTIONS */
void prompt (char*);
void makewindow (void);
/* ------------------------- */

void main ()
{
int   n;
struct text_info entry;
```

Program 8.6 **(continued)**

```
   gettextinfo (&entry);                    /* get entry state */
   textbackground (MAINBACK);                  /* set colors */
   textcolor (MAINFORE);
   textbox (1, 1, 80, 23, 2);        /* outline main screen */
   window (2, 2, 79, 22);                /* set main window */
   clrscr ();                   /* puts background into effect */

   for (n = 1; n < 22; n++) {             /* write some text */
     gotoxy (n + 5, n);
     cprintf ("This is at row %d, column %d", n, n + 5);
   }

   prompt ("Press any key for window...");
   makewindow ();

   prompt ("Press any key to restore original screen...");
   puttext (28, 10, 53, 12, save);

   prompt ("Press any key to quit...");
   window (1, 1, 80, 25);             /* restore entry screen */
   textcolor (entry.attribute);
   textbackground (BLACK);
   clrscr ();
} /* ---------------------- */

void prompt (char *mssg)

{         /* write message to command line and wait */

   window (1, 24, 80, 25);
   textcolor (MSSGFORE);
   clreol ();
   cputs (mssg);
   getch ();
   window (2, 2, 79, 22);
   textcolor (MAINFORE);
} /* ---------------------- */

void makewindow (void)

{           /* make a popup window */
struct text_info  original;

   gettextinfo (&original);              /* get present state */
   gettext (28, 10, 53, 12, save);          /* save image */
   window (28, 10, 53, 12);             /* define window */
   textcolor (BOXFORE);                    /* set colors */
   textbackground (BOXBACK);
   clrscr ();                          /* clear and fill b/g */
   textbox (1, 1, 25, 3, 1);               /* draw box */
   window (29, 11, 52, 11);          /* define text window */
```

Program 8.6 **(continued)**

```
cprintf ("%s", "This is a pop-up window");

/* Restore environment */
textcolor (original.attribute);
textbackground (original.attribute);
window (original.winleft, original.wintop,
        original.winright, original.winbottom);
} /* ----------------------- */
```

Because this program links with the external TEXTBOX.OBJ module compiled earlier, it's necessary to make TBOX with a project file activated via the **Alt-P** command in Turbo C's environment. This file, which you might call TBOX.PRJ, must contain the following minimal entries:

tbox
textbox.obj

The second entry tells the Turbo C linker where to find the **textbox()** routine called by TBOX.C.

The *Turbo C 2.0 User's Guide*, pages 29–37, discusses project files. Read it. Various routines presented in this book—and still others written by yourself or others—must be similarly specified in a project file in order to achieve a successful program make. The world at large will assume henceforth that, as a proficient Turbo C programmer, you know how and when to construct a .PRJ file to resolve external references.

Controlling the Cursor's Appearance

The display manipulation functions in CONIO.H don't provide any way to turn the cursor off and on or to alter its shape, but you can do so outside the normal means. This involves changing values in the ROM BIOS data area discussed in Chapter 7. Here we'll develop a small library containing functions for controlling the cursor appearance.

The cursor shape is a little tricky because it depends on the video device. The default underscore text cursor on color displays starts on scan row 6 and ends on 7, while that on the monochrome screen normally starts at row 11 and ends on 12. This is because a color display's character cell is 8 rows high, and the monochrome's is 14.

You can fetch the current cursor shape from the ROM BIOS fields cursTop and cursBottom. Before changing the shape, it's considerate to set these values aside so that you can restore the cursor to its original state on program termination.

The video hardware makes the cursor blink, and there's no practical way short of turning off the cursor and simulating your own (a lot of work) to make it stop. You can, however, change its shape. Do this by altering the values in cursTop and cursBottom; for example, to make a block cursor that fills the entire cell, change cursTop to **0**. The EGA, however, demands that you go through the ROM BIOS. You can change the values in cursTop and cursBottom, but the EGA doesn't do anything about them unless it's been notified via function 1 in interrupt 10h. Therefore the ROM BIOS variables are good for reference only. The **cursShape()** function in Program 8.7 makes the necessary ROM BIOS call.

There are two ways to hide the cursor. One is to force it to a row that doesn't exist, such as row 26, which is off-screen. The problem with this method is that **cprintf()** and other standard I/O functions then have effects that don't show on the display. The other method is to set bit 5 of the cursor-top variable. Most adapters interpret this as a signal to turn off the hardware cursor and leave it where it is, with the result that console I/O functions operate normally even though the cursor is invisible. (DOS references such as Ray Duncan's *Advanced MS-DOS* warn against this practice, but it must be safe inasumch as the IBM ROM BIOS itself uses it.)

The **cursoff()** and **curson()** functions in Program 8.7 therefore use the second method, ORing and ANDing bit 5 as appropriate, and calling the ROM BIOS to satisfy the EGA.

Program 8.7 is the library source file CURSOR.C, containing routines for controlling the cursor appearance, and Program 8.8 is a header file for this library. Compile CURSOR.C and **#include** CURSOR.H in any program that uses the library. You will need a project file to link with it.

Program 8.7 **Cursor Appearance Functions**

```
/* CURSOR.C: Cursor appearance functions */

#include <dos.h>
#include <biosarea.h>

BIOSDATA far *bios = MK_FP (0x0040, 0);

void cursoff (void)
{                                       /* turn hardware cursor off */
union REGS reg;

   reg.h.ah = 1;
   reg.h.ch = bios->cursTop | 0x20;        /* turn on bit 5 */
   reg.h.cl = bios->cursBottom;
   int86 (0x10, &reg, &reg);
} /* ----------------------- */
void curson (void)
{                                       /* turn hardware cursor on */
union REGS reg;
```

Program 8.7 **(continued)**

```
   reg.h.ah = 1;
   reg.h.ch = bios->cursTop & 0xDF;        /* turn off bit 5 */
   reg.h.cl = bios->cursBottom;
   int86 (0x10, &reg, &reg);
} /* ----------------------- */
void cursShape (int top, int bottom)
{                                          /* change cursor shape */
union REGS   reg;

   reg.h.ch = top;
   reg.h.cl = bottom;
   reg.h.ah = 1;
   int86 (0x10, &reg, &reg);
} /* ----------------------- */
```

Program 8.8 **#Include File for CURSOR Library**

```
/* CURSOR.H: Prototypes for cursor appearance functions */

void cursoff (void);          /* turn hardware cursor off */
void curson (void);           /* turn hardware cursor on */
void cursShape (int top, int bottom);   /* change shape */
----------------------------------------------------------
```

Program 8.9 lists a Turbo C program CURS.C that tests the functions in CURSOR.C. Run this program to see how the cursor appearance functions work on your display.

Program 8.9 **Demonstrating the Cursor Appearance Functions**

```
/* CURS.C: Tests cursor appearance functions */

#include <conio.h>
#include <dos.h>
#include "biosarea.h"
#include "cursor.h"

void main ()
{
int  oldtop;
void wait (void);
BIOSDATA far *bios = MK_FP (0x0040, 0);

   clrscr ();
   cputs ("\r\nCursor is off");
   cursoff ();
   wait ();
```

Program 8.9 (continued)

```
    cputs ("\r\n\r\nCursor is back on");
    curson ();
    wait ();

    cputs ("\r\n\r\nBlock cursor");
    oldtop = bios->cursTop;
    cursShape (0, bios->cursBottom);
    wait ();

    cputs ("\r\n\r\nNormal cursor again");
    cursShape (oldtop, bios->cursBottom);
    wait ();

    clrscr ();
} /* ---------------------- */

void wait (void)
{
    cputs ("\r\nPress any key to continue...");
    getch();
}
--------------------------------------------------------------
```

We've now developed the basic tools for text-handling in Turbo C. The next chapter builds on this one to create professional-quality displays with menu bars, pop-up windows, and pull-down menus.

CHAPTER 9

CREATING THE VISUAL ENVIRONMENT

T his chapter builds on the tools and techniques covered in the last chapter to create the kinds of visual environments associated with high-powered software products. Friendly user interfaces typically use three kinds of visual objects: free-form text screens, menu bars, and pop-ups. The interactive environment of Turbo C contains examples of all three and serves as a convenient point of reference.

A free-form screen is one in which the user or the data being presented have some control over the appearance of the display. The edit screen is an example; you as the user have the ability to move around within it, altering the way it looks by changing its contents.

A menu bar is a list of action items, usually running across the top or bottom of the display. There's one at the top of the Turbo C screen. A menu bar might also appear in a pop-up; this commonly occurs in applications written to run under Microsoft Windows.

The third kind of object, a pop-up, is a window that appears and later vanishes. Pop-ups can take several forms. They share the characteristic that they temporarily overlay part or all of the screen and, when they disappear, the underlying display is restored. Three common examples are pull-down menus, which seem to fall down from a menu bar, help panels, and dialog boxes.

In the last case, the pop-up is a bordered window. A program uses a dialog box to request and receive information that it needs under special circumstances to do its job. An example from Turbo C is the file pick list you get from pressing **Alt-F3.**

We'll examine these things in detail in this chapter and develop methods for working with them.

Structured Displays

A pop-up is, in effect, a subset of the screen ranging from a few rows by a few columns up to the entire visible display. As such, no matter where a pop-up is or what its size, we should be able to describe and manage it in a consistent fashion.

And what are the elements essential for its management? Here's a list:

- Its position and size: coordinates of the left, top, right, and bottom of the pop-up.
- Its border style: 0–2 as defined in the **textBox()** function from Chapter 8.
- Its text attributes: normal and highlighted.
- Its text background: normal and highlighted.
- The border color.
- A pointer to its text content: menu selections and other fixed text. If none, this pointer is NULL.
- A pointer to a buffer for saving the overlaid part of the screen, so that it can be restored in order to make the pop-up disappear.
- A **text_info** structure for saving the state of the display so that it can be restored later.

This suggests a structure describing a pop-up along with a set of routines that operate on that structure, and that's what we're about to develop.

The pop-up structure is as follows:

```
typedef struct {
    int   left, top right, bottom,        /* border loc /*
          style,                          /* border style /*
          normal, hilite,                 /* text colors */
          normback, hiback,               /* backgrounds */
          border;                         /* border color */
    char *text,                           /* pointer to fixed text */
    void *save;                           /* pointer to save buffer */
    struct text_info prev;                /* old video state */
} POPUP;
```

Programs should initialize one such structure for each pop-up, filling in everything except the pointers and the **text_info** structure. It's easiest to do this at declaration. However, your program will need to execute a statement to set the text pointer, since the string's address isn't known until run-time.

Figure the coordinates of a pop-up in terms of full-screen coordinates. The reference values are left and top. Bottom is the sum of top plus one more than the number of text rows in the window. Right is two more than the longest string's length, plus left. For example, the window contains

```
This
is
a
popup
```

and its upper-left corner is at {10, 10}. There are four lines, so the bottom is at 15. The longest string contains five characters, so the right is at 17. This leaves one space between the final letter and the border, which is necessary to keep the cursor from wrapping to the next line and scrolling the window contents.

Creating and Erasing Pop-ups

Now we can develop a set of functions that provide simple calls for manipulating these POPUP objects, thus controlling pop-up windows. The first is **popShow()**, which does the following:

1. Saves the current video state.
2. Sets the window to full-screen mode (the pop-up's location is assumed to be relative to the display as a whole and not to the active window).
3. Checks to make sure the coordinates are in the proper order (left < right, top < bottom), and sorts them if they're not.
4. Saves the area under the new window.
5. Draws the border in the normal background and border foreground colors.
6. Sets the window to the inside of the border and clears it to put the normal text colors into effect.
7. Writes the fixed text, if any.

The opposite of **popShow()** is **popErase()**, which makes a pop-up go away by restoring the underlying display area and resetting the screen to its previous state. As mentioned in the last chapter, you should take care to erase pop-ups in the order opposite their creation, that is, newest to oldest.

Programs 9.1 and 9.2 are the beginnings of a pop-up library that we'll expand through the rest of this chapter. POPUP.H in Program 9.1 is a header file containing information about the actual library routines, which are in POPUP.C, Program 9.2. The header file as shown contains the POPUP structure definition and the two basic functions described above. The listings for some library routines will be repeated later, but it will be necessary to add their prototypes to POPUP.H.

Program 9.1 **Initial Header File for a Pop-up Toolkit**

```
/* POPUP.H: Prototypes and typedefs for POPUP.C library */

extern struct text_info;                      /* from conio.h */

typedef struct {
  int  left, top, right, bottom,    /* border location */
       style,                       /* border style */
       normal, hilite,              /* text attributes */
       normback, hiback, border;
  char *text;                       /* fixed text contents */
  void *save;                       /* pointer to save buffer */
  struct text_info  prev;           /* previous video state */
} POPUP;

typedef struct {
  int  row,                         /* row where bar appears */
       interval,                    /* cols between first chars */
       fore, back;                  /* foreground/background colors */
  char *choice;                     /* pointer to text contents */
} MENUBAR;

void popShow (POPUP *pop);       /* display popup window */

void popErase (POPUP *pop);
          /* Erase popup window, restoring overlaid image */
```

Program 9.2 **Source for Starting the Pop-up Library**

```
/* POPUP.C: Pop-up window library */

#include <stdio.h>
#include <dos.h>
#include <conio.h>
#include <alloc.h>
#include <string.h>
#include "textbox.h"
#include "biosarea.h"
#include "popup.h"

void popShow (POPUP *pop)              /* display popup window */
{
int   bufsize, x;

  gettextinfo (&(pop->prev));     /* save old video state */
  window (1, 1, 80, 25);          /* go to full-screen mode */

  /* Make sure boundaries are in correct order */
  if (pop->left > pop->right) {
    x = pop->left;
    pop->left = pop->right;
```

Program 9.2 **(continued)**

```
    pop->right = x;
  }
  if (pop->top > pop->bottom) {
    x = pop->top;
    pop->top = pop->bottom;
    pop->bottom = x;
  }

  /* Save area under new window */
  bufsize = (pop->right - pop->left + 2) *      /* buf size */
            (pop->bottom - pop->top + 2) * 2;
  pop->save = malloc (bufsize);                 /* get buffer */
  gettext (pop->left, pop->top, pop->right,  /* save image */
           pop->bottom, pop->save);

  /* Draw the border */
  textcolor (pop->border);                      /* border color */
  textbackground (pop->normback);
  textbox (pop->left, pop->top, pop->right,     /* border */
           pop->bottom, pop->style);

  /* Open the window */
  textcolor (pop->normal);             /* set text foreground */
  window  (pop->left+1, pop->top+1,            /* open window */
           pop->right-1, pop->bottom-1);
  clrscr ();
  if (pop->text != NULL)                  /* write fixed text */
    cputs (pop->text);
} /* ----------------------- */

void popErase (POPUP *pop)
          /* Erase popup window, restoring overlaid image */
{
  /* Make sure the window exists */
  if (pop->save == NULL)
    return;                           /* quit if it doesn't */

  /* Restore previous window characteristics */
  window (pop->prev.winleft, pop->prev.wintop,
          pop->prev.winright, pop->prev.winbottom);
  gotoxy (pop->prev.curx, pop->prev.cury);  /* cursor pos */
  textcolor (pop->prev.attribute & 0x0F);    /* old color */
  textbackground (pop->prev.attribute >> 4);   /* and b/g */

  /* Restore overlaid area */
  puttext (pop->left, pop->top, pop->right,
           pop->bottom, pop->save);
  free (pop->save);
  pop->save = NULL;
} /* ----------------------- */

void popCenter (POPUP *win, char *string)
```

Program 9.2 (continued)

```
      /* Center string in window */
{
int   i, tab;

  tab = (win->right - win->left - strlen (string)) / 2;
  for (i = 0; i < tab; i++)
    cputs (" ");
  cputs (string);
} /* ----------------------- */

void popRewrite (POPUP *win, int row, char attrib)
     /* Rewrite pop-up row with new character attribute */
{
int          p, nchars;
union  REGS  reg;
struct text_info text;

  gettextinfo (&text);               /* get current settings */
  nchars = win->right - win->left;        /* popup width */
  for (p = 1; p < nchars; p++) {
    gotoxy (p, row);
    reg.h.ah = 8;                          /* get character */
    reg.h.bh = 0;                           /* in page 0 */
    int86 (0x10, &reg, &reg);            /* via ROM BIOS */
    reg.h.ah = 9;                    /* write back out with */
    reg.h.bl = attrib;                /* hilite attribs */
    reg.h.bh = 0;                            /* page 0 */
    reg.x.cx = 1;                         /* one char */
    int86 (0x10, &reg, &reg);
  }
  gotoxy (text.curx, text.cury);      /* restore cursor */
} /* ----------------------- */

void popHilite (POPUP *win, int row)
     /* Hilight text in popup row */
{
char attrib;

  attrib = win->hilite +
           (win->hiback << 4);        /* hilite attributes */
  popRewrite (win, row, attrib);
} /* ----------------------- */

void popNormal (POPUP *win, int row)
     /* Set text in popup row to normal attribs */
{
char attrib;

  attrib = win->normal +
           (win->normback << 4);      /* normal attributes */
  popRewrite (win, row, attrib);
} /* ----------------------- */
```

Program 9.2 **(continued)**

```
void menubar (MENUBAR *spec)
     /* Write the menu bar described by spec */
{
struct text_info   text;
int                p, s, c = 0;

   gettextinfo (&text);            /* get current video state */
   textcolor (spec->fore);                    /* set colors */
   textbackground (spec->back);
   gotoxy (1, spec->row);               /* start of menu bar */

   for (s = 1; s < text.winright - text.winleft + 2; s++)
     cprintf ("%c", ' ');                /* set background */

   gotoxy (1, spec->row);               /* start of menu bar */
   for (p = 0; spec->choice [p]; p++)   /* copy text to bar */
     if (spec->choice [p] != '\n')
       cprintf ("%c", spec->choice [p]);      /* write char */
     else
       gotoxy (spec->interval * ++c, spec->row);   /* next */

   /* Restore previous state */
   textcolor (text.attribute & 0x8F);       /* color scheme */
   textbackground (text.attribute >> 4);
   gotoxy (text.curx, text.cury);
} /* ---------------------- */
```

Note that **popShow()** places the saved image on the heap, which is an area of uncommitted memory above your program's workspace. Part IV discusses the heap in detail. **popShow()** computes bufsize, the amount of space needed for the image, and acquires the memory with a call to **malloc()**, placing its address in **pop->save**. Gettext() uses this address as its destination.

The program remembers where the image is because it retains the address in the POPUP structure. That's how **popErase()** can restore the overlaid area with **puttext()**. Once the image is restored, it's no longer necessary to keep it, so **popErase()** issues the **free()** statement to deallocate the heap space, then resets the save pointer to **NULL**.

Specifying Fixed Text

Because pop-ups often contain fixed text—for example, a list of menu selections and perhaps a header—it's convenient to specify the elements as a single string. That way you can place a pointer to the string in the text field of the descriptor structure, and **popShow()** will automatically print the text with **cputs()**.

You can use the carriage return/line feed sequence\r\n to separate text elements (Turbo C's conio functions such as **cprintf()** don't translate the usual \n into a full newline, so you have to do it explicitly when using them). Say the text in a pop-up menu is to appear as follows:

```
MENU
Run
Fetch file
Edit
Quit
```

The specification of this menu's fixed text, then, is

```
poptxt[] = "   MENU\r\nFetch file\r\nEdit\r\nQuit";
```

Note that the first element (**MENU**) is preceded by three spaces to achieve centering.

Demonstration: Overlapping Pop-up Windows

Program 9.3 puts this discussion into practice with QUICKPOP.C. The program fills the display with the letter **T** to serve as a visual backdrop. Two successive keypresses produce overlapping pop-ups with calls to **pop-Show()**. The next two keypresses remove them in last-to-first order by calling **popErase()**. A final keypress clears the screen and ends the program. Note how little code it takes to handle the screen changes thanks to the routines in POPUP.C.

To link this program with the routines that support it, you will need a project file containing the entries:

```
quickpop
popup, textbox
```

Program 9.3 **A Pop-up Window Demonstration**

```
/* QUICKPOP.C: Creates and erases two pop-up windows on */
/*    successive keystrokes                             */

#include <stdio.h>
#include <dos.h>
#include <conio.h>
#include "textbox.h"
#include "popup.h"

char    string1 [] = "This\r\nis\r\na\r\npopup",
```

Program 9.3 **(continued)**

```
        string2 [] = "So\r\nis\r\nthis";
POPUP   pop [] = {
          {20, 5, 27, 10, 2,
           BLUE, MAGENTA, CYAN, CYAN, RED, string1},
          {26, 8, 32, 12, 1,
           YELLOW, WHITE, BROWN, BROWN, BLACK, string2}
};

void main ()
{
int     n;

  clrscr ();
  for (n = 0; n < 1920; n++)              /* fill screen */
    cputs ("T");

  for (n = 0; n < 2; n++) {               /* show the popups */
    getch ();
    popShow (&(pop [n]));
  }
  for (n = 1; n >=0; n--) {               /* then erase them */
    getch ();
    popErase (&(pop [n]));
  }
  getch ();
  clrscr ();
}
```

Writing Variable Data to a Pop-up

Pop-ups often need to show variable information. The conio functions make it easy; it's no different from working on a full screen. Use **cprintf()** for formatting the output, and **gotoxy()** to move the cursor to a new location.

Keep in mind that **gotoxy()** works in relation to the upper-left corner of the active window, not of the screen as a whole. Therefore, gotoxy (1, 1) moves the cursor to the window's home position.

Be sure to make the window wide enough to contain the longest possible string plus one.

Centering Text in a Pop-up

For cosmetic reasons, you might want to center text within a pop-up. Examples are a title or a prompt such as **Press any key to continue** . . . . Sometimes variable data looks better centered, too.

Centering is a simple operation. Find the width of the window (from its POPUP structure), subtract the string length, and divide by two. This gives the number of spaces to insert in front of the string in order to achieve centering.

Program 9.4 lists a **popCenter()** function that performs this operation. Add the prototype to POPUP.H.

Program 9.4 **POPUP.C Routine for Centering a String**

```
void popCenter (POPUP *win, char *string)

     /* Center string in window */
{
int   i, tab;

  tab = (win->right - win->left - strlen (string)) / 2;
  for (i = 0; i < tab; i++)
  cputs (" ");
  cputs (string);
} /* ----------------------- */
```

Use **sprintf()** if you need to center a string containing variable information. After building the string, pass it as an argument to **popCenter()**.

Word of caution: Don't put a leading newline (\n) into a string that is to be centered. The routine will insert the leading spaces, but then advance to the start of the next line before writing the text. Consequently, the line will not be centered, and it will appear in the wrong row.

Demonstration: *Showing the Date in a Pop-up*

Program 9.5 is a program POPDATE.C that illustrates centering variable information in a pop-up. The program fills the display with plus signs and then prompts at the bottom of the screen for a keypress. Upon detecting one, it pops up an empty window and then calls **showDate()**. Note that the prompt at the bottom of the display is erased before the window appears, so that the user isn't confronted with "stale" prompts.

This routine calls Turbo C's **getdate()** function to read the system date, converts the results into a string with **sprintf()**, and in turn calls **popCenter()** to center the output. It also sends an invariant prompt message to **popCenter()**, then waits for another keypress.

The second keypress evaporates the pop-up with **popErase()** and produces another prompt at the bottom of the screen. The final keypress clears the display and ends the program.

The project file for this program reads

popdate, popup.obj, textbox.obj, cursor.obj

Program 9.5 **Centering Text in a Pop-Up**

```
/* POPDATE.C: Gives the date and time in a pop-up window */

#include <dos.h>
#include <string.h>
#include <stdio.h>
#include <conio.h>
#include "textbox.h"
#include "popup.h"
#include "cursor.h"

void showDate (POPUP*);          /* local function prototype */

void main ()
{
int     n;
POPUP   pop = {25, 10, 55, 13, 1, YELLOW, 0,
               BLUE, 0, WHITE, NULL, NULL};

   clrscr ();
   for (n = 0; n < 1920; n++)                  /* fill screen */
     cputs ("+");
   cputs ("Press any key to see the date...");
   getch ();                                    /* wait */
   gotoxy (1, wherey ());
   clreol ();                           /* clear prompt line */
   popShow (&pop);                         /* create pop-up */
   showDate (&pop);                        /* show the date */
   popErase (&pop);                     /* erase the pop-up */
   cputs ("Press any key to end...");
   getch ();                                    /* wait */
   clrscr ();
} /* ----------------------- */

void showDate (POPUP *win)

   /* Show date in window */
{
struct date dates;
char message [27], month [13][10] = {
    {""}, {"January"}, {"February"}, {"March"}, {"April"},
    {"May"}, {"June"}, {"July"}, {"August"}, {"September"},
    {"October"}, {"November"}, {"December"}
   };

   cursoff ();
   getdate (&dates);

   sprintf (message, "Today is %s %d, %d",
            month [dates.da_mon], dates.da_day,
            dates.da_year);
   popCenter (win, message);
```

Program 9.5 **(continued)**

```
        sprintf (message, "Any key to continue...");
        popCenter (win, message);
        getch ();
        curson ();
} /* ----------------------- */
```

Highlighting Text

Many applications using pop-ups employ highlighting for prompt lines, to show which menu choice is currently indicated for selection, for warning messages, and so forth. They do this by setting a different foreground/background attribute. The Turbo C environment's pop-ups are an example; the "pointed-at" selection has dark letters on a light background, the opposite of all others.

You can control highlighting by changing the attributes for a row using the POPUP structure's hilite and hiback fields. Scan across the pop-up from left to right, changing the attribute byte for each character position. In window coordinates (relative to the upper-left corner of the pop-up), the first row is 1, the second 2, and so on, and the columns are also numbered from 1 upward.

The Turbo C library doesn't include a function for detecting what's on the screen at a given character position, but the ROM BIOS does. Interrupt 10h, function 8, returns the character at the current cursor position. Function 9 writes a character and attribute to the display. Thus, by advancing across the row one character at a time, you can tell the ROM BIOS to read the current character and rewrite it with the highlighting attributes. The same process applies to removing highlighting and restoring the normal color schemes. Simply substitute the POPUP structure's normal and normback values.

The expression for building an attribute byte used by the ROM BIOS call is

attribute = foreground + (background << 4);

That is, shift the background value left four bits and add it to the foreground. The result is consistent with the attribute structure shown in Chapter 8.

A common application for these functions is in highlighting selections on pull-down menus. When the highlight moves from one selection to another (often but not always in response to a cursor arrow key, as covered in the next chapter), three actions are necessary:

1. Set the currently indicated row back to the normal attributes.
2. Increment or decrement the selection indicator as appropriate.
3. Highlight the newly indicated row.

Program 9.6 introduces three new functions to add to POPUP.H. popRewrite()
is called by the other two; it rewrites a window row using the new attribute
byte, relying on ROM BIOS calls to do its job. popNormal() and popHilite()
both take as arguments the address of the affected POPUP structure and the
row number within the window. For example, say indic is an integer variable
giving the indicated row. On a signal from the user to advance the indicator,
implement the steps above as follows

```
popNormal (&popup, scrn, indic);
++indic;
popHilite (&popup, scrn, indic);
```

Program 9.6 **Setting Highlighted and Normal Attributes**

```
void popRewrite (POPUP *win, int row, char attrib)
     /* Rewrite pop-up row with new character attribute */
{
int       p, nchars;
union  REGS   reg;
struct text_info text;

   gettextinfo (&text);                   /* get current settings */
   nchars = win->right - win->left;         /* popup width */
   for (p = 1; p < nchars; p++) {
     gotoxy (p, row);
     reg.h.ah = 8;                         /* get character */
     reg.h.bh = 0;                           /* in page 0 */
     int86 (0x10, &reg, &reg);              /* via ROM BIOS */
     reg.h.ah = 9;                      /* write back out with */
     reg.h.bl = attrib;                   /* hilite attribs */
     reg.h.bh = 0;                           /* page 0 */
     reg.x.cx = 1;                          /* one char */
     int86 (0x10, &reg, &reg);
   }
   gotoxy (text.curx, text.cury);          /* restore cursor */
} /* ------------------------ */

void popHilite (POPUP *win, int row)
     /* Hilight text in popup row */
{
char attrib;

   attrib = win->hilite +
            (win->hiback << 4);             /* hilite attributes */
   popRewrite (win, row, attrib);
} /* ---------------------- */

void popNormal (POPUP *win, int row)
     /* Set text in popup row to normal attribs */
{
```

Program 9.6 **(continued)**

```
char attrib;

    attrib = win->normal +
            (win->normback << 4);        /* normal attributes */
    popRewrite (win, row, attrib);
} /* ------------------------- */
```

Menu Bars

Another familiar device of professional user interfaces is the menu bar, which usually runs across the top of the window but can run across the bottom, or even somewhere in between. Many software systems use it: Framework, Paradox, Reflex, dBASE, and the pfs family of products, to name but a few. Turbo C's is at the top, and like most of its kind, it names several broad categories of action that, when selected, lead to a pull-down submenu from which the user picks the specific task to be performed.

A menu bar is a much simpler visual object than a pop-up. It's simply one line on the display possessing the following properties:

- The row where it appears.
- The interval in columns between choices' first characters.
- The foreground and background colors.
- The text contents.

This leads naturally to the second descriptor structure that appears in POPUP.H:

```
typedef struct {
    int   row,                    /* row where bar appears */
          interval,               /* cols btwn first chars */
          fore, back;             /* text colors */
    char *choice;                 /* ptr to text contents */
} MENUBAR;
```

As in the case of pop-ups, the text component of the descriptor is a pointer to an initialized string. You can preserve memory space by packing this string with a byte indicating where it is to be broken and the next character written at the following interval. Any nonprinting will do: a convenient one, used here, is the new line sequence (\r \n). Thus the packed string

```
"File\r\nPrint\r\nData\r\nGraph\r\nOptions"
```

is expanded into five separate selections spread evenly across a menu bar.

The interval between selections is simple to figure. If there are n selections, the interval is $^{80}/_n$ on the full 80-column screen. The string above contains five selections, so their interval is $^{80}/_5$ = 16 characters. If the menu bar is to appear inside a window 50 characters wide, then the interval is $^{50}/_5$ = 10 characters.

A complete menu bar specification, then, consists of a string initialization followed by a structure initialization, as in:

```
char menutxt[] =
    "File\r\nPrint\r\nData\r\nGraph\r\nOptions";
MENUBAR bar = {0, 16, BLACK, GREEN, menutxt};
```

This specifies a menu bar containing the selections in menutxt[], with the bar located in row 0, interval between the selections' first characters of 16 columns, and black-on-green.

You can construct this object in a memory screen image with the menubar() function in Program 9.7. Make it the final entry in your POPUP.H file.

Program 9.7 **Function to Display a Menu Bar**

```
void menubar (MENUBAR *spec)
     /* Write the menu bar described by spec */
{
struct text_info   text;
int                p, s, c = 0;

   gettextinfo (&text);                /* get current video state */
   textcolor (spec->fore);                        /* set colors */
   textbackground (spec->back);
   gotoxy (1, spec->row);                   /* start of menu bar */

   for (s = 1; s < text.winright - text.winleft + 2; s++)
     cprintf ("%c", ' ');                      /* set background */

   gotoxy (1, spec->row);                 /* start of menu bar */
   for (p = 0; spec->choice [p]; p++)   /* copy text to bar */
     if (spec->choice [p] != '\n')
       cprintf ("%c", spec->choice [p]);        /* write char */
     else
       gotoxy (spec->interval * ++c, spec->row);    /* next */

   /* Restore previous state */
   textcolor (text.attribute & 0x8F);         /* color scheme */
   textbackground (text.attribute >> 4);
   gotoxy (text.curx, text.cury);
} /* ----------------------- */
```

Note how **menubar()** works. First it gets the current video state, which it needs in order to find out the width of the active window. Next it sets the text colors and goes to the start of the menu bar. The first step in creating the bar is to initialize the row, passing through it printing space characters to set the background color. After that, it copies the text to the bar. The p index keeps track of the source location, while the c variable gives the current selection (0, 1, 2, and so on). Whenever a newline is encountered in the source string, c is incremented and multiplied by the interval to give the new column where output resumes. Thus the routine expands the source string to fill the bar with proper spacing between selections. Afterwards, the routine restores the original text colors and the cursor position for subsequent output.

Menu Bars and Pull-Down Menus: A Skeleton Program

We now have nearly all the software mechanisms in place to develop a sophisticated program driven by a menu bar and pull-down menus. The only things lacking are "pointing" refinements via the keyboard and mouse, which we cover in the next two chapters.

The program we'll develop here is PULLDOWN.C, a skeleton containing a complete menu-driven program that relies on the direct image manipulations we have developed here. The program works like this: It displays a menu bar containing five selections. Type the first letter of any selection and an associated pull-down appears with the first choice highlighted. You can step through the choices by pressing the space bar. To leave the pull-down, press the **Esc** key, and to select an item, press **Enter.**

PULLDOWN doesn't do any useful work beyond providing a working user interface. It's up to you to customize it and flesh it out, chiefly in the **actOn()** function, which we'll discuss later. One selection does work, however, and that's the **Quit** choice in the File menu. To stop the program, type **F,** then space down to **Quit** and press **Enter.**

Now let's discuss the structure and features of the PULLDOWN program.

The first major step in defining a system of menus is to initialize structures and their related strings. Doing so outside the scope of any function, including **main()**, makes these objects visible to all ensuing functions in the compile unit. A sensible way is to define, one by one at the top of the primary file, the text components, followed by their related descriptors. That's what the **OBJECT DEFINITIONS** portion of Program 9.8 does.

The **main()** function has three phases. The first sets up the basic screen and, for purposes of demonstrating how the removal of a pull-down restores the underlying text, writes some text just below the menu bar. The last phase simply cleans up by clearing the screen, homing the cursor, and turning the cursor back on. Most of the real work occurs in the loop that is the middle phase.

This loop drives the menu bar selections. It waits for the user to key one of the selection indicators, then assigns a numeric value that's used to select the pulldown menu. The next step is to call a routine that displays the menu and processes the user's request. This function, doMenu(), returns TRUE if the loop is to reiterate and FALSE if the user has decided to stop (File menu, Quit selection).

The doMenu function changes the status line at the bottom of the display to reflect appropriate instructions, then displays the pull-down. There are three possible actions (which will be expanded in the next two chapters to include others). These are:

- Striking the space bar to move the highlight to the next choice in the pull-down.
- Striking the **Esc** key to abandon the pull-down and revert to the initial (menu bar only) display.
- Striking the **Enter** key to execute the pull-down choice.

The switch() in doMenu() processes these keyboard entries, with the case clauses setting control variables as appropriate to continue the local and main() loops. Note that the CR case either halts all loops (user pressed **Enter** when Quit is chosen from the File menu) or passes control to another function called actOn().

The actOn() function is what you must flesh out if you adapt this user interface to your own application. As written here, it merely displays which choice the user has made. Normally this function would act as a dispatcher via nested switch() statements, as in:

```
switch (pick) {
  case 0:
    switch (indic) {
      case 0: getFile(); break;
      case 1: saveFile (); break;
      case 2: combFiles(); break;
      case 3: backup(); break;
    }
    break;
  case 1:
    switch (indic) {
      case 0: prtReport(); break;
      case 1: prtGraph(); break;
      case 2: prtNewPage(); break;
    }
    break;
  case . . . etc.
```

PULLDOWN.C is long for a sample program. However, as the basis for a complete menuing system, the libraries developed here make it surprisingly compact. The means presented in these chapters enable us to confine it to less than 160 lines of code.

Program 9.8 **A Complete Menuing Skeleton**

```
/* PULLDOWN.C: Skeleton of menu bar with pull-down menus */

/* INCLUDES */
#include <stdio.h>
#include <dos.h>
#include <conio.h>
#include <ctype.h>
#include "textbox.h"
#include "popup.h"
#include "cursor.h"

/* DEFINES */
#if !defined TRUE
#define  FALSE 0
#define  TRUE  !FALSE
#endif
#define  CR   13
#define  SPC  32
#define  ESC  27

/* OBJECT DEFINITIONS */
POPUP full = {1, 1, 80, 25, 0, YELLOW, 0, BLACK};
              /* Full is defined so that we can use
                 popCenter to center prompt in full display */

/* Menu bar */
char  menutext [] = "File\r\nPrint\r\nData\r\nGraph\r\nOptions";
MENUBAR bar = {1, 16, WHITE, BLUE, menutext};

/* Text of pull-down menus */
char  p0text [] = "Retrieve\r\nSave\r\nCombine\r\nBackup\r\nQuit",
      p1text [] = "Report\r\nGraph\r\nNew page",
      p2text [] = "Edit\r\nDelete\r\nInsert\r\nBrowse",
      p3text [] = "Type\r\nView\r\nDelete\r\nSave",
      p4text [] = "Colors\r\nKeyboard\r\nRecalc";

POPUP pop [] = {
      { 1, 2, 11, 8, 1, BLACK, BLACK,
          LIGHTGRAY, GREEN, WHITE, p0text},
      {16, 2, 26, 6, 1, BLACK, BLACK,
          LIGHTGRAY, GREEN, WHITE, p1text},
      {32, 2, 40, 7, 1, BLACK, BLACK,
          LIGHTGRAY, GREEN, WHITE, p2text},
      {48, 2, 56, 7, 1, BLACK, BLACK,
          LIGHTGRAY, GREEN, WHITE, p3text},
      {64, 2, 74, 6, 1, BLACK, BLACK,
```

Program 9.8 **(continued)**

```c
                  LIGHTGRAY, GREEN, WHITE, p4text}
};

/* LOCAL FUNCTIONS */
void prompt (char*);
int  doMenu (int, POPUP*);
void actOn (int, int);
/* --------------------------------------------------- */

void main ()
{
int    repeating, pick;
char   sel;
POPUP *popup;

   textcolor (YELLOW);
   textbackground (BLACK);
   clrscr ();
   menubar (&bar);                          /* display menu bar */

   gotoxy (1, 4);
   cputs
     ("Four of the pull-down menus will overlay this text");

/* Loop to drive menu bar selections */
   do {
     cursoff ();
     repeating = TRUE;                       /* set switch */
     prompt ("Pick menu selection by letter");
     sel = toupper (getch ());               /* get selection */
     switch (sel) {
       case 'F': pick = 0; break;
       case 'P': pick = 1; break;
       case 'D': pick = 2; break;
       case 'G': pick = 3; break;
       case 'O': pick = 4; break;
     }
     popup = &(pop [pick]);              /* select pulldown */
     repeating = doMenu (pick, popup);       /* display it */
   } while (repeating);

/* Clean up at end of job */
   curson ();                               /* restore cursor */
   textcolor (LIGHTGRAY);
   textbackground (BLACK);
   clrscr ();
} /* ----------------------- */

void prompt (char *message)

     /* Display a prompt message at bottom of screen */

{
```

Program 9.8 **(continued)**

```c
struct text_info  screen;

   gettextinfo (&screen);                /* get screen state */
   gotoxy (1, 24); clreol ();            /* clear prompt line */
   popCenter (&full, message);           /* display prompt */
   gotoxy (screen.curx, screen.cury);      /* return cursor */
} /* ----------------------- */


int doMenu (int pick, POPUP *menu)

     /* Display pull-down menu, get selection */
{
int  indic = 1, keepOn = TRUE, looping = TRUE, last;

   prompt ("Space to advance, Enter to select, ESC to quit");
   popShow (menu);                    /* display the pulldown */
   popHilite (menu, indic);         /* highlight first choice */
   last = menu->bottom - menu->top - 1;    /* last menu row */
   do {
     switch (getch ()) {
       case SPC:                              /* advance */
         popNormal (menu, indic);        /* reset to normal */
         if (++indic > last)
           indic = 1;                        /* wrap to top */
         popHilite (menu, indic);         /* hilite next */
         break;
       case ESC:                               /* quit */
         looping = FALSE;
         break;
       case CR:                               /* select */
         if ((pick == 0) && (indic == 5))
           keepOn = FALSE;              /* if picked 'Quit' */
         else
           actOn (pick, indic);        /* act on choice */
         looping = FALSE;
         break;
     }
   } while (looping);
   if (!looping)
     popErase (menu);         /* erase menu when done with it */
   return (keepOn);
} /* ----------------------- */


void actOn (int barchoice, int menuchoice)

     /* stub of dispatcher for acting on menu choice */
     /* merely displays choice for 3 sec in a pop-up */
{
char  report [30];
POPUP action = {25, 12, 55, 14, 2, RED + BLINK, 0,
               LIGHTGRAY, 0, MAGENTA};
```

Program 9.8 **(continued)**

```
sprintf (report, "You selected menu %d, item %d",
         barchoice, menuchoice);
popShow (&action);
popCenter (&action, report);
sleep (3);                               /* hold for 3 sec */
popErase (&action);
} /* ----------------------- */
```

Of course there are other approaches to menus. This is just one. Expand the capabilities of the routines given here as your needs dictate. That's what we're going to do in the next couple of chapters.

CHAPTER 10

KEYBOARD VIRTUOSO

Just as the display is the most important output device of a personal computer, so is the keyboard the most important input. It's not merely a means for entering data, but also the primary device—indeed, the *only* device in most cases—by which a user controls the system. For that reason, mastery of the keyboard is essential to successful software.

The C language in general makes it easy to take the keyboard for granted, and Turbo C is no different. It provides character-at-a-time input functions such as **getch()** (get a character without echo) and **getche()** (same but echo to the display), as well as string-input functions such as **gets()** and **scanf()**, which take advantage of DOS' input-editing operations.

The problem with the standard C functions is that they don't accommodate the peculiarities of the PC-style keyboard: There are no standard functions, for example, to obtain a cursor-control key, a function key, or others such as **PgUp, Home, End,** and so on.

Consequently, this chapter concentrates chiefly on the things that *don't* come built into Turbo C.

Of ASCII and Codes

Since you've been programming for a while, you probably don't need another description of what ASCII is all about. If you do, refer to any of the numerous works for beginning programmers. Here we'll discuss its extensions on PCs.

Formally, ASCII defines only 128 unique characters in the numeric range 0–127. Because an eight-bit byte can represent 256 possible values, the IBM PC and related machines furnish an extended character set that utilizes the upper range of 128 values by turning on the high-order bit. These "extended ASCII" values furnish the box-drawing characters discussed in Chapter 8, plus mathematical symbols, foreign-language characters, and other things unavailable in standard ASCII. This book gives some of them; the rest you can get from the likes of IBM Technical References, language manuals, and, often, word processing product documentation.

To display one of these extended ASCII characters from Turbo C, all you need is the numeric code. For example, if you want to display the Greek letter omega, write

putchar (234);

You can also stuff it into a text string with sprintf():

sprintf (string, "The omega symbol is %c", 234);

Unfortunately, those who designed the PC forgot to make it so easy to capture these special symbols from the keyboard. There is no keystroke or key combination that produces the omega character, a double-scored northwest box corner, or the summation symbol. That doesn't mean it can't be done, but only that it's a little more difficult than displaying these characters. We'll cover this later in the chapter.

The PC also has a special set of keyboard codes that relate to the nonprinting control keys—notably the function keys **F1–F10** (**F1–F12** on newer keyboards), any **Alt**-key combination, and the cursor control keys. They all generate two-byte character sequences in which the first is a null (ASCII 0) followed by a value corresponding to the depressed key. For example, the two-byte sequence 00h, 4Dh (in decimal, 0 followed by 77) indicates that the cursor-right key has been pressed.

In the case of these keys, an ASCII zero indicates that the receiving software must fetch the *next* character to determine which nonprinting key has been operated, as discussed next.

The Keyboard Buffer

Chapter 7 defined the ROM BIOS data area, part of which contains the keyboard buffer. This is a 15-byte circular buffer that stores up ASCII values coming from the keyboard. How it works isn't germane to our discussion here; if you want details, see Bob Jourdain's *Programmer's Problem Solver*, pages 92–93.

What you do need to know is that Turbo C calls the DOS keyboard routines, which in turn call the ROM BIOS interrupt 16h functions to fetch successive values from the keyboard buffer. When the user presses one of the nonprinting control keys, *two* values go into the keyboard buffer: a null followed by the key's value.

Therefore, when your program fetches a null from the keyboard, it should branch to a handler that gets the next value with **getch()** and acts on it not as a normal ASCII code, but as a special case. The next section shows how.

Handling the Non-Printing Control Keys

There's a startling number of nonprinting keys. For example, any **Alt**-letter combination generates a valid two-byte sequence that you can associate with a unique software function. Jourdain covers them all on page 136. Here we'll concentrate on the major ones, for which Table 10.1 lists the second-byte values.

Table 10.1 **Values of the Major Nonprinting Keys**

Lead-in byte is 0, followed by:

Value	Keystroke
16–25	**Alt-Q** through **Alt-P** (top row of letters)
30–38	**Alt-A** through **Alt-L** (middle row)
44–50	**Alt-Z** through **Alt-M** (bottom row)
59–68	**F1** through **F10**
71	**Home** (keypad **7**)
72	**Cursor up** (keypad **8**)
73	**PgUp** (keypad **9**)
75	**Cursor left** (keypad **4**)
77	**Cursor right** (keypad **6**)
79	**End** (keypad **1**)
80	**Cursor down** (keypad **2**)
81	**PgDn** (keypad **3**)
84–93	**Shift = F1–F10**
94–103	**Ctrl = F1–F10**
104–113	**Alt = F1–F10**

Say you've declared **ch** as a character variable. You can handle the special keys with a test such as

```
if ((ch = getch()) != 0) {
   /* handle char normally */
} else
   specKey ();  /* process special key */
```

The **speckey()** routine can then fetch the next character and act on it as appropriate, as in

```
keyVal = getch();  /* get second byte */
switch (keyVal) {
case 59: help(); break;   /* F1 key */
case 60: edit(); break;   /* F2 key */
/*  etc.  */
}
```

Let's translate this discussion into a working program that reports which key has been operated.

Keyboard Sampler

Program 10.1 processes both ordinary keystrokes and extended keys. The **setUpScreen()** function creates a "pretty" display with operating instructions in the upper box and a large text work area in the lower.

The main loop captures keystrokes. If the user presses a normal (one-byte) key, the program displays the generated character. It branches to a subprogram on detecting the ASCII null signifying an extended key. There it uses **getch()** to fetch the second byte from the keyboard buffer. A **switch()** statement identifies the main extended keys: **F1–F10** and those of the keypad. An unspecified keystroke such as **Ctrl-Fn** generates the message **Other ext code**. The program terminates on **Alt-Q**.

Note that the program produces output in columnar format within the work area. The variables **row**, **col**, and **c** manage the output using **gotoxy()**. When the program runs out of screen space—that is, the next item would be beyond the right side of the display—it quits automatically.

Note also the compound statement

```
if (++row==17)
    row = TOP, c += 16;
```

The second line is not an error, but a valid C construction. Multiple statements separated by commas count as a single statement. This construction allows you to resolve two or more independent expressions controlled by the **if()**, but without using curly braces to isolate the block.

Program 10.1 **Keyboard Sampler**

```
/* KEYS.C: Captures and displays keypresses */

#include <stdio.h>
#include <conio.h>
#include <dos.h>
#include "textbox.h"
#include "cursor.h"

#ifndef TRUE
#define FALSE 0
#define TRUE  !FALSE
#endif
```

Program 10.1 **(continued)**

```
/* Local functions */
void setUpScreen (void);
int  extended (void);

void main ()
{
char  key;
int   row = 1, col, repeating, c = 2;

  setUpScreen ();                            /* create work screen */

/* Loop to process keypresses */
  do {
    col = c;
    gotoxy (col, row);                       /* place cursor */
    key = getch();                           /* get next keypress */
    if (key == 0)                            /* if null char */
      repeating = extended ();    /* handle extended code */
    else
      if (key == ' ')
        cputs ("Space");
      else
        putchar (key);                       /* else show char */
    if (++row > 17)
      row = 1, c += 16;
    if (c > 78) repeating = 0;       /* quit if screen full */
  } while (repeating);

/* End of run */
  window (1, 1, 80, 25);
  textcolor (LIGHTGRAY);
  textbackground (BLACK);
  clrscr ();
  curson();
} /* ----------------------- */

void setUpScreen (void)
      /* Build display */
{
  cursoff ();                                /* turn off cursor */
  clrscr ();                                 /* clear entire screen */

  /* Construct instruction box */
  textcolor (WHITE);                           /* set up colors */
  textbackground (BLUE);
  textbox (1, 1, 80, 5, 2);                  /* make a text box */
  window (2, 2, 79, 4);              /* open window inside it */
  clrscr ();                                 /* implement colors */
  gotoxy (32, 1);                            /* print instructions */
  cputs ("Keyboard Sampler");
  gotoxy (16, 2);
  cputs
```

Program 10.1 **(continued)**

```
   ("Press any key and the program reports what it is");
   gotoxy (32, 3);
   cputs ("Quit with Alt-Q");

   /* Construct program workarea */
   window (1, 1, 80, 25);              /* restore full screen */
   textbackground (BLACK);
   textbox (1, 6, 80, 24, 1);          /* surround workarea */
   window (2, 7, 79, 23);              /* open window inside */
   clrscr ();                          /* implement colors */
} /* ----------------------- */

int  extended (void)            /* process extended codes */
{
char  ext;
int   keepOn = 1;                       /* TRUE is default */

   ext = getch();                       /* get second byte */
   switch (ext) {
      case 16: keepOn = 0; break;         /* Alt-Q for quit */
      case 59: cputs ("F1"); break;
      case 60: cputs ("F2"); break;
      case 61: cputs ("F3"); break;
      case 62: cputs ("F4"); break;
      case 63: cputs ("F5"); break;
      case 64: cputs ("F6"); break;
      case 65: cputs ("F7"); break;
      case 66: cputs ("F8"); break;
      case 67: cputs ("F9"); break;
      case 68: cputs ("F10"); break;
      case 71: cputs ("Home"); break;
      case 72: cputs ("Cursor up"); break;
      case 73: cputs ("PgUp"); break;
      case 75: cputs ("Cursor left"); break;
      case 77: cputs ("Cursor right"); break;
      case 79: cputs ("End"); break;
      case 80: cputs ("Cursor down"); break;
      case 81: cputs ("PgDn"); break;
      case 82: cputs ("Ins"); break;
      case 83: cputs ("Del"); break;
      default: cputs ("Other ext key");
   }
   return keepOn;
}
```

Controlling Menu Selections with Cursor Keys

Now that we've seen how to capture and interpret the cursor control keys, we can improve on the menu-handling discussed in the last chapter. Instead of using the space key to advance the highlight bar, we can use the cursor keys to move it up and down and select a choice.

Suppose you have the following menu on the display:

Accounts payable
Receivables
Payroll & Personnel
General ledger
Quit

The usual ground rules for such menus are:

- Pick an entry by typing its unique first letter, or;
- Use the cursor keys to move the highlight to the desired item, then press **Enter** to select it.

Thus, if the highlight is over Receivables and you want to quit, you can either type **Q** or use any of the cursor keys to move to the **Quit** entry and press **Enter**. The up and left cursor keys move the highlight up; the down and right keys move it down. The lighted bar wraps to the opposite end of the menu when it reaches an extreme. Furthermore, in accordance with usual practice, the **F1** key summons help.

You can handle these conditions with a loop that waits for a keypress, then decides what to do with it using a **switch()** statement. The **A**, **R**, **G**, and **P** keys dispatch the appropriate task, while **Q** sets a TRUE/FALSE variable to FALSE, thus signalling the loop to terminate and end the program. Operation of the **Enter** key selects the currently indicated task for execution or, if the lighted bar is over **Quit**, has the same effect as pressing **Q**.

Any cursor control or function key generates a two-byte sequence in which the first is ASCII null, also handled by a case in the **switch()** statement. However, in this event, the program must fetch the second byte and then act on it with a nested **switch()**. In the case of **F1**, it dispatches the help task. The cursor keys are handled by multiple cases, in which up and left are identical and have the same entry point, and down and right have a different common case.

Both switches ignore extraneous keystrokes. For example, **J** has no effect, nor do **Ins** and **F3**. This is accomplished by omitting the default case from the **switch()** constructs.

The **process()** function in Program 10.2 implements these ideas. If the indicator is not on menu row 6 (**Quit**), the run() function is called; otherwise the looping variable is set to FALSE, which signals the function to stop and return. The looping variable also changes to FALSE if the user actually presses **Q**, and the indicated job runs for any other valid letter entered.

At the start of the loop in **process()**, the current selection is highlighted only for as long as the program is waiting for a keystroke, and then it reverts to normal. Why? Because the user will likely press one of the initials (**A**, **R**, **P**, or

G) to select a task, regardless of where the bar is. It wouldn't do to have the program run **Payroll** while **A/P** is still highlighted. Thus, **process()** turns off the highlight as soon as it receives a keystroke.

Because this is a skeleton program, the **run()** function only simulates the execution of a task by flashing up a pop-up showing the task (indicator) number and pausing for a couple of seconds. In reality, you'd probably dispatch different tasks as appropriate from the outer **switch()** in the **process()** function. Each task under this scheme should be a function that performs the following steps:

1. Highlight the selected task on the menu.
2. Save the current display.
3. Run the task itself.
4. Restore the display.
5. Unhighlight the selected task on the menu.
6. Return.

Program 10.2 is the program APPMENU.C, which simulates a hypothetical business application and furnishes a user-friendly skeleton that you can flesh out to suit your needs.

Program 10.2 **A Full-Featured Menuing Program**

```
/* APPMENU.C: Menuing skeleton for a hypothetical appli-  */
/*    cation, showing cursor control in menu selection    */
/* ------------------------------------------------------ */

/* INCLUDES */
#include <stdio.h>
#include <dos.h>
#include <conio.h>
#include "textbox.h"
#include "popup.h"
#include "cursor.h"

/* DEFINES */
#define   CR      13
#define   F1      59
#define   UP      72
#define   LEFT    75
#define   RITE    77
#define   DOWN    80
#ifndef   TRUE
#define   FALSE   0
#define   TRUE    !FALSE
#endif

/* LOCAL FUNCTIONS */
void   process (POPUP*);
void   run (int);
```

```
void  help (void);

/* POP-UP DEFINITIONS */
POPUP menu = {28,  4, 51, 11, 2, BLACK, RED,
                CYAN, BLACK, BLACK};
POPUP jobid = {31, 17, 47, 19, 1, RED + BLINK, 0, GREEN, 0,
                RED};
POPUP helps = {34,  7, 76, 13, 1, LIGHTGRAY, 0, MAGENTA,
                0, LIGHTGRAY};

/* MENU TEXT DEFINITION */
char  *menutext =
"  ** MAIN MENU **\r\n Accounts payable\r\n Receivables\r\n\
 Payroll & Personnel\r\n General ledger\r\n Quit";

/* ------------------------- */

void main ()
{
  /* Set up base screen */
  textcolor (YELLOW);
  textbackground (BLACK);
  clrscr ();
  cursoff ();
  gotoxy (27, 1);
  cputs ("The Empire Corporation, Inc.");

  /* Run the program */
  menu.text = menutext;
  popShow (&menu);                    /* display menu */
  process (&menu);                    /* process choices */

  /* Clean up and quit */
  window (1, 1, 80, 25);
  textcolor (LIGHTGRAY);
  textbackground (BLACK);
  clrscr ();
  curson ();
} /* ----------------------- */

void process (POPUP *menu)   /* Process main menu choices */
{
int  indic = 2, looping = TRUE;
char key;

  do {
    popHilite (menu, indic);    /* hilite indic selection */
    key = toupper (getch ());        /* get a keystroke */
    popNormal (menu, indic);     /* un-hilite selection */
    switch (key) {               /* act on keystroke */

      /* If an alpha selection */
```

Program 10.2 **(continued)**

```c
        case 'A': run (1); break;
        case 'R': run (2); break;
        case 'P': run (3); break;
        case 'G': run (4); break;
        case 'Q': looping = FALSE; break;

        /* If user hit Enter on current selection */
        case CR : if (indic != 6)
                    run (indic-1);          /* run indic task */
                  else
                    looping = FALSE;             /* or quit */
                  break;

        /* If user hit a function or cursor key */
        case 0  : key = getch ();       /* get second byte */
                  switch (key) {             /* act on it */
                    case F1 : help (); break;
                    case UP:
                    case LEFT: if (--indic == 1)
                                 indic = 6;    /* wrap down */
                               popHilite (menu, indic);
                               break;
                    case DOWN:
                    case RITE: popNormal (menu, indic);
                               if (++indic == 7)
                                 indic = 2;      /* wrap up */
                               popHilite (menu, indic);
                               break;
                  }               /* end of nested switch */
        }                         /* end of outer switch */
    } while (looping);
} /* ----------------------- */

void run (int job) /* Simulate running the menu selection */
{
char mssg [20];

    popShow (&jobid);                /* pop up job ident window */
    sprintf (mssg, "Running job %d", job);
    popCenter (&jobid, mssg);        /* identify job number */
    sleep (3);                       /* pretend to run the job */
    popErase (&jobid);               /* delete the job pop-up */
} /* ----------------------- */

void help (void)     /* Pop up help panel if F1 is pressed */
{
char mssg [40];

    popShow (&helps);
    popCenter (&helps, "** H E L P **\n");
    popCenter (&helps, "Select by typing first letter, or\n");
    sprintf (mssg,
```

Program 10.2 **(continued)**

```
                "Move up with %c or %c, down with %c or %c,\n",
             24, 27, 25, 26);
      popCenter (&helps, mssg);
      sprintf (mssg, "then press %c%c", 17, 217);
      popCenter (&helps, mssg);
      cputs ("\n");
      popCenter (&helps, "Press any key to resume . . .");
      getch ();
      popErase (&helps);
} /* ----------------------- */
```

Reassigning Keys

One of the design shortcomings in PCs is the inaccessibility of the extended ASCII characters from the keyboard. The only way to display characters with values above 7Fh (127 decimal) is to generate them within software; there is no keystroke to generate, for example, the Greek letter pi, which is E3h (227 decimal), nor are there keystrokes for the foreign-language symbols (most of those in 80h through ADh). Thus, it's necessary for software to trap keystrokes and reassign values to them.

A simple way is through direct replacement. Say for example that you want to give the user the ability to type the pi symbol. The backwards apostrophe (French accent grave, written "è") is a character of very limited usefulness to most applications, yet it's available directly from the keyboard and thus a good candidate for reassignment.

Your keyboard handler can simply look for this ASCII value (60h) and replace it with the ASCII value for pi (E3h):

```
if ((ch = getch()) == 0x60)
    putchar (0xE3); /* replace with pi */
else
    putchar (ch); /* treat normally */
```

A simple if() is fine for a single keystroke reassignment, but it won't do for multiple substitutions, especially when **Alt-key** combinations are a factor. Let's say you want to write software that accepts and faithfully replays the French language. Here are the key reassignments:

Keystroke	Produces
Alt-A (0 + 30)	a-grave (a), 85h
Ctrl-E (5)	e-acute (e), 82h
Alt-E (0 + 18)	e-grave (e), 8Ah
Alt-C (0 + 46)	cedille (c), 87h

Note that three of the keystrokes produce a null lead-in, while one does not. This complicates reassignment.

A way to overcome the problem is to process keystrokes with a **switch()** inside a function that returns the "final" value after substitutions. The returned value is displayed, emulating echo of keyboard entries. That's what the **keystroke()** function does in the FRENCH.C program shown in Program 10.3.

Program 10.3 **Keyboard Reassignment**

```
/* FRENCH.C: Illustrates keyboard reassignment to produce */
/*     text typed in French. Replacements are:            */
/*            Alt-A      a-grave                           */
/*            Ctrl-E     e-acute                           */
/*            Alt-E      e-grave                           */
/*            Alt-C      cedille                           */
/* ------------------------------------------------------ */

#include <stdio.h>
#include <conio.h>

#define    A_GRAVE    0x85
#define    E_ACUTE    0x82
#define    E_GRAVE    0x8A
#define    CEDILLE    0x87
#define    CR         0x0D

char   keystroke (void);                         /* prototype */

main ()
{
char    ch, input [80];
int     p = 0;

  puts ("\nEDITEUR FRANCAIS:\n");
  puts ("\nEcrivez une ligne");               /* ask for a line */

  do {                                    /* get a line of input */
    if (kbhit) {                             /* wait for keypress */
      ch = keystroke ();       /* get it after substutution */
      if (ch != NULL) {                 /* ignore unknown key */
        putchar (ch);                      /* echo to display */
        input [p++] = ch != CR ? ch : NULL;   /* save it */
      }
    }
  } while (ch != CR);

  puts ("\n\nVOUS AVEZ ECRIT LA LIGNE SUIVANTE:");
  puts (input);                        /* repeat what was typed */
} /* ------------------------ */
char   keystroke (void)    /* substitute keystrokes as reqd */
{
char    key;
```

```
key = getch();                /* get ASCII for keypress */
switch (key) {
  case 5: key = E_ACUTE; break;              /* Ctrl-E */
  case 0: key = getch();       /* get second key on Alt */
          switch (key) {
            case 30: key = A_GRAVE; break;     /* Alt-A */
            case 18: key = E_GRAVE; break;     /* Alt-E */
            case 46: key = CEDILLE; break;     /* Alt-C */
            default: key = NULL;          /* unknown key */
          }  /* end of nested switch */
}  /* end of outer switch */
return (key);
}
```

The program first identifies itself as **EDITEUR FRANCAIS** (a French-language editor), and asks you to **Ecrivez une ligne** (type a line of text). To see it in action, type the line

Je suis élève de la langue français

meaning "I'm a student of the French language." Type the appropriate key combinations to produce the special French characters. The program echoes your keystrokes, making the necessary substutitions. When you press **Enter**, the program reports that **VOUS AVEZ ECRIT** (you have written) followed by the line of input. This full-line echo shows that the substitutions—and not the keystrokes—were stored in the **input[]** string.

A word about the **kbhit()** macro in the **main()** function's input loop: This macro, which is defined in CONIO.H, waits for a keypress. It does not actually fetch the keystroke from the keyboard buffer. Rather, it puts the program in a tight loop until you press a key, and then it allows execution to resume. That's why the first thing **keystroke()** does is to call **getch()**; the ASCII value is still in the buffer. The rest of the program's operation should be clear, based on the discussion earlier in this chapter.

PART III

Computer Graphics in Turbo C

Turbo C 2.0 comes with an extensive set of tools for creating interesting and useful visual effects on computers equipped with more than the minimal Monochrome Display Adapter (MDA), which is suitable only for text displays. This graphics library, while not entirely device-independent, fits itself with a remarkable degree of flexibility to a variety of graphics sub-systems ranging from the early IBM Color Graphics Adapter (CGA) up through the recent and highly versatile Virtual Graphics Adapter, or VGA, which runs chiefly on the PS/2 machines. It also handles non-IBM standards, the Hercules board being the most prevalent.

The Turbo C manuals describe the numerous graphics library functions in detail. You can obtain an excellent quick reference to these functions and constants by listing the GRAPHICS.H file that comes with Turbo C. This is almost indispensible, in fact, when doing graphics programming.

With good documentation already in existence, it would be a waste of time and paper to describe the library again in this book. Instead, what is needed are concrete examples that show how to put the library to work in practical applications, as well as a discussion of computer graphics issues that digs deeper than the product documentation. And that is the stuff of the next several chapters.

We should point out, however, that like so many other pro-gramming topics, graphics is an entire arena of computer science, and there are numerous subjects that we won't cover here. Our aim is to lay a reasonably solid foundation for creating practical graphics.

CHAPTER 11

GRAPHICS 101

The fundamental proposition of graphics is this: All visual objects on a computer screen are composed of small blips of light. To the machine, each one is an individual entity known in computer parlance as a pixel, short for picture element. The eye connects them together to form an image. It might be something as simple as the letter A or as complex as a multicolored topographical map of North America. No matter, the process is the same; the computer software throws little splashes of light and color on the display and leaves it to us to interpret them as "things."

The simplest "thing" is a line segment, which connects point A with point B. If the line is perfectly horizontal, the computer easily represents it with a sequence of pixels, all on the same scan row, between the two points. A perfectly vertical line is similar, except that the pixels are in the same horizontal position on successive scan rows. A diagonal line is a different matter and something of a challenge. Here the pixels occur on successive scan rows, but without the benefit of strict vertical alignment. Figure 11.1 illustrates a typical diagonal line, where an X indicates a lighted pixel and a period is one not lighted.

Figure 11.1 **A Diagonal Line in Computer Graphics**

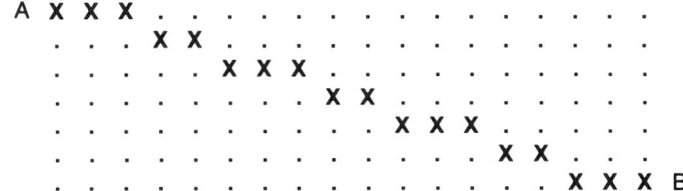

This pixel pattern approximates a diagonal line, but it's not smooth. That's because each pixel on the screen has a fixed position. If you squint at Figure 11.1, your eyes will perceive a reasonably smooth line, which is the best that a digital device can do. The irregularities from one row to the next are called *jaggies,* and they're an unfortunate but inescapable feature of the graphics landscape.

Jaggies appear everywhere in computer graphics. Any object that is not perfectly orthogonal (exactly vertical or horizontal) has them: circles, triangles, polygons, even the letters of text. Examine your screen closely. They're there.

Jaggies are minimized by increasing the resolution of the display, and that's the intent in advancing the technology of computer graphics. The now-obsolete CGA has jaggies in spades; everything seems to be made of stairsteps. Later adapters such as the EGA and VGA have more horizontal positions and more vertical scan rows within the same physical display space. More positions mean higher resolution and thus less apparent jaggies.

In its color graphics modes, the CGA has 320 pixels horizontally by 200 vertically, for a total of 64,000. The VGA presents, in the same display area, 640 × 480 pixels, or 307,200 pixels. Consequently the VGA has 4.8 times the resolution of the CGA or, stated another way, the jaggies are about 20% as apparent as on the CGA.

Look again at Figure 11.1. The line is composed of three pixels on one scan row, two on the next, three on the next, and so on. Figuring out how many pixels per row in order to connect point A with point B is a complex process. There are a number of algorithms for doing this. The most common is Bresenham's, which introduces minimal overhead and is used by the Turbo C graphics library. Nevertheless, it's still a computationally intensive task, and for that reason graphics don't appear with the same lightning speed as text.

The Source of Graphics Images

The display screen of most computers is a cathode ray tube, or CRT, a roughly conical glass tube. The inside of the viewing surface is coated with a phosphorescent substance that glows momentarily when struck by electrons, which emanate from a group of "guns" located in a neck at the back of the tube. Under control of some circuitry, the guns ceaselessly fire this beam in a fixed pattern that sweeps to and fro across the viewing surface.

The beam is carefully synchronized so that it sweeps across any given point on the viewing surface at regular intervals. As the beam crosses a point to be lighted — a pixel location — the guns fire; when a pixel is dark, they don't. The object of the game is to cross all points often enough that the phosphor remains illuminated without flickering.

The sweep speed affects screen resolution. In a CGA, for example, each cycle of the beam horizontally crosses the display 200 times. Thus, there are 200 scan rows, and hence a maximum of 200 pixels stacked vertically. Similarly, the number of times the guns can be fired during a single sweep govern the horizontal resolution.

Display technologies developed after the CGA have higher resolutions, since the controlling electronics have gotten faster, enabling the guns to sweep more times and fire more often. The electronics can also control more guns, leading to a greater number of colors on the screen at one time.

Display adapters get the information they need to control the electron guns from an on-board memory called the video buffer. Through either output commands or direct memory addressing, software writes to the video buffer. The adapter's circuitry then reads this memory and translates what it finds there into actions that control the firing of the guns. And that, in brief, is how graphics get from your program to the display.

But how do you tell the display adapter which pixels to light, and in what colors?

Coordinates

For each type of display there exists an addressing scheme to identify individual pixels. Each pixel position has a row and column number, or X and Y coordinate. This is a concept borrowed from Cartesian geometry, in which the X axis expresses a horizontal position and the Y axis a vertical position. Taken together, the X and Y coordinates represent the location of any point on a plane with respect to a fixed point (the origin, where X and Y are both 0). No doubt you recall this system from high school algebra.

All graphics displays have a common origin, which is the upper left corner of the screen. X grows to the right, while Y grows downward (never mind for now that downward-increasing Y coordinates are backwards from what they taught you in school; we'll deal with this problem later). The resolution of a specific display device and the active graphics mode determine the maximum X and Y values, as Figure 11.2 shows.

Figure 11.2 **Graphics Coordinate Systems**

A. CGA four-color graphics:

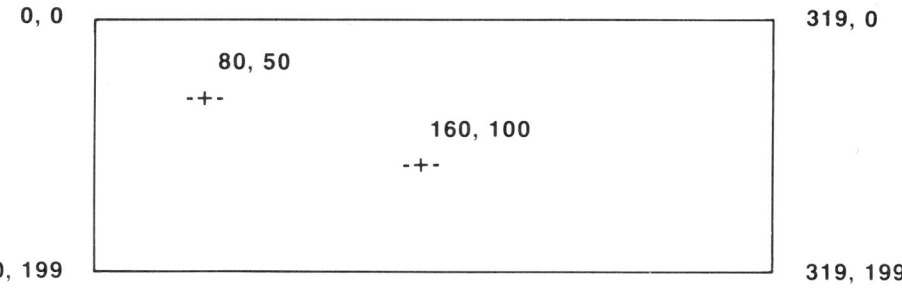

Figure 11.2 **(continued)**

B. EGA 640 × 350 color modes:

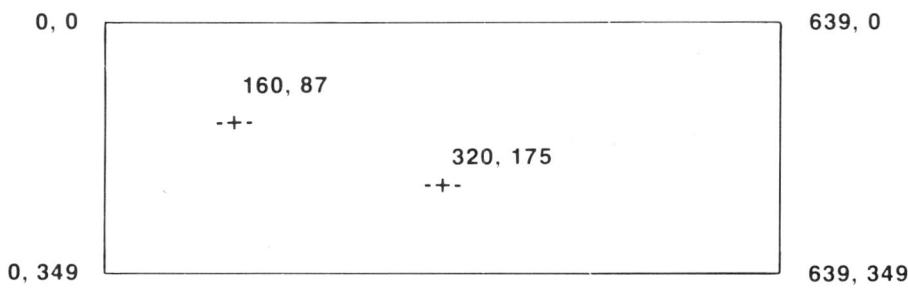

In CGA four-color graphics, the maximum X is 319. Counting the origin itself, then, the width of the screen can hold 320 pixels. The maximum Y is 199, for a total of 200 pixels vertically. Any point can be represented within these two ranges: the center, for example, is at {160, 100}. On the other hand, most EGA graphics modes are 640 wide by 350 high. The VGA (not shown here) can go up to 640 × 480, and other less-common displays have resolutions such as 1,024 × 768 or 800 × 600. Note that by convention, the computer industry describes the resolution of a display in terms of "X by Y" and never "Y by X."

With the Turbo C graphics library, you have the option of letting the **initgraph()** function select the best graphics mode available. The problem with this is that if you're writing programs for distribution—commercially or within a corporation, for example—your software will be confronted with different screen dimensions. For this reason, the library furnishes the highly useful functions **getmaxx()** and **getmaxy()**, which return the highest X and Y respectively for the current graphics mode. We'll use these functions in the graphics programs in this book, and you'll find them useful in your own projects as well.

Using Traditional Coordinates

The device coordinates of a computer screen are upside-down, since the Y value increases toward the bottom of the screen. For many drawing applications, that's not a problem. It complicates matters, though, when doing mathematical plots of the sort you learned in algebra. Fortunately, it's fairly simple to adjust coordinates.

Say you're working on a CGA, whose Y ranges from 0 at the top through 199 at the bottom (Figure 11.2A). Intuition says 0 should be at the bottom and Y should increase upward. In devising the program, you can pretend that the latter is the case, creating a conceptual screen in which the origin is at the lower left corner, as in Figure 11.3. The two inner points are now specified more naturally, so that the point physically higher has a higher Y value.

Figure 11.3 **Traditional Coordinates on the CGA**

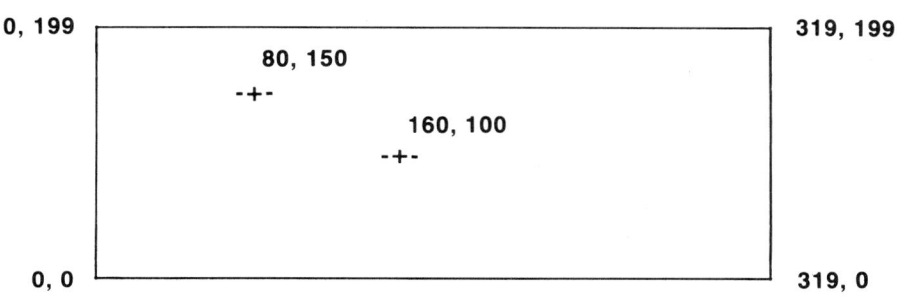

The computer, of course, doesn't know that you've flipped the Y scale, so if you start drawing without telling it, it will produce your plot upside down. All you have to do to make the proper translation is to subtract your Y coordinates from 199 as you output them.

Extending this idea a bit further, you can move the conceptual origin anyplace. In Figure 11.4, for example, it's in the center of the screen.

Figure 11.4 **Relocating the Origin on the CGA**

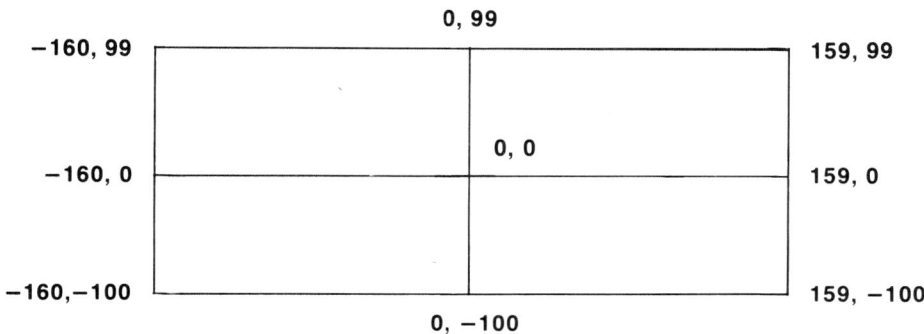

Here you can work in a coordinate system whose extremes are at the four corners of the display. To translate from your coordinates to device coordinates:

1. For X, add the physical location of the X origin. Here it's at 160. Thus the left side of the screen is at device coordinate $-160 + 160 = 0$, and the right side is at $159 + 160 = 319$. Figure 11.2A shows that this is correct.
2. For Y, add the physical location of the Y origin (100 in this case) and subtract from 199. Thus the top of the screen translates to $199 - (99 + 100) = 0$, and the bottom to $199 - (-100 + 100) = 199$.

Virtual Coordinates _____

The techniques we just covered work fine for the CGA, and you can easily adapt them to the EGA and VGA by changing the maximum X and Y values. Often, however, you don't know which adapter your program will use, as in writing software for distribution. If you specify the lowest common denominator—320 × 200 CGA—when entering graphics mode with the **initgraph()** function, your graphics will fill the screen, but they'll put the EGA and VGA into CGA emulation mode, which is grainy and hard on the eyes, and which doesn't take advantage of more up-to-date technology. On the other hand, graphics that use the adapter's capabilities but hard-wire the coordinates to the CGA limits will look pretty silly squished into the upper-left quarter or less of the screen. To make graphics that self-adjust to the display's dimensions, you need to apply another technique called *virtual* (or *normalized*) coordinates.

Virtual coordinates assume arbitrary X and Y scales that are independent of actual device coordinates. In establishing virtual coordinates, you say in effect, "All screens are *n* units wide by *m* units high." You then work within this assumed coordinate system, and translate to device coordinates at output time.

The normal screen for PCs has a height that is 75 percent of its width. Therefore, to get square squares and round circles and other correct proportions, the range of virtual Y coordinates should be 75 percent of the X range. The only common graphics standard that currently provides this ratio in physical device coordinates is the VGA's 640 × 480 mode. Even if you don't have one of these high-end adapters, you can fake "square pixels" on any display using virtual coordinates.

Set the scale to anything you want, observing the 75 percent Y rule: 400 × 300, 640 × 480, 600 × 450, and so on. Your conceptual screen might be as shown in Figure 11.5. Note that Y coordinates increase upwards.

Figure 11.5 **A Screen Using Virtual Coordinates**

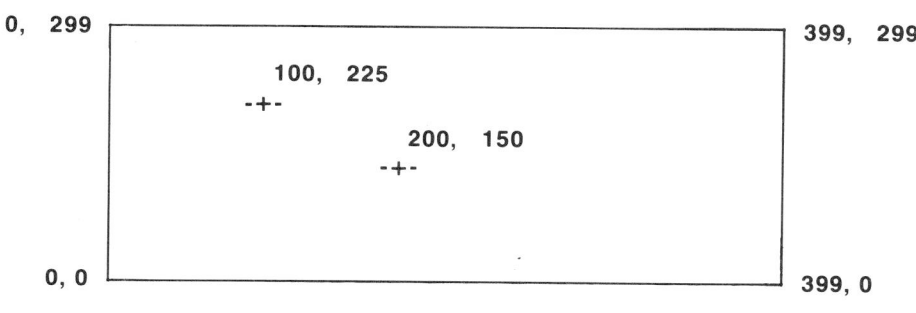

Because the object in using virtual coordinates is to overcome the differences among devices, you can't make any hard assumptions when translating to device coordinates. Instead, query the graphics system with **getmaxx()** and **getmaxy()** to determine the device's physical characteristics, then translate using the following algorithms (where vw and vh are the maximum virtual X and Y, and vx and vy are the virtual coordinates to be translated).

1. For X:

```
px = getmaxx();                         /* physical width in pixels */
xf = (double)(px)/vw;                    /* x translation factor */
dx = (int) (xf) * vx;                        /* device x */
```

2. For Y:

```
py = getmaxy();                         /* physical height in pixels */
yf = (double)(py)/vh;                    /* y translation factor */
dy = (int) (py-(yf * vy));                   /* device y */
```

The most sensible way to handle these calculations, which occur every time you output to the screen, is with functions. The variables **px**, **py**, **xf**, and **yf** should be statics initialized outside the translation functions in order to reduce overhead.

Because many of the graphics programs in succeeding chapters (and ones you write yourself) will use virtual coordinates, let's create a VCOORDS library. Its two major components, header and source, are shown in Programs 11.1 and 11.2. The library furnishes an 800 × 600 virtual display area for Turbo C graphics. A program later in the chapter shows how to use the library.

Program 11.1 **Header File for Virtual Coordinates**

```
/* VCOORDS.C: Header for implementing 800 x 600 virtual
                display area in Turbo C graphics */

#define VH 600              /*height */
#define VW 800              /*width  */

/* GLOBALS DEFINED IN LIBRARY, EXTERNALLY VISIBLE */
extern int    px, py;              /* physical x and y width */
extern double xf, yf;          /* x and y translation factors */

void setFactors (void);      /* compute translation factors */
int dx (int vx);             /* translate virt X to device X */
int dy (int vy);             /* translate virt Y to device Y */
```

Program 11.2 **Library File for Virtual Coordinates**

```
/* VCOORDS.C: Code for implementing 800 x 600 virtual
                display area in Turbo C graphics */

#define VH 600              /* height */
#define VW 800              /* width  */

int    px, py;                     /* physical x and y width */
double xf, yf;                 /* x and y translation factors */

void setFactors (void)      /* compute translation factors */
{                           /* call once at start of program */
  px = getmaxx();
  py = getmaxy();
  xf = (double) (px) / VW;
  yf = (double) (py) / VH;
} /* ---------------------- */

int dx (int vx)             /* translate virt X to device X */
{                                  /* call at output time */
  return ((int) (xf * vx));
} /* ---------------------- */

int dy (int vy)             /* translate virt Y to device Y */
{
  return ((int) (py - (yf * vy)));
} /* ---------------------- */
```

Now that we've covered some of the conceptual aspects of graphics, let's discuss the particulars of working with the Turbo C graphics library.

Working with the Graphics Library

When writing graphics programs, you can use a project (.PRJ) file that includes, as one of its entries, the name of the library file itself: GRAPHICS.LIB. This tells the linker to look in the same directory as your object files for the library; if you forget to include the library name or to load the project file, the linker won't be able to find the library and will report unresolved graphics references. Thus, if you're writing a program called GRAPH1.C, the minimal project file (GRAPH1.PRJ) reads

```
graph1.c graphics.lib
```

with a space or newline separating the two filenames.

The GRAPHICS.DOC file with Turbo C 1.5 suggests an alternative that's preferable: Use the TLIB utility to merge GRAPHICS.LIB with the C libraries you use. The command for this is

```
TLIB CS+GRAPHICS.LIB
```

when merging with the library for the small model. Change the letter following **C** as appropriate for other libraries. After you do this, it's no longer necessary to have a .PRJ file for a single-module program, nor is it necessary to retain a copy of GRAPHICS.LIB in the source directory. The linker resolves graphics references as it processes the C library.

The graphics library is an entire subsystem that isolates programs from the usual low-level tedium of pixel graphics: ROM BIOS calls and the like. It handles all the hardware interfaces for you, via high-level functions. The constants and calls are all spelled out in GRAPHICS.H. Don't try going around the graphics system and calling the ROM BIOS directly, as this is almost a guarantee of catastrophe.

The doorways into and out of graphics mode are initgraph() and closegraph(), respectively. The closegraph() function restores the machine to whatever mode was in effect when initgraph() was called. Because it uses state information saved by initgraph(), closegraph() takes no arguments.

The arguments to initgraph() are pointers to three variables, at least two of which must be initialized before the call is made. In order, these are:

int driver;	Set to one of the members of the graphics_drivers enumeration.
int mode;	Set to one of the members of the graphics_modes enumeration. (Mode doesn't need to be initialized if driver = DETECT, which selects the best mode automatically.)

char path[];   A string indicating the path to the subdirectory containing the .BGI (graphics device driver) files. (You can pass a null string if the .BGI files are in the default directory. Subsequent program examples assume that this is the case.)

If you specifically want to select CGA hi-res (640 × 200 monochrome) graphics mode and the .BGI drivers are in the \BGI directory of drive C, you might declare the variables as

```
int driver = CGA, mode = CGAHI;
char path[] = "C:\BGI";
```

and the call is

```
initgraph (&driver, &mode, path);
```

or alternatively

```
initgraph (&driver, &mode, "C:\BGI");
```

if the **path[]** variable is undeclared. To select autodetect, on the other hand, with the .BGI files in the default directory, the declarations read

```
int driver = DETECT, mode;
```

and the call is

```
initgraph (&driver, &mode, "");
```

It's always wise to check and see if the operation was successful before attempting any graphics output. The **graphresult()** function returns one of the values defined in the graphics__errors enumeration; **grOk** indicates success. Thus a good sequence of instructions surrounding a graphics routine is as follows:

```
initgraph (&driver, &mode, path);
if (graphresult() == grOk) {
/* do graphics stuff */
    closegraph(); /* when done */
} else
    /* report the bad news */
```

The library furnishes two kinds of line-drawing routines called absolute and relative. The absolute routine is line (x1, y1, x2, y2), which draws between the two specified points expressed in device coordinates. If you've done graphics in other languages, this method is probably familiar.

Relative line-drawing uses a conceptual device, the graphics cursor or pen, which when "down" leaves a trail as it moves from place to place, thus drawing lines. Another name for this is turtle graphics. Two sets of instructions move the pen in semirelative and totally relative ways:

Semi-relative:

lineto (x, y);	Draws from the present pen location to the indicated device coordinates.
moveto (x, y);	Like lineto(), but moves the pen without drawing.

Totally relative:

linerel (x, y);	Draws a straight line from the present pen location to a point x and y device units away.
moverel (x, y);	Like linerel(), but without drawing.

The graphics system observes rules of inheritance. The "set" functions, such as setlinestyle() and setcolor(), establish characteristics globally, and all eligible objects created thereafter inherit those characteristics. For example, after you issue the statements

```
setcolor (GREEN);
setlinestyle (DOTTED__LINE, 0, THICK__WIDTH);
```

all lines and all line-drawn objects (rectangles, circles, and so on) will be green (on devices capable of 16-color graphics) and will consist of thick dotted lines. Text will also be green, but not thick and dotted since it's not eligible for those characteristics.

The "get" functions provide means for inquiring about the status of the graphics system: text settings, line settings, current foreground color, screen dimensions, and so on. In addition, if you call initgraph() with the driver argument set to DETECT, the driver and mode variables afterward indicate which adapter is present and its display mode. The values map to the graphics__drivers enumeration and the graphics__modes values, respectively. In this way, you can determine anything you need to know about the display.

Example ───

Program 11.3 is called GEOM.C. It puts some of the ideas of this chapter to work. This program is largely device-independent, using the virtual coordinate system shown in Figure 11.5 to draw some geometric shapes. It produces very similar graphics on the CGA, EGA, and VGA, the only variations being the colors of the objects displayed (different on the CGA than on the others). The objects themselves are the same size on all three, thanks to normalization of coordinates.

When you run this program, you will see a border around the display, which consists of a square resting on a corner in the left half of the screen, and a smaller upright square in the top-right quadrant and a circle in the lower-right quadrant. The program freezes the display until you press a key, then it restores the previous text mode.

Program 11.3 **A Demonstration of Normalized Graphics**

```
/* GEOM.C: Plots some geometric figures using          */
/*          virtual coordinates for device independence */

/* INCLUDES */
#include <stdio.h>
#include <graphics.h>
#include "vcoords.h"

void main ()
{
int     driver = DETECT, mode;
char    path[] = "";

   initgraph (&driver, &mode, path);     /* start graphics */
   if (graphresult() == grOk) {
      setFactors();                      /* initialize variables */
      setcolor (1);
      setlinestyle (SOLID_LINE, 0, THICK_WIDTH);
      moveto (dx   (0), dy   (0));               /* home pen */
      lineto (dx (799), dy   (0));               /* outline screen */
      lineto (dx (799), dy (599));
      lineto (dx   (0), dy (599));
      lineto (dx   (0), dy   (0));

      setlinestyle (DOTTED_LINE, 0, NORM_WIDTH);
      setcolor (2);          /* rectangle, upper right corner */
      rectangle (dx (600), dy (550), dx (760), dy (300));

      setlinestyle (DASHED_LINE, 0, NORM_WIDTH);
      setcolor (3);                  /* tilted square, left half */
      moveto (dx (100), dy (300));
      lineto (dx (300), dy (500));
```

Program 11.3 **(continued)**

```
lineto (dx (500), dy (300));
lineto (dx (300), dy (100));
lineto (dx (100), dy (300));

setlinestyle (SOLID_LINE, 0, NORM_WIDTH);
setcolor (1);
circle (dx (600), dy (150), dx (100));   /* lower right */

getch();                             /* wait for keypress */
closegraph();                        /* leave graphics */
} else
puts ("Graphics not available on this machine");
}
```

Having covered the basics of the Turbo C graphics system, let's develop some practical applications.

CHAPTER **12**

BUSINESS GRAPHICS

W ith the advent of low-cost color graphics capabilities on personal computers, business graphics has become an important aspect of software. Business graphics concerns itself with depicting the relationships among sets of numbers; changes in revenue over time, for example. Because the eye more easily discerns patterns as visual objects than as fluctuations along rows and columns of figures, charts enable people to see trends at a glance. Thus business graphics is a highly effective way of summarizing and presenting complex data so that people can readily understand it.

There are many different kinds of business charts, and whole books have been written about selecting and designing the appropriate type for a given application. Consequently, our thrust here confines itself to programming four common types: bar, line, XY, and pie charts. This will provide a basis that you can build upon in constructing other types.

You will need one of the graphics adapters supported by the Turbo C graphics library in order to run the programs given in this chapter.

Bar Charts

One of the most common applications of business graphics is to compare changes in some measurable commodity—usually money—over time. A bar chart is ideal for this purpose. The lengths of the bars represent quantity, and their positions represent time. Figure 12.1 shows a typical bar chart that, because its bars are vertically oriented, is a variant known as a column chart.

In this case, the heights of the bars correspond to millions of dollars, and time increases to the right. The "colors," represented here by a pattern and a solid, provide another dimension of sorts by indicating budgeted and actual amounts. The bars are paired over their legends to increase clarity, and dotted gridlines serve as registration marks so that the viewer can easily measure the heights of all bars.

Now let's build a similar chart using Turbo C graphics.

Figure 12.1 **Typical Column Chart**

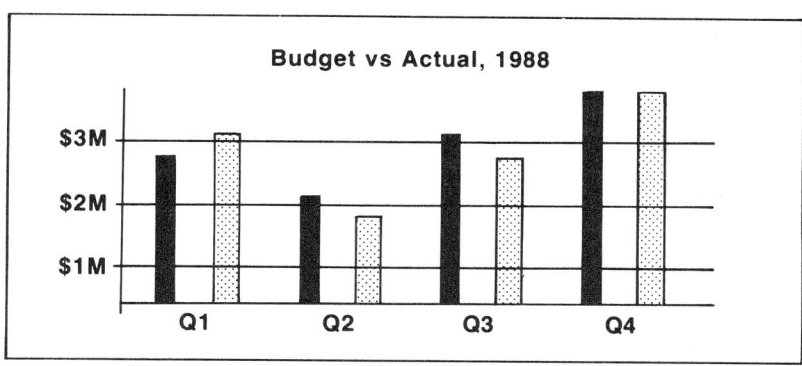

Drawing Bars

Anticipating applications such as this, the Turbo C graphics library furnishes a column-drawing function called—not surprisingly—**bar()**. Its arguments are {x1, y1} and {x2, y2}, representing opposite corners expressed in device coordinates. The bar inherits the fill pattern and color established by the **setfilltype()** function, which we'll also discuss here.

The bars get their heights, of course, from data. Ordinarily, graphics programs acquire the data they chart from an external source: keyboard entry or, more typically, a disk file. For the sake of simplicity, however, the programs developed here have the data built in. This enables us to focus on graphics programming issues without cluttering the listings with file processing routines.

Program 12.1 is BAR1.C, a foundation program that we'll build up into a complete bar chart. It merely displays the bars, then waits for a keypress.

Program 12.1 **Displaying the Bars of a Column Chart**

```
/* BAR1.C: Foundation for a bar chart program */
/*         Just draws the bars based on results data */

#include <graphics.h>
#include <conio.h>
#include "vcoords.h"

int result[][2] = {                    /* budget vs actuals */
          {270, 220},
          {320, 370},
          {180, 160},
```

Program 12.1 **(continued)**

```
            {200, 310}
};

void main ()
{
int   driver = DETECT, mode;
void drawBars (void);

   initgraph (&driver, &mode, "");        /* open graphics */
   if (graphresult() == grOk) {           /* if successful... */
     setFactors ();                       /* set xlation factors */
     drawBars ();                         /* draw the bars */
     getch ();                  /* hold until key pressed */
     closegraph ();
   }
} /* ----------------------- */

void drawBars (void)                       /* draw the bars */
{
int    start, col;

/* draw base line */
   line (dx (40), dy (39), dx (760), dy (39));

/* draw the budget bars first */
   setfillstyle (XHATCH_FILL, 1);
   start = 60;                             /* start at nx 60 */
   for (col = 0; col < 4; start += 180, col++)
     bar (dx (start), dy (40),
         dx (start + 60), dy (40 + result [col][0]));

/* then draw the actuals bars */
   setfillstyle (SOLID_FILL, 2);
   start = 140;
   for (col = 0; col < 4; start += 180, col++)
     bar (dx (start), dy (40),
         dx (start + 60), dy (40 + result [col][1]));
} /* ----------------------- */
```

This program uses virtual coordinates on an 800 × 600 plane with ascending Y, as discussed in the last chapter. We'll develop the program for device independence; the colors are different on an EGA/VGA than on a CGA, but because of virtual coordinates the chart components are the same size on any adapter.

If you have a CGA, you'll see this program's display as having a yellow base line with light green and light red bars. On an EGA or VGA, the line is white and the bars are blue and green. The left bar in each pair is a heavy hatched pattern; the right is solid. This makes it clear that the bars represent different things, even if you don't have a color monitor (for example, when using a Hercules card with a green display).

The **drawBars()** routine first draws the left-hand (hatched) bars. The bars are 60 units wide (in virtual units), beginning at X coordinate 60. Each column is spaced 180 units to the right of its predecessor. The second loop draws the right-hand bars starting 80 to the right of the first and spacing at the same interval. Thus there are 20 X units between the bars comprising a pair, and 40 X units between pairs.

The function calculates each bar height as its data value plus the location of the base line (40). This illustrates the advantage of using virtual coordinates; they measure upward from the base line, exactly as the chart itself appears, and there's no need to know how many scan lines the specific display device has.

Setting the Fill Style

Before each bar-drawing loop, the program calls **setfillstyle()** to establish the characteristics of the ensuing columns. This function takes two arguments. The first is one of the members of the **fill_patterns** enumeration (**EMPTY_FILL**, **SOLID_FILL**, and so on), and the other is a color.

It's important to understand how the color indicator works when programming for device independence. With the CGA, you have only four colors at your disposal, numbered 0 through 3. Zero is the background color and the other three are selected from a color palette. There are four color palettes for the CGA; in auto-DETECT, you automatically get Palette 0, whose colors are:

1. Light green
2. Light red
3. Yellow

You can change the CGA palette to any of the other three color schemes using the **setpalette()** function. Unfortunately you can't change any individual component of a palette, so you're stuck with four preset combinations on the CGA. The highest permissible color index is 3. Pick anything higher and the adapter defaults to the background color, which makes an object drawn in that color invisible.

Therefore, device independent programming means that you can only use three foreground colors, regardless of which adapter is actually present. Later we'll discuss how to get more than simply blue, green, and cyan on the EGA/VGA. Just live with it for now.

In **setfillstyle()**, the pattern indicators are the same for all adapters, and you can also create your own fill style as described later in this chapter. The color argument indicates a true color in the EGA/VGA, but on the CGA it's an index to one of the palette selections.

As the loops show, **setfillstyle()** remains in effect and all subsequent bars inherit its characteristics until you issue the next **setfillstyle()**. This function also sets the inheritance for other filled objects, as covered later.

Writing Text

While charts convey most of their information via nonverbal patterns, they only have meaning when text explains what they show. Run BAR1 again and you'll see what I mean; this chart could be anything, and even the values of the bars are unknown. Therefore it's necessary to attach explanations to charts.

The graphics library comes with five text fonts. The term *font* refers to a typeface or typographical style. To see the different fonts, run the GDEMO program that comes with Turbo C. You'll find that one of them, the Gothic font, is almost completely useless, being purely decorative and jarringly out of place in computer graphics.

The **settextstyle()** function sets the characteristics of text. It takes three arguments:

1. The font, selected from the **font_names** enumeration.
2. The direction, of which there are two choices. **HORIZ_DIR** is normal left-to-right orientation, while **VERT_DIR** rotates the text 90 degrees to the left so that it writes upward.
3. The magnification factor, where 1 is normal, 2 is twice normal size, and so on up to 10. (The small font is barely legible even on a VGA until it's at least 3X.)

Thus, to select sans serif in a horizontal direction at 2X magnification, the call is

    settextstyle (SANS_SERIF_FONT, HORIZ_DIR, 2);

All subsequent text output to the graphics screen inherits these character-istics until the next call to **settextstyle()**.

The Turbo C graphics library has two text output functions: **outtext()** and **outtextxy()**. The first writes a text string starting at the current graphics cur-sor location, and is thus relative output. The second positions the graphics pen, then begins output, making it an absolute routine. In **HORIZ_DIR**, the starting position is the upper-left corner of the first character; if the string is "The," output begins at the start of the bar crossing 'T.' It's at the opposite cor-ner of the string in **VERT_DIR**, or near the open mouth of the e in "The," with the text stretching downward and to the left of the starting point.

Don't try to use **printf()**, **puts()**, or one of the other standard output routines when Turbo C graphics is active. It won't work very well, if at all. If you need to format the output, as when printing a combination of text and numerics, write to a string using **sprintf()**, then call **outtext()** or **outtextxy()** to write the formatted string to the display.

The **textwidth()** function is useful for determining the width of a string. Virtual units don't apply since the function works only in pixels. A typical use is in centering:

```
void center (char *string, int topRow)
{
int start;

   start = (getmaxx() − textwidth (string)) / 2;
   outtextxy (start, topRow, string);
}
```

If you're near the bottom of the screen and uncertain if the text will fit, use **textheight()** as well, as in

```
center (aString, (getmaxy() − textheight (aString)));
```

Now let's illustrate this discussion by adding a title and some labels to the bar chart from BAR1. The new program, BAR2.C, is shown in Program 12.2.

Program 12.2 **Bar Chart with Text**

```
/* BAR2.C: Adds text to the bar chart program */

#include <graphics.h>
#include <conio.h>
#include <stdio.h>
#include "vcoords.h"

int result[][2] = {                         /* budget vs actuals */
          {270, 220},
          {320, 370},
          {180, 160},
          {200, 310}
};

void main ()
{
int   driver = DETECT, mode;
void identify (void);
void drawBars (void);
```

Program 12.2 **(continued)**

```
  initgraph (&driver, &mode, "");          /* open graphics */
  if (graphresult() == grOk) {        /* if successful... */
    setFactors ();                     /* set xlation factors */
    identify ();                    /* write text descriptions */
    drawBars ();                         /* draw the bars */
    getch ();                      /* hold until key pressed */
    closegraph ();
  }
} /* ----------------------- */

void center (char *string, int topRow)    /* center text */
{
int    start;

  start = (px - textwidth (string)) / 2;
  outtextxy (start, topRow, string);
} /* ----------------------- */

void identify (void)                /* add text to chart */
{
char   title[] = "Budget vs Actuals, 1988", label[3];
int    start = 120, labelNo;

  settextstyle (SMALL_FONT, HORIZ_DIR, 5);
  center (title, dy (VH));
  for (labelNo = 1; labelNo < 5; start += 180, labelNo++) {
    sprintf (label, "%dQ", labelNo);
    outtextxy (dx (start), dy (35), label);
  }
  settextstyle (SMALL_FONT, VERT_DIR, 4);
  outtextxy (10, dy (400), "($ Millions)");


} /* ----------------------- */

void drawBars (void)                     /* draw the bars */
{
int    start, col;

/* draw base line */
  line (dx (40), dy (39), dx (760), dy (39));

/* draw the budget bars first */
  setfillstyle (XHATCH_FILL, 1);
  start = 60;                        /* start at nx 60 */
  for (col = 0; col < 4; start += 180, col++)
    bar (dx (start), dy (40),
         dx (start + 60), dy (40 + result [col][0]));

/* then draw the actuals bars */
  setfillstyle (SOLID_FILL, 2);
```

Program 12.2 **(continued)**

```
    start = 140;
    for (col = 0; col < 4; start += 180, col++)
       bar (dx (start), dy (40),
            dx (start + 60), dy (40 + result [col][1]));
} /* ----------------------- */
```

Adding Gridlines

Gridlines are horizontal (and sometimes vertical) reference points, usually occurring at major subdivisions. Here, for example, gridlines should appear at intervals of $100 million. Because they're less important than the data, we'll make them dashed lines.

Calculating the virtual Y for each gridline is relatively easy. Each NY unit represents $1 million, and the baseline is defined as NY = 80. Therefore each incremental $100 million line is at (millions * 100) + BASELINE, where millions is a loop counter stepping at intervals of $100 million.

Gridlines should be labeled so that the viewer knows at a glance what they represent. Because the Y axis already has the label "$ millions," it's necessary only to write the digits 1, 2, and so on. The **outtext** . . () functions can't output numerics directly like **printf()**, so we'll use **sprintf()** to format a string, then write that string with **outtextxy()**.

Program 12.3 shows the new function **gridlines()**, which you can patch in anywhere above **main()**. In **main()** itself, add a call to **gridlines()** just above the **drawbars()** call. (The complete program to date is contained in BAR3.C on the companion disk).

Program 12.3 **Function for Adding Gridlines to the Bar Chart**

```
void gridlines (void)                    /* write gridlines */
{
int    ny, million;
char   mil [2];

    settextstyle (SMALL_FONT, HORIZ_DIR, 5);
    setlinestyle (DASHED_LINE, 0, NORM_WIDTH);
    for (million = 1; million < 5; million++) {
       ny = (million * 100) + BASELINE;
       line (dx (40), dy (ny), dx (750), dy (ny));
       sprintf (mil, "%d", million);
       outtextxy (dx ( 30), dy (ny+15), mil);
       outtextxy (dx (760), dy (ny+15), mil);
    }
}
```

Combined Charts

A combined chart brings together the styles of two or more chart types. A common combined type superimposes a line chart atop a bar chart. The "budget versus actual" plot developed above lends itself to this idea by using a line to represent deviation from budget; when the line is below the baseline, the reporting organization is below budget, and vice-versa.

Program 12.4 **A Combined Bar/Line Chart Program**

```c
/* COMBCHRT.C: Adds line chart to the barchart program */

#include <graphics.h>
#include <conio.h>
#include <stdio.h>
#include "vcoords.h"
#define  BASELINE 80

int result[][2] = {                    /* budget vs actuals */
        {270, 220},
        {320, 370},
        {180, 160},
        {200, 310}
};

/* Prototypes */
void gridlines (void);
void center (char *string, int topRow);
void identify (void);
void drawBars (void);
void plotDeviation (void);
/* ------------------------- */

void main ()
{
int  driver = DETECT, mode;
char path[] = "C:";

  initgraph (&driver, &mode, path);      /* open graphics */
  if (graphresult() == grOk) {           /* if successful... */
    setFactors ();                       /* set xlation factors */
    gridlines ();                        /* draw gridlines */
    identify ();                   /* write text descriptions */
    drawBars ();                         /* draw the bars */
    plotDeviation ();            /* show above/below budget */
    getch ();                    /* hold until key pressed */
    closegraph ();
  }
} /* ------------------------- */
```

Program 12.4 **(continued)**

```c
void gridlines (void)                    /* write gridlines */
{
int    ny, million;
char   mil [2];

   settextstyle (SMALL_FONT, HORIZ_DIR, 5);
   setlinestyle (DASHED_LINE, 0, NORM_WIDTH);
   for (million = 1; million < 5; million++) {
     ny = (million * 100) + BASELINE;
     line (dx (40), dy (ny), dx (750), dy (ny));
     sprintf (mil, "%d", million);
     outtextxy (dx ( 30), dy (ny+15), mil);
     outtextxy (dx (760), dy (ny+15), mil);
   }
} /* ----------------------- */

void center (char *string, int topRow)    /* center text */
{
int    start;

   start = (px - textwidth (string)) / 2;
   outtextxy (start, topRow, string);
} /* ----------------------- */

void identify (void)                     /* add text to chart */
{
char   title[] = "Budget vs Actuals, 1988", label[3];
int    start = 120, labelNo;

   settextstyle (SMALL_FONT, HORIZ_DIR, 5);
   center (title, dy (VH));
   for (labelNo = 1; labelNo < 5; start += 180, labelNo++) {
     sprintf (label, "%dQ", labelNo);
     outtextxy (dx (start), dy (BASELINE-5), label);
   }
   settextstyle (SMALL_FONT, VERT_DIR, 4);
   outtextxy (dx (15), dy (400), "($ Millions)");
} /* ----------------------- */

void drawBars (void)                      /* draw the bars */
{
int    start, col;

/* draw base line */
   setlinestyle (SOLID_LINE, 0, NORM_WIDTH);
   line (dx (40), dy (BASELINE-1),
     dx (760), dy (BASELINE-1));

/* draw the budget bars first */
   setfillstyle (XHATCH_FILL, 1);
   start = 60;                              /* start at nx 60 */
   for (col = 0; col < 4; start += 180, col++)
```

Program 12.4 **(continued)**

```
    bar (dx (start), dy (BASELINE),
         dx (start + 60), dy (BASELINE + result [col][0]));

/* then draw the actuals bars */
  setfillstyle (SOLID_FILL, 2);
  start = 140;
  for (col = 0; col < 4; start += 180, col++)
    bar (dx (start), dy (BASELINE),
         dx (start + 60), dy (BASELINE + result [col][1]));
} /* ------------------------ */

void plotDeviation (void)        /* use line chart to show */
{                                /* deviation from budget */
int    deviation, point, nx, ny;

  setlinestyle (SOLID_LINE, 0, THICK_WIDTH);
  setcolor (3);
  for (point = 0; point < 4; point++) {
  deviation = result [point][1] - result [point][0];
  nx = (point * 180) + 130;
  ny = BASELINE + deviation;
  if (point == 0)
    moveto (dx (nx), dy (ny));
  else
    lineto (dx (nx), dy (ny));
  }
} /* ------------------------ */
```

Program 12.4 shows the program COMBCHRT.C, which is the complete bar-chart program with the addition of the function **plotDeviation()**. This added function works like this: The deviation is actual minus budgeted for each period, which maps to a virtual Y added to BASELINE. That is, if the organization was $30 million below budget, the NY computes as BASELINE + (−30); if $30 million over budget, as BASELINE + 30. The bar pairs are spaced 180 virtual X units apart, with the median between the first pair occurring at NX = 130. The first period moves the graphics cursor to its deviation point, and all subsequent periods draw lines from the last period's data point to the current data point using turtle graphics (the **lineto()** function). The resulting line is superimposed on the column chart. Figure 12.2 shows the combined graph.

Line Charts

Line charts are often interchangeable with bar charts, the difference being that lines of different styles or colors zigzag across the chart at the same heights as the tops of the bars they replace. In the examples above, for in-

Figure 12.2 **Combined Chart Produced by Program 12.4 on an EGA Monitor**

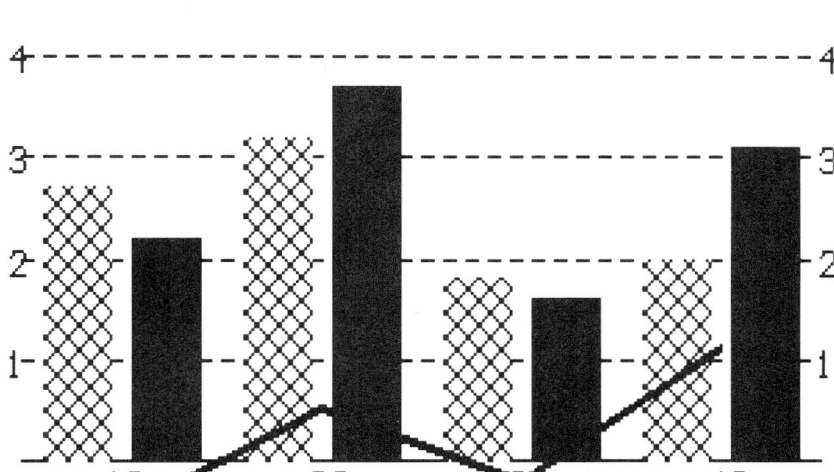

stance, one line would replace the budget bars and another the actuals bars.

A more appropriate use of line charts, however, is in tracing variables through a number of data points where many bars are needed to reveal the "shape" of the data. One example is graphing statistical findings, as in Program 12.5 below. Others are tracking daily prices and displaying price/demand/revenue curves to find the best price for a product.

Program 12.5, INCPLOT.C, illustrates the use of a line chart in plotting the income distribution by age of a statistical sample. The X axis represents age, the Y income, for a group of people between the ages of 20 and 80.

Program 12.5 **A Line Chart Showing Statistical Data**

```
/* INCPLOT.C: Graphs income by age in line chart */

#include <graphics.h>
#include <stdio.h>
#include <conio.h>
#include "vcoords.h"

#define  ORIGIN    100      /* virtual xy origin of graph */
#define  WIDTH     600          /* virtual width of graph */
```

Program 12.5 (continued)

```c
#define   HEIGHT     400             /* virtual height of graph */
#define   YPERK      HEIGHT / 50     /* virt y's per $1K inc */
#define   GRIDCOLOR  1                         /* grid color */
#define   TEXTCOLOR  2
#define   TOTCOLOR   3               /* total income color */

unsigned result [][2] = {                      /* age, income */
   {20, 15},
   {25, 18},
   {30, 21},
   {35, 28},
   {40, 35},
   {45, 41},
   {50, 42},
   {55, 43},
   {60, 44},
   {65, 45},
   {70, 27},
   {75, 21},
   {80, 20}
};

/* Local functions */
void gridlines (int, int);
void identify (char*);
void plotIncome (int, int);
/* ------------------------- */

void main (void)
{
int   n = (sizeof (result) / (sizeof (unsigned) * 2)),
      xs = WIDTH / (n-1), device = DETECT, mode;
char  name[] = "Income Distribution by Age";

   initgraph (&device, &mode, NULL);
   if (graphresult () == grOk) {
     setFactors ();                       /* initialize */
     gridlines (n, xs);              /* score plot area */
     identify (name);                    /* title graph */
     plotIncome (n, xs);         /* plot total income */
   }
   getch ();                       /* hold for keypress */
   closegraph ();
} /* ------------------------- */

void gridlines (int n, int xs)       /* Draw gridlines */
{
int   x, y;
char  label [3];

   setlinestyle (SOLID_LINE, 0, THICK_WIDTH);
```

Program 12.5 **(continued)**

```
    setcolor (GRIDCOLOR);
    rectangle (dx (ORIGIN), dy (ORIGIN),
            dx (ORIGIN+WIDTH), dy (ORIGIN+HEIGHT));
    setlinestyle (DASHED_LINE, 0, NORM_WIDTH);
    for (x = 0; x < n; x += 2) {           /* draw/mark x's */
      line (dx ((x * xs) + ORIGIN), dy (ORIGIN),
          dx ((x * xs) + ORIGIN), dy (ORIGIN+HEIGHT));
    }

    for (y = 10; y < 50; y += 10) {        /* draw/mark y's */
      line (dx (ORIGIN), dy (YPERK * y + ORIGIN),
          dx (ORIGIN+WIDTH), dy (YPERK * y + ORIGIN));
    }

    setcolor (TEXTCOLOR);
    for (x = 0; x < n; x++) {              /* label age lines */
      sprintf (label, "%d", result [x][0]);
      outtextxy (dx ((x * xs) + ORIGIN - 10),
              dy (ORIGIN-10), label);
    }

    for (y = 0; y < 60; y += 10) {    /* label income lines */
      sprintf (label, "%2d", y);
      outtextxy (dx (ORIGIN - 40),
              dy (YPERK * y + ORIGIN + 10), label);
    }
} /* ------------------------- */


void identify (char   *title)              /* Identify graph */
{

 settextjustify (CENTER_TEXT, CENTER_TEXT);
 moveto (dx (VW / 2), dy (VH - 20));
 outtext (title);
} /* ------------------------- */

void plotIncome (int n, int xs)
{
int    x, y;

  setcolor (TOTCOLOR);
  setlinestyle (SOLID_LINE, 0, NORM_WIDTH);
  y = YPERK * result [0][1] + ORIGIN;
  moveto (dx (ORIGIN), dy (y));
  for (x = 1; x < n; x++) {
    y = YPERK * result [x][1] + ORIGIN;
    lineto (dx ((x * xs) + ORIGIN), dy (y));
  }
} /* ------------------------- */
```

The origin (lower-left corner) of the plot area is at {100, 100} in virtual coordinates, extending up and to the right. The result array contains the survey data. After switching into graphics mode, the program calls **gridlines()**.

This function outlines the plot area with a thick line and draws visual reference points as thin dashed lines. It marks every 20 years in age along the X axis and every $10,000 in income along the Y; note how the loops increment and calculate the device coordinates in order to achieve this. A second pair of loops label the axes, again using the ORIGIN as the point of reference. Because **outtextxy()** prints only text, it's necessary to use **sprintf()** to convert numbers to strings.

The **identify()** function centers the chart title at the top. This is a different approach than we used in Program 12.3. The library's **settextjustify()** function establishes a text justification inheritance, which in this case centers all subsequent text output both horizontally and vertically around the current graphics pen position. Consequently, the **moveto()** statement places the pen in the middle of an area above the graph, and the text written by the subsequent call to **outtext()** centers the title around the pen.

The **plotIncome()** function moves the pen to the first data point and then enters a loop that successively draws relative lines from the previous data point to the current one. Again, each point is relative to ORIGIN in virtual coordinates, thus effecting correct placement of the line chart within the plot area.

When the graph is finished, the program freezes it until a keypress, then restores the screen to its previous status.

Bar charts effectively track one or two variables through a few data points, and line charts follow one to several variables through many data points. When the data points are very close together or continuous, as in a mathematical function, an XY chart becomes appropriate.

XY Charts

In an XY chart, each data point resolves to a single pixel, hence the name. XY charts are also called "scatter graphs" since the data points can be scattered all over the place when the correlation between the variables (X and Y) is too imperfect to effect a continuum. Statisticians often use XY charts to see if the points form a pattern, indicating a relationship between the variables.

XY charts are also useful for drawing curves based on a mathematical function. The trick is to place the pixels closely enough together to form a continuous line: Every physical X is best, and even closer when there are steep rises and falls in the Y component.

Program 12.6 shows the program FCNPLOT.C, which graphs the equation $y = \cos x + \sin 2x$. It's a three-color chart showing the sum and its two factors. As you watch it drawing the sinuously graceful curves, you're seeing mathematics in action. In addition to demonstrating pixel plotting (in main()) and relative-motion output (in legend()), this chart introduces the concept of a legend that explains the colors.

Program 12.6 **XY Chart of a Mathematical Function**

```c
/* FCNPLOT.C: Graphs the function y = cos x + sin 2x */

#include <math.h>
#include <graphics.h>
#include <conio.h>
#include <stdio.h>
#include "vcoords.h"

#define   PI2       M_PI * 2.0          /* domain of graph */
#define   RADX      (double) PI2 / VW   /* radians/virt X */
#define   BASELINE  VH / 2              /* elevation of baseline */
#define   YFACT     BASELINE / 2.0      /* y conversion */
#define   COSCOLOR  1                   /* color of cosine curve */
#define   SINCOLOR  2                   /* color of sine curve */
#define   PLOTCOLOR 3                   /* color of graph line */

/* Local functions */
void gridlines (void);
void title (char*);
void legend (void);
int  vy (double);
/* --------------------------- */

void main ()
{
int     vx;
double  x, y, cx, sx;
int     device = DETECT, mode;

  initgraph (&device, &mode, NULL);
  if (graphresult() == grOk) {
    setFactors ();
    gridlines ();
    title ("Y = cos X + sin 2X");
    legend ();
    for (vx = 0; vx < VW; vx++) {         /* pixel per vx */
      x  = (double) vx * RADX;      /* convert to radians */
      cx = cos (x);                       /* get cos x */
      putpixel (dx (vx), dy (vy (cx)), COSCOLOR);

      sx = sin (2.0 * x);                 /* get sin 2x */
      putpixel (dx (vx), dy (vy (sx)), SINCOLOR);

      y  = cx + sx;                       /* compute sum */
      putpixel (dx (vx), dy (vy (y)), PLOTCOLOR);
    }
    getch ();                             /* freeze image */
    closegraph ();
```

Program 12.6 **(continued)**

```
  }
} /* --------------------- */

int  vy (double y)         /* convert y into virtual coord */
{
  return (y * YFACT + BASELINE);
} /* --------------------- */

void gridlines (void)                   /* draw grid lines */
{
  setcolor (PLOTCOLOR);
  setlinestyle (SOLID_LINE, 0, NORM_WIDTH);
  line (0, dy (BASELINE), dx (VW-1), dy (BASELINE));

  setcolor (SINCOLOR);
  setlinestyle (DASHED_LINE, 0, NORM_WIDTH);
  line (0, dy (vy ( 1.0)), dx (VW), dy (vy ( 1.0)));
  line (0, dy (vy (-1.0)), dx (VW), dy (vy (-1.0)));
} /* --------------------- */

void title (char *name)                 /* title graph */
{
  setcolor (PLOTCOLOR);
  settextjustify (CENTER_TEXT, CENTER_TEXT);
  moveto (dx (VW / 2), dy (575));
  outtext (name);
} /* --------------------- */

void legend (void)                      /* identify colors */
{
  settextjustify (LEFT_TEXT, CENTER_TEXT);
  setcolor (COSCOLOR);
  moveto (dx (50), dy (20));
  linerel (dx (100), 0);
  outtext (" Cos X");

  setcolor (SINCOLOR);
  moverel (dx ( 30), 0);
  linerel (dx (100), 0);
  outtext (" Sin 2X");

  setcolor (PLOTCOLOR);
  moverel (dx ( 30), 0);
  linerel (dx (100), 0);
  outtext (" Sum");
} /* --------------------- */
```

Note the #defines at the top of FCNPLOT.C. This program follows the trig functions through one complete circle, or two. Consequently it defines the constant PI2 based on **M_PI**, which comes from MATH.H. Because it works in virtual coordinates, the factor to convert a virtual *x* into radians (the angle measurement used by **cos()** and **sin()**) is PI2/VW, where VW is the virtual width of the screen from VCOORDS.H. The chart will show both positive and negative values, so its baseline is placed in the vertical center of the screen, at VH/2. Both the sine and cosine range between -1.0 and 1.0, so their sums could conceivably result in a number between -2.0 and 2.0. For that reason, the factor for converting Y into a virtual coordinate is BASELINE/2.

The vy function performs this conversion. If VH = 600 (from VCOORDS.H), then BASELINE = 300 and YFACT = 150. Suppose $y = -2.0$ when **vy()** is called. It returns $-2.0 * 150 + 300 = 0$, or the bottom of the virtual screen. Similarly, when $y = 2.0$, vy() returns 600, which is the top. The function works, then, for all conceivable values of y.

Gridlines() draws the X axis as a solid line and two dashed lines showing the locations of $y = -1.0$ and $y = 1.0$. Nothing new here, nor is there in **title()**, which identifies the chart at top center.

A legend is an explanation of the chart elements, enabling the viewer to identify at a glance what each element means. Here, the **legend()** function relates line colors to plotted functions. It uses **moveto()** to place the pen near the bottom of the screen, then outputs information with graphics functions that move the pen relative to its resting point following each preceding output.

Main() does most of the work inside a loop that advances through each virtual x. It derives the x for the calculations through multiplication by RADX, resulting in a radians value that becomes the argument to **cos()** and **sin()**. The calls to **putpixel()** plot the curves in their proper colors.

Because the virtual screen has more data points than the physical display device, roundoffs frequently occur. This places two or more pixels at different y's within the same column. While this method is less efficient than stepping x by physical units, it results in curves with fewer and less-apparent gaps where the slope of the curve is steep, or in other words higher resolution and a better appearance.

So far we've discussed data representation in two dimensions: height and width. Now let's look at a one-dimensional way of viewing the components of a whole.

Pie Charts

A pie chart shows the subdivisions of a set of data. An example is breaking down the dollar volume of a company's sales by product line. The whole pie is total sales; each slice gives a visual approximation of the percentage contributed by a given product.

The tool for building a pie chart in Turbo C graphics is the **pieslice()** function. It draws a pie slice based on the following integer arguments:

x	Center X (where the "center" is the point of the slice)
y	Center Y
s	Starting angle (0 ≤ s ≤ 360 degrees, where 0 degrees is at three o'clock)
e	Ending angle (as above)
r	Radius in device units

The .BGI driver for each supported device automatically adjusts for distortion introduced by nonsquare pixels. This means that a whole pie drawn by **pieslice()** calls is round and not stretched vertically no matter which video device runs a graphics program. Consequently, while you can use the virtual coordinate system from VCOORDS, it's not necessary in order to eliminate distortion.

The pie slice inherits the prevailing color and fill pattern. These characteristics are set by a call to **setfillstyle**, which takes integer arguments specifying a fill pattern and a color. There are 11 patterns (0–10) predefined in the **fill_patterns** enumeration in GRAPHICS.H. The twelfth is **USER_FILL**, which refers to a user-defined pattern set by a call to **setfillpattern()**; if you want to define your own fill style, see the **getfillpattern()** description in the Turbo C 1.5 manual.

In general, adjacent slices in a pie should have at least different colors, and varying patterns is a good idea too, since many people are colorblind. Also, the Hercules board doesn't support colors, so patterns are the only way to distinguish between slices. The zero pattern is **EMPTY_FILL**, which is undesirable in most cases. You might also want to hold the solid fill (style 1) aside for a slice to be emphasized. If you're building a pie from an array, you can use the loop counter plus 2 to set the pattern. This assumes, of course, that the pie has nine or fewer slices (more than eight confuses the eye, anyway).

Varying the color can be a problem on the CGA, where you have only three foreground colors (1–3) to work with. A little creative programming using the modulo operator (%) works around the problem. Modulo returns the remainder in integer division. If the counter for the loop that builds the pie chart is i, you can always derive a color in the range 1–3 with the expression

```
color = (i % 3) + 1;
```

As i increments, color takes the repeating values 1, 2, 3, 1, 2, 3, and so on. This leads to the following generalized piechart-building loop:

```
for (i = 0; i < n; i++) {
  if (device == CGA)
    color = (i % 3) + 1; /* colors 1, 2, 3 */
  else
    color = i; /* EGA, VGA, etc. */
```

```
    setfillstyle (i + 2, color);
    ...                                      /* set other values as needed */
    pieslice ( ... );
}
```

This is the general approach used in Program 12.7, the first of two programs that develop methods for building pie charts. You'll find it, with some embellishments, in main().

Program 12.7 **Building a Basic Pie Chart**

```
/* PIE1.C: Builds a basic, unadorned pie chart */

#include <graphics.h>
#include <conio.h>

typedef struct {
  char    region [8];
  int     revenue;
} DATA;

DATA  sales [] = {
  { "Central", 31 },
  { "North",   26 },
  { "South",   19 },
  { "East",    16 },
  { "West",    11 }
};
/* ---------------------------------------------------- */

void main ()
{
int    device = DETECT, mode, cx, cy, i, color,
       stangle = 0, endangle, spread, radius, nreg;
double total = 0.0, pct;
void   title (char*);

  nreg = sizeof (sales) / sizeof (DATA);     /* # regions */

  for (i = 0; i < nreg; i++)      /* figure total revenues */
    total += sales [i].revenue;

  initgraph (&device, &mode, "");
  if (graphresult() == grOk) {
    radius = getmaxy () / 3;          /* radius of slices */
    cx = getmaxx () / 2;                 /* center of pie */
    cy = getmaxy () / 2;
    title ("Sales Results by Region");

    for (i = 0; i < nreg; i++) {    /* loop to make chart */
      if (device == CGA)                       /* set color */
        color = (i % 3) + 1;
```

Program 12.7 (continued)

```
        else
          color = i + 1;
        setfillstyle (i + 2, color);      /* set fill style */

        pct = sales [i].revenue / total;      /* pct total */
        spread = 360 * pct;                   /* slice spread */
        if (i != nreg - 1)
          endangle = stangle + spread;    /* end next slice */
        else
          endangle = 360;                       /* last slice */
        pieslice (cx, cy, stangle, endangle, radius);
        stangle += spread;                /* next slice start */
      }
    getch ();
    closegraph ();
  }
} /* ----------------------- */

void title (char name[])                    /* title chart */
{
  setcolor (3);
  settextjustify (CENTER_TEXT, CENTER_TEXT);
  moveto (getmaxx () / 2, 20);
  outtext (name);
} /* ----------------------- */
```

The basis of this exercise is sales results by region, where there are five regions: Central, North, South, East, and West. Their individual results appear in the array of DATA structures called sales, which substitutes here for an external data file. Note how the program determines the number of regions in the expression yielding the variable **nreg**. If you later add or remove a region, the program automatically adjusts itself to accommodate the change.

One cannot figure the sizes of pie slices until the total is known, since a pie chart always shows percentages of the whole; thus the loop computing total.

After entering graphics mode, the program sets the radius of the slices as one-third of the total display height, yielding a pie occupying two-thirds of the vertical dimension. The center of the pie will be at the center of the screen.

The loop that makes the pie chart follows the general plan discussed above. For each slice, it computes the percent of total sales, then translates that into the slice's spread in degrees. The end angle is the starting angle plus the spread unless this is the last slice. In that case, it's necessary to adjust for cumulative roundoff errors by completing the circle with endangle = 360. After drawing the slice, the program advances the next slice's starting angle to stangle + spread, then reiterates the loop.

This makes a nice pie chart with varying patterns and colors, but it's incomplete. You can't look at the chart and determine which slice belongs to whom. For that you need to add text to the chart.

Adding Callouts to a Pie Chart

Callouts are text labels that explain specific pie slices. They're rather like legends, but with the added characteristic of having a position adjacent to the slice.

PIE2.C in Program 12.8 expands the example by adding the function callout(), which gets control after each slice is drawn. callout() uses trigonometry to calculate an imaginary line bisecting the arc of the slice. It originates at the slice's point and has a radius 10 device units greater than that of the slice itself, thus ending outside the pie. This is the text reference point.

The position of the callout itself relative to the reference point depends on which side of the pie it's on. If it's to the right, the text can begin there. If on the left, however, the callout has to end there in order to avoid intruding into the slice. The Boolean variable left assumes that all callouts are to the right unless proven otherwise. The proof is the bisector's angle; if between 90 and 270 degrees, it's to the left and the Boolean becomes TRUE. Its value determines the starting point (tx) of the text in outtextxy().

Program 12.8 **A Pie Chart with Callouts**

```
/* PIE2.C: Adds callouts to chart from PIE1.C */

#include <math.h>
#include <graphics.h>
#define   FALSE 0
#define   TRUE  !FALSE

typedef struct {
  char    region [8];
  int     revenue;
} DATA;

/* Global data */
DATA   sales [] = {
  { "Central", 31 },
  { "North",   26 },
  { "South",   19 },
  { "East",    16 },
  { "West",    11 }
};

int    cx, cy;
/* ------------------------------------------------- */

void main ()
{
int    device = DETECT, mode, i, color, stangle = 0,
       endangle, spread, radius, nreg;
double total = 0.0, pct;
void   title (char*);
```

Program 12.8 **(continued)**

```
void    callout (int, int, int, int);

  nreg = sizeof (sales) / sizeof (DATA);      /* # regions */

  for (i = 0; i < nreg; i++)      /* figure total revenues */
    total += sales [i].revenue;

  initgraph (&device, &mode, "");
  if (graphresult() == grOk) {
    radius = getmaxy () / 3;              /* radius of slices */
    cx = getmaxx () / 2;                     /* center of pie */
    cy = getmaxy () / 2;
    title ("Sales Results by Region");

    for (i = 0; i < nreg; i++) {    /* loop to make chart */
      if (device == CGA)                    /* set color */
        color = (i % 3) + 1;
      else
        color = i + 1;
      setfillstyle (i + 2, color);      /* set fill style */

      pct = sales [i].revenue / total;    /* pct total */
      spread = 360 * pct;               /* slice spread */
      if (i != nreg - 1)
        endangle = stangle + spread;    /* end next slice */
      else
        endangle = 360;                  /* last slice */
      pieslice (cx, cy, stangle, endangle, radius);
      callout (i, stangle, spread, radius);
      stangle += spread;              /* next slice start */
    }
    getch ();
    closegraph ();
  }
} /* ----------------------- */

void title (char name[])                      /* title chart */
{
  setcolor (3);
  settextjustify (CENTER_TEXT, CENTER_TEXT);
  moveto (getmaxx () / 2, 20);
  outtext (name);
} /* ----------------------- */

void callout (int n, int start, int spread, int radius)
{                           /* attach callout to pie slice */
int    callangle, left = FALSE, tx, ty;
double angle;
char    *text;

  text = sales[n].region;
  settextstyle (SMALL_FONT, HORIZ_DIR, 4);
```

Program 12.8 **(continued)**

```
    callangle = start + (spread / 2);
    if ((callangle > 90) && (callangle < 270))
       left = TRUE;                    /* left side of pie chart */
    angle = (double) callangle * (M_PI/180.0);   /* radians */
    tx = cx + (cos (angle) * (radius + 10));     /* text pos */
    ty = cy - (sin (angle) * (radius + 10));
    if (left)
       tx -= textwidth (text);
    outtextxy (tx, ty, text);
} /* ----------------------- */
```

This chapter has skimmed along the surface of business graphics, but it's covered the main principles and given you techniques that you can build upon.

The next chapter delves more deeply into the rich capabilities of the Turbo C graphics library.

CHAPTER 13

DRAWING OBJECTS

W e now move from the sober realm of business graphics into more lighthearted matters: geometric shapes, arcs, circles, polygons, and the like, along with fillings. To be sure, you can do serious work with these things, but in general it tends to be more fun than business graphics because there are more possibilities and more room for imagination.

We'll discuss the CGA here briefly, but most of the programs in this chapter and subsequent chapters are aimed at the EGA. There are a couple of reasons for this. First, the CGA is rapidly becoming obsolete. Second, the reasons it's becoming obsolete are that it's barely acceptable for anything more than primitive graphics, and the cost of EGA is now within the reach of most computer owners. About the only thing you can say in favor of the CGA is that it's better than no graphics at all. If you want to do serious graphics work, invest in an EGA.

Or better yet, a VGA. It happens that we have a VGA and it's tempting to base some programs on it. However, a VGA can emulate an EGA, and since VGAs are still relatively rare, we'll confine our projects to the more common EGA, which delivers acceptable graphics.

Detecting the Graphics Adapter

Turbo C provides a function called **detectgraph()** that you can call from text mode. It determines the adapter type and its best graphics mode. The ADAPTER.C program in Program 13.1 shows how to use **detectgraph()**.

Program 13.1 **Detecting the Graphics Adapter**

```
/* ADAPTER.C: Reports graphics adapter and default mode */

#include <graphics.h>
#include <stdio.h>

void main ()
{
```

Program 13.1 **(continued)**

```
int adapter = DETECT, mode, lomode, himode;

    detectgraph (&adapter, &mode);
    printf ("\nAdapter = %d", adapter);
    printf ("\nBest mode is = %d", mode);
    getmoderange (adapter, &lomode, &himode);
    printf ("\nModes supported are %d . . %d",
            lomode, himode);
}
```

The key value here is the adapter variable. You set it initially to **DETECT**, then call **detectgraph()**. The function loads the variable parameters with results.

The adapter variable contains one of nine values as follows:

Value	Driver/Adapter
1	CGA
2	MCGA
3	EGA
4	EGA64
5	EGAMONO
6	IBM8514
7	HERCMONO
8	ATT400
9	VGA
10	PC3270

Note that these correspond to the graphics drivers furnished by Turbo C.

For each of these adapter types, there might be from one to six possible modes. The graphics subsystem selects a best mode if there is one, *best* being defined as the one with the highest resolution or the most colors. For example, the EGA supports 640 × 200 in 16 colors with four pages (mode 0), or 640 × 350 in 16 colors with two pages (mode 1). The best mode here is 1, since it yields the highest resolution.

However, you might want to know if other modes are available. In that case, call **getmoderange()**. It returns the lowest and highest possible modes for the given adapter. ADAPTER.C also shows this function in action. Taking advantage of the most appropriate (as opposed to "best") mode would require some complex program logic, but it can be done with nested **switch()** statements.

If you detect a CGA (adapter type 1), you're in trouble if you need to do graphics in more than three colors and/or with fairly high resolution. This is because the CGA's color selection and resolution are poor. All graphics modes in the CGA have 200 scan lines vertically. The monochrome graphics mode (CGAHI, mode 4) produces 640 pixels horizontally, but only a single color against the background. For color modes, you can select among four palettes (CGAC0 through CGAC3) that provide different color schemes. Each palette offers three fixed colors numbered 1 through 3, plus a variable background color indexed as 0. Even if you partition the CGA screen into viewport windows, only one palette can be active at a time for the entire display. This means you have a choice of only three foreground colors at any time. Additionally, the color modes furnish a horizontal resolution of only 320 pixels, which is too coarse for much graphics work. That's why the CGA is of limited usefulness, and is not treated here.

Drawing Objects

The Turbo C graphics library furnishes routines for drawing six geometric objects. These are:

    arc()
    circle()
    drawpoly()
    ellipse()
    line()/lineto()/linerel()
    rectangle()

The line . . . () routines were discussed in the last chapter, as was the concept of the graphics pen (or "turtle").

The routines for arcs, circles, and ellipses are all related in that they specify a center point about which the curve turns at some distance (the radius). A circle is, of course, just that, and an arc is part of a circle. An ellipse can be considered as a circle that is compressed either from the sides or from above and below, resulting in elongation along the vertical or horizontal axis; mathematically, but not in Turbo C, an ellipse could also elongate along an angle. The **ellipse()** function actually draws an elliptical arc that only closes when the starting angle is 0 and the ending angle is 360.

All three routines automatically self-adjust for the aspect ratio—or vertical distortion—of the screen. In all but the VGA's 640 × 480 mode, pixels are taller than they are wide. If self-adjustment didn't occur, a circle would appear as a vertically oriented ellipse on the display. The routines consider that the radius runs along the X axis (center to either nine o'clock or three o'clock), and adjust the Y distance so that it's approximately the same, "approximately" because circles drawn on the EGA by Turbo C are still slightly out of round tending toward the vertical.

This self-adjustment creates a problem when drawing arcs that connect with other elements such as a line. For example, say you're drawing a box with rounded corners. You need to draw horizontal lines that connect the corners, but since the arc routine has adjusted the vertical radius, you don't know exactly where the end point is.

Fortunately, the Turbo C library contains a fix for this problem. GRAPHICS.H contains the structure definition

```
struct arccoordstype {
   int  x, y;
   int  xstart, ystart, xend, yend;
};
```

If you declare a variable of this type and pass its address in a call to **getarccoords()**, the function will fill in information about the last call to **arc()**: x, y contain the center point, **xstart** and **ystart** the starting coordinates, and **xend** and **yend** the ending point of the arc.

Program 13.2, ROUNDBOX.C, illustrates how to use **arc()** and **getarccoords()** to draw a rounded box. Note how each call to **line()** goes from the end of the last arc to a point some distance away, either vertically or horizontally depending on the direction to the next corner.

Program 13.2 Drawing a Rounded Box with Adjusted Arcs

```
/* ROUNDBOX.C: Draws a box with rounded corners */

#include <graphics.h>
#include <conio.h>

#define   RADIUS 30

void main ()
{
struct arccoordstype   arcs;
int                    driver = EGA, mode = EGAHI;

   initgraph (&driver, &mode, "");
   if (graphresult() == grOk) {
     arc (480,  87,   0,  90, RADIUS);        /* upper right */
     getarccoords (&arcs);
     line (arcs.xend,      arcs.yend,
         arcs.xend-320, arcs.yend);

     arc (160,  87,  90, 180, RADIUS);        /* upper left */
     getarccoords (&arcs);
     line (arcs.xend, arcs.yend,
         arcs.xend, arcs.yend+175);

     arc (160, 260, 180, 270, RADIUS);        /* lower left */
     getarccoords (&arcs);
     line (arcs.xend,      arcs.yend,
         arcs.xend+320, arcs.yend);
```

Program 13.2 (continued)

```
    arc (480, 260, 270, 360, RADIUS);      /* lower right */
    getarccoords (&arcs);
    line (arcs.xend, arcs.yend,
          arcs.xend, arcs.yend-175);

    getch();                                /* freeze for keypress */
    closegraph ();
  }
}
```

The **rectangle**() function is the easiest of the object-drawing routines. It draws a rectangle whose opposite corners are at {x1, y1} and {x2, y2}. The object inherits the current line style, color, and thickness. The Turbo C manual states that {x1, y1} must be at the upper-left corner and {x2, y2} at the lower right. In fact, this is not true; you can specify any two opposing corners in any order.

Drawpoly() is the Turbo C implementation of a routine commonly called POLYLINE in graphics literature. It draws a series of n connected lines using an array containing n + 1 coordinate pairs, where **p[0]** contains the starting point of the first segment and **p[n]** the end of the last segment. If **p[n]** is equal to **p[0]**, the polygon is closed. This function is useful for drawing the outline of almost any figure imaginable (see also **fillpoly**() under Filling, below).

Program 13.3 (POLYS.C) draws two polygons. The closed polygon is a tilted hexagon. Note that the first and last points are the same, which achieves closure of the figure. Since a hexagon consists of six sides and six vertices ("corners"), it takes seven points to describe it. The **openPoly** figure also has six sides, but it never closes; no two points are equal in its definition.

Program 13.3 Closed and Open Polygons

```
/* POLYS.C: Draws closed and open polygons */

#include <graphics.h>
#include <conio.h>
#include "vcoords.h"

/* Figures in virtual coordinates */
int hexagon [][2] = {           /* tilted hexagon */
    {100, 300},
    {220, 440},
    {380, 440},
    {420, 300},
    {300, 160},
```

Program 13.3 **(continued)**

```
    {140, 160},
    {100, 300}
};

int openPoly [][2] = {           /* zigzag pattern */
    {440, 240},
    {540, 360},
    {500, 240},
    {600, 360},
    {680, 240},
    {660, 360},
    {740, 240}
};

void main ()
{
int  driver = EGA, mode = EGAHI, n;

  initgraph (&driver, &mode, "");
  if (graphresult() == grOk) {
    setFactors();
    settextjustify (CENTER_TEXT, CENTER_TEXT);
    setcolor (GREEN);
    for (n = 0; n < 7; n++) {       /* convert points to dc */
      hexagon [n][0] = dx (hexagon [n][0]);
      hexagon [n][1] = dy (hexagon [n][1]);
    }
    drawpoly (7, (int far*) hexagon);
    outtextxy (dx (260), dy (500), "Closed");

    setcolor (BLUE);
    for (n = 0; n < 7; n++) {
      openPoly [n][0] = dx (openPoly [n][0]);
      openPoly [n][1] = dy (openPoly [n][1]);
    }
    drawpoly (7, (int far*) openPoly);
    outtextxy (dx (600), dy (500), "Open");

    getch();
    closegraph();
  }
}
```

Because the points are expressed in virtual coordinates, the program must pass through the arrays converting to device coordinates before calling **drawpoly()**. That's what the two loops do.

So much for basic figures. Before we can take full advantage of the graphics library, it's necessary to cover two other fundamentals: line and fill patterns.

Line Patterns

The graphics library furnishes four standard line styles: solid, dotted, center (close dot-dash), and dash. There are also two widths available. A normal line is one pixel wide, a thick line two. You set the line to solid and normal width with the call

    setlinestyle (SOLID_LINE, 0, NORM_WIDTH);

as we've done in several programs so far.

Additionally, you can define your own line pattern with the call

    setlinestyle (USERBIT_LINE, pattern, width);

where the width parameter is one of the two standard widths. The pattern argument is a 16-bit unsigned value in which a 1-bit means pixel-on and a 0-bit means pixel-off. For example, an exaggerated version of the center line pattern—wide spacing between the dot and its surrounding dashes—is 1111 1110 0001 0000, or 0xFE10. A call to set this user-defined pattern is

    setlinestyle (USERBIT_LINE, 0xFE10, NORM_WIDTH);

(or THICK_WIDTH) and thereafter, all ensuing lines drawn with the line() routines or any object-drawing function will inherit your pattern.

To see the line patterns including the one defined above, run **LINES.C** in Program 13.4.

Program 13.4 **Standard and User-Defined Line Patterns**

```
/* LINES.C: Standard and user-defined line patterns */

#include <graphics.h>
#include <conio.h>

char ident [][13] = {
    {"SOLID_LINE"},
    {"DOTTED_LINE"},
    {"CENTER_LINE"},
    {"DASHED_LINE"},
    {"User-defined"}
};

void main ()
{
int  driver = EGA, mode = EGAHI, n, y;
```

Program 13.4 **(continued)**

```
    initgraph (&driver, &mode, "");
    if (graphresult() == grOk) {
      for (n = 0; n < 4; n++ ) {          /* standard patterns */
        setlinestyle (n, 0, NORM_WIDTH);
        settextjustify (LEFT_TEXT, CENTER_TEXT);
        y = (n + 1) * 60;                 /* line and text row */
        line (0, y, 319, y);
        outtextxy (360, y, ident [n]);
      }
      y = (n + 1) * 60;
      setlinestyle (USERBIT_LINE, 0xFE10, NORM_WIDTH);
      line (0, y, 319, y);
      outtextxy (360, y, ident [n]);

      getch ();
      closegraph ();
    }
}
```

If your program forgets which line style is currently in effect, it can find out by calling **getlinesettings()**. This function's argument is the address of a structured variable of the **struct linesettings** type, which is defined in GRAPHICS.H. Its members are linestyle, pattern, and thickness, which correspond directly to the arguments most recently passed in **setlinestyle()**.

Filling

Often you want closed figures to be filled with some pattern and color in order to make them distinct from their surroundings. This is such an important aspect of graphics that Turbo C furnishes six different functions in support of it. Two perform fills, and four control or inquire about the current filling appearance. These functions tend to work best in groups.

Using Standard Shapes and floodfill()

Before you can fill an area, it's necessary to define the pattern and color. GRAPHICS.H defines 12 standard styles, which we discussed in the last chapter. You set one of the standard patterns with **setfillstyle()**, whose arguments are the pattern name (from the **fill_patterns** enumeration or alternatively a digit 0 . . . 11), and a color 0 . . . 15.

You must also draw the figure to be filled if it's one of the standard objects: circle, ellipse, rectangle, and so on. The outline itself inherits the prevailing line color, and it *must* be a solid line.

After setting the fill style and drawing the figure, use **floodfill()** to fill it. The arguments of **floodfill()** are a coordinate pair and the figure's outline color. If the coordinates are within the figure's boundaries, the figure is filled with the pattern and color set via **setfillstyle()**; if the coordinates are outside, the filler surrounds the figure without invading it.

Program 13.5 is (FILLER.C) that illustrates the discussion. Using virtual coordinates, it draws a large box in white at the center of the display and a smaller box, also in white, at the lower-right corner. After setting the fill style to solid and yellow, it fills the center box by specifying inside coordinates. The fill style then changes to interleaved (colored and background pixels alternating on successive rows) and brown, and the program does the fill outside the center box. Note that the fine, checkerboard pattern surrounds the center box. It also flows around the small box, since it encounters a barrier of white that it cannot penetrate.

Program 13.5 A Demonstration of Filling

```
/* FILLER.C: Draws object and fills it using floodfill */

#include <graphics.h>
#include "vcoords.h"

void main ()
{
int    driver = EGA, mode = EGAHI;

   initgraph (&driver, &mode, "");
   if (graphresult() == grOk) {
      setFactors();                        /* init virtual coords */
      setcolor (WHITE);                          /* border color */
      setlinestyle (SOLID_LINE, 0, NORM_WIDTH);
      rectangle (dx (200), dy (200),           /* draw border */
                 dx (600), dy (400));
      rectangle (dx (650), dy ( 50),   /* box in lower right */
                 dx (750), dy (150));

      setfillstyle (SOLID_FILL, YELLOW);      /* inner fill */
      floodfill (dx (400), dy (300), WHITE);       /* fill */

      setfillstyle (INTERLEAVE_FILL, BROWN);  /* outer fill */
      floodfill (dx (50), dy (50), WHITE);         /* fill */

      getch();
      closegraph();
   }
}
```

To inquire about the current fill attributes, call the function **getfillsettings()** and pass the address of a variable bound to **struct fillsettingstype**, which is defined in GRAPHICS.H. It fills in the structure with the numbers of the pattern and color given in the most recent **setfillstyle()** call. If the pattern number is 12, a user-defined pattern is in effect. That's what we discuss next.

Defining Your Own Fill Pattern

setfillstyle() and **getfillsettings()** are the set and inquiry functions, respectively, for the standard fill attributes. If you want to define your own, the corresponding functions are **setfillpattern()** and **getfillpattern()**.

The Turbo C manual gives an example under **getfillpattern()** for constructing a checkerboard, so we won't duplicate it here. The call to implement this is

```
setfillpattern (checkerboard, color);
```

where **color** is a value 1...15.

The inquiry is **getfillpattern()**, whose argument is the address of an eight-byte array that is filled in with the current user-defined pattern. Normally you only call this function when **getfillsettings()** returns 12 in the settings pattern field; you can get the pattern color from the color field returned by **getfillsettings()**. Therefore, **getfillpattern** is seldom called, the only time being when you want to modify a user-defined pattern on the fly.

Using the *fillpoly()* Function

The **fillpoly()** function combines the best of all worlds in one operation. It draws a polygon (which should be closed) and fills it with a pattern and color. The outline of the polygon is in the prevailing line style and color, and the filling is in the pattern and color decreed by the most recent call to **setfillstyle()** or **setfillpattern()**. Thus, **fillpoly()** is a combination of **drawpoly()** and **floodfill()**.

The line style must be solid, as in any filled figure. Why? Because the filling algorithm continually tests any obstacle of the barrier color that it encounters. When it finds a hole—even a tiny one—it wiggles through and begins filling the region on the other side. A noncontinuous line presents many apertures. That's why any filled area or any area that is to be surrounded must be "watertight."

Harking back to Program 13.3, you could convert the closed hexagon to device coordinates, then draw it as a solid green object with the following sequence:

```
setlinestyle (SOLID_LINE, 0, NORM_WIDTH);
setfillstyle (SOLID_FILL, GREEN);
fillpoly (7, hexagon);
```

Instead, though, let's draw something more interesting than a simple geo-metric shape.

Figure 13.1 **Outline of a 3D Cube**

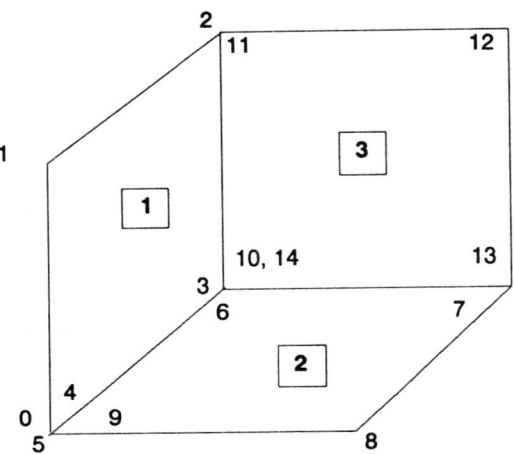

Figure 13.1 shows the outline of a three-dimensional cube that consists of three plane figures, all of which touch each other. There are two parallelograms (labeled 1 and 2 in the figure) and a square. We'll draw a whole bunch of these cubes fitted together like a puzzle with no spaces in between, creating the visual effect of a wall of cubes. That's the purpose of the program CUBES.C in Program 13.6.

Program 13.6 **Drawing a Wall of Cubes**

```
/* CUBES.C: A wall of cubes */

#include <graphics.h>
#include <conio.h>
#define   VERTICES 15

int cube [VERTICES][2] = {
    { 0, 60},
    { 0, 20},
    {40,  0},
    {40, 40},
    { 0, 60},

    { 0, 60},            /* cube 2 */
    {40, 40},
    {90, 40},
    {50, 60},
```

Program 13.6 **(continued)**

```
    { 0, 60},

    {40, 40},                    /* cube 3 */
    {40,  0},
    {90,  0},
    {90, 40},
    {40, 40}
};

/* PROTOTYPE */
void showCube (int, int);
/* ------------------------ */

void main()
{
int  driver = EGA, mode = EGAHI, nc, nr, c = 0, r = 0,
     baseX = 0, baseY = -20;

   initgraph (&driver, &mode, "");
   if (graphresult () == grOk) {
     setlinestyle (SOLID_LINE, 0, NORM_WIDTH);
     setcolor (WHITE);

     c = baseX;
     r = baseY;
     for (nr = 0; nr < 10; nr++) {
       for (nc = 0; nc < 13; nc++) {
         showCube (c, r);
         c += 90;
         r -= 20;
       }
       baseX -= 40;
       baseY += 60;
       c = baseX;
       r = baseY;
     }

     getch ();
     closegraph ();
   }
} /* ----------------------- */

void showCube (int cofs, int rofs)
{
int i, temp [VERTICES][2];

   for (i = 0; i < VERTICES; i++) {
     temp [i][0] = cube [i][0] + cofs;
     temp [i][1] = cube [i][1] + rofs;
   }

   setfillstyle (SOLID_FILL, LIGHTCYAN);
```

Program 13.6 **(continued)**

```
fillpoly (5, (int far*) temp [0]);

setfillstyle (SOLID_FILL, LIGHTBLUE);
fillpoly (5, (int far*) temp [5]);

setfillstyle (SOLID_FILL, CYAN);
fillpoly (5, (int far*) temp [10]);
}
```

The cube array at the top of the program defines the vertices of the three figures comprising the cube. Note that each figure is closed; that is, its last point coincides with its first. The **showCube()** function draws the figures with three calls to **fillpoly()**. A call to **setfillstyle()** precedes each **fillpoly()** in order to set the facet's fill color.

The nested loops in **main()** control the placement of successive cubes. There are two sets of control values. BaseX and baseY define the position of the first cube in a row, while c and r govern the locations of the row's subsequent cubes. As a row grows, the shape and dimensions of the figures require that each cube be 90 units to the right and 20 above its predecessor (this program uses device coordinates). Consequently the row slants upward. The next row's first cube needs to be 40 units to the left and 60 below the starting cube of the previous row, hence the updates to baseX and baseY in the outer loop. The loops draw more cubes than the screen can contain, so many are not visible. This is necessary because the rows slant upwards while the initial cubes for each row stairstep down and to the left. The program has to draw enough cubes to fill the entire viewing area of the display.

Each call to **showCube()** passes the column and row offsets for the cube to be drawn. The loop in **showCube()** then adds these values to the X and Y coordinates of each vertex in the cube array, storing the results in the **temp** array. Thus, **temp** contains the actual device coordinates for the current figure, and those are the array elements passed to **fillpoly()**.

Capturing and Restoring Graphics Images

The Turbo C graphics library furnishes a set of routines for making and reproducing "snapshots" of the screen or a portion thereof: **imagesize()**, **getimage()**, and **putimage()**. Like real-life snapshots, these images are rectangular. The **imagesize()** function tells how many bytes of memory are needed to hold the image within an area delineated by the northwest and southeast corners. **getimage()** copies a portion of the screen to a memory buffer, and **putimage()** writes a buffered image anywhere on the display. The latter two routines are thus the graphics counterparts to **gettext()** and **puttext()**, except that they require far pointers to the save buffer. Graphics literature often refers to the **getimage()** and **putimage()** operations as "bitblt" (pronounced bit blit), meaning a high-speed bit-image transfer.

Use **imagesize()** to determine the amount of space needed to contain an image you want to capture. It takes into account the video mode (different modes use varying numbers of bits per pixel) when calculating the space requirement, and returns that value. You can then use it to allocate space on the heap with **farmalloc()**. Example:

```
nbytes = imagesize (left, top, right, bottom);
buffer = (unsigned far*) farmalloc ((long) nbytes);
```

(where buffer is declared as unsigned far *buffer).

Having allocated a heap buffer of the appropriate size, you can save the image with

```
getimage (left, top, right, bottom, buffer);
```

To copy the image to a new location on the screen, write

```
putimage (newleft, newtop, buffer);
```

If you have no further use for the image, release the buffer space from the heap with

```
farfree (buffer);
```

Bitblts are useful for replicating a rectangular image many times. The program DIAMONDS.C in Program 13.7 illustrates this. It draws a four-color diamond inside a white-line square at the upper-left corner of the display, then waits for a keypress. When you hit any key, the program copies the diamond to successive locations until the diamonds fill the screen in a linoleum pattern. The display freezes until you press another key to end the program.

Program 13.7 Using Bitblts to Replicate an Image

```
/* DIAMONDS.C: Demonstrates getimage/putimage */

#include <graphics.h>
#include <conio.h>
#include <alloc.h>

#define MAXX    62
#define MAXY    48
#define HALFX   MAXX / 2
#define HALFY   MAXY / 2
```

Program 13.7 **(continued)**

```
void main ()
{
int  driver = EGA, mode = EGAHI, size, x, y;
unsigned far *image;
void makeFigure (void);

   initgraph (&driver, &mode, "");        /* open graphics */
   if (graphresult () == grOk) {
     makeFigure ();                       /* draw basic figure */
     getch ();                                         /* wait */

     size = imagesize (0, 0, MAXX, MAXY);     /* get size */
     image = (unsigned far*) farmalloc        /* get space */
            ((long) size);
     getimage (0, 0, MAXX, MAXY, image);      /* save image */

     /* copy image to fill screen */
     for (y = 0; y < 330; y += MAXY)
       for (x = 0; x < 640; x += MAXX)
         putimage (x, y, image, COPY_PUT);

     getch ();
     farfree (image);
     closegraph ();
   }
} /* ---------------------- */

void makeFigure (void)
{
   setlinestyle (SOLID_LINE, 0, NORM_WIDTH);
   rectangle (0, 0, MAXX, MAXY);
   moveto ( HALFX,      0);
   linerel (-HALFX, HALFY);
   linerel ( HALFX, HALFY);
   linerel ( HALFX,-HALFY);
   linerel (-HALFX,-HALFY);
   linerel (  0, MAXY);
   line    (  0, HALFY, MAXX, HALFY);

   setfillstyle (SOLID_FILL, YELLOW);
   floodfill (HALFX-1, HALFY+1, WHITE);

   setfillstyle (SOLID_FILL, GREEN);
   floodfill (HALFX+1, HALFY+1, WHITE);

   setfillstyle (SOLID_FILL, BLUE);
   floodfill (HALFX+1, HALFY-1, WHITE);

   setfillstyle (SOLID_FILL, RED);
   floodfill (HALFX-1, HALFY-1, WHITE);
} /* ---------------------- */
```

Note that over half the code in this program creates the image. It takes only six lines—the capture the copy loop—to save it and write it back out to numerous locations.

Using Multiple Display Pages

Four of the standard Turbo C graphics drivers support multiple display pages. These are the drivers identified as EGA, EGAMONO, HERCMONO, and VGA. HERCMONO supports two pages, and the others four.

When an adapter furnishes more than one page, you can select which one is visible and which is active. The active page is the one to which the graphics output routines write. The implication is that you can construct an image "behind the scenes," on a page that is not currently visible.

For example, you might issue the following instructions:

```
setvisualpage (0);
setactivepage (1);
```

Thereafter, all graphics calls (**bar()**, **circle()**, **line()**, **floodfill()**, and so on) write to page 1 as the user looks at page 0. When the new image is finished, show it to the user with

```
setvisualpage (1);
```

This causes an instantaneous switch of display memories; the new screen appears at the speed of the screen refresh, which occurs too rapidly for the eye to detect. The effect is magical to the viewer.

Multiple pages open a number of possibilities. For example, you can build different pictures, text/graphics screens, or business graphs in separate pages and toggle among them with a keypress or other signal. As the next section illustrates, multiple pages also have important implications for animation effects.

Animation

The combination of **get/putimage()** and multiple display pages opens the way to limited animation effects: "limited" because the IBM PC isn't as good for arcade-style graphics as some other computers. Still, you can use them to create some interesting visual effects.

The secret is in having two pages with identical backdrops. One is always active and the other visible. While the viewer looks at the visual page, erase the moving object's image from the active page and place the image at its new location. Then switch pages and repeat.

Program 13.8 illustrates simple animation with a truck that drives along a country road, crossing the screen from right to left; that's why it's called TRUCK.C. This program works with the virtual coordinates developed in the last chapter. It will only run with an EGA or VGA adapter attached to a color monitor, since it uses two display pages.

The program first draws an identical backdrop in pages 0 and 1. Page 0 is still visible after page 1 is set up, so the program constructs the truck image out of sight in page 1 Two images are actually required. The blank image is the area under the truck; it's used to "erase" the truck image. Note that both captured images extend a few pixels to the right of the truck's actual dimensions. This ensures that, as the image position moves left, all of the remainder behind it gets erased.

Once the truck is captured with **getimage()** and erased by overlaying it with the blank, the program begins the animation. It does this with a loop. The loop is controlled by the variable p, which decrements from right to left and determines the placement of the images. In the first iteration, page 1 is active and page 0 is visible. After the image is blanked and the truck is copied to it, the pages exchange places and the process repeats with page 0 active and page 1 visible. This goes on until the truck's nose reaches the left border of the screen.

At the conclusion of the journey, the program releases the image spaces from the heap with a pair of **farfree()** calls, restores the system to text mode, and quits.

Program 13.8 Simple Animation with Multiple Display Pages

```
/* TRUCK.C: Animation using a truck */

#include <graphics.h>
#include "vcoords.h"
#include <conio.h>
#include <alloc.h>

void drawBackground (void);
void drawTruck (void);

void main ()
{
int      p, driver = EGA, mode = EGAHI,
         active = 1, visual = 0;
unsigned size;
void far *truck, far *blank;

   initgraph (&driver, &mode, "");
   if (graphresult() == grOk) {
     setFactors ();           /* initialize virtual coords */
```

Program 13.8 **(continued)**

```c
    if ((driver == EGA) || (driver == VGA)) {   /* can run */

     /* Set up basic screen in pages 0 and 1 */
     for (p = 0; p < 2; p++) {
        setactivepage (p);                      /* page for output */
        drawBackground ();                       /* create basic screen */
     }

     /* Do the rest of the setup out of sight on page 1 */
     /* Get the background without the truck */
     size = imagesize (dx (400), dy (320),
                       dx (510), dy (260));
     blank = (void far*) farmalloc             /* get space */
             ((long) size);
     getimage (dx (400), dy (320),             /* capture */
              dx (510), dy (260), blank);

     /* Draw and capture truck image */
     drawTruck ();                             /* draw the truck */
     truck = (void far*) farmalloc             /* get space */
             ((long) size);
     getimage (dx (400), dy (320),             /* capture image */
              dx (510), dy (260), truck);

     /* Erase truck image from page 1 */
     putimage (dx (400), dy (320), blank, COPY_PUT);

     /* Move truck across screen */
     /* (At entry, page 1 is active, page 0 is visual) */
     for (p = 700; p > 0; p -= 4) {
        putimage (dx (p), dy (320),    /* clear image area */
                 blank, COPY_PUT);
        putimage (dx (p), dy (320),    /* copy truck image */
                 truck, COPY_PUT);
        active = (active == 1) ? 0 : 1;   /* switch pages */
        visual = (active == 1) ? 0 : 1;
        setvisualpage (visual);
        setactivepage (active);
     }
     farfree (truck);
     farfree (blank);
     closegraph ();
    } else {                          /* if neither EGA nor VGA */
     closegraph ();
     cprintf ("Unable to run: Single-page adapter");
    }
  }
} /* ---------------------- */

void drawBackground (void)

     /* Set up background for animation */

{
```

Program 13.8 **(continued)**

```
    setbkcolor (GREEN);                        /* green foreground */
    setcolor (LIGHTBLUE);
    setfillstyle (SOLID_FILL, LIGHTBLUE);
    rectangle (0, dy (600), dx (800), dy (400));
    floodfill (dx (400), dy (500), LIGHTBLUE);   /* blue sky */

    setcolor (BROWN);
    setfillstyle (SOLID_FILL, BROWN);
    rectangle (0, dy (300), dx (800), dy (250));
    floodfill (dx (400), dy (275), BROWN);     /* brown road */
} /* ----------------------- */

void drawTruck (void)

        /* Draw the truck image */
{
    setcolor (LIGHTGRAY);                       /* box */
    setfillstyle (SOLID_FILL, LIGHTGRAY);
    rectangle (dx (440), dy (315), dx (500), dy (280));
    floodfill (dx (480), dy (300), LIGHTGRAY);

    setcolor (RED);                             /* cab */
    setfillstyle (SOLID_FILL, RED);
    rectangle (dx (400), dy (295), dx (439), dy (280));
    floodfill (dx (420), dy (290), RED);
    line (dx (420), dy (295), dx (420), dy (305));
    line (dx (420), dy (305), dx (439), dy (305));
    line (dx (439), dy (305), dx (439), dy (295));

    setcolor (DARKGRAY);                        /* wheels */
    setfillstyle (SOLID_FILL, DARKGRAY);
    circle (dx (410), dy (280), dx (10));
    floodfill (dx (410), dy (280), DARKGRAY);
    circle (dx (480), dy (280), dx (10));
    floodfill (dx (480), dy (280), DARKGRAY);
} /* ----------------------- */
```

Viewports

Turbo C furnishes an analog to text windows that is called, in graphics, a viewport. They're similar in that they both define a subset of the screen in which the origin is at the upper-left corner. In text, the coordinates of the origin are {1, 1} and in graphics, {0, 0}. When both are created, the cursor (text or graphics as appropriate) moves to the origin.

A viewport differs from a text window, of course, by being a graphics area. There is one other difference as well: clipping. In a text window, the edges are barriers beyond which the cursor cannot move. This might or might not be true of a graphics viewport depending on how you set it up.

Clipping means that the cursor stops drawing when it reaches a viewport edge. It may move beyond the edge, but the results aren't visible. The same is true of fills; they go only to the edge of the clipped viewport and not beyond. On the other hand, if you specify no clipping when you open a viewport, then the results of graphics operations outside the viewport *are* visible.

You specify which type you want with the clipflag argument to the **set-viewport()** function. A zero value (logical FALSE) turns clipping off, and a nonzero (TRUE) value turns it on.

The VIEWSTAR.C program in Program 13.9 illustrates both clipped and unclipped viewports. The program labels and opens two viewports, drawing a star enclosed by a pentagon in each. The viewport on the left is clipped, so that the figure (which is too wide to fit in either viewport) gets truncated at the right edge. The right-hand viewport, on the other hand, doesn't have clipping, so the figure continues outside its boundaries.

Program 13.9 Clipped and Unclipped Viewports

```
/* VIEWSTAR.C: Writes stars into viewports */

#include <graphics.h>
#include <conio.h>

/* Clipping flags */
#define   NOCLIP 0
#define   CLIP   !NOCLIP

/* Star figure */
int star [][2] = {
    {30, 120}, {130, 120}, {160, 50}, {80, 0}, {0, 50}
};

/* Prototypes */
void drawStar (void);
void label (void);
void clippedPort (void);
void unclippedPort (void);

/* ------------------------------------------------------- */

void main ()
{
int  driver = EGA, mode = EGAHI;

  initgraph (&driver, &mode, "");
  if(graphresult () == grOk) {
    label ();
    clippedPort ();
    unclippedPort ();
    getch ();
    closegraph ();
  }
```

Program 13.9 (continued)

```
} /* ----------------------- */

void drawStar (void)

    /* draw pantagon enclosing star */
{
int  pivot, vert;

  for (pivot = 0; pivot < 5; pivot++)
    for (vert = 0; vert < 5; vert++)
      line (star [pivot][0], star [pivot][1],
            star [vert][0], star [vert][1]);
} /* ----------------------- */

void label (void)

    /* label the display elements */
{

  /* Top first */
  settextstyle (TRIPLEX_FONT, HORIZ_DIR, 4);
  settextjustify (CENTER_TEXT, CENTER_TEXT);
  outtextxy (getmaxx () / 2, 20, "Viewports");

  /* Viewports */
  settextstyle (DEFAULT_FONT, HORIZ_DIR, 1);
  outtextxy (170, 100, "Clipped");
  outtextxy (440, 100, "Not clipped");
} /* ----------------------- */

void clippedPort (void)

    /* Create clipped viewport */
{
  rectangle (99, 119, 241, 241);                   /* outline */
  setviewport (100, 120, 240, 240, CLIP);       /* viewport */
  setcolor (GREEN);                            /* green star */
  drawStar ();                                     /* draw it */
  setviewport (0, 0, getmaxx (),    /* revert to full scrn */
            getmaxy (), CLIP);
  setcolor (WHITE);                              /* and white */
} /* ----------------------- */

void unclippedPort (void)

    /* Create unclipped viewport */
{
  rectangle (369, 119, 511, 241);
  setviewport (370, 120, 510, 240, NOCLIP);
  setcolor (RED);
  drawStar ();
  setviewport (0, 0, getmaxx (), getmaxy (), CLIP);
} /* ----------------------- */
```

In text modes, clrscr() is a catch-all function that clears the current window. Graphics modes provide two different clearing functions: cleardevice() clears the entire graphics screen without leaving the current mode, while clearviewport() clears only the active viewport. Thus, if you open a viewport and want to get rid of any underlying graphics, issue the clearviewport() statement.

cleardevice() wipes the entire display clean without affecting any other settings. The current color remains in effect, and so does the current viewport. If you have a viewport active and issue cleardevice(), the screen blanks, but the next graphics output is relative to the viewport's origin and in the color most recently specified by setcolor().

Graphics provides the function getviewsettings(), which is a parallel to gettextinfo(). It fills in a variable of struct viewporttype with information about the active viewport. See the manual for further details.

More on Drawing Polygons

The star array in VIEWSTAR.C (Program 13.9) shows a brute-force way to define a polygon: specify the vertices directly. This method obviously works, since we got stars in the resulting display. However, it lacks not only elegance, but flexibility. The specification of the vertices also incorporates a phenomenon called *aspect ratio*. There's a better way to compute closed polygons.

About Aspect Ratio

Most displays exhibit a vertical distortion caused by nonsquare pixels. This distortion is *aspect ratio*. The virtual coordinates developed in the last chapter and used in this one as well are one way to deal with the aspect ratio. These virtual coordinates establish an artificial display area whose height is 75 percent of its width.

Another way of handling the aspect ratio is to factor it into calculations involving Y coordinates. The aspect ratio is computed as

pixel width / pixel height

The resulting value is a floating-point number representing the amount of vertical correction necessary to make squares square, circles round, and so on. In other words, when applied to any vertical measurement (Y value), the aspect ratio removes the distortion.

Turbo C provides the function getaspectratio(), which by indirection returns two values representing the physical width and height of a pixel. The setup for this function is rather clumsy, because you have to pass far pointers to two integers. Example:

```
void main ()
{
int far *xa, far *ya, xasp, yasp;
double ratio;

   xa = &xasp, ya = &yasp;
   getaspectratio (xa, ya);
   ratio = (double) xasp / (double) yasp;
   . . .
}
```

The values **xasp** and **yasp** are normalized to 10,000. That's always the value returned for **yasp**, while **xasp** is always less than 10,000. For the EGA in 640 × 350 graphics mode, **xasp** is 7,750. The aspect ratio is thus 0.775: in other words, we have to take 77.5 percent of vertical measurements in order to square them with horizontal distances and remove distortion.

Now let's see how this applies to polygons.

Computing Regular Polygons

The vertices of a regular closed polygon are simply points spaced at even intervals around an imaginary circle. The outline of the polygon is obtained by joining these points, as in a square or a hexagon.

All vertices are equidistant from the center of the circle they lay on. In fact, if you create a polygon with a great many vertices, it will approximate a circle. It's valid to describe a true circle as a polygon with infinitely many vertices. Consequently, the trigonometry of circles is useful for creating polygons.

The distance from the center to the edge of the circle is its radius, or r. The angle to the point is customarily represented by the Greek letter theta. Thus, if the origin is at coordinates {0, 0}, the coordinates for a point r units away at angle i are found as follows:

$$x = r \cos theta$$
$$y = r \sin theta$$

Suppose you want to define a hexagon. The number of sides is six, so the arc for each vertex is 360/6 = 60 degrees. The successive values of theta are thus 0, 60, 120, . . . , 360. However, computer graphics throws in a couple of small complications.

The first is that the sin() and cos() functions don't work with degrees, but instead with radians. *Radians* is a measure of angular motion based on pi (3.1415927). A full circle is 360 degrees, or 2*pi radians. Therefore a half circle is pi radians, and the number of radians per degree is pi/180.0 = 0.0174532. If we call this value RAD, we can convert degrees of i into equivalent radians with

    radians = degrees * RAD;

At this point, then, the coordinates are derived from

    x = r cos (radians)
    y = r sin (radians)

But we're not done yet. The assumed center is at {0, 0}, which is fine for computation but no good for graphics. Why? Because it's at the upper-left corner of the screen, so all we can actually see of the plotted polygon is its southeast corner. We have to offset the resulting coordinates to some useful location on the display. Let's call this point {CX, CY}, which can be any arbitrary place. If we want to place the polygon in the center of the EGA screen, the offsetting coordinate pair is {320, 175}. Consequently, the coordinates are now found with

    x = CX + (r cos [radians])
    y = CY + (r sin [radians])

Finally, we need to adjust for aspect ratio. Assuming that this has already been calculated and the result placed in a floating-point value called *aspect*, we can compute the Y coordinate as

    y = CY + (r sin [radians] * aspect)

This sequence of events, if placed within a loop, calculates a regular polygon. But there's one further hitch: if you start at zero degrees, the apex of the polygon (its "top") will always be at the three o'clock position with respect to the center. This produces silly-looking figures that have an odd number of sides; a pentagon, for example, is precariously balanced on its apparent right point, and has no discernible base. Since the Y coordinate system of the display is upside down, the points rotate clockwise, which is opposite to the direction of conventional geometry. Therefore, to produce proper-looking upright polygons, start at 270 degrees.

If you want to create a polygon of n vertices that can be drawn with the Turbo C drawpoly() function, allocate a two-dimensional array of n + 1 points and load it with the following procedure:

```
int v [16][2], a;
double angle = 270.0, interval, radians;

  interval = 360.0 / sides;
  for (a = 0; a <= sides; a++) {
    radians = angle * RAD;
    v [a][0] = CX + (int)(r * cos (radians));
    v [a][1] = CY + (int)(r * sin (radians) * aspect);
    angle += interval;
  }
  drawpoly (sides, v);
  . . .      /* etc. */
```

Note that the terminating condition of the loop is $a <=$ sides. It's different if you want to draw a polygon with all points joined, as in the star from Program 13.9. In that case the terminating condition is $a <$ sides. You can see why by inspecting the **drawStar()** routine in VIEWSTAR or the final loop in the **draw()** function in Program 13.10. The pivot value in these loops is one of the vertices from 0 to sides – 1, while the nested loop draws lines from every other point (including itself) to the pivot. This joins all points, so that the n + 1 vertex isn't required.

Demonstration

Program 13.10 puts this discussion of regular polygons into practice. POLYGONS.C draws a series of jewel-like polygons having 4 to 15 sides into 12 viewports. It joins all vertices in each polygon, with the color of the polygon and its viewport outline derived from the number of sides. The workings of this program should be clear from the preceding discussion and the comments.

Program 13.10 Drawing Regular Polygons

```
/* POLYGONS.C: Draws polygons from 4 to 15 sides */

#include <graphics.h>
#include <math.h>
#include <conio.h>
#include <stdio.h>

#define CX     80                        /* center X, Y */
#define CY     73
#define RAD    0.0174532         /* radians per degree */
#define RADIUS 50

void viewport (int, int, int);
```

Program 13.10 **(continued)**

```c
void draw (int);

void main ()
{
int   driver = EGA, mode = EGAHI, sides = 4, r, c, x, y;

   initgraph (&driver, &mode, "");
   if (graphresult () == grOk) {
     settextjustify (CENTER_TEXT, CENTER_TEXT);
     for (r = 0; r < 3; r++) {
       y = r * 116;
       for (c = 0; c < 4; c++) {
         x = c * 159;
         viewport (x, y, sides);
         draw (sides);
         ++sides;
       }
     }
   }
   getch ();
   closegraph ();
} /* ----------------------- */

void viewport (int x, int y, int sides)

     /* Open viewport, outline it */
{
char number [3];

   setviewport (x, y, x + 159, y + 116, 1);
   setcolor (sides - 1);
   linerel (   0, 114);
   linerel ( 157,   0);
   linerel (   0,-114);
   linerel (-157,   0);
   sprintf (number, "%d", sides);
   outtextxy (79, 10, number);
} /* ----------------------- */

void draw (int sides)

     /* Draw a polygon with all points joined */
{
int    color, v [16][2], a, p, xasp, yasp,
       far *xa, far *ya;
double angle = 270.0, interval, radians, aspect;

   xa = &xasp, ya = &yasp;
   getaspectratio (xa, ya);        /* aspect ratio of display */
   aspect = (double) xasp / (double) yasp;

   color = sides - 1;                      /* color of this figure */
   setcolor (color);
```

Program 13.10 **(continued)**

```
interval = 360.0 / sides;

for (a = 0; a < sides; a++) {        /* compute vertices */
    radians = angle * RAD;                    /* in radians */
    v [a][0] = CX + (int)(RADIUS * cos (radians));
    v [a][1] = CY + (int)(RADIUS * sin (radians) * aspect);
    angle += interval;                       /* next angle */
}

for (p = 0; p < sides; p++)           /* join all vertices */
    for (a = 0; a < sides; a++)
        line (v [p][0], v [p][1], v [a][0], v [a][1]);
} /* ------------------------ */
```

This chapter has by no means exhausted the rich potential of the Turbo C graphics library for drawing fascinating visual objects, but it has developed a sound basis for your further experiments.

Now let's move on to a method of drawing complex curves.

CHAPTER **14**

DRAWING CURVES

One of the classic difficulties in graphics programming is representing curves. Examples are curlicues, handwriting, and the shapes of real-world objects with curved surfaces. This chapter presents one of the most practical solutions—the Bezier method—which enables you to express a complex curve in terms of a few points.

The method takes its name from its inventor, P.E. Bezier (pronounced "bay-zee-AY"), a mathematician working for Renault in France, who developed it in the early 1970s. It's one of a group of mathematical curios called cubic splines, all of which have the same general objective of describing curves. The Bezier proposition is that a polygon can approximate a curve, which wends its way among the vertices like the Voyager spacecraft navigating among the outer planets. If the polygon closes back to its origin, the curve is also closed, such as a circle or an ellipse. An open polygon, on the other hand, describes a curve with two end points. The curve only touches the end points, with the other vertices exerting an influence over its path. Figure 14.1 shows a Bezier curve.

Figure 14.1 **Bezier Curve Formed by the CURVE.C Program in Program 14.3**

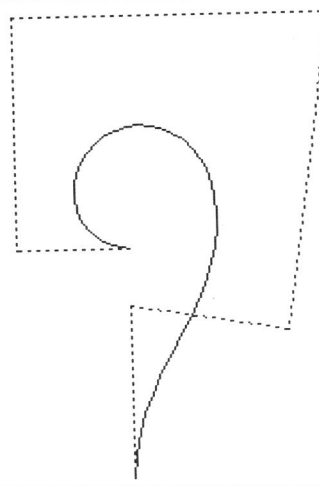

How a Bezier Curve Works_____

A science fiction analogy helps explain how a Bezier curve works. Suppose a spacecraft is moving from one galaxy to another. As it travels, it encounters other celestial bodies whose gravity pulls it away from a straight line. All the objects in the universe influence its path to some extent, but the nearest ones have the most effect. When it finally arrives at its destination, the spaceship's track will have described a complex, constantly varying curve.

In the course of the journey, the craft's position at any instant is represented by two kinds of information. One is its coordinates, which are x, y, and z (for horizontal, vertical, and depth, respectively) and give its absolute location with respect to some point. The other is a value called u in the calculations in Program 14.1. This is a relative indicator ranging from 0 to 1, representing the percentage of the total distance that the craft has to travel from start to finish. When u = 0.0, the craft hasn't left yet; when u = 1.0, it's arrived; and when u = 0.5, it's halfway there. Thus, if you were the navigator, you could determine your position at any time by deriving the coordinates from u, which is, in effect, the controlling variable of the voyage. Bezier furnishes a formula for doing this.

Calculus 101 _____

Unfortunately, no one has yet come up with a way to do more than the most primitive graphics without resorting to heavy math, and Bezier curves are no exception. The Bezier equation for a curve is

$$P(u) = \sum_{i=0}^{n} p_i \, B_{i,n}(u)$$

In other words, for any point u, the location is the sum of $n + 1$ control-point factors proceeding from point 0. This factor is a blending function

$$B_{i,n}(u) = C(n,i) \, u^i \, (1 - u)^{n-i}$$

which in turn is derived from the binomial coefficient

$$C(n,i) = n!/(i!(n-i)!)$$

So much for the equations. Now let's talk about what they do.

The blending function is where the real work of the Bezier method gets done. It calculates a "gravity factor" for each control point relative to the current u. The closer a control point, the more "gravity" it has and thus the more it influences the outcome, which is the coordinates. When u = 0, the metaphorical spacecraft is still at the point of origin, or p[0], and no other points have any say-so about its position. As it leaves the origin, p[1] begins to pull it. Halfway between p[0] and p[1], both points have the same influence. However, p[2] also attracts the craft enough to pull it away from a straight line between p[0] and p[1], and other points beyond p[2] also draw it in diminishing proportion to their distance. As it approaches the end point, there is nothing beyond to draw it away, and so it arrives.

The blending function is merely a mathematical statement of this effect. For each control point, it returns a fractional value by which the coordinates of that control point are multiplied. The sums of these x, y, and z products are the coordinates of the position at u.

And by drawing lines between successive us, we make a map of the route, which is the Bezier curve based on the control point layout.

Hulls

The power of Bezier curves lies in their ability to represent a complex curve with a few points expressed in coordinates. The simplest curve is described by three points: the origin, the destination, and one intermediate vertex. The outcome in this case is a smooth arc from origin to destination, tending toward the intermediate point.

More interesting curves result from several points laid out in an order that very roughly approximates the desired trajectory, as in Figure 14.1. That curve derives from seven control points. The straight lines join the points in order, forming an open polygon, or *hull* as it's often called. Normally, of course, you wouldn't draw the hull itself, since the object of the game is the curve. However, we show the hull here so that you can see how it provides an intuitive notion of the curve's shape.

Bezier curves are insensitive to orientation. It happens that in Figure 14.1, the origin is at the center of the curl and the destination at the far right. However, if we had specified the control points in the opposite order, exactly the same curve would have resulted.

As mentioned earlier, a hull can be closed, producing a circle or something like it. Figure 14.2 illustrates a closed Bezier curve. The hull has six control points. The four corners are obvious. Less so are the origin and destination, which are coincident at bottom center where the circle and hull meet. If you pulled one of the corners of the hull out or pushed it in, the Bezier curve would form a misshapen circle.

Figure 14.2 **A Closed Bezier Curve**

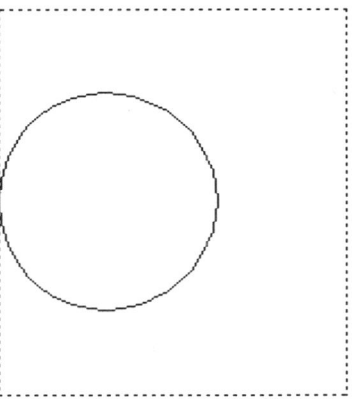

Implementing the Bezier Algorithm

Programs 14.1 and 14.2 are the header and source files for a library that partially implements the Bezier algorithm, "partially" because, although the Bezier algorithm can create three-dimensional curves, the method given here only works in two dimensions. The reason is that 3D graphics is a subject for a thick book beyond the scope of this one. If you want to learn more, see *Principles of Interactive Computer Graphics* by W. Newman and R. Sproull (New York: McGraw-Hill, 1979). The Bezier algorithm in Program 14.2 is based in part on Newman and Sproull, pages 315–319, who provide lucid explanations and Pascal listings for some of the more opaque concepts of this dense topic.

Program 14.1 **Bezier Library Header File**

```
/* BEZIER.H: Prototypes for drawing Bezier curves in 2D */

/* Return coordinates for current 'u' */
void bezierFcn (double *x, double *y, double u,
               double  coeff[], int n, int p[][2]);

/* Draw a Bezier curve */
void drawBezier (int p[][2], int npts, int segments);
```

Program 14.2 **Bezier Library Source Listing**

```c
/* BEZIER.C: Functions for drawing Bezier curves in 2D    */
/*    Assumes display is in graphics mode via a .BGI file */
/* ----------------------------------------------------- */

double fact (int q)

      /* Return q factorial */
{
int    f = 1, c;

  for (c = q; c > 1; c--)
    f *= c;
  return (f);
} /* ---------------------- */

double c (int n, int i)

      /* Binomial coefficient used in blending function */
{
  return (fact (n) / (fact (i) * fact (n - i)));
} /* ---------------------- */

double blend (int i, int n, double u, double binomial)

      /* Bernstein blending function */
{
double partial;
int    j;

  partial = binomial;
  for (j = 1; j <= i; j++)
    partial = partial * u;
  for (j = 1; j <= (n - i); j++)
    partial = partial * (1.0 - u);
  return (partial);
} /* ---------------------- */

void bezierFcn (double *x, double *y, double u,
                double  coeff[], int n, int p[][2])

      /* Return coordinates for current 'u' */
{
int    i;
double b;

  *x = *y = 0;
  for (i = 0; i <= n; i++) ¼
    b = blend (i, n, u, coeff [i]);
    *x = *x + (b * p [i][0]);
    *y = *y + (b * p [i][1]);
```

Program 14.2 **(continued)**

```
  }
} /* ----------------------- */

void drawBezier (int p[][2], int npts, int segments)

     /* Draw a Bezier curve */
{
int    i, oldx, oldy;
double u, x, y;
double coeff [20];   /* should be big enough for any curve */

  for (i = 0; i < npts; i++)    /* compute binomial coeffs */
    coeff [i] = c (npts-1, i);
  for (i = 0; i <= segments; i++) {
    u = (double) i / segments;
    bezierFcn (&x, &y, u, coeff, npts-1, p);
    if (i == 0)
      oldx = x, oldy = y;
    else {
      line (oldx, oldy, (int) x, (int) y);
      oldx = x, oldy = y;
    }
  }
} /* ----------------------- */
```

The segments argument passed to **drawBezier()** is the basis for u in the calculations. It defines how many line segments make up the complete curve. The **drawBezier()** function controls curve-drawing with the loop

```
for (i = 0; i <= segments; i++) { . . .
```

and calculates u as i / segments. Therefore $0.0 \leqslant u \leqslant 1.0$, representing a percentage of the complete transit from origin to destination.

Three of the five subroutines in BEZIER.C are directly useful to application programs. The **drawBezier()** function is probably the only one you'll ever call, but it's conceivable that you might want to call **bezierFcn()** for purposes such as marking points on the curve—say every 10 percent of its length, or its midpoint. Given the desired point in terms of u, **bezierFcn()** will return the coordinates. The other one, **fact()**, is a general mathematical function that returns the factorial of an integer.

Putting It to Work

You've already seen the output from the demonstration program Program 14.3, CURVE.C. It's the curlicue shown in Figure 14.1. This program uses the Bezier library to draw the curve in a virtual coordinate space.

Program 14.3 **A Program to Draw a Bezier Curve**

```c
/* CURVE.C: Draws a Bezier curve and its hull */

#include <graphics.h>
#include <conio.h>
#include "vcoords.h"
#include "bezier.h"

#define NPOINTS 7

int pt[][2] = {
    {400, 270},
    {400, 120},
    {100, 120},
    {100, 540},
    {510, 480},
    {475, 270},
    {700, 270}
};

void main ()
{
int driver = DETECT, mode, n;

  /* Set up screen in graphics mode, virtual coords */
  initgraph (&driver, &mode, "");
  if (graphresult () == grOk) {
    setFactors ();

    /* Convert virtual coords in vector array to device */
    for (n = 0; n < NPOINTS; n++) {
      pt [n][0] = dx (pt [n][0]);
      pt [n][1] = dy (pt [n][1]);
    }

    /* Draw the hull outline */
    setlinestyle (DOTTED_LINE, 0, NORM_WIDTH);
    setcolor (2);
    moveto (pt [0][0], pt [0][1]);
    for (n = 1; n < NPOINTS; n++)
      lineto (pt [n][0], pt [n][1]);

    /* Draw the Bezier curve */
    setlinestyle (SOLID_LINE, 0, NORM_WIDTH);
    setcolor (3);
    drawBezier (pt, NPOINTS, 40);

    /* Hold image for keypress, then quit */
    getch ();
    closegraph ();
  } else
      cputs ("Unable to enter graphics mode");
}
```

The program itself is quite simple and self-explanatory. It puts the display adaptor into the best graphics mode available, initializes the virtual coordinate system, and converts the hull array (**pt[]**) into device coordinates. After that it outlines the hull in one color and draws the Bezier curve in another. The program then waits for a keypress and terminates.

Joining Curves _____

The nature of Bezier curves is such that a change in any hull vertex changes the path of the entire curve. If you're working on a complex shape, it's usually easiest to decompose the object into a number of small curves and join them together. That way you can tweak individual parts of the shape without introducing undesired side effects elsewhere.

In order to achieve a smooth joint between curves, there are two rules. First, make the end points of the adjacent curves coincident. That is, one curve ends at exactly the same point that the next begins. The second is to create continuity in the adjoining hulls across the joint.

Say for example that you have two hulls called A and B, and that A, which flows into B, has six control points. To achieve continuity, A[4], A[5] (coincident with B[0]), and B[1] must all lie on the same plane, so that a straight line passes through all of them. The span from A[4] through B[1] should be fairly long, so that the curves have room to sweep gracefully to their coincident end points. This avoids an abrupt kink that would disrupt the flow.

Figure 14.3 **Joining Two Curves** _____

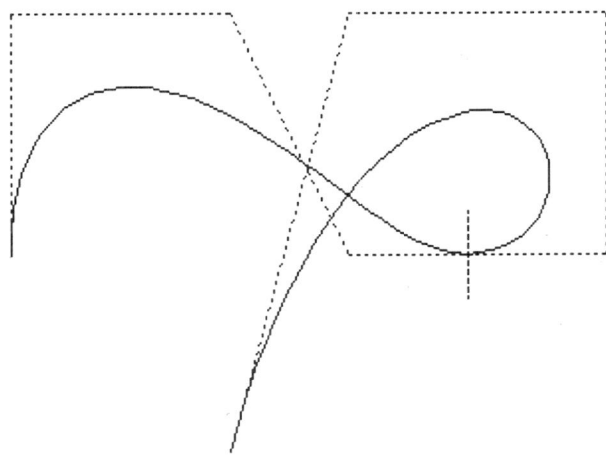

Figure 14.3 illustrates this. Both hulls are outlined in dotted lines. A vertical line marks the joint, which is in the bottom center of the right-hand polygon. Curve A sweeps up from the left side of the screen and down to the end point, where curve B picks up and crosses back over A. If you study and run the TWOCURVS.C program in Program 14.4, you'll see that curve A is drawn in green and curve B in yellow. This is to identify more clearly that you're looking at two curves and where, in their smooth transition, one ends and the next begins.

Program 14.4 **Program to Draw the Adjoining Curves in Figure 14.3**

```
/* TWOCURVS.C: Draws two joined curves on the CGA */

#include <graphics.h>
#include <conio.h>
#include "bezier.h"

#define NPOINTS   5
#define SEGMENTS 40

int a [][2] = {                    /* hull for first curve */
    { 10, 110},
    { 10,   0},
    {120,   0},
    {180, 110},
    {240, 110}
}, b [][2] = {                     /* ... and for second */
    {240, 110},
    {310, 110},
    {310,   0},
    {180,   0},
    {120, 199}
};

void main ()
{
int   driver = CGA, mode = CGAC0, n;

    /* Get into graphics mode */
    initgraph (&driver, &mode, "");
    if (graphresult () == grOk) {

        /* Draw the first hull */
        setlinestyle (DOTTED_LINE, 0, NORM_WIDTH);
        setcolor (1);
        moveto (a [0][0], a [0][1]);
        for (n = 1; n < NPOINTS; n++)
            lineto (a [n][0], a [n][1]);

        /* Mark the joint */
        linerel (0,  20);
        linerel (0, -40);
        linerel (0,  20);
```

Program 14.4 **(continued)**

```
        /* Draw the second hull */
        for (n = 1; n < NPOINTS; n++)
          lineto (b [n][0], b[n][1]);

        /* Draw the first curve */
        setlinestyle (SOLID_LINE, 0, NORM_WIDTH);
        setcolor (2);
        drawBezier (a, NPOINTS, SEGMENTS);

        /* ... and the second */
        setcolor (3);
        drawBezier (b, NPOINTS, SEGMENTS);

        /* Hold for keypress and quit */
        getch ();
        closegraph ();
    } else
        cprintf ("Unable to enter graphics mode");
}
```

Program 14.5 carries the idea of joining curves a little further. The output looks like balloons on a string. Four are above the string and three below. This program actually alternates between two Bezier curves that are identical except for their orientations. Both curves are based on the vertical center of the virtual display, which provides a plane for achieving smooth joints.

As the main loop of the program reiterates, it relocates each curve by calling the **advance()** function, which adds the fixed INTERVAL to the X coordinates. The curves occupy 110 virtual X units along the base plane, so the downward hull is initialized with X values 110 greater than the upward array. Thus, one iteration moves each alternating curve right by 220 virtual X units, which is the value of INTERVAL.

The **fill()** function finds the middle of the closed circular object formed by the Bezier curve. It does this by calculating the X and Y coordinates midway between the second and fourth points, which are opposite corners of the hull defining the curlicue. This point is the origin for a **floodfill()** that gives each "balloon" its color.

Program 14.5 **A Series of Joined Bezier Curves**

```
/* BALLOON.C: Draws balloons with joined Bezier curves */

#include <graphics.h>
#include <conio.h>
#include "bezier.h"
#include "vcoords.h"
```

Program 14.5 **(continued)**

```
#define NPOINTS    6
#define SEGMENTS  30
#define INTERVAL 220

int up [][2] = {                              /* upward balloon */
    {  0, 300}, {140, 300}, {140, 480},
    {-30, 480}, {-30, 300}, {110, 300}
},
    dn [][2] = {                              /* downward balloon */
    {110, 300}, {250, 300}, {250, 120},
    { 80, 120}, { 80, 300}, {220, 300}
};

void main ()
{
int  driver = DETECT, mode, n;
void advance (int m[][2]), fill (int m[][2]);

  initgraph (&driver, &mode, "");
  if (graphresult() == grOk) {
    setFactors();
    setfillstyle (SOLID_FILL, 2);
    setcolor (3);

    /* Convert points to device coords */
    for (n = 0; n < NPOINTS; n++) {
      up [n][0] = dx (up [n][0]);
      up [n][1] = dy (up [n][1]);
      dn [n][0] = dx (dn [n][0]);
      dn [n][1] = dy (dn [n][1]);
    }

    /* Draw first curve */
    drawBezier (up, NPOINTS, SEGMENTS);
    fill (up);
    advance (up);

    /* Draw two more of each curve */
    for (n = 0; n < 3; n++) {
      drawBezier (dn, NPOINTS, SEGMENTS);
      fill (dn);
      advance (dn);
      drawBezier (up, NPOINTS, SEGMENTS);
      fill (up);
      advance (up);
    }

    /* Hold for keypress */
    getch ();
    closegraph ();
  } else
```

Program 14.5 **(continued)**

```
    cputs ("Unable to enter graphics mode");
} /* ------------------------- */

void advance (int m[][2])

    /* Advance the X coords by fixed interval */
{
int   i;

  for (i = 0; i < NPOINTS; i++)
    m [i][0] += dx (INTERVAL);
} /* ------------------------- */

void fill (int m[][2])

    /* Fill each balloon with color */
{
  floodfill ((m [1][0] + m [3][0]) / 2,
             (m [1][1] + m [3][1]) / 2, 3);
}
```

Art with Bezier Curves

Because the Bezier algorithm was developed chiefly to help in the design of automobiles, it lends itself to forms of artistic expression that would otherwise be difficult or impossible with a computer. We live amidst irregular, complex curves, and since art imitates life, the Bezier algorithm gives us a means of replicating the visual world around us.

Figure 14.4 provides an example. It depicts an amphora, a graceful urn shape much in favor in the ancient Mediterranean world and still popular for flower vases. This picture, drawn on an EGA monitor, consists entirely of repetitions of the same basic Bezier curve. The alternating green and blue stripes give a sense of form and depth to the vase, making it appear highly realistic. Although an amphora is itself a complex object, the application of a Bezier curve made the writing of a program to draw it amazingly easy; it took a little over an hour.

The first step was to design the Bezier curve that outlines the right side of the vase. After some experimentation, we arrived at a five-point hull with the following points expressed in virtual coordinates:

100,	500
– 80,	420
220,	300
180,	100
40,	100

Figure 14.4 **A Vase Consisting Entirely of Bezier Curves**

Having designed the curve, it was largely a matter of applying trigonometry, then tweaking the program to improve performance.

The trick in this case is to "rotate" the Bezier hull around a reference point—the horizontal center of the display—redrawing the curve at intervals close enough together to form a solid object. We can do this with trigonometry. If a circle is r units from its center, then the X coordinate where a line at angle theta intersects with it is found by the equation

$$X - r \cos theta$$

The variable r is, of course, the radius of the circle.

And what is the radius in this case? The X coordinate of each hull point. By rotating the hull at degree intervals and recalculating its X's according to the equation, then drawing a Bezier curve based on them, we eventually construct the image of the amphora. Because the center X of the vase is assumed to be 0 (the left edge of the screen), it's necessary to add an offset to each derived X that relocates it somewhere on the display. In this case, we added the physical center of the screen, which is obtained with

$$cx = getmaxx() / 2;$$

after entering graphics mode. You can see how it works in Program 14.6.

Program 14.6 **Program to Draw a Vase with a Bezier Curve**

```c
/* VASE.C: Draws a vase using Bezier curves */

#include <graphics.h>
#include <math.h>
#include <conio.h>
#include "vcoords.h"
#include "bezier.h"

#define NPOINTS   5           /* number of points in hull */
#define SEGMENTS 15           /* segments in Bezier curve */
#define DEG2RAD  M_PI / 180.0     /* degrees to radians */

int ref[][2] = {              /* reference points for curve */
    {100, 500},
    {-80, 420},
    {220, 300},
    {180, 100},
    { 40, 100},
};

void main ()
{
int    driver = DETECT, mode, n, step = 5;
int    pt[5][2], angle, cx, color = 1;
double cosine;

    /* Set up to run */
    initgraph (&driver, &mode, "");
    if (graphresult () == grOk) {
      setFactors ();
      setlinestyle (SOLID_LINE, 0, THICK_WIDTH);
      setcolor (color);
      cx = getmaxx () / 2;   /* vertical centerline of vase */

      /* Widen image if CGA. No change otherwise */
      if (driver == CGA)
        for (n = 0; n < NPOINTS; n++)
          ref [n][0] *= 2;

      /* Convert reference coords to device coords */
      for (n = 0; n < NPOINTS; n++) {
        ref [n][0] = dx (ref [n][0]);
        pt [n][1] = ref [n][1] = dy (ref [n][1]);
      }

      /* Draw the vase as curves radiating around CX */
      for (angle = 0; angle < 90; angle += step) {
        if ((angle % 20) == 0) {   /* flip color each 20 deg */
          color = (color == 1) ? 2 : 1;
          setcolor (color);
          if (angle == 20)          /* speed/fill optimization */
            step = 2;
          if (angle == 60)
```

Program 14.6 **(continued)**

```
        step = 1;
    }
    cosine = cos (DEG2RAD * angle);
    for (n = 0; n < NPOINTS; n++)          /* compute x's */
        pt [n][0] = dx ((int) (cosine * ref [n][0])) + cx;
    drawBezier (pt, NPOINTS, SEGMENTS);  /* right curve */
    for (n = 0; n < NPOINTS; n++)
        pt [n][0] = cx - (pt [n][0] - cx);  /* left shape */
    drawBezier (pt, NPOINTS, SEGMENTS);      /* draw it */
    }

    /* Hold image for keypress, then quit */
    getch ();
    closegraph ();
    } else
        cputs ("Unable to enter graphics mode");
}
```

After observing the program in action, it became obvious that some tweaks were necessary to improve performance and appearance. They occur in the drawing loop. The program flips between colors 1 and 2 every 20 degrees, which was intended from the onset of the design. Two aspects of the algorithm were added later: speed/fill optimization, and the drawing of the inverse curve.

The drawing loop enters the if() statement every 20 degrees, so that's a convenient point to implement other optimizations that would otherwise impede execution. At very low angles—less than 20 degrees—the program proceeded to build the amphora at a finger-drumming rate. So we set the stepping value of the angle at five degrees initially. Beyond 20 degrees, however, a five-degree interval caused gaps in the image because each new Bezier curve passed too far from its predecessor, leaving black streaks on the vase. So we reset the stepping interval to two degrees. The same problem recurred above 60 degrees, resulting in the reduction of the interval to one degree. The consequence of these optimizations is that the program builds a solid amphora at a relatively constant rate.

Originally, also, the program moved through a full 180 degrees. It takes time to transform the hull points with trigonometry, and the right side is the mirror image of the left. Therefore it made sense to simply shift the transformed points from the right side to the left side and redraw the curve. That's the thrust of the loop labeled "left shape."

The result is what you see in Figure 14.4. It still takes a minute or so to draw the complete image on an AT without an 80287 floating-point unit, but this is about a third of the time it took initially.

It's difficult to imagine how one could draw an amphora—or any other such complex object taken from the real world—without Bezier curves.

It usually takes some experimentation to get a curve the way you want it, but the Bezier method gives you a powerful means for describing complex shapes with a few data points that have an intuitive feel about them. Because Bezier curves were developed in response to the need for CAD tools to design cars, they're eminently well suited to computer art, and a fascinating object of study as well.

This concludes our discussion of graphics in Turbo C. So far we've dealt with external programming issues: disks and files in Part I, the user interface in Part II, and graphics in Part III. The next section does an about-face to peer inward at something we can't see, but that is equally as important in building advanced applications: strategies for manipulating large amounts of dynamic data.

PART IV

Dynamic Memory

Many C applications deal with large amounts of data whose format is known in advance but whose quantity is not. Here are a couple of examples:

1. In a windowing environment, it's necessary to save the current screen before writing a new window, so that you can later restore the display to its previous appearance. We saw cases of this in Part II. It's often impossible to predict how many screen images you might have to save when the user is capable of popping up menus, dialog boxes, help panels, and so forth. The problem is solved by building an image stack in dynamic memory.
2. An effective method for gaining instant access to any given record within a file is to index the file on a key value. When you want to fetch a specific record, you look up its key in the index, and an associated field tells you where the record is within the file so that you can use direct access to get to it. It is usually impossible to know in advance how many records a file contains. Therefore a dynamic index structure is appropriate.

There are plenty of other uses for dynamic memory as well. These two examples give a flavor for its importance.

This part of the book begins with a discussion of the concepts and tools for dynamic memory allocation. Chapter 16 covers singly linked lists, which embody many of the basic principles that serve as the foundation for the more complex structures later. Chapter 17 examines doubly linked lists, queues (FIFO structures), stacks (LIFO structures), and circular lists. Chapter 18 looks at binary trees, which offer extremely efficient means for organizing and searching large quantities of data. Finally, Part IV concludes with a discussion of irregular data structures.

These five chapters are not intended as a comprehensive treatment of dynamic data structures, but rather as an introduction to the most common ones. Weighty and learned tomes have been written on the subject. Perhaps the best known, and an excellent resource if you want exhaustive coverage, is *The Art of Computer Programming,* by Donald E. Knuth (Addison-Wesley, 1973). This multivolume series is known among software engineers simply (and affectionately) as Knuth.

Another caveat: Most of the program examples in this book are workaday functions that you can apply directly to your own projects. Those in this part of the book are instead conceptual in nature. This is because operations on linked lists are highly application-dependent; we search on specific criteria, develop structures for defined purposes, and so on. Therefore, you must adapt the concepts to suit your own objectives.

Having said that, let's get on with it.

CHAPTER 15

DYNAMIC ALLOCATION

Dynamic memory is the portion of the computer's memory that belongs to your program, but is not committed to any specific purpose such as code or static data. This uncommitted memory, often called the "heap," is dynamically available because a program can grab and release pieces of it as needed.

DOS itself is memory-resident, and on the IBM PC and compatibles, there are usually other resident programs (TSRs—Terminate and Stay Resident) as well: Sidekick, ProKey, device drivers of one kind and another, and so forth. The running program takes up some additional memory, and it needs a stack for calling subprograms and passing parameters. The sum of committed memory might add up to a couple of hundred K. All the rest (total installed main memory on the machine less committed memory) is available to the program through dynamic allocation. For example:

Total main memory		640K*
Less:		
DOS	35	
TSRs	85	
Running program	56	
Stack segment	64	
Subtotal		240K
Available for dynamic allocation		400K

* Note that expanded/extended memory (EMS) is not included in "main memory" since it takes special techniques to use addresses beyond 640K. Chapter 24 discusses EMS in detail.

In other words, about two-thirds of memory (400/640) is uncommitted in this case and is available to the program as dynamic space. That's a lot of memory that you can use for dynamic data workspace.

The nature of the heap varies according to which of the six Turbo C memory models you use. The models' memory segmentation diagrams appear on pages 349–352 of the *Turbo C 2.0 User's Guide*. Note that the small and medium models each have two, a near and a far heap, between which is the stack. The tiny model has only a near heap, while the three large data models—compact, large, and huge—have only a far heap ("near" and "far" depending on which side of the stack they're on from the viewpoint of the code).

These two heaps are very different. The near heaps available in the small code models should only be used for small amounts of dynamic storage. Why? Because they share a 64K memory segment with the stack. The stack is a constantly changing structure that grows downward from the top of the 64K segment, while dynamic memory grows upward from the bottom of the same segment. It is impossible to predict the size of the stack at any given moment; it grows as functions are called and shrinks when they return. A large amount of dynamic storage and deeply nested calls will result in a collision between the stack and the heap, causing the program to fail.

The far heap, on the other hand, is a stable amount of dynamically available memory that is not shared with anything else. Thus a program using the far heap will only run out of dynamic memory when, indeed, all the space has been used up.

Consequently, for large amounts of dynamic memory, use the far heap. Don't use the tiny model at all unless you have little code, little data, few function calls, and few dynamic memory requirements.

Turbo C offers means for utilizing dynamic space. The C functions **calloc()** and **malloc()**, plus their **far** counterparts, are all variations on the theme "gimme some free memory." We'll discuss how to use them and what their differences are later in the chapter.

First, though, let's review one of the most confusing aspects of C notation.

Addresses and Pointers _____

The Intel processor family, which includes the 8088, 8086, 80286, and 80386 (the latter two running in real mode), uses two 16-bit words to represent a memory address. This scheme is called segmented addressing. The first word is the segment, which is a 16-byte paragraph computed as

    actual address mod 16

The second word is the data offset, a value that offsets from the segment paragraph address to find the location of the variable in question. The notation is:

Segment	:	Offset
0120	:	00C3 (in hex)
0288	:	0195 (in decimal)

The upshot of all this is that any memory address on the IBM PC and compatible machines is a 32-bit value. However, only 20 of the full 32 bits are needed to gain access to a memory location. This is because of an 80×86 architectural concept known as segment registers.

There are four segment registers, as follows:

Register	Points to
CS	Code segment
DS	Data segment
SS	Stack segment
ES	Extended segment

Each register gives the starting paragraph address of its relevant 64K segment.

Using the small-code group as an example, when the program begins to run, DOS loads the CS register with the start of the code segment, DS with the start of the data segment, SS with the start of the near heap, and ES with the start of the far heap. In this model, the size of the first three segments is fixed at 64K each, which means that these registers never change during program execution.

Consequently, in the small-code group, the only part of the address that you need to locate any program element is the 16-bit offset. The machine code adds this to the appropriate segment register to derive the actual address. To fetch a static data value, the machine code adds the offset to the DS register; to jump to an executable location, it adds the offset to the CS register; and so on.

These 16-bit offsets are all that the small-code group needs to locate anything fixed within the domain of the program. They are called *pointers,* or more precisely within the context of Turbo C, *near pointers.* A near pointer is a 16-bit offset from a segment register whose content is fixed for the duration of the program's execution.

Matters are more complicated when dealing with the far heap. The ES register points to the start of the far heap, but since this is an area greater than 64K, all addresses within the far heap are not necessarily direct offsets from it. If you have exactly 64K of allocated space, then any address is indeed an offset from ES, but when you proceed beyond that point, a different segment applies. Consequently, the full 32-bit address must be used to find objects on the far heap. These are called *far* or *huge pointers* in Turbo C, and they must be declared as such when, as in the small-code models, they are not the default pointer size.

A program written for the small memory model might have the following declarations:

```
OBJTYPE *nearptr;
OBJTYPE far *farptr;
```

Both pointers point to an object of type OBJTYPE, but the first is a 16-bit entity that will offset from the SS register on the near heap, while the second is a 32-bit pointer giving the full address of an object on the far heap. The **far** modifier overrides the default pointer size for the compilation model.

The Turbo C compiler automatically develops pointers of the appropriate size—16 or 32 bits—depending on the memory model. In the large model (64K data but any amount of code), for example, pointers to static data are 16 bits offset from DS while pointers to executable code are 32 bits.

You might wish to override the default pointer size the other way, that is, by making a near code pointer within the large model, thus forcing the compiler to generate a 16-bit pointer where it would normally create one of 32 bits. Such a declaration might read

   void near somefcn (void)

In this case, **somefcn()** takes no arguments, returns no value, and is accessed via a 16-bit pointer offset from the current CS register. The effect is to make **somefcn()** callable only within the current 64K code segment; it is not accessible from outside the segment, since other segments will have different settings for the CS register. Why do this? To reduce overhead. It takes fewer machine cycles to handle a 16-bit offset ("short jump") than a 32-bit address ("long jump"). This is particularly useful for recursive functions, and can significantly improve program performance.

Turbo C has two kinds of 32-bit pointers, called *far* and *huge*. Both contain segment and offset portions and can be used interchangeably. The difference is that huge pointers are normalized. A far pointer contains a paragraph address in the segment portion and any value up to 64K in the offset; by contrast, a huge pointer's offset is limited to values in the range 0 through 16, while the nearest lower paragraph address appears in the segment. In other words, a normalized pointer has as much of the address information as possible packed into the segment portion, and only a value ranging from 0 through 0Fh in the offset portion.

This suggests a tradeoff. Because far pointers are not normalized, you cannot compare them and expect reliable results. The following two hex addresses are equivalent:

   093B : 0011
   093C : 0001

However, they are not equal. Thus, if you compare them with

   if (ptra == ptrb)

the comparison will fail even though the pointers indicate the same memory location.

Normalization forces all 32-bit huge pointers to contain the nearest paragraph in the segment. The second pointer above is normalized. As a result, if **ptra** and **ptrb** are both declared as huge, the comparison will return valid results. The tradeoff is overhead. Normalization of huge pointers executes additional compiler-inserted code every time a huge pointer is modified.

One way to get the best of both worlds is to use **far** pointers as a matter of course and cast them to **huge** prior to a comparison, as in

```
OBJTYPE far *ptra, *ptrb;
{
  . . .
  ptra = (OBJTYPE huge*) ptra;
  ptrb = (OBJTYPE huge*) ptrb;
  if (ptra == ptrb) . . .
}
```

Indirection

Indirection is a technique used in C and other languages such as Pascal to get at a data object indirectly, that is, through the use of a pointer rather than by direct reference.

The notation for pointers and addresses frequently confuses C programmers. Some reading tricks help to alleviate these problems.

When you declare the variable

```
int count;
```

you tell the compiler to assign a memory location symbolically referred to as count, which will hold a 16-bit value of type **int**. There is no ambiguity about this matter; **count** is an integer variable that you can manipulate directly with instructions such as

```
count++;
```

Now suppose you declare the variable

```
int *count;
```

Here **count** is a pointer to an integer. In other words, **count** is the symbolic name for a variable that contains a pointer to an integer, and not the integer itself. The expression

```
*count++;
```

can be read "increment the integer pointed to by **count**," or more concisely, "increment **count's** referent." Similarly, you can use the referent in more complex expressions, such as

```
fpcount = double (*count);
mod2 = *count % 2;
if (*count) . . .
```

Read these statements as

"**fpcount** becomes **count's** referent cast as a double"
"**mod2** becomes **count's** referent modulo 2"
"if **count's** referent is not equal to 0"

The **if()** statement above has a very different meaning if you don't include the asterisk. The statement

```
if (count) . . .
```

means "if **count** points to nothing" or, equivalently, "if **count** is a null pointer."
A pointer usually acquires a value through assignment. Three kinds of pointer assignments are appropriate. Given that **count** and another are declared as pointers and **var** as a variable of a compatible type, then:

Null assignment	count = 0;
Pointer-to-pointer	count = another;
Address-to-pointer	count = &var;

In the first case, **count** (and not its referent) is being initialized to a null value to indicate that the pointer is not currently in use; that is, **count** points to nothing. (NOTE: A pointer declared as static is automatically initialized to **NULL**. An auto pointer—that is, one declared in a function and thus existing on the stack—must *always* be initialized to **NULL** unless something is assigned to it before its first reference in the function.) In the second case, another is also a pointer to an integer, and the address it contains is being transferred to **count**. In the last case, the address or offset of **var** is being loaded into **count**, such that **var** becomes **count's** referent. After this instruction executes (and as long as nothing further is done to **count**), the following two instructions are exactly equivalent:

```
var      + = 2;
*count   + = 2;
```

This should help clear up another confusion about C notation. The * operator means "the referent of" whereas **&** means "the address of."

Dynamic Memory Allocation: Single-Heap Memory Models

This section discusses dynamic storage in memory models that have a single heap, that is, all but the small and medium models. If you're using either of those two, this discussion applies to the near heap only, and you should refer to the next major section for coverage of the far heap.

The prototypes for the Turbo C dynamic allocation functions are in the header file alloc.h. If your program does dynamic allocation, place the following line near the top of the source listing:

```
#include <alloc.h>
```

Allocating and Using Dynamic Memory

Dynamic allocation is the process of acquiring and using the free memory of the computer. The process is:

1. Request the amount of memory you need.
2. Store the returned pointer to the object.

Thereafter, you can use the pointer to access the data much as you access any other variable.

As an example, suppose you're working with cubes, which have the attributes of length, width, and height. You might declare a structure type to describe them as follows:

```
typedef struct {
    int  length, width, height;
} CUBETYPE;
```

For any object placed on the heap, there must be a pointer available to the program so that it can locate the object. In this case, you might declare the pointer as

```
CUBETYPE *cube;
```

meaning that "cube is a pointer to an object of CUBETYPE."

There are two options for acquiring the heap space for the object: malloc() and calloc. While they take different arguments, the chief difference is that malloc() does not initialize the allocated space, while calloc does (that is, it sets the allocated space to all zeros). Thus, space acquired with malloc() is guaranteed to contain garbage, but it's slightly faster than calloc. On the other hand, **calloc** is more suited for allocating array space on the heap.

Only one argument is passed to **malloc()**, which is the size in bytes of the space requested. It works fine in this case, where you only want to set aside space for one object of CUBETYPE, and as long as you don't care if the space is uninitialized. Given the declarations above:

```
cube = malloc (sizeof (CUBETYPE));
```

This instruction computes the size of the **CUBETYPE** object and passes it to **malloc()**. When **malloc()** returns the pointer, which is of type void, the compiler binds it to **CUBETYPE** (the declared data type of the receiving variable) and assigns it to **cube**.

The call to **calloc** entails two arguments: the number of objects to allocate, and the size of each. Obviously, all objects must be of the same type in a given call to **calloc**, suggesting an array. The call is

```
cube = calloc (1, sizeof (CUBETYPE));
```

which accomplishes the same thing as the call to **malloc()**. If you wanted to set aside space for three **CUBETYPE** structures, you would substitute **3** for **1** in the argument list.

Both **malloc()** and **calloc** return a pointer to the allocated space if successful, and **NULL** (a pointer containing all zeros) when not. It's good practice to check the results after each allocation request with a statement such as

```
if (cube == NULL) . . .
```

If this test proves true, about the only thing you can do is gracefully end the program, unless you want to go to heroic lengths to keep it running.

Whichever function you use, and assuming a **NULL** pointer isn't returned, you can now store values in the allocated structure. Once again, there are two alternatives in the notation. To place **3** into the length member, you can write either

```
(*cube).length = 3;
```

or

```
cube->length = 3;
```

The choice is one of personal preference; ours is the second, and thus the arrow notation appears in this book.

Once the structure members have been assigned values, you can use them in expressions like normal variables, for example, volume = cube->length * cube->width * cube->height;

and

partial = cube->height * factor;

Releasing Heap Space

Dynamically allocated space is automatically released when the program ends. If a program runs for a long time, though, you might wish to release space when it's no longer needed, thus making that memory available for future allocation requests and preventing the heap from filling up with forgotten junk. The **free()** function exists for that purpose.

To use **free()**, simply pass the pointer to the object you want to discard. Continuing the example from the previous discussion, you can release the space occupied by the structure with

free (cube);

Determining How Much Heap Space Is Available

You can determine in advance if your dynamic allocation request can be satisfied by issuing the **coreleft()** call. This function takes no arguments and returns the size (expressed in 16-byte paragraphs) of the unused space above the highest object currently on the heap. In the small-code group, **coreleft()** returns an unsigned integer, in the compact group, large, and huge models, a long.

Dynamic Allocation: Split-Heap Models _____

The preceding discussion of dynamic allocation covers heap utilization in the tiny, compact, large, and huge memory models, and the near heap in the small and medium models. This section deals with dynamic allocation of the far heap in the large and huge models, which have two heaps separated by the stack.

In general, when using the small and medium models, use the near heap for small amounts of dynamic data that are frequently referenced, and the far heap for large or numerous dynamic objects. As an example, you might build some short lookup tables in the near heap, where the access overhead entails only a 16-bit pointer offset from the SS register, and in the far heap construct a large binary tree processed in the manner of a high-speed data file.

Because the default pointer size in the small and medium models is 16 bits, it's necessary to explicitly declare pointers to the far heap with the far or huge modifier, thus yielding a full 32-bit address pointer. Figure 15.1 summarizes the tradeoffs between these two pointer categories.

Figure 15.1 **Tradeoffs Between Far and Huge Pointers**

	Comparison	Speed
FAR	Inaccurate	Fast
HUGE	Accurate	Slow

Thus, in the small and medium models, declare a pointer **ncube** to the **CUBETYPE** structure on the *near* heap as

CUBETYPE *ncube;

but a pointer **fcube** to the same structure on the *far* heap as

CUBETYPE far *fcube;

or

CUBETYPE huge *fcube;

depending on which kind of 32-bit pointer you need.

Allocating and freeing space on the far heap in the small and medium models take special function calls in Turbo C, which are equivalent to those already discussed. The differences are that the function names are prefixed with "far" and returned values are 32-bit addresses that must be cast to far or huge pointers (to a long for the amount of remaining memory). The argument lists are the same for each counterpart. Figure 15.2 lists them.

Figure 15.2 **Comparable Dynamic Memory Functions**

Near or only heap	Far heap
malloc()	farmalloc()
calloc()	farcalloc()
free()	farfree()
coreleft()	farcoreleft()

Thus, to request space for 10 structures of type **CUBETYPE** on the far heap and assign to **fcube** the pointer to the first one, write

```
fcube = (CUBETYPE*) farcalloc (10, sizeof (CUBETYPE));
```

or alternatively,

```
fcube = (CUBETYPE*) farmalloc (sizeof (CUBETYPE) * 10));
```

Thereafter, access to members of the structure(s) is the same as before, for example

```
fcube->height = 5;
```

If you've allocated multiple structures in the same call, you can gain access to a member of the fifth with an expression such as

```
(fcube+4)->width += 2;
```

The effect of this expression is to find the fifth structure by numerically adding **sizeof(CUBETYPE)*4** to the pointer, then offsetting by the position of the width member within the structure, and finally adding **2** to the value contained there. You can do the same thing with multiple objects allocated on the near or only heaps in other memory models.

Other operations are also equivalent. For example, to free the space occupied by the 10 structures pointed to by **fcube**, issue the call

```
farfree (fcube);
```

and to find out how much free space is left on the far heap,

```
longfree = farcoreleft();
```

Summary

This chapter has presented background information concerning the various memory models in Turbo C and the means for allocating dynamic heap space within them. Before getting into practical applications, there are a few key points to emphasize.

1. A program using the heap must maintain at least one pointer that serves as a gateway to the data stored on the heap. (The following chapters show how to get to subsequent dynamic objects.)

2. There are tradeoffs between far and huge pointers, which are summarized in Figure 15.1.
3. Eight intrinsic functions govern basic dynamic allocation in Turbo C, all of whose prototypes are in both **alloc.h** and **stdlib.h**.

Figure 15.3 lists the major intrinsic functions by Turbo C memory model and the pointer size or data type that they return, where:

16P = 16-bit pointer
32P = 32-bit pointer
N/A = not applicable to memory model
int = integer value
long = long integer

Figure 15.3 **Basic Dynamic Allocation Functions**

	Small-code			Large-data		
	T	S	M	C	L	H
malloc()	16P	16P	16P	32P	32P	32P
calloc()	16P	16P	16P	32P	32P	32P
free()	16P	16P	16P	32P	32P	32P
coreleft()	int	int	int	long	long	long
farmalloc()	N/A	32P*	32P*	N/A	N/A	N/A
farcalloc()	N/A	32P*	32P*	N/A	N/A	N/A
farfree()N/A	32P*	32P*	N/A	N/A	N/A	
farcoreleft()	N/A	32P*	32P*	N/A	N/A	N/A

The following several chapters provide practical applications of this material.

CHAPTER 16

SINGLY LINKED LISTS

This chapter covers singly linked lists, which are the simplest kind of dynamic data structure. The basic building block of any linked list is an object called a *node,* so we begin by discussing what a node is, and then proceed into the structure and manipulation of singly linked lists.

The term *node* crops up all over computer science. Its basic meaning is "a definable entity." In the context of dynamic memory, a node is one complete data object placed on the heap. Chapter 15 defined a structure type called CUBETYPE and showed how to allocate heap space for it and how to use it in various ways. In the strictest sense, an object of CUBETYPE, placed on the heap, is a node.

The trouble with CUBETYPE is that it doesn't lead anywhere. It is one thing, period. As Chapter 15 noted, there must be a pointer to every object on the heap, lest the software be unable to locate it. We can allocate some number of objects at one time, thus effecting an array, and access them via arithmetic with the common pointer, as in

```
(fcube+n)->member
```

However, this is an unsatisfactory method when the number of nodes is unknown in advance, as when building a dynamic list from keyboard input or a disk file.

A better method is to build the dynamic list naturally, as it grows, where each node points to its successor so that a logical chain develops: this node leads to the next, which leads to the next, and so on to the end of the list. In an alphabetic context:

AAAA leads to
AAAB leads to
AAAC leads to

. . .

ZZZY leads to
ZZZZ which is the end of the list

That is what a linked list does. Minimally, it furnishes a **static**, which points to the head (starting node) of a list. Each node thereafter provides a pointer to its successor, so that software can pursue the chain throughout the entire list and detect when it has reached the end.

Why is this important? For three reasons. First, only one pointer needs to be stored in the data segment to gain access to the entire list. Second, the size of the list can vary dynamically from one access to the next—nodes can be inserted, appended, or deleted—and the only external effect is the time it takes to pass through the list. Finally, different node types can be placed in succession on the heap depending on the order of dynamic allocation requests. You might have three different lists intermingled on the heap: types A, B, and C, all of which are of different lengths. The order could be A, C, B, B, A, C, A, B . . . . If the order is properly constructed via pointers, each type A leads to the next type A, each B to the next B, and so on, irrespective of their physical arrangement in memory.

The essential element of a linked list node, therefore, is that it contain a pointer to the next node in succession. Singly and doubly linked lists, queues, stacks, and circular lists, covered in this chapter, and binary trees, covered in the next, all adhere to this principle in one way or another. They furnish a single **static** pointer as a gateway to the list and a mechanism for locating related nodes.

Singly Linked Lists: Background

The least versatile but most understandable form of dynamic data structure is the singly linked list (SLL). We say "singly linked" because there is one and only one path through the nodes, leading from the head to the tail. In other words, a single link—a pointer—joins each node to the next in the list.

It is possible to have a list consisting of nodes that contain only a pointer to the next node. However, this is not very practical inasmuch as the purpose of a linked list is to store data, and the pointers are merely a means for getting at that data. For that reason, the minimal node in a SLL consists of two components: a data field and a pointer field. Figure 16.1 depicts such a node.

Figure 16.1 **Minimal Node for a Singly Linked List**

Data	Pointer

For the sake of illustration, let's say that each node occupies 10 bytes of storage and the SLL is on the near heap, thus using 16-bit pointers. In that case, then, the list might appear conceptually as shown in Figure 16.2. Each node's offset appears to the left, thus showing how the pointer field provides a path from one node to the next. Note that the last node's pointer field is set to **NULL**. That's because it leads nowhere; in other words, it signifies the end of the list.

Figure 16.2 **Conceptual Diagram of a Singly Linked List**

1000	Data	Pointer 1010
1010	Data	Pointer 1020
1020	Data	Pointer 1030
1030	Data	Pointer 1040
1040	Data	Pointer NULL

Now suppose that another object not belonging to this list is placed on the heap. This "foreign object" begins at offset 1050 and occupies some amount of space: let's say 32 bytes from 1050 through 1081. What happens if you then add a new node to the tail of the SLL? The **NULL** pointer in the old tail is changed to point to the new node. Thus, while the foreign object exists physically, it is not a barrier to expansion, and as far as traversing the list is concerned, it effectively does not exist at all. Figure 16.3 illustrates this and shows how differing objects can be placed on the heap without interfering with each other.

The only declared data element that absolutely must exist outside the list is a pointer to the head, so that the software can find where the path through the list begins. In this example, the head pointer contains the offset 1000. To traverse the list, the software first acquires the value of the head pointer and uses it to locate the first node, then uses a loop or a recursive call to access successive nodes. In each iteration, it grabs the pointer field from the current node to find the next node. We will deal with this in more concrete terms when we get to the discussion of operations on singly linked lists.

Traversal of the list ends when the pointer field contains **NULL**. This is a signal to the program that there are no more nodes. For example, if you had a loop to print out all the data components, the loop would terminate when it fetched the pointer to the next node and found that it was NULL. As another example, if you're adding a new node, it's necessary to update the old tail's

Figure 16.3 **Adding a Node Beyond a Foreign Object**

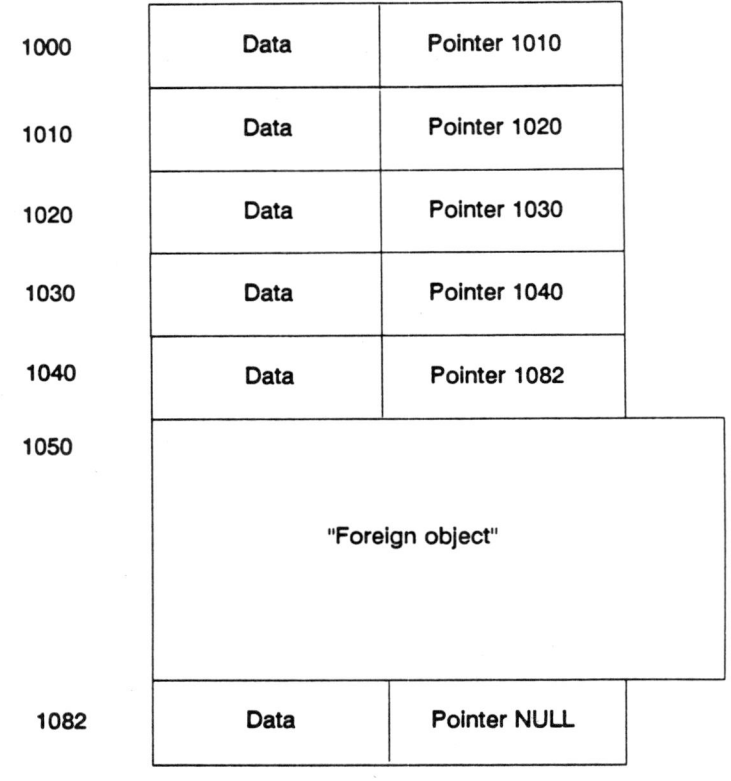

pointer so that it points to the new member of the list. Therefore, you follow the path until you hit a **NULL** pointer, allocate the new node, stuff its address into the pointer field of the old tail, and then use that pointer to initialize the new node.

It would seem that very long lists require a time-consuming traversal to find the old tail each time a new node is added. However, you can save this traversal time by keeping an external pointer not only to the head, but also to the current tail. That way you can go directly to the tail without having to look for it. It's also easier to load data into the new SLL node with a tail pointer. We'll illustrate this in the next section.

Declaring a Node Type

In the next section, we'll need an example on which to build some working code, and this is where we'll create the node type for that purpose. Let's say we want to build a SLL containing the first names of some people. Most first names are relatively short, so the data component will be a 10-character string. The other field will be the mandatory pointer to the node type.

The pointer must be bound to the data type of the node, thus requiring a recursive definition. We can accomplish this in C using the optional tag field in a structure definition, as the following **typedef** shows.

```
typedef struct ntag {
    char name [ 10 ];
    struct ntag *next;
} SLNODE;
```

Now that we have a sample application in mind and a node type to implement it, let's begin building and manipulating a singly linked list.

Operations on Singly Linked Lists

As mentioned above, SLLs are somewhat limited in their capabilities. You can think of them as being analogous to sequential disk files; there is only one direction through it (top to bottom), and the data appear in the order in which they were acquired and can't be easily rearranged. The chief advantage of an SLL over a sequential disk file is that it's much faster to work with.

It's also relatively simple, and for those reasons SLLs are frequently used for lookup tables of unpredictable size. As an example, most compilers use SLLs to construct symbol tables built and frequently referred to during the compilation process. Each node contains a variable's name, its data type, its dimensions (if an array), and other information. Plus, of course, a pointer to the next node. Because there is no way to anticipate the number of symbols a given source program might contain, a dynamic data structure such as an SLL is a perfect solution to the problem of keeping all this information in a place that is readily accessible: on the heap. You might never write a compiler, but chances are that your programs often need to build and refer to tables.

Building an SLL

We have repeatedly mentioned that the one essential data element external to a linked list is a pointer to the head. This is ordinarily a global pointer variable bound to the node type.

When the program begins execution, the linked list does not exist. Therefore the head pointer should be immediately initialized to **NULL**. The easiest way to do this is at declaration, as in

```
main()
{
SLNODE *head = NULL;
. . .
```

Any other pointers to the linked list should also be born initialized. For example, if you plan to maintain a tail pointer, you should code something like this:

```
SLNODE *head = NULL, *tail =NULL;
```

An even easier way to accomplish the same thing is to declare the SLL pointers at the top of the program, before **main()** and outside the scope of any other function. This makes them **static** variables, which the compiler automatically initializes. Example:

```
SLNODE *head, *tail;
main()
{ . . .
```

Initialization of the SLL pointers, if followed through by testing for **NULL** pointers in the code, helps to guarantee that the program won't go wandering because of a pointer containing garbage.

The SLL comes into existence with the allocation of its first node. In this case, the head pointer must be reset to indicate the starting node and, if maintained, the tail pointer must also be set to the same value. Adding a node to an existing list is an almost identical process, the only difference being that the head pointer remains unchanged. The steps are as follows:

1. Allocate the new node.
2. If a tail node already exists, update its pointer field to indicate the new node.
3. Set the tail pointer to the new node, and set the head pointer to the same value if it is **NULL**.
4. Set the new node's pointer field to **NULL**.

After that, you can load the data component using the tail pointer.

Because adding nodes to SLLs is an operation you might want to perform at different points in a program—possibly involving more than one list—this procedure lends itself to a subprogram. Using double indirection, the function can automatically alter the head and tail pointers appropriately, thus relieving the caller of the responsibility for maintaining its own pointers.

Program 16.1 lists the function **addsl()**, which performs the steps outlined above. Because it updates pointers, **addsl()** requires the addresses of the head and tail pointers (using the **&** operator) as its arguments. It returns a pointer to the new node.

Program 16.1 **Adding a Node to a Singly Linked List**

```
void addsl (SLNODE **h, SLNODE **t)

      /* Add node to tail of SLL */
{
SLNODE   *new;

  new = (SLNODE*) malloc (sizeof (SLNODE));
  if (*t != NULL)
    (*t)->next = new;   /* update old tail's pointer field */
  if (*h == NULL)
    *h = new;                /* set head pointer if necessary */
  *t = new;                         /* update tail pointer */
  (*t)->next = NULL;     /* blank new tail's pointer field */
} /* ------------------------- */
```

Thus you see that with one algorithm, you can start the SLL and build it by adding new nodes at the tail. The **addsl()** function is sufficiently generalized that it could control the growth of several independent lists all using the same node type, merely by passing it different pointers.

Traversing a Singly Linked List

Traversal of an SLL is not usually an end unto itself, unless you're merely seeking the tail in the absence of a specific tail pointer. Ordinarily you pass through the nodes, pausing to perform some operation on each one: searching for a data value, listing the node's contents, and so on. Whatever, the basic process is always the same. Expressed in C:

```
SLNODE *n; /* local pointer */

  n = headptr;
  while ( n != NULL ) {
    /* perform the operation */
    n = n->next;
  }
```

The local pointer **n** is necessary since you don't want to corrupt any static pointers such as **head**. In the first step, **n** is pointed to the head of the list. The **while** loop executes only as long as **n** is not **NULL**; it will not execute at all if the list doesn't exist, i.e. if **head** is **NULL**. The first part of the loop does whatever you want to do with the node currently pointed to by **n**. The important part is the instruction

```
n = n -> next;
```

The **n** pointer advances to the next node by grabbing the pointer field from the current node. Using Figure 16.3 as an example, if **n** contains 1020, it acquires the pointer field from the node at 1020 and thus advances to 1030. This is the value **n** contains when the loop reiterates. When **n** points to 1082, it grabs **NULL** from the **next** field and the loop does not repeat because the **while** test fails.

Program 16.2 lists the function **freelist()**, which frees all the space occupied by an SLL. In this case, the argument is a pointer to the head of the list, and the operation performed during the traversal is to **free()** each node in succession. In effect, **freelist()** erases the SLL from the heap.

Program 16.2 Erasing a Singly Linked List from the Heap

```
void freelist (SLNODE *h)

        /* Delete list from heap */
{
SLNODE *n;

    n = h;                              /* point to head of SLL */
    while (n != NULL) {                 /* until end of list... */
      free (n);                         /* free current node */
      n = n->next;                      /* go to next node */
    }
} /* ------------------------ */
```

Application: Building, Listing, and Deleting an SLL

Now let's look at a complete program that demonstrates an SLL. This program (SLLDEMO1.C, Program 16.5) builds a linked list of five nodes, asking you to type a person's first name into the data field of each one. As it runs, it reports the amount of memory left on the near heap and the values of the **head** and **tail** pointers. When you have furnished the five names, the program displays them by traversing the list, and then erases the list from the heap with another traversal. It ends by reporting the amount of memory left on the heap. Note that the **showlist()** and **freelist()** functions differ only in the single operation each performs.

Program 16.3 Demonstration of SLL Operations

```
/* SLLDEMO1.C: Builds and traverses a SLL */

#include <stdio.h>
#include <alloc.h>
#include <conio.h>

typedef struct ntag {                   /* SLL node structure */
```

Program 16.3 (continued)

```
  char          name [10];
  struct ntag *next;
} SLNODE;

SLNODE *head, *tail;                /* static list pointers */
/* ------------------------------------------------------- */

void main ()
{
int   i;
void showlist (SLNODE*), freelist (SLNODE*),
        addsl (SLNODE**, SLNODE**);

  for (i = 0; i < 5; i++) {
    addsl (&head, &tail);
    printf ('\nMemory left = %u", coreleft ());
    printf ('\nhead = %p, tail = %p", head, tail);
    printf ('\nEnter a name... ");
    gets (tail->name);
  }
  showlist (head);
  freelist (head);
  printf ('\nMemory left after freeing = %u\n",
          coreleft ());
} /* ----------------------- */

void addsl (SLNODE **h, SLNODE **t)

      /* Add node to tail of SLL */
{
SLNODE  *new;

  new = (SLNODE*) malloc (sizeof (SLNODE));
  if (*t != NULL)
    (*t)->next = new;   /* update old tail's pointer field */
  if (*h == NULL)
    *h = new;              /* set head pointer if necessary */
  *t = new;                    /* update tail pointer */
  (*t)->next = NULL;    /* blank new tail's pointer field */
} /* ----------------------- */

void showlist (SLNODE *h)

      /* Traverse list and display names */
{
SLNODE *n;
  puts ('\n\nList of names in nodes:");
  n = h;                         /* point to head of SLL */
  while (n != NULL) {            /* until end of list... */
    printf ('\n%s", n->name);       /* display name and */
    n = n->next;                    /* go to next node */
  }
} /* ----------------------- */
```

Program 16.3 (continued)

```
void freelist (SLNODE *h)

      /* Delete list from heap */
{
SLNODE *n;

  n = h;                              /* point to head of SLL */
  while (n != NULL) {                 /* until end of list... */
    free (n);                           /* free current node */
    n = n->next;                         /* go to next node */
  }
} /* ------------------------ */
```

Searching a Singly Linked List

This is again a traversal operation, but with one important difference: It returns a pointer to the node in which the match is found, or **NULL** if there is no match.

As mentioned earlier, one of the chief uses of SLLs is in lookup tables. There are two basic things we do with tables:

- Determine if a key value is valid.
- Find out additional information about a key value.

An example of the first case is validation of keyboard entries. Suppose you're writing a payroll system in which the key value is the employee Social Security number. Each time the operator types a new timecard entry, it's necessary to determine if the Social Security number is valid. Consequently, your program could search an SLL containing all employee Social Security numbers. If there is no match in the list, the operator has made an error. This is detected by a **NULL** pointer being returned from the search routine. Detecting it, the program can request re-entry.

We can also draw an example of the second case from business applications: getting additional information about a key value. The SLL nodes might contain customer account numbers, billing and shipping addresses, and credit ratings. When the order entry operator types the account number, a search of the SLL automatically fills in the billing and shipping addresses and verifies that the customer has a credit rating sufficient for the terms of sale. If no match is found for the account number, the operator made a mistake.

We could present numerous other examples, but you get the idea. By checking the pointer to the node matching the key value, your program can determine validity and other information from the lookup table, and if the pointer is **NULL**, it indicates an error.

An SLL search function requires two arguments: a pointer to the head of the list, and the key value to be matched with a data element within the nodes. The key value must be of the same data type as the node's data element, or else the search results will be unreliable. The search function must return a pointer to the matching node or **NULL** depending on the outcome.

To illustrate in a simplistic manner, let's say we want to validate keyboard entries of the first names of people. If the operator types **Susan** but there is no **Susan** in the SLL table, the lookup routine returns **NULL**. On the other hand, a non-**NULL** returned value indicates a valid entry. Program 16.4 implements these requirements.

Program 16.4 **Searching a Singly Linked List**

```
SLNODE *findsl (SLNODE *h, char *key)

      /* Search SLL for key, return pointer to node */
{
SLNODE *n;

  n = h;
  while (n != NULL) {
    if (strcmp (key, n->name) == 0)
      break;
    n = n->next;
  }
  return (n);
}
```

Deleting a Node

Just as lists grow, sometimes they also shrink, as in removing entries from a lookup table when they're no longer valid or useful. This is a little trickier than traversal, because we not only follow pointers, but rearrange them. Further complicating matters is the possibility that the node being deleted is either the head or the tail of the list, thus requiring an update of the involved static pointer via indirection.

A deletion normally involves a search: "Delete the node whose data field contains the name Bob." First you have to find the node, then you can delete it. It would appear that you can use findsl() for this, but alas, there's a catch; you have to be able to locate the node preceding the one to be deleted. The next couple of paragraphs explain why.

Let's say you have a list containing three nodes, as shown in the "Before" part of Figure 16.4, and you're going to delete the one containing Bob. You begin searching the list at the head. No match, so you save the address of this node and follow its pointer field to the next node, where you find what you're looking for.

Figure 16.4 **Deleting a Node Within a List**

Before

1000	Alice	1010
1010	Bob	1020
1020	Cathy	NULL

After

1000	Alice	1020
1020	Cathy	NULL

The deletion itself is quite simple. You take the pointer field from Bob's node and copy it into Alice's (which explains why you have to keep track of the last node you checked). Though not necessary, it's good practice to deallocate Bob's node with **free()**.

The "After" portion of Figure 16.8 shows the effect. Within the scope of the list, Bob's node has ceased to exist because Alice's pointer field now links to Cathy's node, thus bypassing Bob's. Note that the list is physically the same size as before, since Cathy hasn't moved. It's just that Bob's former node is now dead space.

You can tell if you're about to delete the head of the list by comparing the node's pointer with the head pointer. (NOTE: if you're using one of Turbo C's large-data models, be sure the pointers are **huge**). If they're equal, you're deleting the head of the list.

Two possible conditions arise when deleting the head: either there are other nodes, or it's the only remaining one. Whichever, you're going to have to change the head pointer. The question is, to what?

If another node follows the head, it becomes the new head of the list, so copy the **next** field from the node into the head pointer. Figure 16.5 depicts this situation before and after the deletion.

Figure 16.5 **Deleting Head of List**

Before

Head→ 1000	Alan	1010
1010	Beth	1020
Tail → 1020	Carl	NULL

After

Head→ 1010	Beth	1020
Tail → 1020	Carl	NULL

On the other hand, if this is the only remaining node, the list will cease to exist as a result of the deletion. In that event, set the head pointer to **NULL**. These alternatives can be handled with the C expression

head = (head->next != NULL) ? this->next : NULL;

Deleting the tail is similar. Again, you can find out if the deleted node is at the end of the list by comparing its pointer with the tail pointer. If they're equal, change the preceding node's pointer field to **NULL** and put the address of the preceding node into the tail pointer, or **NULL** if you're deleting the only node left on the list.

Figure 16.6 shows deletion of the tail when there is still another node left to assume its position at the end of the list.

Figure 16.6 **Deleting Tail of List**

Before

Head → 1000	Alan	1010
1010	Beth	1020
Tail → 1020	Carl	NULL

After

Head→ 1000	Alan	1010
Tail → 1010	Beth	NULL

The length of this discussion might make it seem that deleting a node is a process of bewildering complexity, but in fact there are only four circumstances:

- Deleting a node inside the list
- Deleting the head
- Deleting the tail
- Deleting the only remaining node

Because C is a terse language, the actual code to accomplish the task is quite brief, as Program 16.5 shows.

Program 16.5 **Function to Delete any SLL Node**

```
void delsl (SLNODE **h, SLNODE **t, char *key)

        /* Delete node indicated by key from SLL */
{
SLNODE *this, *last = NULL;

   /* First find node to be deleted */
   this = *h;
   while (this != NULL) {
      if (strcmp (this->name, key) == 0)        /* if found */
         break;                          /* break out of while loop */
      last = this;                       /* else remember this node */
      this = this->next;                  /* and go to next */
   }
   if (this == NULL)  {                        /* no match */
      puts ("\nNOT FOUND");                /* so tell 'em */
      return;                              /* and quit */
   }

   /* Node is found, so delete it */
   if (this != *h)                        /* not deleting head */
      last->next = this->next;      /* so bypass deleted node */
   else                          /* maybe we are deleting head */
      *h = (this->next != NULL)
            ? this->next : NULL;   /* if so update head ptr */
   if (this == *t)                        /* deleting tail */
      *t = last;                      /* so update tail ptr */
   free (this);                       /* deallocate space */
} /* ----------------------- */
```

Tying It Together

Program 16.6 lists SLLDEMO2.C, which implements all the operations on SLLs discussed in this chapter. This program builds on the one in Program 16.3. The chief difference is that, once the SLL is complete, the program prompts you for a name to delete from the list. If you type a valid name, the program removes the node, and otherwise it reports **NOT FOUND**. After each attempt, the current list contents are redisplayed. You can end execution by pressing **Enter** in response to the name prompt.

Program 16.6 SLL Operations Including Search and Delete

```c
/* SLLDEMO2.C: Builds a SLL, then selectively deletes    */
/*       based on key entered by user                    */

#include <stdio.h>
#include <alloc.h>
#include <conio.h>
#include <string.h>

typedef struct ntag {                    /* SLL node structure */
  char        name [10];
  struct ntag *next;
} SLNODE;

SLNODE *head, *tail;                      /* static list pointers */
/* ---------------------------------------------------- */

void main ()
{
int  i;
char name [10];
void showlist (SLNODE*), freelist (SLNODE*),
        delsl (SLNODE**, SLNODE**, char*),
        addsl (SLNODE**, SLNODE**);

  for (i = 0; i < 5; i++) {
    addsl (&head, &tail);
    printf ("\n Memory left = %u", coreleft ());
    printf ("\n head = %p, tail = %p", head, tail);
    printf ("\n Enter a name... ");
    gets (tail->name);
  }
  showlist (head);

  do {
    printf (\n\nName to delete? ");
    gets (name);
    if (name [0] != 0) {
      delsl (&head, &tail, name);
      puts ("±n");
      showlist (head);
    }
  } while (name [0] != 0);

  printf ("±nhead = %p, tail = %p±n", head, tail);
  freelist (head);
} /* ---------------------- */
```

Program 16.6 **(continued)**

```
void addsl (SLNODE **h, SLNODE **t)

     /* Add node to tail of SLL */
{
SLNODE  *new;

  new = (SLNODE*) malloc (sizeof (SLNODE));
  if (*t != NULL)
    (*t)->next = new;   /* update old tail's pointer field */
  if (*h == NULL)
    *h = new;               /* set head pointer if necessary */
  *t = new;                      /* update tail pointer */
  (*t)->next = NULL;       /* blank new tail's pointer field */
} /* ---------------------- */

void showlist (SLNODE *h)

     /* Traverse list and display names */
{
SLNODE *n;

  puts ("\n\nList of names in nodes:");
  n = hh;                        /* point to head of SLL */
  while (n != NULL) {            /* until end of list... */
    printf ("\n%s", n->name);       /* display name and */
    n = n->next;                    /* go to next node */
  }
} /* ---------------------- */

void freelist (SLNODE *h)

     /* Delete list from heap */
{
SLNODE *n;

  n = h;                         /* point to head of SLL */
  while (n != NULL) {            /* until end of list... */
    free (n);                       /* free current node */
    n = n->next;                    /* go to next node */
  }
} /* ---------------------- */

void delsl (SLNODE **h, SLNODE **t, char *key)

     /* Delete node indicated by key from SLL */
{
SLNODE *this, *last = NULL;

  /* First find node to be deleted */
  this = *h;
  while (this != NULL) {
```

Program 16.6 **(continued)**

```
    if (strcmp (this->name, key) == 0)         /* if found */
        break;                           /* break out of while loop */
        last = this;                     /* else remember this node */
        this = this->next;                   /* and go to next */
    }
    if (this == NULL) {                           /* no match */
        puts ("\nNOT FOUND");                /* so tell 'em */
        return;                                /* and quit */
    }

    /* Node is found, so delete it */
    if (this != *h)                        /* not deleting head */
        last->next = this->next;     /* so bypass deleted node */
    else                           /* maybe we are deleting head */
        *h = (this->next != NULL)
            ? this->next : NULL;    /* if so update head ptr */
    if (this == *t)                         /* deleting tail */
        *t = last;                        /* so update tail ptr */
    free (this);                          /* deallocate space */
} /* ---------------------- */
```

Because they're simple to construct and manage, SLLs are widely used for lookup tables. However, there are some problems with SLLs. As we've seen, deleting a node is somewhat cumbersome. Also, you can only move in one direction through the list. It's possible, but awkward, to insert a node somewhere within an SLL; we haven't covered it here because the doubly linked lists covered in the next chapter make insertions easier, as well as fixing some of the other issues related to SLLs.

CHAPTER 17

DOUBLY LINKED LISTS

If a singly linked list is analogous to a one-way street, then a doubly linked list (DLL) is comparable to a two-way street. That is, it provides two parallel paths through the node structure, one from the head to the tail, the other from tail to head. While the structure of a DLL is more complex than an SLL, the ability to traverse bidirectionally and to find out where any node's neighbors are allows you to create much more versatile, efficient dynamic data structures.

Each node in a DLL contains two pointers to its own type, one pointing to the next node in sequence, the other to the one previous. This effects a two-way street, as the following list shows:

In the Node Named	Previous Points To	Next Points To
D	C	E
E	D	F
F	E	G
G	F	H

If you're in node E and you want to move down the list, you follow the **Next** pointer to get to node F. Conversely, you can follow the **Prev** pointer to move up the list to Node D.

This bidirectional capability is important in creating and searching ordered lists—lists that are sorted according to their data content. A common example is alphabetic ordering, as in:

Alice
Bill
Charlie
. . .
Xavier
Yvette
Zeke

The nodes of this list might contain other data elements, such as sales figures, phone numbers, and so forth, but the nodes are arranged by alphabetic order of names. The field that determines the order—the name field in this case—is called the *key*.

SLLs lend themselves nicely to static lists that are ordered by some principle such as time of arrival or key sequence, then searched linearly each time a lookup is done. DLLs, on the other hand, are better suited for applications in which nodes are constantly being added to and deleted from the list, and/or in which the list must either be maintained without searching, or searched in either direction from the most recently visited node. Examples are circular lists, stacks, and queues, which we'll discuss later in this chapter.

DLL Nodes

The minimal practical node for a DLL consists of:

- At least one data-conveying component.
- At least two pointers to its own node type.

The two pointers are for the upward and downward paths to neighboring nodes. We say "at least two," since a node can contain other pointers as well, even to other node types. Figure 17.1 depicts a minimal node for a DLL containing 15-character strings.

Figure 17.1 **Node for a Doubly Linked List**

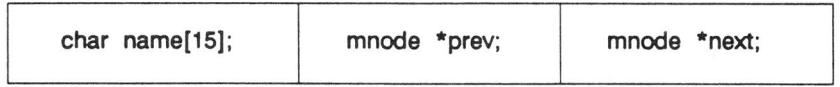

| char name[15]; | mnode *prev; | mnode *next; |

As with the SLL nodes covered in the last chapter, the physical order of fields within the node doesn't matter.

You can define this node in Turbo C using a **typedef** as follows:

```
typedef mnode {
    char name [15];
    struct mnode *prev, *next;
} MINNODE;
```

From this definition, you can declare pointer variables such as

    MINNODE *head, *tail, *new;

that allow you to manipulate list nodes. When using the far heap, you can also apply modifiers as in

    MINNODE huge *head, far *tail, *huge new;

Refer to the section of the Turbo C user's guide dealing with near, huge, and far pointers for more information on these modifiers and why they're important.

The Circular DLL Model

Like an SLL, a DLL can have a head and tail that are the extremes of the list. In this case, the upward path is terminated in the head node when head-> prev == NULL and the downward path when tail->next == NULL, using C notation. To simplify matters, though, this chapter focuses on a type of DLL called a circular list.

Life is easier inside a circular DLL than in a list with terminal nodes for several reasons. Chiefly, the processes for insertion are virtually identical whether the new node is at the head, the tail, or in between. Also, one simple test tells when you've traversed the list no matter which direction you're moving: no need to look for different **NULL** pointers depending on direction.

Conceptually, a circular list wraps around on itself and has no definable start and end. The list grows and shrinks dynamically, with its "circumference" defined by the number of nodes it contains at any given moment. The program needs only to remember the address of one node somewhere in the circular list (we'll call it *head*) to gain access to the entire structure. If the list contains three nodes, its pointer arrangement is as follows:

Node Name	Previous Points To	Next Points To
Head	Tail	Middle
Middle	Head	Tail
Tail	Middle	Head

Thus you can traverse the list upward from the head or downward from the tail. All nodes, then, are effectively "middle."

If you're searching the list for an element that it potentially doesn't contain, you have to compare pointers to determine when you've completely traversed the list. Otherwise you'll end up in the deadly embrace of an infinite loop, forever running in circles through the list with no exit. This makes it essential, when using the far heap from small-code models and any time in the large-data models, to declare or cast the compared pointers as huge. This guarantees their normalization and thus true equality when being compared.

What about the situation in which a circular DLL consists of only one node? In that case, the pointers are as follows:

Node Name	Previous Points To	Next Points To
Head	Head	Head

Here an attempt to traverse the list immediately brings you back to the point of origin.

Now say you add a node that becomes the effective tail. The pointers rearrange as follows:

Node Name	Previous Points To	Next Points To
Head	Tail	Tail
Tail	Head	Head

No matter which way you go, you'll move to the other node and from there back to the origin.

It doesn't matter in any dynamic data structure where the nodes are located physically on the heap. They might be contiguous or scattered all over the place in random physical order. The computer doesn't take longer to jump over 30,000 bytes than over three. Thus, by dealing with pointers, we work in concepts of order rather than in physical arrangement. In effect, we don't care where the nodes are as long as we have reliable pointers to them.

Now let's consider the question of where one inserts a new node in a circular list. The answer is: That depends. There are three general forms of list management that govern the placement of new nodes:

- LIFO (Last In First Out) or stack organization makes the most recently added item the first available. This is the in-basket concept, in which the most recently delivered letter gets taken off the pile first and the old stuff gets older. In this case, the new node always becomes the head of the list. When an item is removed, the head shifts to the next-older node.
- FIFO (First In First Out) or queue organization is analogous to standing in line at the bank. You join the end of the line and work your way to the front. In a circular FIFO list, new nodes are inserted above the head or, in other words, at the tail. When a node is removed, the whole line moves forward one position.

- Ordered lists pay no attention to the time of arrival, but instead to the collating sequence of keys. In this case, it's necessary to search the list and determine where the new node belongs, then rearrange the pointers to accommodate it.

Each of these list disciplines has practical applications in software. LIFO keeps track of interrupted tasks so that you always return to successively lower levels. FIFO queues up events in their order of arrival, so that all events have an equal chance for service. Ordered lists are primarily applicable to lookup tables.

Operations on DLLs

In discussing operations on DLLs, we'll use ordered lists as the example since they are the most flexible form of list discipline. You can adapt the algorithms to other DLL concepts.

Starting the List

To manage a circular DLL, you need only one pointer to the node type; we'll call it *head* in this discussion, and it points to some node that is an entry point to the list. Since we're dealing here with ordered lists, head should point to the node containing the key lowest in sequence ("Alice" in the example given earlier). Head thus remains fixed unless we insert a lower-order node: Aaron, for example.

As a practical matter, it's advisable to declare the entry to the list as a global variable in Turbo C, that is, a static declared outside any function and ahead of **main()**. Example:

```
typedef ntype {
      . . .
} NTYPE;

NTYPE *head;

main()
{
      . . .
}
```

This assures that head is initialized to **NULL** before you ever use it, and that local functions can refer to the pointer directly, saving the trouble and overhead of passing it as an argument. An alternative when head is a local variable declared inside a block is

```
main ()
{
NTYPE        *head = NULL;
    . . .
}
```

The thrust is that you *must* initialize the pointer to a zero value. That way you have a reliable value to test in order to determine if the list exists; garbage is a false indicator.

When you allocate the first node in the list, or any other node for that matter, you have to fetch its pointer from the return value of **malloc()** (or **calloc()** or **farmalloc()** or whatever other allocation routine you use). Thus, if you have declared

```
NTYPE *new;
```

assign the returned pointer to new with

```
new = malloc (sizeof (NTYPE));
```

After that you can store a value in the node with

```
*new = someval;
```

As a general rule, list-building routines should assign any new node's address to a working pointer such as **new**, store data in the node, and then check to see if this is the first node in a list. If so, assign the value of **new** to head, as in

```
if (head == NULL)
    head = new;
```

That way the head of the list is automatically set by the routine.

Once this process completes, you have the beginnings of a list that you can expand either by appending nodes to the tail, or by inserting between two existing nodes. In circular lists, there's not much difference. A new node at the tail goes between the old tail and the head, whereas a node inserted elsewhere goes between nodes at a position determined by the order of keys. Let's discuss these two methods in order.

Appending a Node at the Tail

It's simplest to grow a list by inserting new elements immediately above the head: that is, between the head and the old tail. The result is, of course, an "unordered" list (in fact it's ordered by the sequence of arrival rather than by key values, which is sometimes what you want, as in the queues and stacks discussed later in this chapter).

The process for doing this is:

1. Allocate the new node, assigning the resulting pointer to **new**.
2. Put data into the new node.
3. Copy head->prev to new->prev.
4. Set head->prev to the new pointer.
5. Copy new->prev->next to new->next.
6. Set new->prev->next to the **new** pointer.

Steps 3 through 6 rearrange the pointers to effect insertion of the new node between the head and the old tail. Figure 17.2 depicts this process with before and after views of the lists (where parentheses around a name indicate "pointer to the node containing that person's name").

Figure 17.2 **Appending a New Tail to a DLL**

Before:

Data	Prev	Next
Zeke	(Yvette)	(Alice)
Alice	(Zeke)	(Bob)

After:

Data	Prev	Next
Zeke	(Yvette)	(Carla)*
Carla	(Zeke)	(Alice)
Alice	(Carla)*	(Bob)

*Pre-existing pointers changed by the insertion

Now if the list is traversed from the head back to the head, Carla is the last key encountered. That's appropriate, since she arrived most recently and is therefore at the tail.

Inserting a Node Based on Key Value

This method has the effect of sorting data, since it inserts each incoming node into the list based on the relative values of keys. The steps are as follows:

1. Allocate the new node and assign the returned pointer to **new**.
2. Put the data into the new node.
3. Determine where to insert the new node by traversing the list comparing keys.
4. Rearrange the pointers to effect insertion.

Step 3 differentiates this process from the one described previously. Step 4 is the same as steps 3 through 6 above.

Data often come into a program in random order; the person doing data entry types names or numbers, a measurement device propagates values, or whatever, without regard to sequence. Insertion based on a key value is a sensible way to order data as it arrives.

Step 2 puts the data into the new node. To find the proper position of the node, then, simply traverse the list starting at the head and compare keys. Usually you sort data into ascending order. Thus, when

new->key > compared->key

(as in C > B), keep looking. When

new->key < compared->key

the search is over and you have found the point of insertion; it's between the compared node and the one preceding. At that point:

1. Copy compared->prev into new->prev.
2. Set compared->prev to the new pointer.
3. Copy new->prev->next into new->next.
4. Set new->prev->next to the new pointer.

Note that this differs from the algorithm in the previous section only in that compared is substituted for **head**.

In searching a circular list for the insertion point, you have to be alert to one other possibility: that no element in the existing list has a higher value than the new key. If you don't watch for this, you'll run in circles forever inside the list. You can detect this condition by checking the compared node's pointer against **head**. If the two are the same, you've completely traversed the list without finding a higher key than that of the new node. Therefore, re-encountering the head is the same as finding the point of insertion, and the new node belongs at the tail.

Similarly, it's possible that the new node has a key lower in order than the existing head, as when the present head's key is Alice and the new node's is Abel. In that case, the new node goes between the former head and the current tail, but it becomes the new head. Rearrange the pointers as already discussed, but also update the global head pointer to point to the new node. You can detect this condition by checking **compared** against **head**: if they are the same, compare keys. If the new node's key is less than that of the head, change the global head pointer.

Application: Building an Ordered List

Now let's tie this discussion together with a demonstration program. We'll call it MAKEDLL.C, and Program 17.1 lists it. The purpose of this program is to accept last and first names from the keyboard and organize them into an ordered list sorted by last name. Each time you finish typing a name, the list appears in sorted order on the screen, as in

```
Last name? Perez
First name? Dennis
Ellsworth, Don
Hoffman, Doug
Needham, Nancy
Perez, Dennis
Randall, Peggy

Last name?
```

You can signal the program that the input is finished by pressing the **Enter** key in response to the **Last name?** query. At that point, the entire list appears on the screen, and the program saves it in alphabetic order by last name into a text file called NAMES.DLL.

As you'll see in the next section, it saves programming complexity to sort the data on entry, as we've done in Program 17.1. When you read the file or load it into a DLL as we do later, it's already in order.

If you need test data, here are the names in the order we typed them into MAKEDLL. Later examples use these names for table searching. As in the real world, the names follow no particular order.

```
Ellsworth, Don
Needham, Nancy
```

Randall, Peggy
Hoffman, Doug
Perez, Dennis
Quion, Nadine
MacDonald, Laureen
Cady, Frank
Katz, Michael
Marcus, Larry
Irvine, Ed
Austin, Avis
Wallis, Angela
Lindho, Joe
Chow, Doris

Program 17.1 **Demonstration: Building an Ordered List**

```c
/* MAKEDLL.C: Build DLL from keyboard input. On receiving */
/*    blank last name, save list in file NAMES.DLL         */

#include <stdio.h>
#include <alloc.h>
#include <string.h>
#include <conio.h>

#define  MAXSTR  15
#ifndef  TRUE
#define  TRUE  1
#define  FALSE 0
#endif

typedef struct dnode {
  char          LastName[MAXSTR], FirstName[MAXSTR];
  struct dnode  *prev, *next;
} DNODE;

/* LOCAL FUNCTION PROTOTYPES */
DNODE   *GetData (void);
DNODE   *FindInsert (DNODE *new);
void    InsertNode (DNODE *new);
void    ShowList (void);
void    BuildList (void);
void    StoreList (void);
void    ShowList (void);

/* GLOBALS */
DNODE   *head;
/* ------------------------- */

void main ()
{
  BuildList();
```

Program 17.1 (continued)

```
  StoreList();
} /* ----------------------- */

void  BuildList (void)           /* Build DLL from kbd input */
{                                /* Done when GetData returns NULL */
DNODE   *new;

  do {
    new = GetData ();
    if (new != NULL)
      InsertNode (new);
    ShowList ();
  } while (new != NULL);
} /* ----------------------- */

DNODE *GetData (void)        /* Capture data from kbd, put in */
                  /* new node. Return node address or NULL */
{                           /* if nothing was entered by user */
char   name[MAXSTR];
DNODE *new = NULL;

  cputs ("\nLast name?  ");
  gets (name);                            /* get last name */
  if (name[0]) {
    new = (DNODE*) malloc (sizeof (DNODE)); /* alloc node */
    strcpy (new->LastName, name);      /* put in last name */
    cputs ("First name? ");
    gets (new->FirstName);              /* get first name */
  }
  return (new);                   /* return pointer or NULL */
} /* ----------------------- */

DNODE *FindInsert (DNODE *new)
                          /* Find point where new->key fits */
{            /* into list, or quit on re-encountering head */
char    found = FALSE;
DNODE   *this;

  this = head;
  do {
    if (strcmp (new->LastName, this->LastName) < 0)
      found = TRUE;                 /* found insertion point */
    else
      this = this->next;              /* try the next node */
  } while (!found && this != head);
  return (this);
} /* ----------------------- */

void  InsertNode (DNODE *new)
{                                  /* Insert new node into list */
DNODE   *ins = NULL;

  if (head == NULL) {               /* If first node in list */
```

Program 17.1 **(continued)**

```
      head = new;                        /* set head pointer */
      head->prev = head->next = head;    /* point to itself */
   } else {
      ins = FindInsert (new);          /* Find insertion point */
      new->prev = ins->prev;             /* Rearrange pointers */
      ins->prev = new;
      new->next = new->prev->next;
      new->prev->next = new;
      if (strcmp (new->LastName, head->LastName) < 0)
         head = new;                   /* If new head, change head */
   }
} /* ---------------------- */
void  ShowList (void)    /* Display list as entered so far */
{
DNODE  *this;

   if (head != NULL) {
      this = head;
      do {
         printf ("\n%s, %s", this->LastName, this->FirstName);
         this = this->next;
      } while (this != head);
      putchar ('\n');
   }
} /* ---------------------- */
void  StoreList (void)      /* Store DLL in file NAMES.DLL */
{
FILE   *f;
DNODE  *this;

   if (head != NULL) {
      f = fopen ("NAMES.DLL", "w");
      this = head;
      do {
         fputs (this->LastName, f);
         fputc ('\n', f);
         fputs (this->FirstName, f);
         fputc ('\n', f);
         this = this->next;
      } while (this != head);
      fclose (f);
   }
} /* ---------------------- */
```

Searching a DLL

Search an unordered DLL the same way you would an SLL: top to bottom
following the **next** pointers and comparing each node's key with the value
sought (the "argument"). Alternatively, you could go the other way in the
chain furnished by the **prev** pointers. Neither direction has an advantage

over the other since an unordered list is random by definition. On average, a search passes through half the list to discover the object it's seeking. The head of an unordered circular list is merely an arbitrary, known entry point, and you know that you've completely but fruitlessly traversed the list when the chain of pointers takes you back to the head.

The search of an ordered list is more intelligent. Assuming the keys are in ascending order and you're following the **next** pointers, each key comparison produces one of three possible outcomes that form the basis for deciding what to do next. These are:

1. Argument > node's key. Continue the search.
2. Argument = node's key. The search is successful.
3. Argument < node's key. Abandon the search.

A fourth condition is returning to the head. This happens when the argument is greater than any key in the list. It has the same effect as item three.

Program 17.2 illustrates this algorithm using the DNODE structure defined in Program 17.1. It is a function that returns the address of the node containing the argument, or **NULL** if unsuccessful, and can be used as a model for your applications.

Program 17.2 **Function to Search an Ordered List**

```
DNODE *match (char *arg, DNODE *head)
{
DNODE *this;
int    result;
char   found = FALSE;

  this = head;
  do {                                          /* traverse list */
    result = strcmp (arg, this->LastName)    /* comp keys */
    if (result > 0)           /* if arg lower in alpha order */
      this = this->next;                  /* continue searching */
    else
      if (result == 0)
        found = TRUE;                         /* found match */
      else
        return (NULL);                        /* else abandon */
  } while (!found && (this != head));
  return (this);
} /* ---------------------------- */
```

Deleting a Node

Before deleting a node, of course, you have to know where it is. A common way is to search the list for the key value you want to delete, using a routine similar to Figure 17.3 to get the pointer to the node. If the returned pointer isn't **NULL**, you merely rearrange adjacent pointer fields and free the heap space; this is exactly the opposite of inserting a node. Program 17.3 illustrates the effect on adjacent pointers when a node is removed.

Figure 17.3 **Pointer Rearrangements for Deleting a Node**

Before:

Data	Prev	Next
Ethel	(David)	(Frank)
Frank	(Ethel)	(George)
George	(Frank)	(Heather)

Delete ──────▶ points to the Frank row.

After:

Data	Prev	Next
Ethel	(David)	(George)*
George	(Ethel)*	(Heather)

* Changed pointers

Described in C notation, the pointer shuffling is:

```
del->next->prev = del->prev;
del->prev->next = del->next;
```

In other words, from the deleted node, drop the **prev** pointer to the next node and lift the **next** pointer to the previous node.

Note that the list doesn't physically close up when a node is deleted; nothing actually moves, but the pointers instead bypass the removed node, effectively forgetting that it ever existed.

Now let's consider two special cases: You're deleting the only node in the list, and you're deleting the head when other nodes still exist. Both cases in fact involve deleting the head, which requires an update to the global head pointer. In the first instance, the deletion erases the list altogether, so you set the head pointer to **NULL**. In the second, you promote the next node to be the head.

You can find out which case you're dealing with by comparing **del->next** (or **del->prev**) with **del** itself. If the two are equal (remember to use huge pointers if working on the far heap), the node is the last on the list. You can bypass pointer rearrangements in that event, resetting the head pointer to **NULL** and freeing the node's space.

If **del** equals **head**, and **del->next** and **del** are not equal, you're deleting the head of a list containing at least two nodes. Therefore, rearrange pointers, advance the global head pointer to **del->next**, and free the old node space.

Program 17.3 **Function for Deleting a Node**

```
void delnode (DNODE *del, DNODE **head)
{
  if (del == NULL) return;              /* already deleted */
  if (del == *head)                     /* then deleting head node */
    if (del == del->next) {             /* if the only node... */
      *head = NULL;                     /* erase the list */
      free (del);
      return;                                    /* and quit */
    } else
      *head = del->next;       /* else promote next to head */
  del->next->prev = del->prev;          /* rearrange pointers */
  del->prev->next = del->next;
  free (del);                           /* deallocate space */
} /* ------------------------ */
```

Program 17.3 lists a model function **delnode()** that summarizes this discussion. Note the use of double indirection in passing the head parameter; this is so that you can pass a change to the head pointer's value back to the caller. The double-indirection argument ****head** passes the address of the pointer to the head node. Therefore the single-indirection statement

   *head = del->next;

changes the pointer itself.

Call this function after using **match()** or some equivalent function to locate the node you want to delete. For example, to remove the node containing the last name Porter, write:

   delete = match ("Porter", head);
   delnode (delete, &head);

Now let's put these techniques to work in a program.

Application: Finding and Deleting Nodes in an Ordered DLL

Program 17.1 presented the program MAKEDLL.C, which put names typed at the keyboard into a circular DLL and later saved them in the disk file NAMES.DLL. This application—Program 17.4—uses that file in a somewhat opposite manner; it's a seek and destroy mission that loads the file into a DLL, then locates the nodes containing your keyboard entries and removes them from the DLL (though not from the disk file itself).

The program asks you for a last name. After finding the associated node, it displays the person's full name and asks if that's the node you want to delete. Type **Y** for yes and anything else for no. The program then deletes the node if appropriate and redisplays the entire list as it now stands.

Program 17.4 **Demonstration: Finding and Deleting DLL Nodes**

```c
/* DELDLL.C: Demos searching and deleting nodes in a DLL */

/* INCLUDED FILES */
#include <stdio.h>
#include <alloc.h>
#include <string.h>
#include <conio.h>

/* CONSTANTS */
#define    MAXSTR   15
#ifndef    TRUE
#define    TRUE   1
#define    FALSE  0
#endif

/* TYPES */
typedef struct dnode {                    /* DLL node structure */
   char          LastName[MAXSTR], FirstName[MAXSTR];
   struct dnode  *prev, *next;
} DNODE;

/* LOCAL FUNCTION PROTOTYPES */
void    BuildList (void);
void    ShowList (DNODE*);
void    InsertNode (DNODE*);
DNODE   *FindInsert (DNODE*);
void    Delete (void);
DNODE   *match (char*, DNODE*);

/* GLOBALS */
DNODE     *head;
/* --------------------------- */

void main ()
{
  BuildList ();
  Delete ();
} /* ---------------------- */

void  BuildList (void)          /* Build DLL from disk file */
{
FILE    *f;
DNODE   *new;
char    last[MAXSTR], first[MAXSTR];

  f = fopen ("NAMES.DLL", "r");              /* Open file */
  if (f == NULL) {                           /* error */
```

Program 17.4 **(continued)**

```c
      puts ("Unable to open NAMES.DLL");
      exit (1);
   }
   while (!feof (f)) {                    /* while not end of file */
      fscanf (f, "%s%s", last, first);            /* get data */
      if (!feof (f)) {
         new = (DNODE*) malloc (sizeof (DNODE));
         strcpy (new->LastName, last);
         strcpy (new->FirstName, first);
         InsertNode (new);                    /* put into list */
      }
   }
   fclose (f);                         /* close file at end */
} /* ----------------------- */

void  InsertNode (DNODE *new)      /* Insert node into DLL */
{
DNODE   *ins = NULL;

   if (head == NULL) {                      /* First node in list */
      head = new;                           /* set head pointer */
      head->prev = head->next = head;       /* point to itself */
   } else {
      ins = FindInsert (new);   /* else find insertion point */
      new->prev = ins->prev;               /* rearrange pointers */
      ins->prev = new;
      new->next = new->prev->next;
      new->prev->next = new;
      if (strcmp (new->LastName, head->LastName) < 0)
         head = new;     /* change global pointer if new head */
   }
} /* ----------------------- */


DNODE   *FindInsert (DNODE *new)
{                                 /* Find where new->key fits */
char   found = FALSE;
DNODE *this;

   this = head;
   do {
      if (strcmp (new->LastName, this->LastName) < 0)
         found = TRUE;                 /* found insertion point */
      else
         this = this->next;            /* else try the next node */
   } while (!found && this != head);
   return (this);
} /* ----------------------- */

void ShowList (DNODE *head)        /* Show list on screen */
{
DNODE   *this;

   this = head;
```

Program 17.4 **(continued)**

```c
   do {
      cprintf ("\r\n%s, %s", this->LastName, this->FirstName);
      this = this->next;
   } while (this != head);
   putchar ('\n');
} /* ----------------------- */

void    Delete (void)     /* Sub to delete nodes on request */
{
char    reply = 'N', name[MAXSTR];
DNODE   *del = NULL, *start;

   do {
      clrscr();
      cputs ("\r\nCURRENT CONTENTS OF LIST:");
      ShowList (head);
      start = head;
      cputs ("\r\n\n\nName to delete? ");
      gets (name);                        /* get name from keyboard */
      while (name[0] && reply != 'Y') {
         del = match (name, start);    /* find node with name */
         if (del) {
            cprintf ("\r\nFound %s %s", del->FirstName,
                      del->LastName);
            cputs ("\r\nDelete this one? (Y/N)... ");
            reply = toupper (getch());
            if (reply == 'Y') {
               del->prev->next = del->next;      /* remove node */
               del->next->prev = del->prev;
               if (del == head)        /* if deleting head node */
                  head = del->next;              /* repoint head */
               free (del);
            } else
               if (del->next != head)  /* if not wrapping back */
                  start = del->next;       /* resume at next node */
               else
                  start = NULL;                /* else stop search */
         } else {
            cprintf ("\r\nUnable to find %s", name);
            cputs ("\r\n\nPress any key to continue... ");
            getche();
            reply = 'Y';                /* to stop while() loop */
         }
      }
      reply = 'N';                      /* to re-enable while() loop */
   } while (name[0]);
} /* ----------------------- */

DNODE *match (char *name, DNODE *list)
                                       /* find name in list */
{
DNODE   *this;
int     found = 0;
```

Program 17.4 (continued)

```
if (list != NULL) {
  this = list;
  do {
    if (strcmp (name, this->LastName) == 0)
      found = 1;
    else
      this = this->next;
  } while ((this != head) && !found);
}
if (!found)
  this = NULL;
return this;
} /* ------------------------- */
```

Stacks and Queues

Stacks and queues differ from other linked lists not in their structure and mechanics, but in the way they're used. So far we've considered unordered and key-sorted lists. In stacks and queues, the organizing principle is order of arrival in and retrieval from the list. Thus they represent two alternative forms of list management.

A queue is like a conveyor belt: things go in one end and come out the other. Another analogy is a line of people waiting at the grocery checkout; you join at the end and eventually you get your turn to pay.

In software, queues are often used to hold requests for service until it's convenient to service them. An example is an interrupt from an external device. The interrupt arrives while the system is busy doing other things, so it puts a record of the interrupt into a queue ("enqueues" it) and goes on about its business. Later, it gets around to servicing interrupts, of which there might be several. The software pulls the oldest off the queue first ("dequeues" it), takes care of it, then gets the next, and so on until the queue is drained or some distraction arises.

Consequently, a queue lines things up in order of arrival, and furnishes them to the software in the same order. Queues are also called FIFO buffers, short for First In, First Out.

You effect a queue by always adding new nodes to the tail, and always fetching and deleting the head when you take a node out of the list. Program 17.4 illustrates this.

A stack works on the opposite principle; the last item added is the first to be retrieved. An analogy is the in-basket on your desk at work. Everything goes on top of the existing contents, and when you want something to do you take off the most recently arrived thing first. If you always pulled from the bottom of the pile, you'd be maintaining a queue, but that's not the way it usually works. Stacks also go by the name LIFO, for Last In, First Out.

Stacks are essential for retracing the path out of a sequence of events, and are thus used throughout software. An example close to C programmers is retreating from a series of subroutine calls. The **main()** function calls **fcn1()**, which calls **fcn2()**. When **fcn2()** completes, it returns to **fcn1()**, and eventually **fcn1()** returns to **main()**. Out of sight inside its works, the program maintains a stack where it places the return address each time your C code calls a function. The **return()** statement or the closing curly brace of a subroutine pulls the return address from the top of the stack so that execution can resume where it left off when you called the function.

Stacks are so common that there is a vocabulary surrounding them. Placing an item on the stack is called *pushing.* Thus, in the example above, you push a return address onto the stack before calling a subroutine. Taking it off the stack later is called *popping,* as in "pop the return address off the stack."

There are several ways to manage a stack. In the context of this chapter, which is as good a method as any other, you can operate a stack by always pushing and popping the head node. Conceptually the stack grows upward and shrinks downward by activity at its top.

Popping and dequeuing are the same thing, since the object at the head is removed and the list shrinks toward its "lower" end. The distinction is that in popping from a stack, you get the most recent item, while in dequeuing you fetch the oldest thing.

Program 17.4 lists a program called STAQUE.C. It's an entertaining demonstration of queue and stack operations. As you key in a line of text, the program enqueues and pushes each character in separate dynamic structures. When you press **Enter**, the program dequeues the characters to reconstruct your input in the order of arrival. After that, it pops characters and writes them to the screen in the reverse order that characterizes a stack. The queue- and stack-affecting subprograms (**enqueue()**, **dequeue()**, **push()**, and **pop()**) implement the discussion.

Note that this program also proves a point mentioned earlier in the chapter: Two or more linked lists can be physically intermingled on the heap without fear of confusion. Examining the flow of Program 17.5, you can see that stack and queue nodes alternate. Yet they don't confound each other since proper pointer management keeps the lists separate and uncorrupted.

Program 17.5 Demonstration: Stack and Queue Operations

```
/* STAQUE.C: Queue and stack operations */

#include <stdio.h>
#include <alloc.h>
#include <conio.h>

#define ENTER 13
```

Program 17.5 (continued)

```
#define BKSPC   8

typedef struct chnode {
  char          ch;
  struct chnode *prev, *next;
} CHNODE;

/* Globals */
CHNODE  *stack, *qhead, *qtail;

/* Prototypes */
CHNODE *enqueue (char, CHNODE*);
CHNODE *dequeue (char*, CHNODE*);
CHNODE *push (char, CHNODE*);
CHNODE *pop (char*, CHNODE*);

/* ------------------------- */

void main ()
{
char  ch;

  /* Get the data, put into queue and stack */
  clrscr();
  cputs ("Queues and stacks\r\n");
  cputs ("Type something:\r\n");

  /* NOTE: following is not a complete keyboard processor */
  do {
    ch = getche ();                       /* get char and echo */
    if (ch != ENTER) {        /* until Enter is pressed... */
      qtail = enqueue (ch, qtail);        /* enqueue char */
      if (qhead == NULL)
        qhead = qtail;             /* set queue head if first */
      stack = push (ch, stack);            /* push char */
    }
  } while (ch != ENTER);

  /* Read from the queue */
  cputs ("\r\n\nYour input taken from the queue:\r\n");
  while (qhead != NULL) {
    qhead = dequeue (&ch, qhead);     /* dequeue next char */
    if (qtail == NULL)                /* reset head if last */
      qhead = NULL;
    putchar (ch);                           /* print char */
  }

  /* Read from the stack */
  cputs ("\r\n\nYour input taken from the stack:\r\n");
  while (stack != NULL) {
    stack = pop (&ch, stack);           /* pop next char */
    putchar (ch);                          /* print it */
```

Program 17.5 **(continued)**

```
    }
    cputs ("\r\n");
} /* ----------------------- */

CHNODE *enqueue (char c, CHNODE *tail)
    /* add node to end of queue, return pointer to new tail */
{
CHNODE *newtail;

    newtail = malloc (sizeof (CHNODE));    /* allocate node */
    newtail->ch = c;                            /* save char */
    if (tail) tail->next = newtail;      /* update old tail */
    newtail->prev = tail;          /* set new tail's pointers */
    newtail->next = NULL;
    return newtail;
} /* ----------------------- */

CHNODE *dequeue (char *c, CHNODE *head)
           /* remove node from head of queue, return next */
{
CHNODE *newhead = NULL;

    if (head) {                          /* if queue exists... */
        *c = head->ch;                      /* give back char */
        newhead = head->next;
        newhead->prev = NULL;     /* update backward pointer */
        free (head);                   /* deallocate space */
    } else
        *c = NULL;                 /* else no char to return */
    return newhead;
} /* ----------------------- */

CHNODE *push (char c, CHNODE *top)
        /* push char onto stack, return new top of stack */
{
CHNODE *newtop;

    newtop = malloc (sizeof (CHNODE));    /* allocate space */
    newtop->ch = c;                           /* save char */
    if (top) top->prev = newtop; /* update old top of stack */
    newtop->next = top;           /* set new node's pointers */
    newtop->prev = NULL;
    return (newtop);
} /* ----------------------- */

CHNODE *pop (char *c, CHNODE *top)
                  /* pop char from stack, return new top */
{
CHNODE *newtop = NULL;

    if (top) {                           /* if stack exists... */
        *c = top->ch;                       /* send back char */
```

Program 17.5 **(continued)**

```
    newtop = top->next;
    newtop->prev = NULL;        /* update backward pointer */
    free (top);                            /* free space */
  } else
    *c = NULL;                   /* else no char to return */
  return newtop;
} /* ---------------------- */
```

Conclusion

This chapter has explored some of the possibilities that doubly linked lists offer for creating highly flexible dynamic data structures. We've touched on unordered lists, but most of our attention has been focused on three types of ordered structures: sorted by key, queues, and stacks. DLLs lend themselves to ordered sequences of nodes much more readily than SLLs, since insertion of a node between two that already exist is painless. Therefore, as a practical matter, if your data are inherently unorganized and you don't care, use an SLL for it; otherwise, use a DLL.

The circular lists covered here are much easier to use in organizing a key-ordered list than are DLLs with terminal nodes. It's probably a little easier to use terminal-node lists with queues and certainly with stacks, but the circular model erects few inconveniences in any case and is a workable solution for most DLL applications.

The trouble with both SLLs and DLLs is that searches must always proceed in a sequential manner. Ordered DLLs offer the option of bailing out early when you detect that the key you're looking for isn't in the list. Still, in both types of lists, if the list contains n items, it takes $n/2$ comparisons on average to find what you want. In very large lists, this can potentially consume a significant amount of time. So can the problem of ordering a DLL, which is not ordered unless you specifically undertake to make it so.

Let's move on now to binary trees, dynamic structures similar to DLLs that are inherently ordered and offer a dramatically faster search path.

CHAPTER 18

BINARY TREES

T he nodes of a binary tree look the same as those of a doubly linked list in that they include two pointers, one to a "higher" node and the other to one that is "lower." The similarity ends there. A linked list is sequential, much like a string of pearls where one follows another. A binary tree, on the other hand, is hierarchical, such that the path divides into two at each node. The import of this difference will become apparent as we proceed.

A binary tree is inherently ordered according to its key, making the concept of sorting implicit in the organization. Every time you add a new element, the node is inserted into its proper position within the hierarchy and the overall structure of the tree adjusts accordingly. The tree also changes its structure when you delete a node. And because searches traverse the tree—not sequentially as in a linked list, but along paths that are continually dividing—movement through a binary tree is blazingly fast. Binary trees are perfectly suited to organizing and searching very large amounts of data.

There are many practical applications for binary trees. One example is a spelling checker, which has to order huge numbers of words and find any one in the bat of an electronic eye. Another is a database management system, which organizes records indexed by key fields. Your programs might use binary trees to arrange customer ledgers by account number, phone lists by name, mailing labels by ZIP code, or a library's card catalog by accession number. The uses for ordering data by a key are limitless.

Paradoxically, the concept of a binary tree is fairly simple and the algorithms extremely efficient, but the underlying details are difficult unless you are thoroughly indoctrinated in the self-defining world of recursion. We'll cover some concepts first, and then get into the details.

Organization of a Binary Tree

A binary tree takes its name from its resemblance to a biological tree turned upside down. Turn over Figure 18.1 and you'll see it clearly. Some of the taxonomy associated with binary trees also comes from the biological model: root, branch, and leaf.

Figure 18.1 **A Typical Binary Tree**

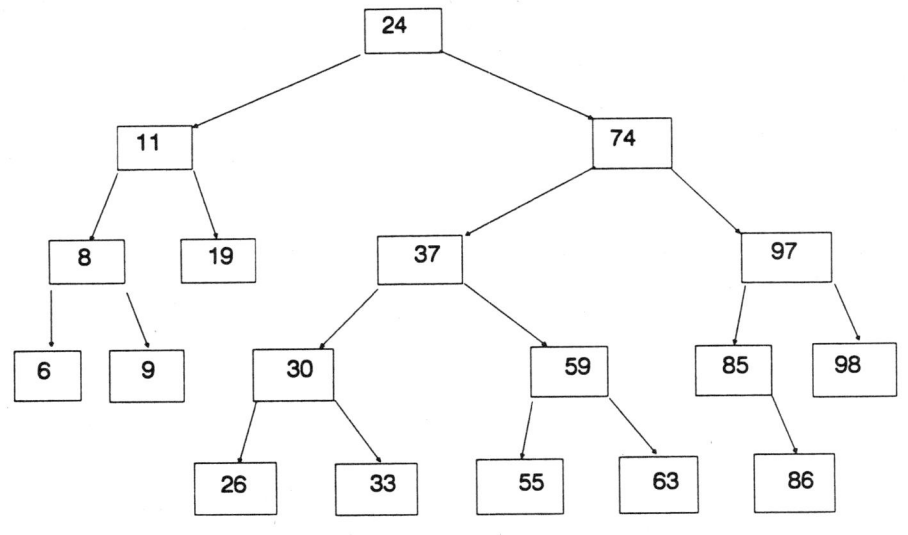

Each of the nodes in Figure 18.1 shows its key value so that you can see how keys order the structure. The topmost node contains key 24; it's called the *root*, and it serves as the point of entry to the tree much as the head does in linked lists.

Two *branches* flow from the root. The subtree to the left contains keys that are all less than the root's key, while those in the right-hand subtree are greater than the root's.

The subtrees follow the same ordering principle. Taking the left subtree as an example, the nodes to the left of its root all have keys less than 11, while the nodes to the right have keys greater than 11 but less than 24, the value of the tree's main root. The sub-subtree beginning at 8 is similarly organized, as are all structural components of a binary tree.

Terminal nodes (6, 9, 19, 26, and so on) are called *leaves* because, like the leaves on a tree, they are the ends of the paths and lead nowhere beyond. Note that, unlike linked lists, a binary tree has no definite end, or *tail*. Instead, its many paths all culminate eventually in leaf nodes. A leaf can be detected because both of its linkage pointers are **NULL**.

The term *binary* comes, in this case, from the less-than/greater-than organization. From any given node, the path to subsequent nodes depends on whether the sought key is less than or greater than the current node's key. It might also be equal, in which case the search ends successfully.

Efficiency of Binary Trees

The tree in Figure 18.1 contains 18 nodes. If these same nodes were in a linked list, on average it would take nine compares per search to find a given value. This is based on the assumption that all nodes have an equal chance of being selected, so the "average" node would be in the middle of the list. Therefore 18/2 = 9 searches on average.

The computation is somewhat more complex in a binary tree. It also depends on the structure of the individual tree; if the tree in Figure 18.1 had different key values, the tree would have a different structure. This leads to the general observation that every binary tree is unique, and because it is a dynamic data structure that automatically adjusts its own configuration to accomodate the insertion and deletion of nodes, uniqueness extends down to the level of any given moment in a particular tree's existence. Still, since we know how this tree is organized, we can compute the average number of compares to reach a specific node.

Typical Case

Figure 18.2 illustrates that the tree consists of five levels. The level number is equivalent to the number of compares it takes to reach that level. That is, if the argument is 24, the first compare finds a match at the first level. Similarly, if the argument is 26, we have to compare it with 24, 74, 37, 30, and finally 26 to find a match; 26 is on level 5, and it takes five compares to get there.

Therefore we can estimate a weighted average based on the number of nodes per level times the level number. The right-hand column in Figure 18.2 shows the number of nodes at each level. The total number of compares to reach all nodes is:

$$(1*1) + (2*2) + (3*4) + (4*6) + (5*5) = 66$$

Since there are 18 nodes, the average number of compares to find any given node is 66/18 = 3.67.

In other words, searching this binary tree is almost three times as efficient as searching for the same key in a linked list. And this is a small tree. As the amount of data increases, the average number of compares rises very slowly in contrast to linked lists, where it grows at exactly half the rate of increase in the number of nodes. For example, adding two nodes at level 4—keys of 17 and 21, for example—would increase the average number of compares from 3.67 to 3.7, while in a linked list it would go from 9 to 10. Thus you can see that the search efficiency for a binary tree is dramatically better even for a small amount of data, and it keeps getting better as the amount of data increases.

Computer scientists such as Knuth have devoted a great deal of mathematical energy to this subject. The general conclusion is that it takes something on the order of [LOG$_2$N]-1 searches to find a node within the average tree. The point is that reasonably balanced binary trees are well suited for organizing large amounts of data.

Figure 18.2 **Levels of the Binary Tree**

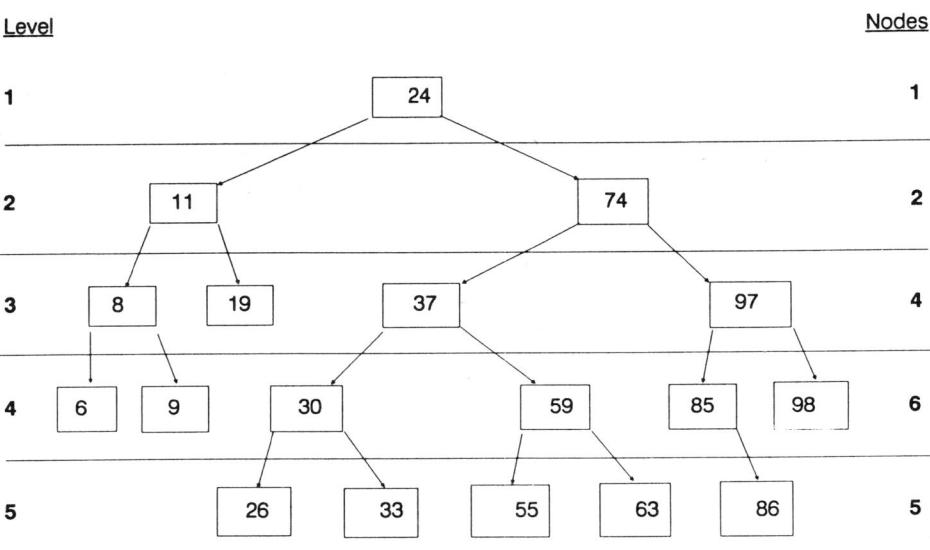

Level   Nodes

| Level | | Nodes |

Best Case

The best case in the organization of a tree is illustrated by the subtree beginning at node 37 in Figures 18.1 and 18.2 Here every possible path reaches a leaf at the same level, or in other words the subtree is perfectly symmetrical or "balanced."

Unfortunately, most binary trees aren't perfectly balanced. We'll consider some extreme cases of imbalance in a moment. A reasonable degree of balance occurs when keys arrive in random order, so that the tree grows more or less uniformly along all possible paths. Usually this is "good enough." There are techniques for forcing a tree into symmetry. The best-known is the AVL method, named for two Russian mathematicians—G.M. Adelson-Velski and E.M. Landis—who developed it in 1962. Such techniques go far beyond the scope of this book, but they're worth investigating if you're faced with a gigantic tree problem; Knuth covers them.

In this book we'll assume that keys arrive in random order and achieve a fairly balanced tree that will deliver better performance than an equivalent linked list.

Worst Case

Figure 18.3 shows three trees exhibitng the worst possible binary structures, which we call linear, zigzag, and mixed linear. In all cases, each node has only one path away from it. Such trees are said to be *degenerate*, as though they were somehow morally reprehensible. As for performance, they are no different from ordinary linked lists, and their efficiency is exactly equal.

Figure 18.3 **Degenerate Trees**

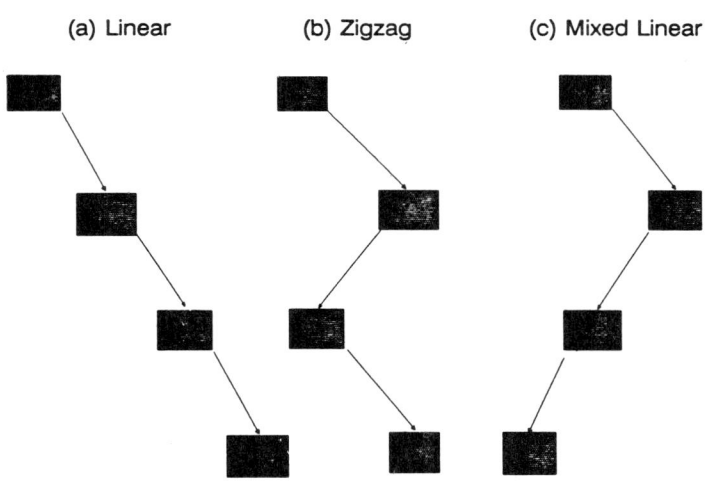

From this you can conclude that, in the worst case, a binary tree will deliver the same search performance as a linked list. Sadly, it's quite easy to build a worst-case binary tree. The secret of reasonable balance is random arrival of keys; a binary tree built from previously ordered data inevitably results in a worst-case structure.

Later we'll cover a method called pre-order traversal that enables us to save and rebuild a binary tree, thus potentially avoiding the construction of a worst-case organization.

Now let's consider the building blocks of binary trees.

Node Structure

The nodes of a binary tree are identical to those of a doubly linked list; that is, the minimal node consists of:

- A data element that can serve as a key.
- Two pointers bound to the node type.

The node can, of course, contain nonkey data elements as well. The difference between binary tree and DLL nodes is in how we employ the pointers.

By convention, the pointers are referred to as **LLink** and **RLink**, where **LLink** points to the "left" (a node whose key is of lesser value) and **RLink** points to the "right" (greater key). In the root of Figures 18.1 and 18.2, **LLink** leads to the node containing 11, and **RLink** leads to 74. Figure 18.4 shows a convenient visualization of the node structure.

Figure 18.4 **Conceptual Structure for a Node**

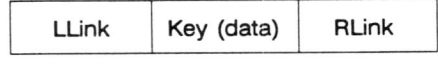

In C, you could define this node as follows:

```
typedef struct binnode {
    int                    key;
    struct binnode * LLink, *RLink;
} BINNODE;
```

Note that, as in the other node types discussed in the preceding chapters, the order of fields doesn't matter. Thus the node format defined here has the same content as, but a different order of elements from, the node depicted in Figure 18.4.

Building a Binary Tree

The first data presented to a routine that builds a new binary tree becomes the root node. Say we're building the tree depicted in Figure 18.1. In that case, the first data value—hence the first key—is 24, which becomes the "splitting value" of the tree that ensues.

Maybe the next key that comes to the tree is 74. It's greater than 24, so the root's **RLink** is set to point to the node containing 74, and the tree takes the form shown in Figure 18.5.

Figure 18.5 **Starting the Binary Tree**

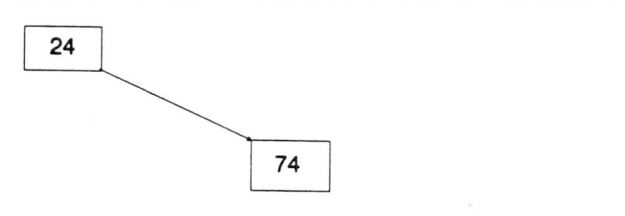

Perhaps the next value to arrive is 11. To find its rightful place, we begin searching the tree at the root. Because 11 < 24 and the root's **LLink** is **NULL**, we set **root->LLink** to point to the new node, with the result that appears in Figure 18.6.

Figure 18.6 **Adding a Third Node to the Tree**

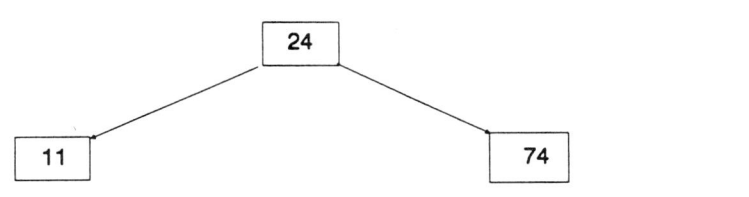

Now we get the key value 37 and things become more interesting as we search for its home. Starting at the root, 37 > 24, we follow **RLink** to key 74. There we discover that 37 < 74. This node's **LLink** is **NULL**, so we set it to point to the new node and a tree takes shape as in Figure 18.7.

Figure 18.7 **A Tree Begins to Form**

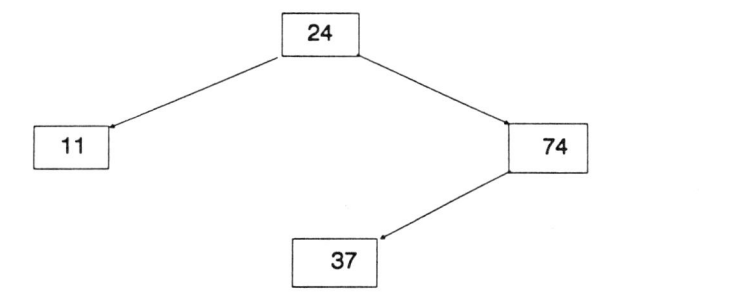

The next incoming value is 59. Again starting at the root, 59 > 24, 59 < 74, and 59 > 37. Because the **RLink** at 37 is **NULL**, the tree takes the new shape in Figure 18.8.

Figure 18.8 **The Tree Continues to Grow as Nodes Arrive**

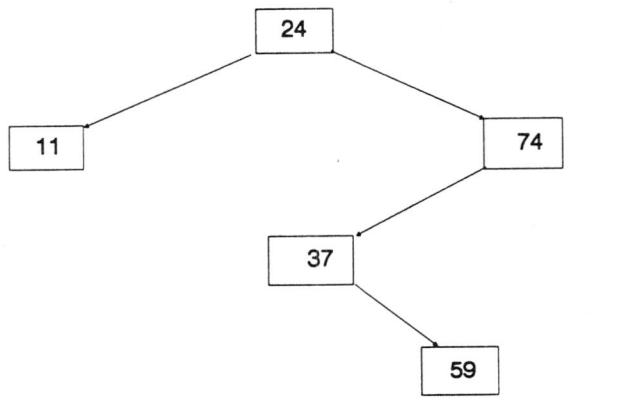

This process continues along the same lines for as long as new nodes keep arriving. Each new node falls into the **LLink** or **RLink** path from its "parent" (higher-level node), and is added to the tree as a leaf.

Duplicate Keys

Conceivably an application could have duplicate keys in a binary tree. An example is a system that tracks daily sales orders using the customer account number as the key; the same customer might place two or more orders in the same day, resulting in duplication of the key in the tree.

Binary trees are capable of dealing with this problem, but it's not a good idea. Why? Because searches will always stop at the first encounter with the key being sought. You have to introduce considerable overhead to look at secondary criteria and decide whether or not to continue the search. This might cancel out the benefits of using binary trees.

A better approach is to use a key that you're confident is unique in all cases. In this example, organize and search on the customer purchase order number instead of the internal account number. It might be unlikely that any given customer will place two or more separate orders using the same PO number, and statistically improbable that two different customers will generate the same PO number in any given day.

Binary trees work best when all keys are unique.

Traversing a Tree _____

As with lists, the process of moving through a tree and accessing each of its nodes is called *traversing*. This is a purely sequential operation in a list; it's considerably more complicated in a tree, which has a complex organization.

There are three ways to traverse a binary tree: in-order, pre-order, and post-order, referring to the sequence in which the contents of individual nodes are accessed. Each has application to real-world programming problems, and we'll discuss some of those applications as we cover the three methods.

In-Order Traversal

In-order traversal follows the tree according to the collating sequence of its keys (A through Z or whatever). A common usage is in printing out a sorted listing of node contents. For example, if the tree is keyed on employee names, in-order traversal will automatically produce an alphabetized list of employees. In-order traversal of the tree in Figure 18.1 follows the order

```
    6
    8
    9
   11
   19
   24
   . . .
   86
   97
   98
```

The **LLink** pointer of every node points either to another node having a lower key value, or it is **NULL**. If you enter at the root and follow the chain of **LLinks** until you encounter a **NULL** pointer, you have reached the lowest-valued leaf in the tree. The in-order algorithm, then, always strives to the left until it can go no further. At that point, it reports the data, then follows **RLink** and begins striving to the left again. When all **RLinks** have been followed in a subtree, the process backs up to the next higher level and follows its **RLink** to a node where it again strives to the left. This continues until all **RLinks** have been exhausted, or in other words until there's nowhere left to go. In Figure 18.1, this happens at the node whose key is 98.

While this and the other traversal algorithms sound complex, it takes only three lines of code to do it using the mysterious magic of recursion. We'll cover the "how" later in the chapter.

Pre-Order Traversal

The most important value in a binary tree is its root key. Secondary in importance are the root keys of subtrees. These pivotal values, if preserved in the proper order with respect to all other keys, enable us to save a binary tree's contents in a disk file and later reconstruct the tree in its present form. That's what pre-order traversal is all about: preserving the tree's contents for later reconstruction.

Why would you want to save the tree's structure as well as its data? Suppose you have a large, reasonably well-balanced table that is used by several applications, or is called in from disk once a day for updates and reference. If you save it with in-order traversal, you end up with an ordered list. The next time you bring it in, you will build a degenerate tree whose performance is no better than a linked list. In other words, the balance and thus the advantage of the tree are destroyed by saving it in-order. That's why saving it pre-order is important.

Like in-order, pre-order tends to the left and only resorts to the right when its leftward path dead-ends in a **NULL LLink**. The difference is the order in which it accesses the data as it traverses. In-order processes the node's data contents whenever it switches from the **LLink** path to the **RLink**. On the other hand, pre-order processes the contents when it first enters a node, and *then* it attempts to move left. When it runs into a **NULL LLink**, it grabs the first **RLink** it can find and again strives leftward. For the tree in Figure 18.1, the pre-order is:

```
24
11
8
6
9
19
74
. . .
97
85
86
98
```

If you take these values and manually reconstruct the tree, you will build a configuration exactly like that shown in Figure 18.1.

Post-Order Traversal

Post-order is most commonly employed when traversing a tree to dispose of its elements, that is, when deleting the tree from the heap. You might do this to free up heap space for other uses when the tree is no longer needed ("garbage collection").

In post-order, the action associated with the traversal (disposal, output, or whatever) occurs when you leave the node for the final time to move upward in the tree. Thus, the post-order traversal of Figure 18.1 operates on the nodes in this order:

```
6
9
8
19
11
26
33
30
. . .
98
97
74
24
```

Traversal Summary

In all three traversal algorithms, a transition occurs between **LLink** and **RLink** at some point in every node. The terms pre-, in-, and post- refer to the time when action (typically output of data) occurs with respect to this transition.

- In pre-order, the action occurs before the transition. Thus, pre-order accesses a parent node first, then all its left-hand children, then all on the right.
- In-order takes action during the transition, as the algorithm moves from **LLink** to **RLink**. Consequently, in-order accesses all the left-hand children, then the parent, then all the right-hand children.
- Post-order operates on the data after the transition, accessing all the left-hand children, all the right-hand children, and finally the parent. As a result, when deleting a tree with post-order, the root node is the last to go.

Later we will translate this discussion into C code.

Searching the Binary Tree

As mentioned earlier, a search path in a binary tree tends to be very short because it follows a hierarchy that divides continuously. In a perfectly balanced tree of 65,536 nodes, for example, it would take no more than 16 attempts to locate any given key.

Searching a binary tree is a matter of comparing the key value sought (argument) against the current node's key. There are three possible outcomes:

1. Argument = key   The search succeeds and ends.
2. Argument < key   Follow **LLink**.
3. Argument > key   Follow **RLink**.

A fourth outcome results when the argument is not in the tree; that is, when you're looking for a key that doesn't exist. You know that's the case when the search is barred by a **NULL** pointer.

Perhaps the first argument you search for in Figure 18.1 is 37. Entering the tree at the root, you find that 37 > 24, so you follow **RLink**. There, 37 < 74, so you follow **LLink**. The next node contains a match, so the search ends successfully.

Next you look for 18. Since 18 < 24, you follow **LLink**. In the next node, 18 > 11, sending you per **RLink** to the node containing 19. Following the determination that 18 < 19, your progress is halted since **LLink** is **NULL** in this node. Therefore, the key sought is not in the tree.

The process, then, is to compare values and, if not equal, to move left or right depending on the outcome until you either find a match or come to a dead end.

Since searching is the most common operation in binary trees, it's clear that the search procedure needs some way to report results back to the caller. There are two possible outcomes: found and not found. If found, you usually want to do something else, such as printing or otherwise using nonkey data items from the node; if not found, you need to know that too, so that you can display a "no match" message or take some contingency action.

This suggests a function returning a pointer to the found node, or **NULL** if the search was unsuccessful.

Our thoughts are now turning from the theoretical to the practical, so let's translate this discussion into code.

Binary Trees in Action

First we need to establish a context for the following examples since, like linked lists, binary trees are application-dependent with respect to details. Let's say you're accumulating a database that relates part numbers to their descriptions.

For instance, if the part number is 5432, the database furnishes the description **Resistor, 4 ohm**. Part names in this application consist of strings up to 20 characters in length. The key field is the part number, which is also a character field with a length of 6.

We can define the node structure in C as follows:

```
typedef struct {
    char        nbr[6]; /* part , key field */
    char        name[20];
} DATAPART;

typedef struct partnode {
    DATAPART            part;
    struct partnode *LLink, *RLink;
} PARTNODE;
```

Note that we've developed two structures here, in which DATAPART becomes a substructure within PARTNODE. Why? Because later we might want to save the DATAPART on disk without also storing the pointers from PARTNODE. The use of nested structures lets us refer to the substructure and its members in an intuitive manner. The whole substructure can be referred to as **node->part**, while the part number field is **node->part.nbr**. Figure 18.9 visualizes the structure defined by typedef DATAPART.

Figure 18.9 **Visualizing the PARTNODE Structure**

nbr[6]	name[20]	*LLink	*RLink

Perhaps the most important variable in the program is

```
PARTNODE *root = NULL;
```

which will eventually point to the root of the binary tree.

Having defined the major elements, we can implement a binary tree. First, though, let's review recursion, which is essential in understanding how to traverse binary trees.

Recursion

Recursion in software means that a function calls itself ("recurs"). This might seem a strange thing for a function to do, but in fact it's merely a variation on the theme of looping. Because it uses the stack for storing and passing information from one invocation to the next, recursion is particularly well suited to navigation within a complex structure such as a binary tree.

Here we'll look at a simple example that does nothing useful except to illustrate how recursion works. Later in the chapter you'll have plenty of exposure to practical applications.

When one function calls another, it places its arguments on the stack, followed by some control information and the return address at which execution is to resume after the called routine completes. A recursive call acts in exactly the same way. If eight bytes of data go on the stack each time the function is called, and the function calls itself recursively three times, then it places a total of 24 bytes on the stack. Each time the function resumes recursively, it can fetch the arguments from the stack that were placed there by the most recent call, using them as it would if called from outside. In effect, the function doesn't know it's been called by itself. Therefore there's nothing peculiar about its operation.

Since recursion is like looping, the same rule applies: you must have some condition that stops the recursion. When that happens, the function returns to its prior invocation, which in turn returns to its predecessor, and so on, each time removing the data placed on the stack before it was called. Eventually it returns to a caller outside itself, thus ending the recursion.

Now let's look at a simple recursive function:

```
void recur (int n)
{
   if (n != 0)
      recur (n-1);
}
```

Say you call this function with

```
recur (2);
```

The if() condition is true, so **recur()** calls itself passing n-1, which is now **one**. This is the second invocation, and again the if() test succeeds and **recur()** calls itself, this time passing **0** as the argument.

Now the terminating condition is satisfied. The function is at the second level of recursion; that is, it called itself with **1**, then with **0** as an argument. It must now back out of the levels. The return address for the first-level call is effectively at the closing curly brace, to which the second level returns. This causes the first level to return, and now the highest level, which was called from outside, reverts control to the original caller. And that's how it works.

Other conditions can also terminate the recursive calling sequence. Later we'll see functions that stop calling themselves on hitting a **NULL** pointer.

This example, of course, doesn't do anything except call itself. Real recursive functions do something before invoking themselves, afterwards, or both, and some that work on binary trees call themselves more than once.

Building a Binary Tree _____

Ideally the routine that controls the acquisition of data and the building of the binary tree should be short, relying on a function elsewhere in the program to handle the details of structuring the tree. Program 18.1 contains an example.

Program 18.1 **Controlling Data Capture and Tree Building**

```
do {                          /* repeat the following... */
  puts ("\n-----------------------------------------\n");
  puts ("Part number? (ENTER to end data entry) ");
  gets (number);
  if (strlen (number) > 0) {
    puts ("\nPart description? ");
    gets (name );
    if (root == NULL)
      root = newnode (number, name, root, root);
    else                            /* ignore result */
      newnode (number, name, root, root);
  }
} while (strlen (number) > 0);
```

This fragment of code keeps getting inputs from the keyboard until the user presses **Enter** in lieu of a part number, thus signalling the end of input. When the root pointer is **NULL**—that is, when the tree doesn't yet exist—the routine calls the **newnode()** function, whose return value is assigned to the root pointer. This establishes the existence of the tree. Thereafter, the routine calls **newnode()** for each new entry, but ignores the pointer it returns by not assigning it to anything. The **if()** block within the loop prevents the creation of an empty node when the user signals end of input.

Having defined a context and role for the tree-building function **newnode()**, we can proceed to develop it. The reason for passing the address of the root node twice as an argument in Program 18.1 will become clear later.

The function heading reads

PARTNODE *newnode (char *arg, char *name,
PARTNODE *parent, PARTNODE *node)

where **arg** is a pointer to the key value (part number) of the node to be added and **name** points to the new part name. The function returns a pointer of type PARTNODE, pointing to the node it added to the tree.

The first order of business is to determine where the node belongs. For this we can use a recursive search:

```
if (strnicmp (arg, node->part.nbr, KEYLEN) < 0)
    node = newnode (arg, name, node, node->LLink);
else
    node = newnode (arg, name, node, node->RLink);
```

Each time we enter a node, we compare the argument with its key. If less than, we proceed to the left by passing this node's **LLink**, and otherwise we go right by passing **RLink** to the next invocation of **newnode()**. Note that the call passes the current node's address to the next invocation's parent argument; that's because this node is the parent of the next we visit. In this manner, by comparing the argument against successive keys and passing on to **LLink** or **RLink** as appropriate, the process intelligently follows branching paths to the place where the new node belongs.

The recursive search algorithm above is not yet complete, though, because it has two problems:

1. It doesn't recognize an empty tree in which no root node exists.
2. There's no way to end the search.

The second is of paramount concern in recursive functions in general, lest the function keep calling itself forever (or until the program crashes from running out of stack space). A recursive function with no exit, or with exit conditions that can never be satisfied, is conceptually similar to an endless loop: bad news. And because recursive exits are usually less intuitively obvious than loop terminations, you have to code them carefully. In this case, the recursion must when the linkage pointer passed as the node argument is **NULL**. That happens automatically on the first call to **newnode()**, since the **NULL**-initialized value of root is passed. Thereafter, when a tree of at least one node exists, the node argument becomes **NULL** when we pass along a **NULL LLink** or **RLink** from the parent. This signifies the end of the search path.

The body of the recursive function **newnode()**, then, must be able to recognize when the search has ended, so that it can create and connect the new leaf in its proper place. The condition is whether or not the node parameter is **NULL**. Expressed in C notation, the overall logic of the function is

```
if (node != NULL)
    /* continue recursive search */
else
    /* make and connect the new node */
```

Program 18.2 lists the implementation of this logic within the context of the parts database.

Program 18.2 **Adding a New Node to a Binary Tree**

```
PARTNODE *newnode (char *arg, char *name,
                   PARTNODE *parent, PARTNODE *node)
{                                  /* insert new node into tree */

   if (node != NULL)       /* find location for node in tree */
      if (strnicmp (arg, node->part.nbr, KEYLEN) < 0)
         node = newnode (arg, name, node, node->LLink);
      else
         node = newnode (arg, name, node, node->RLink);
   else {                           /* new leaf's position found */
      node = (PARTNODE *) malloc (sizeof (PARTNODE));
      node->LLink = NULL;          /* leaf ptrs are always NULL */
      node->RLink = NULL;
      strncpy (node->part.nbr, arg, KEYLEN);    /* init leaf */
      strncpy (node->part.name, name, NAMELEN);
      if (strnicmp (arg, parent->part.nbr, KEYLEN) < 0)
         parent->LLink = (PARTNODE *) node;
      else
         parent->RLink = (PARTNODE *) node;
   }
   return (node);
} /* ------------------------ */
```

Tree Traversal

Tree traversal is the process of moving through an entire binary tree in an orderly fashion and doing something with each node's contents. The three methods, discussed earlier, are in-order, pre-order, and post-order. Traversal entails a lot of up-and-down movement along complex paths; you have to keep track of where you came from so that you can retreat from lower levels. Were it not for recursion, which uses the stack to store this information, traversal routines would be impossibly complicated. With recursion, it's simple.

The following three figures are templates that you can adapt to your own tree-following projects. The **output** and **free()** statements are the only application-dependent portions of the functions. The rest you can use directly, without modification.

In-Order

In-order traversal produces the contents of the tree sorted into ascending order by key: the field **part.nbr** in this case. Program 18.3 shows an **inOrder()** function that lists the node contents in key order to an output device.

Program 18.3 **Function to Output a Tree in Key Order**

```
void inOrder (FILE *dev, PARTNODE *node)
{                                   /* print tree in sorted order */

    if (node != NULL) {
        inOrder (dev, node->LLink);          /* keep going left */
        fprintf (dev, "\n%.6s    %s",         /* output data */
             node->part.nbr, node->part.name);
        inOrder (dev, node->RLink);          /* now go right */
    }
} /* ------------------------- */
```

Refer to Figure 18.1 to follow how this function works. The call from outside that initiates the ordered output process is

    inOrder (root);

which passes a pointer to the root of the tree (24). Because the node pointer is not **NULL**, the first recursive call passes **node->LLink** from node 24, which leads to node 11. Successive calls keep passing **LLink** from the current node, eventually arriving at node 6.

This node is a leaf, so its **LLink** is **NULL**. Therefore on the next invocation, node is **NULL** and the **if()** test fails, causing the invocation to return to node 6. The return address for that level points to the **fprintf()** statement, so the contents of node 6 go to the output device. Now the function calls itself passing **RLink**. Because **RLink** in node 6 is also **NULL**, the newly called level returns immediately, enabling the level that points to node 6 to return also. Having returned to the next-higher level, the data from node 8 goes to the output device and the process repeats passing node 8's **RLink**.

This goes on through all the left-hand subtree, processing 6, 8, 9, 11, and 19, and finally returning to the root, where the data associated with key 24 is output. Now the function moves to the right-hand subtree using **root->RLink**. Because of the tendency to strive left, the next node is key 26, and so it goes in the same manner until we finally reach node 98. There are no **RLinks** left to follow, so all recursive levels return, each to its caller, until the top-level call returns control to the program.

The thrust of this process is that the contents of any given node are processed only when all lesser values (to the left) have been processed, and before moving on to the greater values to the right. The result is strict ordering by key.

Pre-Order

In contrast to key sequence, pre-order produces nodes based on their position within the hierarchy. It does this by following the tree in the same order, but processing contents as soon as it enters a node rather than waiting until it returns to the node from its left-hand children. Consequently it processes the contents of the present node, then all its children to the left, then all those to the right. This is simply a matter of resequencing the statements, as Program 18.4 shows.

A common use of pre-order traversal is to save a tree in a disk file so that it can be reconstructed later with the same hierarchy, and that's how we use it here. Needless to say, the file must already be open and ready to receive data before calling the function for the first time.

Program 18.4 **Function to Save a Tree in Hierarchical Order**

```
void preOrder (FILE *file, PARTNODE *node)
{                                   /* save file in tree order */

  if (node != NULL) {
    fprintf (file, "%s\n%s\n", node->part.nbr,
      node->part.name);                      /* write to file */
    preOrder (file, node->LLink);             /* now go left */
    preOrder (file, node->RLink);            /* and then right */
  }
} /* ------------------------ */
```

Post-Order

Post-order defers action on a given node until it has visited all the children both left and right. Thus, it doesn't do anything with the current node until it's ready to return to the parent. As with pre-order, this is a matter of changing the sequence of statements. Here we put the work-performing statement after the two recursive calls.

Program 18.5 performs the task most commonly associated with post-order traversal: removing an entire binary tree from the heap and freeing the space. If this is not clean-up work at the end of a program run, it's advisable to reinitialize the root pointer so that you can't later use it to barge into corrupted space and cause the program to go haywire. The sequence

postOrder (root);

root = NULL;

effectively disarms the root pointer.

Program 18.5 **Function to Delete an Entire Tree from Memory**

```
void postOrder (PARTNODE *node)
{                                   /* deletes tree from heap */
  if (node != NULL) {
    postOrder (node->LLink);                 /* do all to left */
```

Program 18.5 **(continued)**

```
        postOrder (node->RLink);       /* then all to right */
        free (node);                   /* then free this node */
    }
} /* ----------------------- */
```

Sample Application

It's time to tie together the discussion with a working program that is the first of a pair implementing binary trees. This program (MAKETREE.C in Program 18.6) does the following:

1. Captures data from the keyboard and builds a binary tree from it.
2. When data entry is done (hit **Enter** instead of typing a part number), lists the nodes in key order.
3. Writes the data in hierarchical order to a disk file named BINARY.TRE.

The subsequent program (DELNODES.C in Program 18.8) will fetch the data from disk, rebuild the tree, and let you search for and delete selected nodes by key.

Here are the records I entered into the database:

3730	Aquarium tank
3026	Gravel
5955	Floating thermometer
6359	Aquarium pump
3330	Air distributor
5563	Tank cover
2630	Underwater filter

Program 18.6 **Sample Program to Create, List, and Save a Tree**

```
/* MAKETREE.C: Builds a binary tree, lists it, and saves  */
/*             to a file                                   */
/* ------------------------------------------------------- */
/* INCLUDES */
#include <stdio.h>
#include <io.h>
#include <fcntl.h>
#include <string.h>
#include <alloc.h>
#include <conio.h>

/* CONSTANTS */
#define EJECT   12                    /* printer page eject */
```

Program 18.6 (continued)

```c
#define KEYLEN    6              /* length of key string */
#define NAMELEN  21              /* length of descr field */
#define TREEFILE "BINARY.TRE"        /* output filename */

/* TYPES */
typedef struct {                        /* substructure */
  char      nbr [KEYLEN];    /* part #, key field for node */
  char      name [NAMELEN];       /* part description */
} DATAPART;
typedef struct partnode {          /* tree node definition */
  DATAPART          part;
  struct partnode  *LLink, *RLink;
} PARTNODE;

/* LOCAL FUNCTION PROTOTYPES */
PARTNODE *newnode (char *arg, char *name,
                   PARTNODE *parent, PARTNODE *node);
void inOrder (FILE *dev, PARTNODE *node);
void preOrder (FILE *file, PARTNODE *node);
void postOrder (PARTNODE *node);

/* --------------------------- */

void main ()
{
PARTNODE   *root = NULL;
char       number [KEYLEN];
char       name [NAMELEN];
FILE       *output = stdout; /* change to stdprn for paper */

/* GET DATA AND BUILD LIST */
  clrscr();
  do {
    puts ("\n---------------------------------------\n");
    cputs ("Part number? (ENTER to end data entry) ");
    gets (number);
    if (strlen (number) > 0) {
      cputs ("\nPart description? ");
      gets (name );
      if (root == NULL)
        root = newnode (number, name, root, root);
      else                             /* ignore result */
        newnode (number, name, root, root);
    }
  } while (strlen (number) > 0);

/* PRINT OUT ALL NODES IN ORDER BY KEY */
  fputs ("\r\nAll nodes in key order:", output);
  inOrder (output, root);              /* list tree in order */
  if (output == stdprn)
    fputc (EJECT, output);          /* eject page if printer */

/* SAVE TREE IN HIERARCHICAL ORDER IN DISK FILE */
```

Program 18.6 **(continued)**

```
    output = fopen (TREEFILE, "w");          /* open file */
    preOrder (output, root);                 /* save tree */
    fclose (output);                         /* close file */

/* DELETE TREE FROM HEAP */
    postOrder (root);
    root = NULL;
} /* ----------------------- */

PARTNODE *newnode (char *arg, char *name,
                   PARTNODE *parent, PARTNODE *node)
{                                /* insert new node into tree */

    if (node)              /* find location for node in tree */
        if (strnicmp (arg, node->part.nbr, KEYLEN) < 0)
            node = newnode (arg, name, node, node->LLink);
        else
            node = newnode (arg, name, node, node->RLink);
    else {                      /* new leaf's position found */
        node = malloc (sizeof (PARTNODE));
        node->LLink = NULL;       /* leaf ptrs are always NULL */
        node->RLink = NULL;
        strncpy (node->part.nbr, arg, KEYLEN);    /* init leaf */
        strncpy (node->part.name, name, NAMELEN);
        if (parent)
            if (strnicmp (arg, parent->part.nbr, KEYLEN) < 0)
                parent->LLink = (PARTNODE *) node;
            else
                parent->RLink = (PARTNODE *) node;
    }
    return (node);
} /* ----------------------- */

void inOrder (FILE *dev, PARTNODE *node)
{                              /* print tree in sorted order */

    if (node != NULL) {
        inOrder (dev, node->LLink);          /* keep going left */
        fprintf (dev, "\r\n%.6s    %s",         /* output data */
            node->part.nbr, node->part.name);
        inOrder (dev, node->RLink);          /* now go right */
    }
} /* ----------------------- */

void preOrder (FILE *file, PARTNODE *node)
{                                /* save file in tree order */

    if (node != NULL) {
        fprintf (file, "%s\r\n%s\n", node->part.nbr,
            node->part.name);                /* write to file */
        preOrder (file, node->LLink);        /* now go left */
        preOrder (file, node->RLink);        /* and then right */
```

Program 18.6 **(continued)**

```
  }
} /* ---------------------- */

void postOrder (PARTNODE *node)
{                                    /* deletes tree from heap */
  if (node != NULL) {
    postOrder (node->LLink);              /* do all to left */
    postOrder (node->RLink);             /* then all to right */
    free (node);                        /* then free this node */
  }
} /* ---------------------- */
```

Searching a Binary Tree

A search commences at the root and proceeds to successively lower levels in the tree, following branches until it either finds a match or doesn't. The sought key doesn't exist when further searching is blocked by a **NULL** pointer. Because movement is strictly downward, searching isn't a recursive process.

Comparison is the basis for searching. In every node there are three possible outcomes:

Argument = key   Successful
Argument < key   Go left
Argument > key   Go right

A fourth is no match, detected by a **NULL** pointer blocking the way.

There is no point in searching unless you do something as a result. If a match exists, you output the data, plug a field into a computation, or take some other action. Consequently, the search function should return a pointer to the matching node, or **NULL** if there is no match. That way you can use the returned pointer to access the matching node or undertake recovery action, whichever is appropriate.

You might use this function (**search()** in Program 18.7) as follows:

```
gets (key);
this = search (key, root);
if (this == NULL)
   /* not found */
else
   /* it was found */
```

Program 18.7 **Searching a Binary Tree**

```
PARTNODE *search (char *arg, PARTNODE *node)
{                                      /* find matching node */
  while (strnicmp (arg, node->part.nbr, KEYLEN) != 0)
    if (node == NULL)
      return (NULL);
    else
      node = (strnicmp (arg, node->part.nbr, KEYLEN) < 0) ?
             node->LLink : node->RLink;
  return (node->active ? node : NULL);
} /* --------------------- */
```

Deleting a Binary Tree Node

Algorithms exist for deleting nodes from binary trees. One of the most common is to "promote" the nearest-valued leaf to replace a deleted parent. The problem is that such algorithms must be able to rearrange the entire tree if necessary, and that entails great complexity.

A simpler solution, given here, is to flag a deleted node and thereafter simply ignore its data content in **output** operations. This doesn't actually remove the node, of course, but it gives you an indicator to test. The node's key is still available for traversal comparisons.

You can do this by adding the field

char active;

to the node structure and initializing it as **TRUE**. Later, to effectively delete the node, you change the field to **FALSE**. Functions such as **inOrder()** can test it, as in

if (node->active)
    printf (. . .);

and find out whether to list the node's content or not. Similarly, the exit statement of the **search()** function can be written as

return (node->active ? node : NULL);

which returns a pointer to the found node if it's active and **NULL** if marked as deleted.

This solution has the disadvantage that it adds overhead to tree traversals and searches. The overhead, however, is trivial compared with the saving in complexity obtained by using a simple method for deleting nodes.

Moreover, you can use the deleted nodes to construct an audit trail at the end of processing, producing a report that shows which items were deleted from the database. An audit trail is often mandatory in tightly controlled applications such as finance. The audit trail routine simply reverses the check in **inOrder()**, printing deleted nodes and ignoring those still active with the test

```
if (!(node->active))
    printf ( . . . );
```

Now let's see how this discussion of searching and deleting tree nodes fits into a working program.

Sample Application, Part Two _____

This application continues the exercise begun above with Program 18.6. There we created and saved a database in disk file BINARY.TRE. Now we'll read that file back into a binary tree and list the contents by key order, then do selective deletions of entries.

The program contains a function **stripnl()**, which overcomes a problem introduced by the **preOrder()** function in Program 18.6 that wrote the file. It uses a **fprintf()** format that embeds newline characters (\n) in the text. The objective is to make it easy to distinguish individual strings when reading BINARY.TRE. The problem is that **fgets()** retains these newlines, and since they weren't present in the original data, we have to take them out. The **stripnl()** function does this by replacing the newline with a null terminator, or setting the last valid character position to null if the data completely fill the available space, thus preventing a runaway string on output.

Using DELNODES.C in Program 18.8, you can select a key to delete by answering the questions on the display. The program always precedes the Q&A session by displaying all nondeleted nodes on the basis of the **node->active** field's status. Before doing the deletion, the program finds the node and verifies that it's the item you want to delete. Answer with **Y** or **N**. The program also tells you if you've typed a key that doesn't exist or that has been deleted, which are effectively the same thing.

This process continues until you press **Enter** without any preceding data in response to the request for a key to delete. The program then displays an audit list of deleted items and quits. It does *not* save the changes in BINARY.TRE; if you want it to, add a **preOrder()** routine that checks the status of **node->active** before writing the data back to the file.

Program 18.8 **Sample Program to Find and Delete Nodes in a Binary Tree**

```
/* DELNODES.C: Search and delete nodes from binary tree */

/* INCLUDES */
#include <stdio.h>
#include <string.h>
#include <conio.h>
#include <ctype.h>
#include <alloc.h>

/* CONSTANTS */
#define EJECT    12                    /* printer page eject */
#define KEYLEN    6                    /* length of key string */
#define NAMELEN  22                    /* length of descr field */
#define FNAME    "BINARY.TRE"          /* input filename */
#define BAR      "\n-------------------------------------"
#ifndef TRUE
#define FALSE    0
#define TRUE     !FALSE
#endif

/* TYPES */
typedef struct {                       /* substructure for data */
   char    nbr[KEYLEN];        /* part #, key field for node */
   char    name[NAMELEN];              /* part description */
} DATAPART;
typedef struct partnode {              /* tree node definition */
   DATAPART        part;
   struct partnode *LLink, *RLink;
   char            active;
} PARTNODE;

/* LOCAL FUNCTION PROTOTYPES */
PARTNODE  *newnode (char *arg, char *name,
                PARTNODE *parent, PARTNODE *node);
void inOrder (PARTNODE *node);
void auditTrail (PARTNODE *node, FILE *device);
PARTNODE *search (char *arg, PARTNODE *node);
void delete (PARTNODE *node);
void stripnl (char *str, int maxlen);
/* -------------------------------- */

void main ()
{
FILE     *file;                                /* input file */
PARTNODE *root = NULL, *this;   /* pointers to tree nodes */
char     key[KEYLEN];                          /* input key */
char     name[NAMELEN];                /* part descriptor */
char     reply;                     /* keyboard interaction */
FILE     *audit = stdout;   /* change to stdprn for paper */

/* OPEN INPUT FILE AND BUILD TREE */
   if ((file = fopen (FNAME, "r")) == NULL) {
```

Program 18.8 **(continued)**

```c
    printf ("\nUnable to open input file %s", FNAME);
    exit (1);
  }
  do {                                     /* until eof... */
    fgets (key, KEYLEN, file);            /* get part number */
    if (!feof (file)) {
      stripnl (key, KEYLEN);              /* remove newline */
      fgets (name, NAMELEN, file);        /* get part name */
      stripnl (name, NAMELEN);            /* remove newline */
      if (root == NULL)                   /* start tree */
        root = newnode (key, name, root, root);
      else                                /* else add to it */
        this = newnode (key, name, root, root );
    }
  } while (!feof (file));
  fclose (file);                          /* then close input file */

/* SEARCH AND DELETE SELECTED NODES */
  do {
    puts (BAR);
    puts ("Items currently in tree:");
    inOrder (root);                       /* list entire tree */
    putchar ('\n');
    cputs ("Key of item to delete? (Enter if done) ");
    gets (key);
    if (strlen (key) != 0) {
      this = search (key, root);     /* find match in tree */
      if (this == NULL) {
        puts ("\nItem not found");
        puts ("\nPress any key to continue... ");
        getch ();
      } else {
        printf ("\nItem number is %s\n", this->part.name);
        cputs ("Delete this item? (y/n) ");
        reply = toupper (getche ());
        if (reply == 'Y')
          delete (this);
      }
    }
  } while (strlen (key) != 0);

/* PRODUCE AUDIT TRAIL */
  fputs (BAR, audit);
  fputs (
      "\r\nAudit trail: Following items removed from tree:",
      audit);
  auditTrail (root, audit);
  if (audit == stdprn)
    fputc (EJECT, audit);
  putchar ('\n');
} /* --------------------- */
```

Program 18.8 **(continued)**

```
PARTNODE *newnode (char *arg, char *name,
                    PARTNODE *parent, PARTNODE *node)
{                                    /* insert new node into tree */
  if (node)               /* find location for node in tree */
    if (strnicmp (arg, node->part.nbr, KEYLEN) < 0)
      node = newnode (arg, name, node, node->LLink);
    else
      node = newnode (arg, name, node, node->RLink);
  else {                          /* new leaf's position found */
    node = malloc (sizeof (PARTNODE));
    node->LLink = node->RLink = NULL;     /* leaf pts NULL */
    node->active = TRUE;              /* mark node as active */
    strncpy (node->part.nbr, arg, KEYLEN);   /* init leaf */
    strncpy (node->part.name, name, NAMELEN);
    if (parent)
      if (strnicmp (arg, parent->part.nbr, KEYLEN) < 0)
        parent->LLink = (PARTNODE*) node;
      else
        parent->RLink = (PARTNODE*) node;
  }
  return (node);
} /* ---------------------- */

void inOrder (PARTNODE *node)
{       /* output list of non-deleted nodes in key order */
  if (node != NULL) {
    inOrder (node->LLink);
    if (node->active)
      printf ("\n%.6s       %s", node->part.nbr,
              node->part.name);
    inOrder (node->RLink);
  }
} /* ---------------------- */

void auditTrail (PARTNODE *node, FILE *device)
{         /* output list of deleted nodes in key order */
  if (node != NULL) {
    auditTrail (node->LLink, device);
    if (!(node->active))
      fprintf (device, "\r\n%.6s       %s", node->part.nbr,
              node->part.name);
    auditTrail (node->RLink, device);
  }
} /* ---------------------- */

PARTNODE *search (char *arg, PARTNODE *node)
{                                   /* find matching node */
  while (strnicmp (arg, node->part.nbr, KEYLEN) != 0)
    if (node == NULL)
      return (NULL);
    else
      node = (strnicmp (arg, node->part.nbr, KEYLEN) < 0) ?
```

Program 18.9 **Searching a Binary Tree**

```
                node->LLink : node->RLink;
   return (node->active ? node : NULL);
} /* ----------------------- */

void delete (PARTNODE *node)        /* mark node as deleted */
{
   node->active = FALSE;
} /* ----------------------- */

void stripnl (char *str, int maxlen)     /* remove newline */
{
int    length;

   length = strlen (str);
   if (length > maxlen)
     str [maxlen] = '\0';
   else
     str [length-1] = '\0';
} /* ----------------------- */
```

Binary trees provide a sophisticated technique for ordering large amounts of data and performing lightning-fast searches. Recursion simplifies the complexity of traversals in hierarchical structures. While less intuitive than lists, reasonably balanced trees deliver many times the performace, and have the added benefit that they automatically sort the data into order by key.

Now let's wrap up our coverage of dynamic data structures by considering lists in which the nodes are of inconsistent sizes.

CHAPTER 19

IRREGULAR DYNAMIC DATA STRUCTURES

T he preceding chapters have given the impression that dynamic data structures must always consist of nodes that have a uniform size. In fact that's not so, but for the sake of understanding we've let the impression stand. Now that you're well indoctrinated in handling lists and trees, we can deal with one of the realities of software, which is that requirements seldom pay much attention to tidy rules.

There are numerous situations in which dynamic structures must have the flexibility to deal with variable-length data. A typical example, which we'll use as the case study in this chapter, is a queue. What might we place in a queue? Anything from individual characters typed at the keyboard up to data streams of several hundred or even several thousand bytes arriving from disk or over a serial port. A *queue*, you'll recall from Chapter 17, is a place where we stick things that we want to put off until later. Therefore, almost by definition, a queue is a list of data objects whose sizes are infinitely variable and cannot possibly be anticipated in advance.

There are other examples. DOS itself manages all of the computer's transient memory—the space where programs and their associated data areas live—as a giant singly linked list whose nodes vary in size. For a discussion, see Duncan, pages 179–181. This approach differs from the one discussed here, but it bears study if you're interested in investigating the subject further.

The method we present in this chapter involves two dynamic structures. One is a queue consisting of predefined nodes that manages undefined—variable length—nodes also located on the heap. Each fixed-length "directory" node points to the variable-length data node it controls. The two node types are physically mingled on the heap, but because the entire structure relies on pointers, we don't care where the actual nodes are located in memory.

The Big Picture

We're going to queue keyboard entries for deferred processing. The keyboard entries arrive at random times, go into the queue, and are pulled from it at your convenience to be printed in the order entered. The random times occur whenever you choose to respond to a query from the program. The variability is the number of characters you key, which can be from one to 80 characters. The deferred processing is a listing of the strings, which appears whenever you press **Enter** (without typing any data) in response to a query. A simple application, perhaps, but one whose elements are readily understandable, and that you can adapt to your own more complex requirements.

Each time you finish typing a line of text at the keyboard, two objects come into existence. The first is the fixed-length directory node, whose constituent parts appear in Figure 19.1. This node goes into a circular DLL managed as a queue—FIFO buffer—as the new tail. (Recall that in a queue, we always add to the tail and draw from the head.) The objective here is to create a list that is easy to manage, and fixed-length objects are always easier to deal with than those of variable length. The queue itself serves as a directory to the more complex variable-length objects.

Figure 19.1 **Visualization of a Directory Node**

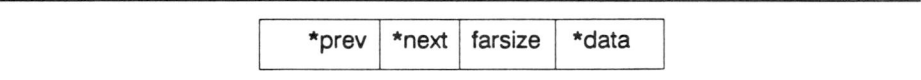

We'll define this node template as

```
typedef struct obj {
    struct obj        *prev, *next;
    unsigned          strsize;
    char              *data;
} OBJ;
```

The **prev** and **next** fields are pointers to other nodes of the same format, and are used customarily in the management of the circular DLL. The **strsize** field gives the number of bytes—up to 64K—in the data string, and the **data** field is a pointer to the string itself.

The data string is, of course, the variable-length object, whose sheer cussedness demands that we go to these lengths to manage it.

When you've entered several strings and enqueued them using this approach, you might have a directory/data combination that looks something like Figure 19.2.

Figure 19.2 **Relationships of the Two Dynamic Structures**

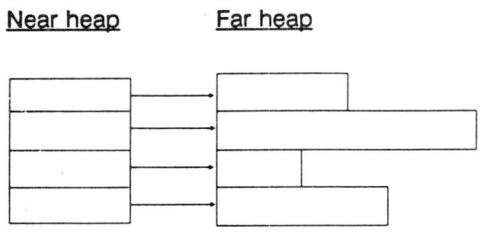

Near heap   Far heap

Each fixed-length directory entry points to a variable-length object in one-to-one correspondence. Because the program uses the directory entries to manage the variable-length objects, it need only refer to the involved directory node. The purpose of using a separate directory is, after all, to simplify managnt of the variable-length data elements.

Building the List Structures

Here is the algorithm for constructing the two parallel data structures, expressed in pseudo-code:

```
repeat
  get data from keyboard;
  if datalength > 0
  begin
    put new directory node in queue;
    update queue head pointer if first node;
    store size of data in directory node;
    allocate data object;
    store pointer in directory node;
    copy input data to data object;
  endif;
while datalength > 0;
```

Program 19.1 expresses this high-level algorithm in C notation.

Program 19.1 **Creating the Parallel Structure**

```
do {
  puts ("\n\nEnter a string (Enter to quit)");
  gets (string);
  if ((datasize = strlen (string)) != 0) {
    new = enqueue (queue, datasize, string);    /* allocate */
```

Program 19.1 **(continued)**

```
    if (queue == NULL)              /* set queue if first */
      queue = new;
    printf ("\n   Fixed-length node is at %p", new);
    printf ("\n   String node is at  %p", new->data);
    printf ("\n   Copied %d characters to string node",
      new->strsize);
  }
} while (datasize > 0);
```

The **enqueue()** function holds no surprises; it's like enqueue operations we've seen in Chapter 17, with the exception that it sets up the new tail node with the datasize argument and creates the variable-sized data node.

Listing the Queue

After several keyboard entries, you'll have a directory-to-data relationship something like Figure 19.2. That is, the heap contains a circular DLL consisting of a number of fixed-length directory nodes, each of which controls a corresponding variable-length data node. Continued construction of these two related lists ends when you press **Enter** in response to a prompt from the keyboard.

At that point, deferred processing occurs in the form of listing the strings you've entered in chronological—FIFO—order. In pseudo-code, this algorithm is

```
while queue is not empty do
begin
  print the next data string from the queue;
  remove head of queue;
  update queue pointer;
enddo;
```

This is implemented under the heading DATA OUTPUT SECTION in Program 19.2 (VARLIST.C), which illustrates how an ordinary linked list can manage the more complex aspects of implicitly unordered, variable-length data.

Program 19.2 **Demonstration of the Discussion**

```
/* VARLIST.C: Dynamic data structs with variable-sized nodes */

/* INCLUDES */
#include <stdio.h>
#include <alloc.h>
```

```
#include <dos.h>
#include <string.h>

/* TYPES */
typedef struct obj {
  struct obj *prev, *next;              /* local node pointers */
  unsigned    strsize;                  /* size of string object */
  char        *data;                    /* pointer to string object */
} OBJ;                            /* directory object definition */

/* LOCAL FUNCTION PROTOTYPES */
OBJ *enqueue (OBJ*, int, char*);
void allocstr (OBJ*);
void copy2far (OBJ*, char*);
void copy2near (OBJ*, char*);
void shownext (OBJ*);
OBJ *drain (OBJ*);
/* ---------------------------------------------------------- */

void main ()
{
char string[80];                        /* string I/O variable */
int  datasize;                          /* size of input string */
OBJ  *queue = NULL, *new;          /* ptrs to directory objects */

/* DATA ENTRY SECTION */
  do {
    puts ("\n\nEnter a string (Enter to quit)");
    gets (string);
    if ((datasize = strlen (string)) != 0) {
      new = enqueue (queue, datasize, string);   /* allocate */
      if (queue == NULL)                /* set queue if first */
        queue = new;
      printf ("\n   Fixed-length node is at %p", new);
      printf ("\n   String node is at  %p", new->data);
      printf ("\n   Copied %d characters to string node",
        new->strsize);
    }
  } while (datasize > 0);

/* DATA OUTPUT SECTION */
  puts ("\n\n\nStrings in order typed:");
  while (queue) {                  /* while queue is not empty.. */
    printf ("\n%s", queue->data);         /* show next item */
    queue = drain (queue);          /* remove head of queue */
  }
  puts ("\n\n");
} /* ---------------------- */

OBJ *enqueue (OBJ *q, int strsize, char *str)
{                       /* place new directory entry in queue */
OBJ *this;
```

Program 19.2 **(continued)**

```c
    this = malloc (sizeof (OBJ));                    /* allocate */
    if (q == NULL)                          /* if first in queue */
      this->prev = this->next = this;       /* points to itself */
    else {                                  /* insert as new tail */
      this->prev = q->prev;                 /* in circular queue */
      this->next = this->prev->next;
      this->prev->next = this->next->prev = this;
    }
    this->strsize = strsize + 1;     /* add one for null termin */
    this->data = malloc (this->strsize);   /* get string space */
    strcpy (this->data, str);              /* copy string to it */
    return (this);
} /* ----------------------- */

OBJ *drain (OBJ *q)                       /* remove head of queue */
{
OBJ  *next;

    free (q->data);                        /* release string space */
    if (q == q->next) {                    /* if last entry in queue... */
      free (q);
      return (NULL);
    } else {                               /* remove node from head */
      q->next->prev = q->prev;
      next = q->prev->next = q->next;
      free (q);
      return (next);                       /* return next node */
    }
} /* ----------------------- */
```

Conclusion

This part of the book has covered a number of techniques for dealing with unpredictable quantities and sizes of data using dynamic data structures. The purpose has not been to provide exhaustive coverage, but rather to lay a solid foundation on which you can build with informed experience.

PART V

Using the DOS Environment in Turbo C

MS-DOS/PC-DOS, the disk operating system of the IBM PC and equivalents, furnishes a number of services to application programs. We've already used several of them: dynamic allocation, the DTA, low-level calls using **int86()**. Indeed, many functions unique to Turbo C, such as **findfirst()/findnext()**, **fnsplit()**, and **gettime()**, are merely DOS services "sugar-coated" in C syntax.

This final part of the book deals with some of the more complex and exotic features of the DOS environment. After covering some background material—much of it useful and interesting in its own right—we'll delve into interrupts, and calling other application written in Turbo C.

The techniques given here, coupled with those already covered, will enable you to write powerful advanced software.

CHAPTER 20

UNDERSTANDING
.EXE FILES

The machine language programs produced by Turbo C are in .EXE format, one of the two kinds of executable files under DOS. An understanding of the .EXE format is essential to the rest of the material in this book, so this chapter explains how they work.

As you're well aware, the primary way to start a program in DOS is to type its name at the command level. You may not be aware of what DOS does to execute that command, or of the important role played by a system-level data structure called the Program Segment Prefix.

How DOS Loads Command Files

Three types of files in addition to the COMMAND.COM shell contain DOS commands: .BAT, .COM, and .EXE. DOS handles each one differently, and follows a present sequence in attempting to process the command.

Let's say you type the command

SKLRGX

in response to the system prompt (normally C: on a machine with a hard disk). Command lines are inputs to the command interpreter shell COMMAND.COM, which gets loaded as a memory-resident program whenever the machine reboots. **SKLRGX** is not a built-in command, so the shell, having determined this, begins a series of activities to locate a disk file whose base name is **SKLRGX**. The disk search begins in the current directory, and goes in order through all other directories specified by the most recent DOS PATH command.

The shell first searches for **SKLRGX.COM**. A .COM file is the memory image of an executable program in machine language. That is, a .COM file can be loaded anywhere in memory and executed without further modification (subject to a bit of setup described later). A .COM file is somewhat limited: its code and data segments cannot exceed 64K apiece, and there are other constraints as well. It's intended chiefly for small programs such as DOS utilities. (Turbo C generates .COM files from the tiny model.)

Failing to locate **SKLRGX.COM**, the shell next searches for **SKLRGX.EXE**. Like a .COM, an .EXE file (usually pronounced "eksey") contains executable machine language, but in a different form. DOS has to do more work to load and start an .EXE file; more on this later. The size of an .EXE file's data and code segments can equal all of memory, which makes it suitable for large software systems.

If neither **SKLRGX.COM** nor **SKLRGX.EXE** exists along the search path, DOS looks for **SKLRGX.BAT**. A .BAT file is not directly executable, but instead contains one or more commands to be processed in sequence. It is thus a *batch command* file, and the shell performs the actions it specifies as though each command had been typed at the DOS prompt.

When all searches prove fruitless, the shell responds with the familiar message

Bad command or file name

which means, "I give up."

The shell works directly with the contents of .BAT files, treating each entry as though it had just been typed from the keyboard (with the exception that it fills in numerically sequenced placeholders such as **%1** and **%2** with corresponding command-line arguments). For .COM and .EXE files, the shell builds the environment block, loads the contents into memory starting at the next available segment, and fills in the Program Segment Prefix, a data structure accompanying each executable program.

For .EXE files, DOS also performs some other setup steps. The linker embeds instructions in the .EXE file's header record (described later) so that the DOS program loader knows what to do. Chiefly this entails resolving addresses using a process called *segment fix-ups*. A single chunk of executable code cannot exceed 64K in size, so a large .EXE file contains several such chunks. The linker crams them together to conserve disk space, so the loader has to pull the chunks apart and align each one on the next segment (16-byte paragraph) boundary. Using data in the header record, the loader also resolves the addresses of far pointers in the code so that they become absolute segment/ offset memory references.

The Program Segment Prefix (PSP), common to both .COM and .EXE files, contains information that either DOS or the program itself needs. DOS fills it in as it loads the program, then passes control to the program's entry point and starts it running. When the program terminates, DOS uses information from the PSP to restore the environment.

Contents of the PSP

The PSP is a 256-byte reserved area with a fixed format. In general, the first 92 (5Ch) bytes are inviolable; you can read them, but don't change anything unless you want to crash the machine. The remaining 164 bytes might or might not contain useful information, and you can usually use them for passing data among processes when the validity of the DS register is suspect.

So what's in those first 92 bytes? The following table lists the contents by hex offset:

Offset	Contains
00–01	Int 20h, DOS call for program termination. Of no practical value to Turbo C programs.
02–03	Segment address of the end of available memory.
04	Reserved byte.
05–09	Long call to Int 21h, the primary entry to the DOS functions. Of no value to Turbo C programs.
0A–0D	Address of the routine to get control when this program terminates, taken from the vector for Int 22h. Normally this is a COMMAND.COM routine, but a program can stuff its own routine in the vector, then start (*spawn*) another program. This field in the spawned program's PSP contains the address of the first program's routine, which will gain control when the spawned process completes. When the original program completes, DOS grabs this value and stuffs it back into the interrupt vector so that control reverts to the next-higher level's termination routine.
0E–11	Address of the Ctrl-Break routine in use before this program began, obtained from the vector for Int 23h. A program can set its own Ctrl-Break routine, so DOS uses this value to make sure the vector is properly restored on exit.
12–5	Address of the critical error handler in use before this program began, obtained from the vector for Int 24h.
16–2B	Reserved for DOS.
2C–2D	Segment address of the environment block. Chapters 21 and 22 cover the environment block.
2E–5B	Reserved for DOS.
5C–6B	A file control block for the first file specified on the command line (empty if none). Turbo C doesn't use this FCB, so the memory is available for your program to use if necessary.
6C–7F	File control block for the second file specified on the command line. As above.
80	Length in bytes of the command line arguments, if any.
81–FF	Command line arguments, if any. (80–FF are also shown in some DOS references as the default DTA. Turbo C programs allocate their own DTA.) You can use C's standard **argc/argv[]** method to fetch command line arguments (also called the *command tail*) out of this area more conveniently than by accessing the PSP directly.

Program 20.1 contains a C structure defining the PSP, which you can place in a file PSP.H.

Program 20.1 **Program Segment Prefix Structure**

```
/* PSP.H: Defines the program segment prefix structure */

typedef struct {
    unsigned    int20h,             /* pgm term call (no value) */
                topofmem;           /* segment of top of memory */
    char        res1,                      /* reserved by DOS */
                int21h [5];             /* no value in Turbo C */
    long        oldtermvec,     /* old int 22h interrupt vector */
                oldcbvec,         /* old Ctrl-Break int vector */
                oldcritvec;     /* old critical error int vector */
    char        res2 [22];                  /* reserved area */
    unsigned    envblock;       /* segment of environment block */
    char        res3 [46],                  /* reserved area */
                avail [36],         /* FCB's: open memory */
                cmdtaillen,     /* length of command tail */
                cmdtail [127];          /* command tail text */
} PSPSTRUC;
```

Getting the Address of the PSP

Turbo C furnishes two methods for obtaining the PSP's address. DOS.H defines the global variable __psp, which automatically acquires the PSP segment address when your application starts running. The PSP is always at offset 0 within its segment, so you can construct a far pointer to it with a statement such as

```
mypsp = MK__FP (__psp, 0);
```

This method works for DOS 2.0 and above.

DOS 3.0 and above have a call that returns the PSP's segment address, and Turbo C has the corresponding "sugar-coated" function getpsp(). It returns an unsigned integer. Both __psp and getpsp() are available in DOS 3.0 and result in the same value, so it's hard to see what advantage getpsp() has for software writers.

You can get the DOS version from two other global variables defined in DOS.H, which are __osmajor and __osminor. If you're running DOS 2.1, for example, __osmajor = 2 and __osminor = 1. Another variable called __version is also available, but less convenient to use. If you're determined to use getpsp() when available, you can write

```
if (__osmajor > 2)
  psp = MK__FP (getpsp(), 0);
else
  psp = MK__FP (__psp, 0);
```

Program 20.2 is a program that reads a few items of interest from its own PSP and lists them on the display.

Program 20.2 **Fetching Information from the PSP**

```
/* PSP.C: Displays information from the PSP */

#include <dos.h>
#include "psp.h"
#include <stdio.h>
#include <conio.h>

void main ()
{
PSPSTRUC far *psp;

    clrscr();
    psp = MK_FP (_psp, 0);
    puts ("PSP Contents for This Program:");
    printf ("Top of memory (segment)         %04X:0000\n",
            psp->topofmem);
    printf ("Environment block (segment)     %04X:0000\n",
            psp->envblock);
    printf ("Old int 22 vector               %lp\n",
            (void far*) psp->oldtermvec);
    printf ("Old ctrl-Break vector           %lp\n",
            (void far*) psp->oldcbvec);
    printf ("Old critical error vector       %lp\n",
            (void far*) psp->oldcritvec);
}
```

Much of the interaction with the PSP occurs in connection with TSR (Terminate and Stay Resident) and spawned programs, which we discuss in later chapters. In other programs, the PSP's upper, uncommitted areas are useful when you need some free memory, as in saving the results of an interrupt.

Getting Information About .EXE Files

As mentioned earlier, the linker stores loading information in a complex structure at the start of the .EXE file. This structure, called the *header record*, consists of a 14-word fixed portion followed by a variable-length relocation table.

There's seldom any reason to snoop around the relocation table, but it's instructive and sometimes useful to read the fixed-length data at the start of the .EXE's header record. This record contains the following information, given hex offsets:

Offset	Content
00	.EXE file signature, always 5A4Dh. Identifies the file as an .EXE.
02	File length MOD 512: the remainder after dividing the file into 512-byte pages.
04	Number of 512-byte pages in the file, plus one.
06	Number of entries in the relocation table.
08	Number of 16-byte paragraphs in the header record.
0A	Minimum number of paragraphs required for the heap and stack.
0C	Maximum number of paragraphs desired for the heap and stack.
0E	Segment displacement of the stack module.
10	Initial setting of the stack pointer (SP).
12	Word checksum. Used internally by the loader to make sure the file is complete.
14	Initial setting of the IP register. This is the program's entry point.
16	Segment displacement of the entry point. Used to set the CS register.
18	Byte offset of the relocation table.
1A	Overlay number. Zero if this is a standalone program or the root of an overlay system.

The segment displacement fields give a paragraph offset from the originating segment of the program. For example, if the field at record offset 16h contains 1Ah and the loader decides to start the program space at segment 200h, then the initial setting of the CS register will be 21Ah.

Program 20.3 lists EXEINFO.C, which inspects the header record of any .EXE file. It lists some fields directly and calculates values from others, such as the number of bytes in the header and in the module as a whole. The program accepts a filename on the command line, and if you don't furnish one, it asks for it. You must furnish the .EXE suffix when typing the filename. EXEINFO.C checks the signature to make sure the file is an .EXE. If not, it tells you so and quits with no further action.

Program 20.3 Listing Information About an .EXE File

```
/* EXEINFO.C: Displays contents of any .EXE header record */

#include <dos.h>
#include <conio.h>
#include <io.h>
#include <fcntl.h>
#include <errno.h>
#include <string.h>
#include <process.h>
#include <stdio.h>

#define   EXESIG 0x5A4D

typedef struct {
  unsigned
    signature,                      /* Fixed at 5A4Dh for .EXE */
    modSize,                                 /* size mod 512 */
```

Program 20.3 (continued)

```
        nPages,              /* number of 512-byte pages */
        relocItems,          /* number of relocation table items */
        headerSize,          /* header size in 16-byte paragraphs */
        minHeap,             /* minimum number of paras in heap */
        maxHeap,             /* max number of paras in heap */
        stackDispl,          /* segment displacement of stack */
        initSP,              /* initial value of SP register */
        checksum,            /* internal checksum for module */
        entryPoint,          /* setting of IP register to begin */
        codeSeg,             /* code segment displacement */
        relocTable,          /* offset of reloc table in file */
        overlayNbr;          /* overlay number, 0 if root */
} HEADREC;

void main (int argc, char *argv[])
{
int     handle, nbytes = sizeof (HEADREC);
char    filepath [80];
HEADREC header;

    /* Get file path from command line or console */
    clrscr ();
    if (argc < 2) {
      puts ("\nFilename (include .EXE extension)... ");
      gets (filepath);
    } else
      strcpy (filepath, argv[1]);

    /* Open the file */
    handle = open (filepath, O_RDONLY | O_BINARY);
    if (handle == -1) {
      puts ("\n\nERROR: ");
      switch (errno) {
        case ENOENT: puts ("Path or filename not found");
                     break;
        case EMFILE: puts ("Too many open files"); break;
        case EACCES: puts ("Permission denied");   break;
        case EINVACC: puts ("Invalid access code"); break;
      }
      puts ("\nProgram terminated");
      exit (1);
    }

    /* Get the header record */
    _read (handle, &header, nbytes);

    /* Show its contents */
    if (header.signature != EXESIG) {
      printf ("\n%s is not an .EXE file", filepath);
      puts   ("\nProgram terminated");
    } else {
      printf ("\nInformation about file %s:\n", filepath);
```

Program 20.3 **(continued)**

```
    printf ("\nOverlay number                        %u",
      header.overlayNbr);
    printf ("\nModule size: in pages                 %u",
      header.nPages);
    printf ("\n              in bytes                 %lu",
      (long) ((header.nPages-1) * 512L) + header.modSize);
    printf ("\nRelocation: number of items           %u",
      header.relocItems);
    printf ("\n            table offset               %04Xh",
      header.relocTable);
    printf ("\n.EXE header: in paragraphs             %u",
      header.headerSize);
    printf ("\n             in bytes                  %lu",
      (long) (header.headerSize * 16L));
    printf ("\nHeap/stack: min paragraphs             %u",
      header.minHeap);
    printf ("\n            max paragraphs             %u",
      header.maxHeap);
    printf ("\nStack: segment displacement           %04Xh",
      header.stackDispl);
    printf ("\n       initial SP offset              %04Xh",
      header.initSP);
    printf ("\nProgram code segment displacement     %04Xh",
      header.codeSeg);
    printf ("\n        entry point offset            %04Xh",
      header.entryPoint);
  }
  puts ("\n");
}
```

So much for .EXE files, the output of Turbo C programs in all memory models except tiny. Earlier we mentioned the environment block. Let's see what that's about.

CHAPTER 21

ENVIRONMENT VARIABLES

DOS has a feature that's like Rodney Dangerfield: It don't get no respect. At least not from users. Those who develop more than casual software for DOS learn to appreciate this little-known corner of the operating system. Since the purpose of this book is to lead you toward advanced programming, it's appropriate to discuss it here.

The feature is the environment block. It's a group of text strings buried in the operating system's memory space. These text strings are called *environment variables*, and they're used for several purposes:

- To provide running programs with general information about the system, such as the directory search path.
- To pass specific information from one program to another.
- To tell a program how its installation was configured, so that it can find its support files and learn about other selections the user made at set-up time.

DOS has several commands that place information in the environment block: **SET**, **PATH**, and **PROMPT**, among others. You can enter these commands at the DOS prompt, or through a command file, or—as we'll see shortly—with a program.

For example, the AUTOEXEC.BAT file on our computer reads as follows:

```
QUIKBUF2 AT 256 E P
PATH=\DOS;\MOUSE;\BIN;\BRIEF;\DQ;\SHELL;
set bpath=;c:\brief\macros
set bhelp=c:\brief\help
set bcprg="clipper %%s -m"
set bpackages=prg:r
set bflags=-i120k1l78M57t -mKP -Dega
mouse 2
menu
click
dos_edit
```

```
prompt $p$g
ng\ng
```

Some of these statements start up memory-resident programs: QUIKBUF2 (an EMS-based print spooler), MOUSE, MENU, and CLICK (supporting the Logitech Mouse), DOS__EDIT (a public-domain DOS shell), and NG (the Norton Guides). The rest set environment variables.

We can list the contents of our environment block by typing the **SET** command and pressing **Enter**. Here's what I get:

```
COMSPEC=C:\COMMAND.COM
PATH=\DOS;\MOUSE;\BIN;\BRIEF;\DQ;\SHELL;
BPATH=;c:\brief\macros
BHELP=c:\brief\help
BCPRG="clipper %s -m"
BPACKAGES=prg:r
BFLAGS=-i120k1l78M57t -mKP -Dega
PROMPT=$p$g
```

The **COMSPEC** variable gives the path to the command interpreter (usually COMMAND.COM). It's automatically set by DOS at startup. All the rest are the results of statements in AUTOEXEC.BAT, a command file that DOS processes whenever we power up or reset the machine. **PATH** gives the sequence of directories that DOS searches when we type a command that isn't in the current directory. **PROMPT** determines the appearance of the DOS prompt; pg means that when we're logged into the TURBOC directory, the prompt shows up as

```
C: TURBOC>
```

All the rest pass specific information to applications.

In particular, note **BHELP** and **BFLAGS**. Both pertain to BRIEF, a program editor I often use for languages other than Turbo C, Turbo Pascal, and the Microsoft QUICK languages, all of which have their own editors. **BHELP** tells BRIEF where to find the HELP files. **BFLAGS** looks like gibberish, but it tells BRIEF which installation options we've selected. The point is that environment variables are to be used by programs, not by humans.

This example illustrates the format of environment variables, which is

```
NAME = <variable information as text>
```

The name of each string must be unique. If you want to add a new variable to the environment, it has to have a name that doesn't already exist. Reusing a variable name has the same effect as in a program. For example, say you type

SET BFLAGS = xyz

and later on you start **BRIEF**. It won't recognize the text string, which is now **xyz**, so the installation options you selected are no longer operative since the original setting of **BFLAGS** has been replaced.

In addition to commands and .BAT files, you can also fetch and set environment variables from within Turbo C programs using the functions **getenv()** and **putenv()**.

Getting Environment Variables

Turbo C's **getenv()** function searches the environment for a specific variable name. Its argument is a pointer to a string containing the environment variable name you want to look for. Wildcard characters such as * are not valid, so you have to be specific. **getenv()** returns a pointer to the environment string matching the argument, or **NULL** if the environment block doesn't contain a variable so named.

The following program (GETPATH.C) illustrates the use of **getenv()** in searching the environment for the string set by the DOS **PATH** command.

```
/* GETPATH.C: Search environment block for PATH */

Include <stdio.h>
Include <stdlib.h>
Include <conio.h>

void main ()
{
char *vname = "PATH", *vstr;

if ((vstr = getenv (vname)) != NULL)
   cprintf ("%s", vstr);
else
   cputs ("No PATH found");
}
```

On our system, the program's output is

\DOS;\MOUSE;\BIN;\BRIEF;\DQ;\SHELL;

which corresponds to the **PATH** command in AUTOEXEC.BAT. If we type **PATH** at the DOS prompt level, we get a similar response, except that it's prefixed by **PATH=**. The Turbo C function assumes that you knew what variable name you were looking for when you issued **getenv()**, and so doesn't feed it back in the response.

Perhaps we should pause to consider what the symbols in the search path signify. The backslash (\) means "another directory," while the semicolon says "stop here and go back to the root." The root is the main directory of the disk; it's where you go when you type

CD \

Thus, the sequence \DOS;\MOUSE means "look in the \DOS directory and if you don't find it there, go back to the root and then to the \MOUSE directory."

Adding a String to the Environment

The **putenv()** function is the opposite of **getenv()**; it adds a new string to the environment, and it can also modify or delete an existing environment variable. Its argument is a string (or a pointer to one) containing the variable's complete text in the form

VNAME = text

For example,

putenv ("HOMEDIR = \\APPS");

sets the environment variable as shown (the double backslash resolves to a single character). If you decide to delete this variable later, you can issue the statement

putenv ("HOMEDIR =");

This removes all reference to HOMEDIR from the current environment.

putenv() returns **0** if successful and **−1** if not. The main reasons for failure are an improperly formatted string (no equals sign) and running out of environment space.

Program 21.1 lists CHENV.C, which illustrates manipulation of an environment variable called TEST_STRING. The program declines to run if TEST_STRING is a legitimate environment variable. Otherwise, it sets up a string by this name with **putenv()**, fetches it with **getenv()**, changes it to something else with another **putenv()** and fetches the new string, and finally deletes it from the environment. At each stage, it reports what it's done.

Program 21.1 **Manipulating an Environment String**

```c
/* CHENV.C: Set/change/delete an environmental variable */

#include <stdio.h>
#include <stdlib.h>
#include <conio.h>
#include <process.h>

void main ()
{
char   *vbl, variable[] = "TEST_STRING", new [80];

  /* See if the variable already exists */
  clrscr ();
  if ((vbl = getenv (variable)) == NULL)
    printf ("Variable %s does not currently exist",
      variable);
  else {
    printf ("Current contents of %s = %s",
      variable, vbl);
    puts
      ("\nProgram ended to avoid corrupting environment\n");
    exit (1);
  }

  /* Set the new environment */
  sprintf (new, "%s=new environment string", variable);
  if (putenv (new) == -1) {
    puts ("\nUnable to add new string. Program ended.\n");
    exit (1);
  }

  /* Check for new string */
  if ((vbl = getenv (variable)) == NULL)
    puts ("\n\nNew variable not found");
  else
    printf ("\n\nNew variable is %s=%s", variable, vbl);

  /* Change environment string */
  sprintf (new, "%s=different string", variable);
  putenv (new);

  /* Get changed string */
  if ((vbl = getenv (variable)) == NULL)
    puts ("\n\nChanged variable not found");
  else
    printf ("\n\nChanged string is %s=%s", variable, vbl);

  /* Remove string from environment */
  sprintf (new, "%s=", variable);
  if (putenv (new) == -1)
    puts ("\n\nUnable to remove string from environment");
  else
    puts ("\n\nRemoved string");
}
```

Passing Information via the Environment

When DOS starts a .COM or .EXE file running, it copies its environment into a new memory space and sets a pointer to it in the PSP. Thus, the running program owns its own copy of the environment, and any changes the program makes with **putenv()** are to this copy and not to the caller's. This prevents a program from altering the system environment and possibly causing the computer to suddenly start acting in unexpected ways.

As we'll discuss in Chapter 22, a process that starts another program running is a "parent," and the job it starts is a "child." The DOS shell program COMMAND.COM is therefore the ultimate parent of all processes on a PC. However, Program A (a child of DOS) can start Program B running, in which case A becomes a parent, B is its child, and DOS is—metaphorically—the grandparent of B.

In this scheme, DOS passes a copy of its environment to A. Perhaps A changes the environment, then initiates B via a call to the appropriate Turbo C routine (**spawn()** or **exec()**, discussed in Chapter 22). During start-up processing, B acquires a copy of A's modified environment. In this way, A can pass information to B, which B obtains with **getenv()** and acts on.

Note that this is a one-way communication path: parent to child only. The child has a copy of the environment and doesn't know where its parent's is. Any changes the child makes are to its own environment. They cease to exist when the child terminates, since DOS releases the memory occupied by the child's environment. Thus the parent's environment is unaffected by the activities of its child (unlike a human parent's).

This is both good and bad. It's good because it keeps the system environment from getting cluttered with old and potentially hazardous stuff. It's bad because you can't run a program that tailors the environment for a bunch of other programs, unless they're all children of the first one. However, there is a way to set environment variables globally and make them a permanent part of the system. That's what we discuss next.

Setting Global Environment Variables

The only way to set an environment variable that's globally available is at the DOS prompt level with the SET command. The variable then becomes a part of DOS' environment as long as the system remains powered up, and it's automatically passed to all children.

It's impractical, of course, to expect a user to type a **SET** command every time he or she wants to run your software. However, there's a way around this. Lines in .BAT files are treated as DOS commands, so if you add **SET** commands to a .BAT file and then run that .BAT file, they have the same effect as if typed manually. The one .BAT file that is guaranteed to run every time you start the computer is AUTOEXEC.BAT.

Consequently, you can place **SET** commands into AUTOEXEC.BAT. The contents of those commands become a permanent part of the DOS environment.

The names of environment variables should be unique enough that there's little chance someone else has already claimed them, and that they don't conflict with keywords such as **PATH, COMSPEC,** and **PROMPT.** The contents of the strings can be anything you like, so long as it's text and doesn't contain an embedded null terminator (ASCII 0).

A Working Example

A common use of environment strings in commercial software packages is to pass configuration information to the application's program(s). This can include directory paths specified by the user, as well as installation parameters such as **BFLAGS** shown earlier. Run an install program that appends **SET** commands to AUTOEXEC.BAT, then have the user reboot the computer to put those commands into effect. Thereafter, the variables are always part of the system environment. The program they configure can then read the appropriately named variables with **getenv()** and adapt itself accordingly.

Programs 21.2 and 21.3 illustrate this idea by simulating an application (APP.C) and its installation program (APPINST.C). Type and run APP.C first, without doing the "installation." The program checks for an environment string called APPPARMS to find out what the screen colors are. If it fails to find the string (because the installation hasn't yet been performed), it refuses to run and tells the user what needs to be done to earn its cooperation.

Program 21.2 A Simple Application Requiring Configuration Information from Environment Strings

```
/* APP.C: Application stub: reads installation info from  */
/*        global environments set by AUTOEXEC.BAT         */
/* Run this program after APPINST.C                       */
/* ------------------------------------------------------ */

#include <stdio.h>
#include <conio.h>
#include <stdlib.h>

void main ()
{
char   fore, back, *string, parms[] = "APPPARMS",
       path[] = "APPPATH";

   /* Get screen installation choices */
   if ((string = getenv (parms)) == NULL) {
     puts ("First run APPINST to install this application");
     puts ("\n(You must reboot the computer afterwards)");
     puts ("\nProgram ended");
     exit (1);
```

Program 21.2 **(continued)**

```
}

/* Set up screen with installed colors */
fore = string [0];
back = string [1];
textcolor (fore - '0');
textbackground (back - '0');
clrscr ();

/* Label screen */
gotoxy (27, 1);
puts ("* * APPLICATION SCREEN * *±n±n±n");

/* Show configuration info */
printf ("Foreground color = %c", fore);
printf ("\n\nBackground color = %c", back);
string = getenv (path);
printf ("\n\nPath to application is %s", string);

/* Wait for keypress and end */
puts ("\n\n\nPress any key to end . . .");
getch ();
textcolor (LIGHTGRAY);
textbackground (BLACK);
clrscr ();
}
```

After the installation is completed, APP sets up the screen with the configuration choices, shows what they are, and displays the other configuration information. It waits for a keypress, then restores the default screen and quits. But first you have to do the installation, which is what APPINST.C in Program 21.3 handles.

This program asks the user to furnish three installation options: the directory path to the application, and the screen foreground and background colors. First, though, it makes a backup copy of AUTOEXEC.BAT (or creates a new file by that name if one doesn't exist). The backup is made by renaming the file AUTOEXEC.OLD, then creating a new AUTOEXEC.BAT and copying everything from .OLD into it. The new .BAT file is left open and ready for the **SET** statements that the program will add.

The program does nothing to ensure that the application path is reasonable (this is just a "pretend" installation, after all). A real installation program should make sure the path actually exists and give the user guidance if not. Here it simply writes a **SET** command to the new .BAT file.

The acquisition of colors is a little smarter. It makes sure the user enters valid choices. When that's done, the program adds another **SET** command, closes the file, and quits. Observe the notice to reboot; that part's not "pretend," but instead required to implement the new environment strings.

You need a project or make file to link APPINST with TEXTBOX.OBJ, a library developed earlier in this book.

Program 21.3 An Installation Program that Modifies the AUTOEXEC.BAT File

```
/* APPINST.C: Sample installation program */
/* Writes installation options into AUTOEXEC.BAT */

#include <stdio.h>
#include <conio.h>
#include <errno.h>
#include <process.h>
#include "textbox.h"

void main ()
{
FILE *old, *new;
char fore = 'x', back = 'x', c, path [80],
     cmd [100];
int  n, col = 49, row = 12, p, cx, cy;

   /* Identify the program */
   clrscr ();
   gotoxy (26, 1);
   puts ("* * INSTALLATION PROGRAM * *\n");

   /* Make a backup copy of AUTOEXEC.BAT */
   if (rename ("\\AUTOEXEC.BAT", "\\AUTOEXEC.OLD") == -1) {
     switch (errno) {
       case ENOTSAM:
       case ENOENT:
         puts ("\nAUTOEXEC.BAT being created");
         new = fopen ("\\AUTOEXEC.BAT", "a");
         break;
       case EACCES:
         puts ("\nUnable to continue");
         puts ("\nFile access error");
         puts
           ("\nPossible conflict with existing AUTOEXEC.OLD");
         puts ("\nProgram ended");
         exit (1);
         break;
     }
   } else {                         /* Copy contents to new file */
     puts
       ("\nYour AUTOEXEC.BAT has been saved in AUTOEXEC.OLD");
     old = fopen ("\\AUTOEXEC.OLD", "r");
     new = fopen ("\\AUTOEXEC.BAT", "a");
     while (!feof (old)) {
       c = fgetc (old);
       fputc (c, new);
     }
     fclose (old);
   }
```

Program 21.3 **(continued)**

```
/* Get application path, put into file */
puts ("\n\nName of directory containing application? ");
gets (path);
sprintf (cmd, "\nSET APPPATH=%s", path);
fputs (cmd, new);
printf ("\n\nAdded command: %s", cmd);

/* Get color combo for APP screen */
puts ("\n\n\nColor selection:");

/* First build a box showing colors */
cx = wherex(); cy = wherey();              /* note position */
textbox (col, row, col+10, row+5, 2);
for (n = 0; n < 8; n++) {                   /* display colors */
  textcolor (LIGHTGRAY);                    /* digit color */
  gotoxy (col+1, row+n+1);
  cprintf ("%d", n);
  textcolor (n);                            /* bar color */
  for (p = 0; p < 2; p++)
    cprintf ("%c", 219);
  if (n == 3)
    col += 6, row -= 4;
}
/* Now get color choice from user */
textcolor (7);                             /* default foreground */
gotoxy (cx, cy);                           /* restore cursor */
puts ("\n\nForeground color? ");
do {
  fore = getche ();
  if ((fore < '0') || (fore > '7')) /* verify selection */
    puts ("\nInvalid choice - try again: ");
} while ((fore < '0') || (fore > '7'));
puts ("\n\nBackground color? ");
do {
  back = getche ();
  if ((back < '0') || (back > '7'))
    puts ("\nInvalid choice - try again: ");
} while ((back < '0') || (back > '7'));

/* Add to file */
sprintf (cmd, "\nSET APPPARMS=%c%c", fore, back);
fputs (cmd, new);
printf ("\n\nAdded command: %s±n±n", cmd);

/* Close and quit */
fclose (new);
puts ("Press Ctrl-Alt-Del to complete installation\n");
}
```

Now you can run APP and see how it adapts itself to the configuration parameters in the new environment strings.

After you've completed this exercise, copy AUTOEXEC.OLD back to AUTOEXEC.BAT to undo the changes made by APPINST. The strings do no harm, but they'll continue to occupy memory needlessly unless you get rid of them.

Environment variables can add a lot of power and flexibility to your software, and quite painlessly. We'll revisit them in the next chapter, where we see how to run child processes from within Turbo C programs.

CHAPTER 22

RUNNING ONE PROGRAM FROM ANOTHER

As application programs increase in complexity and sophistication, it's sometimes necessary for one program to run others. An example is giving your user the ability to leave the application temporarily in order to operate at the DOS-prompt level, then return to the application (as in the File/OS shell menu selection of the Turbo C environment). Other examples are executing DOS commands from within programs, using overlays or other programs in the manner of overlays (as in running a test program from within the Turbo C environment), and chaining two or more programs to form a jobstream.

Turbo C furnishes three functions for executing other programs from within your applications:

- **system**() is the simplest. It executes any DOS command.
- The **spawn** . . . () functions invoke and run another program as a child process. Depending on the mode argument, **spawn** . . . () works either like **system**() or like **exec**(), described next.
- The exec . . . () functions chain to another program, thus overlaying the memory space occupied by the invoking application. There is no return to the parent.

Thus, the three functions furnish two different strategies for invoking another program: with and without return. This chapter describes the alternatives.

Using system()

If you don't intend to port your applications to other C compilers, **system**() is the easiest call to use for invoking child processes that are to return to the parent. A child process can be any DOS command: one built into the COM-

MAND.COM shell, a .BAT file, or an executable program in the .COM or .EXE format. You can also use it to drop into the DOS environment and return to the application with the **EXIT** command.

The ability to call on DOS intrinsic commands (those built into COM-MAND.COM) can save you a lot of work. If you want to give your software users a listing of the files on the A: drive, you can write the statement

```
system ("DIR A:");
```

and the program, when it comes to this statement, executes the quoted command as though typed at the DOS prompt level. Similarly, if you want to copy all the files from drive A: to the current subdirectory (as in an installation program), the statement is

```
system ("COPY A:*.*");
```

This is much simpler than writing unique routines to list the directory, copy files from one drive to another, and so on.

The downside of this method is that the commands behave exactly the same as if typed at the DOS level. For example, the copy command lists on the screen all files copied. A way around this is to redirect the normal screen output to a disk file, as in

```
system ("COPY A:*.* > JUNK.XYZ");
```

The output is thus written to JUNK.XYZ in the current directory.

Another potential problem is that you can lose the current directory for the application. Consider the following sequence of statements:

```
system ("md \\NEWAPP");
system ("cd \\NEWAPP");
system ("COPY A:*.*");
```

This leaves the system in subdirectory \NEWAPP. That can be a real problem if the application subsequently creates and manipulates other files that it expects to be located in its own subdirectory.

The solution is to use **getdisk()** and **getcwd()** to load the current working drive and directory into variables *before* initiating the sequence above. Afterwards, you can use **setdisk()**, **sprintf()**, and another **system()** call to return to the proper directory:

```
int drive;
char direc [64], mainpath [64];
```

```
drive = getdisk ();
getcwd (direc, 64);
system ("md \\NEWAPP");
system ("cd \\NEWAPP");
system ("COPY A:*.*");
setdisk (drive);
sprintf (mainpath, "cd %s", direc);
system (mainpath);
```

The call to **sprintf()** creates the command string that carries the system back to the directory of origin. Note that **system()** takes an argument that is either a literal string or a pointer to a string containing a valid DOS command (both of which the compiler resolves to a pointer anyway).

The **system()** function invokes a copy of COMMAND.COM (or an alternative DOS command interpreter on machines such as Hewlett-Packard PCs) using the COMSPEC environment variable. As a result, it behaves exactly like COMMAND.COM at the DOS prompt level, including the execution of intrinsic commands plus .BAT, .EXE, and .COM files. The executable files (.EXE and .COM) can be in the current directory or in any other directory that is along the PATH environment string. For example, say your program is running out of directory \MYAPP and PATH\DOS;\SYSTEM, with CHKDSK residing in \SYSTEM. If your program issues the statement

```
system ("CHKDSK /F");
```

the CHKDSK program will be executed, since COMMAND.COM searches the directory path for it. Note also that it's valid to pass command-line arguments such as **\F** in **system()** calls.

The **system()** function returns an integer indicating its status, where **0** = success. You can check the status, as in

```
if (system (cmd) == 0)
  /* operation was successful */
else
  /* it wasn't */
```

Unfortunately, the returned status doesn't indicate whether the DOS command itself was successful. If you send an invalid command as an argument to **system()**, the message

```
Bad command or file name
```

appears on the display, but **system()** returns **0** anyway. Therefore the returned status isn't of much use, and you can safely ignore it most of the time.

The one situation in which it's advisable to check the return code from **system()** is at its first invocation in the program. A non-zero value probably means that there isn't enough memory to load and execute the command interpreter. The upshot is that if the first invocation doesn't work, none will and the program must therefore either take defensive action or notify the user of the problem.

Opening a Doorway to the DOS Command Level

In programs with a user interface environment, it's a considerate touch to furnish a doorway to the DOS command level. This enables the user to run programs and execute commands at will, then return to the application by typing the **EXIT** command. **EXIT** is an intrinsic command that tells COM-MAND.COM to quit and restore control to its parent; it has no effect if COM-MAND.COM is not functioning as a child process.

A simple **system()** call takes the user to the DOS prompt level from a program:

```
system ("C:\\COMMAND");
```

This loads a copy of COMMAND.COM from the C drive's root directory and passes control to it. COMMAND.COM signals that it's alive by displaying a copyright notice and presenting the normal DOS prompt. The parent program remains in memory in a state of suspended animation while COM-MAND.COM has control. The user proceeds as though the parent program had ended. However, when the user types **EXIT,** the copy of COMMAND.COM relinquishes control and the parent program resumes running at the statement following the **system()** call. The memory occupied by COMMAND.COM returns to the general memory pool and is thus available for other use.

The difference between this and executing a command via **system()** is that the command is passed through the interpreter for execution, while this approach take the user into the interpreter itself. The similarity is that, in both cases, COMMAND.COM is the parent of the running application, which is the parent of a second copy of COMMAND.COM, which in its turn may be the parent of a process executed in response to a command.

Graceful Exits and Returns

Before invoking a child process that will return, it's usually advisable to save the parent's visual context (the current display), then give the new program a clean slate to work on by clearing the screen. On return, you can restore the visual context and resume execution of the parent. Running an external program doesn't affect the parent's data, but it does corrupt the display. This simple way of handling the visual context provides intuitive boundaries between parent and child.

Demonstration: A DOS Shell

Program 22.1 is a simple DOS shell that illustrates the points covered so far. While it lacks some of the glitzy features of commercial DOS shells such as XTREE, the program is a complete and useful utility.

It lists 10 common intrinsic DOS commands on a menu. The other two menu selections are for command-line mode and to quit the program. You select a choice by typing its associated number and pressing **Enter.** In most cases, the program then prompts for the command line arguments and executes the completed command via a **system()** call. If you select **11** (command line), the program takes you into COMMAND.COM and you operate at the DOS prompt level until you type **EXIT.**

Most of this program's work is done in the **processCommand()** function. Four of the menu choices don't require a separate display, working instead in the background without visual effects; these are **CHDIR, DEL, MKDIR,** and **RENAME.** The rest entail switching to a fresh screen while they run, then restoring the shell's visual context upon a keypress.

Note the **showdir()** function also. It displays the current drive and directory in a box near the top of the display. This function is initially called from **main()** during the set-up phase. **processCommand()** also calls it if the user changes directories with menu selection **1** or returns from command-line mode, in which he or she might have changed directories. **showdir()** dynamically sizes the directory window and its surrounding text box according to the length of the current directory path.

DOSSHELL has a lot of visual appeal on a color monitor, since it uses colors liberally. The program relies heavily on techniques and routines for managing pop-up windows, which Chapters 8 and 9 presented.

Program 22.1 **A DOS Shell Utility**

```
/* DOSSHELL.C: A simple DOS shell program */
/* Compile and link with Turbo C tiny model */

#include <stdlib.h>
#include <stdio.h>
#include <conio.h>
#include <dos.h>
#include <dir.h>
#include <string.h>
#include "textbox.h"
#include "popup.h"

/* Application screen descriptor */
```

Program 22.1 **(continued)**

```
POPUP scrn = {0, 1, 80, 25, 0, YELLOW, MAGENTA,
                BLACK, CYAN, 0};

/* DOS screen descriptor */
POPUP dos = {0, 1, 80, 25, 0, LIGHTGRAY, 0, BLACK};

/* Popup descriptor for command line arguments */
POPUP arg = {2, 21, 79, 23, 1, RED, 0, BLACK, 0, GREEN};

/* POPUP descriptor for current directory */
POPUP dir = {0, 3, 0, 5, 2, MAGENTA, 0, BLACK, 0, CYAN};

/* List of commands */
char cmd [][16] = {
    {"CHDIR"}, {"COPY"}, {"DATE"},       {"DEL"},
    {"DIR"},   {"MKDIR"}, {"RENAME"},     {"SET"},
    {"TIME"},  {"TYPE"},  {"Command line"}, {"Quit"}
};

void buildScreen (void);
void processCommand (int);
char *getargs (int);
char *noargs (int);
void showdir (void);

/* -------------------------------------------------- */

void main ()
{
int    curdrive, choice;
char   curdir [64], oldpath [67], entry [3];

  /* Get current drive and directory */
  curdrive = getdisk ();
  getcwd (curdir, 64);

  /* Set up screen */
  buildScreen ();
  showdir ();

  /* Loop for DOS commands */
  do {
    gotoxy (30, 22);
    clreol ();
    cputs ("Select by number . . . ");
    gets (entry);              /* string input from keyboard */
    choice = atoi (entry);          /* convert to number */
    if ((choice > 0) && (choice < 13))
      processCommand (choice);
  } while (choice != 12);

  /* Restore entry drive and path, then quit */
  setdisk (curdrive);
```

Program 22.1 **(continued)**

```
   sprintf (oldpath, "CD %s", curdir);
   system (oldpath);
   textcolor (LIGHTGRAY);
   textbackground (BLACK);
   clrscr ();
} /* ------------------------ */

void buildScreen (void)

            /* Build display and menu */
{
int  row = 7, col = 23, n;

   clrscr();
   popShow (&scrn);
   popCenter (&scrn, "* * * D O S   S H E L L * * *");
   popHilite (&scrn, 1);
   textcolor (GREEN);
   textbox (20, 5, 60, 19, 2);
   gotoxy (35, 5);
   cputs (" COMMANDS ");
   textcolor (scrn.normal);

   /* Show list of commands */
   for (n = 0; n < 12; n++) {
     if (n == 6) col += 19, row -= 12;      /* column break */
     gotoxy (col, row + (n * 2));           /* next position */
     textcolor (scrn.hilite);
     cprintf ("%2d ", n + 1);
     textcolor (scrn.normal);
     cputs (cmd [n]);
   }
} /* ------------------------ */

void processCommand (int choice)

      /* Execute command selected by user */
{
char   *command;

   switch (choice) {
     case  1:
     case  4:
     case  6:
     case  7: command = getargs (choice);
              system (command);
              break;
     case  2:
     case  3:
     case  5:
     case  8:
     case  9:
     case 10: command = getargs (choice);
```

Program 22.1 **(continued)**

```
                 popShow (&dos);
                 system (command);
                 cputs (
                 "\n\nPress any key to return to shell . . .");
                 getch ();
                 popErase (&dos);
                 break;
      case 11: popShow (&dos);              /* Go to COMMAND.COM */
                 system ("\\COMMAND");
                 popErase (&dos);
                 break;
  }
  if ((choice == 1) ||             /* if changed directories */
      (choice == 11))      /* or went to DOS command level */
    showdir ();
} /* ----------------------- */

char *noargs (int choice)

      /* Build command line without arguments */
{
char cmdline [5];

  sprintf (cmdline, "%s", cmd [choice-1]);
  return (cmdline);
} /* ---------------------- */

char *getargs (int choice)

      /* Build command line with arguments */
{
char cmdline [80], arglist [80];

  popShow (&arg);
  cprintf ("%s ", cmd [choice-1]);
  gets (arglist);
  sprintf (cmdline, "%s %s", cmd [choice - 1], arglist);
  popErase (&arg);
  return (cmdline);
} /* ----------------------- */

void showdir (void)

      /* Show current directory */
{
char   path [64];
int    i;
struct text_info win;

  if (dir.save != NULL)      /* delete unneeded save area */
    free (dir.save);
  gettextinfo (&win);                /* get current window info */
```

Program 22.1 **(continued)**

```
window (1, 1, 80, 25);          /* set up full screen mode */
for (i = dir.top; i <= dir.bottom; i++) {
   gotoxy (1, i);
   clreol ();                    /* clear old dir display area */
}
getcwd (path, 64);                          /* get current dir */
i = strlen (path) + 14;
dir.left = ((80 - i) / 2);              /* size new window */
dir.right = 80 - dir.left;
popShow (&dir);                                  /* show it */
cprintf (" Directory: %s", path);
window (win.winleft, win.wintop,    /* restore old window */
        win.winright, win.winbottom);
gotoxy (win.curx, win.cury);       /* and cursor position */
textcolor (win.attribute & 0x0F);          /* and colors */
textbackground (win.attribute >> 4);
} /* ----------------------- */
```

Using Spawn . . . ()

The Turbo C manual explains the **spawn** . . . () family of functions in considerable detail, so we won't give much space to them here. In general, **spawn** . . . () requires one to three suffixes selected from these four: l, v, p, and e. These suffixes specify methods for passing arguments to the child, the search path, and the child's environment. There are eight possible combinations of suffixes. The same is true of the **exec** . . . () functions covered later.

One of the most important things to note about the **spawn** is the *mode* parameter. There are three:

P__WAIT suspends the parent's activity until the child completes. This mode makes **spawn** . . . () equivalent to the **system()** function, except when passing a new environment (discussed below).

P__NOWAIT ostensibly keeps the parent running while the child executes. This is a Unix mode that doesn't to DOS, which cannot support multiprocessing. Consequently, don't use it.

P__OVERLAY brings the child process into the memory space occupied by the parent. You can't return to the parent from a child called in P__OVERLAY mode. This mode is equivalent to the **exec** . . . () functions discussed later in this chapter.

Because the **spawn** . . . () functions in P__WAIT mode are more complicated than **system()**, there usually isn't much point in using them. The main exception is when passing a new environment to the child.

Communicating with a Child Process

It's frequently necessary for a parent to pass information to the child process it invokes. This information might be quite simple, such as the name of a file containing data to be processed, or as complicated as the data itself along with instructions as to what's to be done. It depends on the application. The environment can be as large as 32K.

As discussed in Chapter 21, the environment consists of a set of null-terminated text strings each having the form

VARNAME =   text

A program can obtain the address of a specific variable name's string using the getenv() function.

If you want to pass the parent's environment to the child without modification, use the system() function. It has no provision for altering the environment, so the child simply inherits the same environment as the parent has.

On the other hand, if you want to pass your own environment strings, you have to use one of the spawne..() (or exece..()) functions. The e-suffixed functions take an argument that is an array of character pointers, with each element pointing to a null-terminated environment string. A **NULL** pointer in this array indicates the end of the list. The pointed-to strings need not be in contiguous memory; before initiating the child program, DOS collects them all in the child's environment block and sets the PSP pointer.

How the Child Obtains Information from the Parent

When the child gets control, it can fetch environment strings just as the parent does, with getenv(). Because getenv() searches the environment for the variable whose name appears as an argument, the child process must be conditioned to "know" the names of the strings it needs.

Similarly, the parent invoking the child through a **spawn** or **exec** call can pass simulated command-line arguments. The l (literal) and v (vectored) suffixes govern how the arguments are passed: separately or as an array of pointers similar to the environment argument, respectively. This is another way of sending information to the child. The child must know which method (l or v) the parent uses, so that it can process the command line appropriately. The examples in this chapter use the v method.

Figure 22.2 is a program called CHILD.C, which we'll use twice in this chapter. The first time we'll call it with the spawnvpe() function in P__WAIT mode. When the child runs to completion, the parent regains control, thus treating CHILD.C as a sort of glorified subroutine. The second time we'll call it with **execvpe()**. In that case, there is no return since the child overlays and thus replaces the parent.

Program 22.2 **A Child Process**

```
/* CHILD.C: Child process                              */
/* This program is invoked by a spawn...() or exec...() */
/*    call. Lists arguments passed and the environment  */
/*    strings COMSPEC, PROMPT, PATH, and XYZ            */

#include <stdlib.h>
#include <conio.h>

void main (int argc, char *argv[])
{
int   n;
char  *estr, *var[] = {"COMSPEC", "PROMPT", "PATH", "XYZ"};

   cputs ("\r\n\nIn child process, arguments are:");
   for (n = 0; n < argc; n++)
     cprintf ("\r\n  argv [%d] = %s", n, argv [n]);

   cputs ("\r\n\nChild's environmental strings are:");
   for (n = 0; n < 4; n++) {
     estr = getenv (var [n]);
     cprintf ("\r\n  %s = %s", var [n],
             estr == NULL ? "(nonexistent)" : estr);
   }
   exit (EXIT_SUCCESS);
}
```

CHILD.C expects to find an array of vectors pointing to the command-line arguments. It also expects its environment to contain the three "standard" strings COMSPEC, PATH, and PROMPT, plus a fourth unique string XYZ, which presumably contains control information passed from the parent via the environment. The program simply outputs the information from the parent and quits, but it illustrates the fetching of command-line arguments and environment strings in a child process. It also gives us a real program to call in the following exercises.

If you run this program from the DOS prompt, the output will look something like this:

```
In child process, arguments are:
  argv [0] = C:\TC\CHILD.EXE

Child's environmental strings are:
  COMSPEC = C:\COMMAND.COM
  PROMPT = $p$g
  PATH = \DOS;\MOUSE;\BIN;\BRIEF;
  XYZ = (nonexistent)
```

There are actually no command-line arguments, but a program always receives a 0th argument from DOS giving the complete path that invoked it (only in DOS 3.0 and later). That's what **argv [0]** is. Among the environment strings, the one to notice on this printout is XYZ. There is no such string in the current environment, so the program reports it as nonexistent. Later, when the Programs 22.3 and 22.4 invoke CHILD, they'll pass an XYZ environment string, so CHILD will report its value.

Preparing to Invoke a Child Process

It's necessary to do some setup before invoking a child process with the **spawn** and **exec** functions. Often you can make all the preparations with initialized variable declarations; the Turbo C manual's treatment of these two functions shows examples. It takes more work if you want to pass along certain of the parent's environment strings and others of your own.

The **getenv()** function returns the variable associated with an environment string, but not the string name and equals sign. Consequently, you have to reconstruct each full string. The easiest way to do this is with **sprintf()**:

```
char path [80], prompt [80], comspec [80],
    xyz[] = "XYZ=7890", *envp [5];

sprintf (path, "PATH=%s", getenv ("PATH));
sprintf (prompt, "PROMPT=%s", getenv ("PROMPT"));
sprintf (comspec, "COMSPEC=%s", getenv ("COMSPEC"));
```

These statements build properly formatted environment strings that can be passed along to the child.

Once the strings are built, put pointers to them into an array of character pointers such as ***envp[]**:

```
envp [0] = comspec;
envp [1] = path;
envp [2] = prompt;
envp [3] = xyz;
envp [4] = NULL;
```

Note that the string pointers are not in the same order as that of declaration. Also, the **xyz** string is an initialized variable that we're adding to the child's environment. The list *must* end with a **NULL** pointer, hence **envp[4]**. The variable **envp** (without subscripts) then becomes a pointer to an array of environment pointers passed with a **spawne..()** or **exece..()** call. DOS uses it to build the child's environment block.

SPAWN.C in Program 22.3 illustrates the setup and calling of CHILD (Program 22.2). First the program displays its own environment, then it performs the steps just described to construct a new environment for the child. SPAWN also passes command-line arguments via the vector of pointers declared in *args[].

Program 22.3 **Calling a Child and Returning From It**

```
/* SPAWN.C: Passes modified environment to child process */

#include <stdio.h>
#include <stdlib.h>
#include <conio.h>
#include <process.h>
#include <dos.h>
#include <errno.h>

void main ()
{
char   newvar[] = "XYZ=7890",    /* New environment string */
       *envp [5],                /* pointers to env strings */
       childpath[] = "CHILD.EXE",        /* path to child */
       *args[] = {"CHILD.EXE",   /* command line arguments */
                  "A1", "A2", NULL},
       comspec [64], path [64], prompt [64];
int    status;

  /* Show current environment */
  clrscr ();
  cputs ("In parent, original environment is:\r\n");
  system ("SET");

  /* Get current environment strings for child */
  sprintf (comspec, "COMSPEC=%s", getenv ("COMSPEC"));
  sprintf (path, "PATH=%s", getenv ("PATH"));
  sprintf (prompt, "PROMPT=%s", getenv ("PROMPT"));

  /* Load pointer array for environment strings */
  envp [0] = comspec;
  envp [1] = path;
  envp [2] = prompt;
  envp [3] = newvar;
  envp [4] = NULL;

  /* Spawn the child */
  status = spawnvpe (P_WAIT, childpath, args, envp);
  cprintf ("\n\n\nIn parent, spawn status = %d", status);

  /* Check for, report error */
  if (status == -1) {
    cputs ("\r\nError occurred:\r\n");
    switch (errno) {
      case E2BIG:   cputs ("Argument list too long"); break;
```

Program 22.3 **(continued)**

```
        case EINVAL:   cputs ("Invalid argument"); break;
        case ENOENT:   cputs ("Bad path or filename"); break;
        case ENOEXEC:  cputs ("Exec format error"); break;
        case ENOMEM:   cputs ("Not enough memory"); break;
    }
  }
} /* ---------------------- */
```

Because SPAWN invokes the child process using **spawnvpe()** in **P__WAIT** mode, termination of the child restores control to the parent. You see this happen when the program reports the spawn status. An error message only appears if **spawnvpe()** indicated failure by returning **-1**; in that case, the child process will not have run, and the message explains why.

The amount of memory not claimed by the parent program constrains the size of a child. For example, say you have 500K of available memory (after claims by DOS and TSRs), and the aggregate total memory requirement of the parent program is 300K: code, data, stack, and heap. That leaves 200K available for all the memory requirements of the child. If that's not enough, **spawn** in **P__WAIT** mode returns **-1** and **errno** is set to **ENOMEM**, indicating insufficient memory to load and run the child.

The alternative in that case is to allow the child to overlay the parent. You can do it either by setting a **spawn** function to **P__OVERLAY** mode, or by using an **exec** function.

Using EXEC . . . ()

Almost everything we've said about the **spawn** functions applies equally to the similar **exec** functions: same suffixes, same methods for passing information to the child, same error conditions. There's only one major difference: child processes called with **exec** always overlay the parent. This difference makes **exec** less flexible than **spawn**, because the **exec** functions lack the P__WAIT/P__OVERLAY options.

There's good news and bad news about child processes that overlay their parent. The good news is that they're less memory-constrained; the child receives the same helping of memory as its parent. The bad news is that you can't return to the parent when the child runs to completion; once the child has control, there's no going back. Thus, this method of invoking child processes is more properly called *chaining*.

One of the defects of Turbo C is that it doesn't provide true overlay management in the same sense as other languages such as Turbo Pascal 3.0. The best you can do is to simulate it using the **spawn** functions in **P__WAIT** mode. Thus, if you're used to a language that supports true overlays (portions of code that can be brought into a memory pool set aside for them, and that have access to the parent's subroutines and data), don't be deceived by the term *overlay* as used here. It means that the child literally overlays the parent, which makes the parent cease to exist as a running process. That's what the **exec** functions do, and also **spawn** in **P_OVERLAY** mode.

And that's why it's more correct to refer to this method as chaining. A chain is a one-way sequence of programs, each invoking the next, which replaces its parent. Taken as a whole, the sequence of programs constitutes what they call a jobstream in the mainframe world: a chain of related programs that follow a logical progression.

If a return to the original parent is necessary, you can construct a circular chain. For example, A calls B, which calls C, which calls A. And because the **exec** functions allow each parent along the line to pass information to its child, via both command-line arguments and the environment, it's possible (though tricky) to make the re-invoked parent appear to resume running where it left off. That's software engineering stuff well beyond the scope of this book, but it should serve to open your imagination to the enormous power available in program chaining.

On a less grandiose scale, let's see an exec function in action. EXEC.C in Program 22.4 is very similar to Program 22.3 (SPAWN.C). Because an **exec** function doesn't return unless there's a problem, this program omits the status variable and, right after the **execvpe()** call, goes into error reporting. The **exec** functions support a few error conditions that **spawn** doesn't, so they've been added here. And finally, there's a goodbye message announcing that the program is chaining to a child process. Note that after the child finishes running, the chain ends and the system reverts to the DOS prompt. That's because there's no return from an overlay.

Program 22.4 **Chaining to a Child Process**

```
/* EXEC.C: Uses exec() to invoke a child process */

#include <stdio.h>
#include <stdlib.h>
#include <conio.h>
#include <process.h>
#include <dos.h>
#include <errno.h>

void main ()
{
char  newvar[] = "XYZ=7890",    /* New environment string */
      *envp [5],                /* pointers to env strings */
      childpath[] = "CHILD.EXE",         /* path to child */
      *args[] = {"CHILD.EXE",   /* command line arguments */
              "A1", "A2", NULL},
      comspec [64], path [64], prompt [64];
```

Program 22.4 **(continued)**

```
/* Show current environment */
clrscr ();
cputs ("In parent, original environment is:\r\n");
system ("SET");

/* Get current environment strings for child */
sprintf (comspec, "COMSPEC=%s", getenv ("COMSPEC"));
sprintf (path, "PATH=%s", getenv ("PATH"));
sprintf (prompt, "PROMPT=%s", getenv ("PROMPT"));

/* Load pointer array for environment strings */
envp [0] = comspec;
envp [1] = path;
envp [2] = prompt;
envp [3] = newvar;
envp [4] = NULL;

/* Chain to the child */
cputs ("\r\nChaining to child process\r\n");
execvpe (childpath, args, envp);

/* This code runs only if there was an error */
cputs ("\r\nError occurred:\r\n");
switch (errno) {
  case E2BIG:    cputs ("Argument list too long"); break;
  case EACCES:   cputs ("File access denied");     break;
  case EMFILE:   cputs ("Too many open files");    break;
  case EINVAL:   cputs ("Invalid argument");       break;
  case ENOENT:   cputs ("Bad path or filename");   break;
  case ENOEXEC:  cputs ("Exec format error");      break;
  case ENOMEM:   cputs ("Not enough memory");      break;
}
} /* ----------------------- */
```

Despite the somewhat daunting appearance of the Turbo C manual's coverage of **spawn** and **exec** functions, it's not particularly difficult to invoke one program from another. Yet this capability adds great power and flexibility to your applications.

CHAPTER 23

WRITING INTERRUPT
SERVICE ROUTINES

The ability to service and otherwise manipulate interrupts opens the
door to great power and flexibility. It allows your software to take control — and tailor the operation — of the machine to suit its purposes.

Writing interrupt service routines is not the simplest programming task,
but neither is it the dark art that it has the reputation for being. You need
plenty of documentation before you take it on, because to tinker with interrupts is to perform surgery on the delicate innards of the system. The *DOS
Technical Reference* is a good place to start. Ray Duncan's *Advanced MS-DOS*
and Bob Jourdain's *Programmer's Problem Solver* both contain excellent ad-
vice. So does a book by Michael Hyman with the verbose title *Memory Resident Utilities, Interrupts, and Disk Management with MS & PC DOS* (Portland,
OR: MIS Press, 1987). All three commercial books provide step-by-step
guides for handling interrupts. Thus equipped with a tried and proven plan,
writing an interrupt service routine (ISR or simply *handler*) becomes a matter
of fleshing it out with specifics.

This chapter is not a comprehensive treatment of the subject. Rather, it
serves as an introduction to interrupts and furnishes some simple working
examples. For more information, see one of the works cited, or any other in-
depth coverage of DOS systems programming.

What Is an Interrupt?

An interrupt is an event that demands the immediate attention of the processor. When an interrupt occurs, the processor stops what it's doing, branches to a routine that services the interrupt, and then resumes where it left
off. An ISR is thus a special kind of subroutine.

There are two kinds of interrupts: hardware and software. A hardware interrupt is typically generated by some system element outside the control of
the running program. Examples are a keypress, a character arriving at a
serial port, a tick of the system clock, and an intolerable error such as divi-

sion by zero. A software interrupt is generated on purpose by the running program. The most common example, which is sometimes referred to as an executive call, is when a program requests service from DOS. The calling program loads information into registers, triggers the interrupt, and usually expects some kind of returned value that it uses subsequently.

These are two very different kinds of interrupts. Hardware interrupts are unpredictable, and the running program seldom knows that one has occurred. A hardware ISR usually takes the minimal actions of saving incoming data if necessary, and setting a flag to indicate that the interrupt has occurred. It's the responsibility of other routines to process the results of the interrupt at their convenience. On the other hand, software interrupts treat the called handler as a subroutine. A software ISR interprets the information passed in registers, takes the requisite action, and sends back an answer.

The great majority of software interrupts entail Int 21h, which is the gateway to DOS services, and Int 10h for the ROM BIOS video services. There are many others less commonly used, each tied to a particular interrupt number. Additionally, some optional services are available through device drivers tied to interrupts. For example, if a mouse is installed, it's manipulated via Int 33h, and EMS through Int 67h. The latter two are interrupts reserved by informal industry standards.

DOS tends to cluster most of the hardware interrupts in Int 0 through Int 1F, and to tie some undocumented interrupts to Int EEh through Int FFh.

What do these hex numbers mean? They identify the interrupt, and also serve as an index to a special system data structure called the interrupt vector table.

The Interrupt Vector Table

The steps that occur in response to an interrupt are intimately tied to the computer's processor. In fact, they're built into the silicon so that the processor doesn't have to follow a program in order to know what to do.

The processors that propel the PC family of machines all handle interrupts in a consistent way. When an interrupt occurs, the CPU saves the current context (all the registers), then uses the interrupt number to find the address of the handler associated with that interrupt. It loads the address into its CS and IP registers, so the next instruction to be executed is the entry point of the handler. The handler itself is software somewhere in the machine's address space (either in RAM or ROM). This software runs until the processor encounters an IRET instruction, which tells it to return from the interrupt. The processor then reloads the context of the interrupted process, which restores control at the point where the interrupt occurred.

The processor finds the address of the handler by using the interrupt number to index into the interrupt vector table. This is a list of 256 far pointers (vectors) beginning at memory address zero. Since a far pointer occupies four bytes, the table is 1,024 bytes in length, running from 0:0 through 0:03FFh. The processor multiplies the interrupt number by four to calculate the appropriate offset. For example, the vector for Int 0 is at 0:0, and for Int 1 at 0:4. When Int 1 occurs, the processor grabs the vector at 0:4 and branches to that address.

By implication, the existence of 256 vectors limits the PC to 256 possible interrupts numbered 0 through FFh. That's a lot of interrupts. DOS, the ROM BIOS, and assorted TSRs and device drivers take up about a hundred, leaving some 150 vacant slots in the table. If you write your own interrupt handler, you can take over any vacant vector as your own.

The problem is identifying an unclaimed vector.

Inspecting the Interrupt Vector Table

The interrupt vector table is initialized during machine startup, partially by the ROM BIOS and partially by the DOS bootstrap program. Therefore the disposition of unused vectors is up to the implementor. Some PCs I've worked on—notably those running DOS 2.n and an early ROM BIOS—left the unused vectors as **NULL** pointers, or in other words, as zero values. Others point the unclaimed vectors at an IRET buried somewhere in memory.

The latter approach makes more sense. That way, a spurious or misdirected interrupt simply returns without doing anything. A **NULL** pointer, on the other hand, can send the machine into never-never land. However, an unused pointer initialized to an IRET is indistinguishable from one that points to a real routine, unless you know for sure that it's unclaimed. One way to do this is to physically inspect the table. If there are scads of vectors all having the same value, they're the unused ones.

Turbo C furnishes the function **getvect()** for fetching an interrupt vector. This function returns the far pointer plucked from the specified vector. You can use it to determine the address of the handler associated with the interrupt number passed as its argument.

Program 23.1 illustrates the use of **getvect()** and also furnishes the useful utility SHOWVECS.C. This program lists the entire interrupt vector table, showing 64 vectors per panel. There are thus four panels, and the program steps through the interrupts in sequence. You can press **Q** to quit, or advance to the next panel with any other keystroke. Note that SHOWVECS uses the **#include** file TEXTBOX.I, which was developed in Part II.

Program 23.1 **A Utility for Inspecting the Interrupt Vector Table**

```c
/* SHOWVECS.C: Lists contents of interrupt vector table */

#include <conio.h>
#include <dos.h>
#include <ctype.h>
#include <stdlib.h>
#include "textbox.h"

#define ICOLOR YELLOW
#define VCOLOR GREEN

void drawBoxes (void);
void showVectors (int);

void main ()
{
int  screen;
char reply;

  clrscr ();
  drawBoxes ();
  for (screen = 0; screen < 4; screen++) {
    textcolor (ICOLOR);
    gotoxy (23, 1);
    cputs ("CONTENTS OF INTERRUPT VECTOR TABLE");
    showVectors (screen * 64);
    gotoxy (20, 24);
    clreol ();
    textcolor (ICOLOR);
    if (screen != 3) {
      cputs ("Q to quit, any other key to continue...");
      reply = toupper (getch());
      if (reply == 'Q') {
        textcolor (LIGHTGRAY);
        textbackground (BLACK);
        clrscr();
        exit (EXIT_SUCCESS);
      }
    } else {
      cputs ("           Press any key to end");
      getch ();
    }
  }
  textcolor (LIGHTGRAY);
  textbackground (BLACK);
  clrscr ();
} /* --------------------- */

void drawBoxes (void)

      /* Draw boxes around the vector lists */

{
```

Program 23.1 **(continued)**

```
int  col = 4, box;

  textcolor (VCOLOR);
  for (box = 0; box < 4; box++) {
    textbox (col, 3, col+17, 20, 1);
    col += 18;
  }
} /* ------------------------ */

void showVectors (int start)

     /* List 64 vectors beginning at start */
{
int  inter, row = 4, col = 6, listed = 0;
void far *vect;

  for (inter = start; inter < start + 64; inter++) {
    gotoxy (col, row++);
    textcolor (ICOLOR);
    cprintf ("%02Xh ", inter);

    vect = getvect (inter);
    textcolor (VCOLOR);
    cprintf ("%04X:%04X", FP_SEG (vect), FP_OFF (vect));

    if (++listed == 16) {
      col += 18;
      row -= 16;
      listed = 0;
    }
  }
} /* ------------------------ */
```

As you run this program, note that there's a lot of vacant real estate past the middle of the vector table, especially around Int A0h. If you need a vector, it's probably safe to grab any arbitrarily selected one somewhere in this vicinity. But check first. Load up every TSR (memory-resident program, such as Sidekick) that you can lay your hands on, then run SHOWVECS and pick an unclaimed vector.

An alternative to using an unclaimed vector is interrupt chaining—that is, calling the handler that owns a vector—which we'll discuss later.

Vector Management

Once you've identified the vector you want to use, you can put a pointer to your routine in it. But first, *save the current vector*. Fetch it with **getvect()** and tuck it into a safe place, preferably a global variable.

Why the italics? Because it's absolutely essential that you restore the old vector before terminating the program. If you fail to do this, the vector will continue to point at where your handler used to be; the next time that interrupt fires, the system will surely malfunction and probably crash. Restoring changed vectors puts the original handler back into service.

For a normal program (not a TSR), a good way to ensure orderly termination with restoral of the changed vector(s) is to use the Turbo C **atexit()** function. This registers one or more subroutines that are automatically called when the program ends. For example, say you declare the global variables

```
void interrupt (*oldvec)();
int myvec;
```

and load the pointer with

```
oldvec = getvect (myvec);
```

(where **myvec** has been set to the interrupt number you've claimed). Your program then includes a function such as:

```
void endofjob (void)
{
   setvect (myvec, oldvec);
}
```

Early in **main()**, register the function using the statement

```
atexit (endofjob);
```

Then, even if you have multiple termination points in the program (using **exit()** calls, plus normal termination at the end of **main()**), the **endofjob()** function will gain control and restore the changed vector to its original state.

Dos and Don'ts of ISRs

Interrupt service routines have certain special requirements that other kinds of subprograms don't. This is because they are, in effect, extensions of DOS and thus don't behave like normal application programs. They have many dos and don'ts that the books cited earlier describe in detail. Here we'll cover a few of the important ones.

Use the Interrupt Keyword

An ISR has special characteristics that normal functions don't. The Turbo C compiler knows to assign these characteristics to a function when it is defined using the keyword **interrupt**, as in

```
void interrupt myint (void)
{
  /* do interrupt stuff */
}
```

An interrupt function comes equipped with machine code that automatically saves all registers before its enclosed code gets control, and restores them on completion. The last statement of an interrupt function is **IRET**, which restores the system context and resumes execution where the interrupt occurred.

An interrupt function is by definition a far function, regardless of the Turbo C memory model in use. A reference to its address generates a 32-bit segment:offset value.

Do the Minimum Possible

An interrupt steals time from the running application. Therefore the less time it takes to do its job, the better. If you look at the ROM BIOS listing in the Technical Reference Manual for your machine, you'll see that the ISRs there are typically a dozen or two lines of assembly code. One or two lines of C code can easily generate the equivalent amount of machine language.

Say you're writing an ISR that accepts incoming data from a remote device attached to a serial port. An effective ISR in this case wakes up when a character is at the port, gets it, stuffs it into a buffer, and sets a flag to indicate that data are awaiting processing. Elsewhere, your application can check the flag periodically and, if it's on, flush the buffer by copying its contents elsewhere. The ISR's only responsibility is to save the data and tell somebody that it's done so.

User-written ISRs are highly application-dependent, of course, and they vary widely in their purposes. The point is that they should do as little as necessary to service the interrupt, in order to avoid stealing too much time from the task they've interrupted.

Use Volatile External Variables

If an ISR sets a flag and saves data someplace, those variables have to be accessible to the host software. An ISR can declare local variables just like a normal subprogram, but they're allocated on the stack and cease to exist when the ISR returns. Consequently, local variables are not externally visible, and they're perishable.

This means that when an ISR needs to pass information to the running program, it has to use an external variable that is global to the host software. Turbo C furnishes a special declaration modifier *volatile* for this purpose. Volatile is a flag indicating that the variable can be modified by some element outside the program's direct control: an interrupt, in this case. Always tag global variables that are affected by ISRs as volatile, and declare them in the heading of the program that contains the ISR. Program 23.2 later in this chapter contains an example.

Don't Do Any I/O

The business of an ISR is to service interrupts, not generate them. By definition, an I/O operation generates other interrupts. This can upset DOS so much that it crashes the system.

The reason is that DOS is a single-user, single-tasking operating system, and thus its routines are not re-entrant. With certain exceptions, only one interrupt can be in process at a time. If your interrupt is the one that's active and it tries to generate other interrupts, the machine stack can become corrupted and critical variables overlaid, causing the operating system to lose its way. When DOS gets confused, the machine either goes berserk or locks up.

Chain Interrupts

Any time you grab an interrupt vector, you potentially inhibit the activation of the ISR that's normally accessible through that vector. Sometimes you do this deliberately, as when replacing a built-in system ISR with one of your own. In most cases, however, the ISRs you write merely enhance existing system services by adding functionality. For example, Terminate and Stay Resident (TSR) utilities usually watch for the "hot key" that activates them by inserting some process into the keyboard interrupt-handling sequence. The keyboard handler operates normally except when the hot key is pressed.

In such cases, your ISR must chain to the process it replaced when it seized the interrupt vector. Depending on how it fits into the interrupt-handling sequence, it can chain either before or after it performs its job. (It might also decide not to chain at all if special circumstances arise, such as the arrival of a hot key.)

Since you must save the old vector anyway, you can accomplish chaining by using that pointer as a function variable. Example:

```
void interrupt myrtn (void)
{
. . . /* do the routine's job */
if (oldvec)
(*oldvec) (); /* chain ints */
}
```

In this case, the routine performs its job and then chains to the ISR it displaced from the table. Looking for a hot key is only slightly more complicated. Example:

```
void interrupt my__kbd__handler (void)
{
  if (__AX == HOT__KEY)
    activate__special__rtn();
  else
    if (old__kbd__vec)  /* chain */
      (*old__kbd__vec) ();
}
```

Here the routine inspects register AX for the hot key; if present, it activates the special routine associated with the hot key, and if not, it chains to the regular keyboard handler. The hot key itself never gets passed through, because it would confuse the program receiving keyboard input.

The next section implements this discussion with a working example.

Using the System Timer Tick

PC-type machines furnish user access to the system timer via Int 1Ch. This vector is normally set to point at an IRET, but you can take control of it if your software needs a real-time clock.

Note that Int 8 is also associated with the system timer. It's not advisable to monkey with this interrupt. The ROM BIOS relies on it to keep the master time-of-day clock and calendar up to date, to turn the floppy disk motor off after a certain interval, and for other purposes. The system may go to sleep, or at least forget to do things, if you take control of Int 8. Always use Int 1Ch instead, which is there just for you (Int 8 chains to it).

The system timer ticks 18.2044 times per second. This seems like an insane interval, but there's a reason. There are 3,600 seconds in an hour, and $18.2044 \times 3,600 = 65,536$, the maximum number obtainable in a 16-bit word. The system counts ticks and knows that an hour has passed when the counter reaches its terminal value.

Program 23.2, TICKER.C, illustrates an application of the timer tick interrupt. Each time the interrupt fires, the program's handler increments the ticks variable. That's all it does, consistent with the general rule that an ISR should remain active for the absolute minimum amount of time possible.

Program 23.2 **Harnessing the Timer Tick Interrupt**

```c
/* TICKER.C: Uses system timer ticks (Int 1Ch) to measure */
/*      how long a process runs                            */

#include <dos.h>
#include <math.h>
#include <conio.h>
#include <stdlib.h>

/* Globals */
void interrupt (*oldvec)();    /* save area for old vector */
volatile long ticks;                    /* for use by ISR */

/* Prototypes */
void interrupt tickisr (void);
void install (void);
double elapsed (void);
/* ----------------------------------------------------- */

void main ()
{
double v, x = 2.13579e+123, etime;
int    n;

  clrscr ();
  install ();                          /* install the handler */

  cputs ("Finding 5000 natural logarithms");
  ticks = 0L;                            /* reset the timer */
  for (n = 0; n < 5000; n++)
    v = log (x);
  etime = elapsed ();
  cprintf ("\r\n Total duration was %.6f seconds", etime);
  cprintf ("\r\n Average per operation was %.6f seconds",
        etime / 5000);

  cputs ("\r\n\nFinding 5000 square roots");
  ticks = 0L;
  for (n = 0; n < 5000; n++)
    v = sqrt (x);
  etime = elapsed ();
  cprintf ("\r\n Total duration was %.6f seconds", etime);
  cprintf ("\r\n Average per operation was %.6f seconds",
        etime / 5000);

  setvect (0x1C, oldvec);    /* restore timer tick vector */
} /* ----------------------- */

void interrupt tickisr (void)

     /* This ISR runs every time the system timer ticks */
{
  ticks++;                            /* update tick counter */
  if (oldvec)
```

Program 23.2 **(continued)**

```
    (*oldvec) ();                          /* chain interrupt */
} /* ---------------------- */

void install (void)

        /* This routine installs the tick ISR in Int 1Ch */
{
  oldvec = getvect (0x1C);                /* save old vector */
  setvect (0x1C, tickisr);                   /* install new */
} /* ---------------------- */

double elapsed (void)

    /* This routine returns elapsed time of nticks in sec */
{
  return ((double) ticks / 18.2044);
} /* ---------------------------------------------------- */
```

After installing the **tickisr()** routine in the interrupt vector table, this program calculates 5,000 natural logarithms and 5,000 square roots, reporting the total elapsed time and the average time for each test. It begins a test by zeroing the ticks variable. As the ensuing loop executes, it is interrupted 18.2 times per second by the timer tick, but because a tick is a hardware interrupt, the loop resumes each time where it left off. At the end of the loop, the program uses the value in ticks to compute and report the elapsed time in seconds and fractions. At completion, TICKER unhooks the local ISR from the vector, restoring the old pointer.

Writing a Software Interrupt Handler

Chances are that you'll never have occasion to write a software-callable ISR. Such handlers are usually the exclusive domain of the operating system and related low-level subsystems such as the ROM BIOS. But if you do, there are a couple of things you need to know about them.

A software interrupt almost always returns something to its caller. Conceptually this is like a value-returning function such as

    int somefcn (. . .)

but with an important difference: **somefcn()** returns its result on the stack, whereas a software ISR sends back its result in a register.

A Turbo C function of type **interrupt** ordinarily comes with built-in code to save and restore all registers. This is a convenience to programmers writing the more common hardware handlers; you don't have to worry about corrupting registers and inadvertently clobbering the interrupted process. The problem is that it erects a seemingly impenetrable barrier against returning a register with different contents, that is, sending back a result.

But there's a way around it. You can declare all the registers as arguments to the interrupt function. This gives you access to them. As a simplistic example, say your handler always returns the digit **3** in register BX. Here's how to write it:

```
void interrupt myisr (bp, di, di, ds, es,
    dx, cx, bx, ax, ip, cs, flags)
{
    bx = 3;
}
```

So what happens here? When the compiler sees all these register arguments, it makes them accessible to the enclosed code. The arguments simply associate names with the register values that the compiler pushes onto the stack. Thus the assignment finds the stack entry corresponding to the BX register and modifies it appropriately. That being the end of the function, the exit-processing code restores the registers and executes an IRET, and the interrupting process resumes. It can pull the returned value from the register using the Turbo C pseudo-variable name __BX. Here's how the calling routine does it:

```
geninterrupt (MYINT);
result = __BX;
```

In this case, **MYINT** is a constant that defines the interrupt associated with myisr().

Program 23.3 illustrates the use of a software interrupt. This program, SOFTINT.C, calls a software ISR associated with Int A0h that fetches the machine identification byte and returns it in register **BX**. The program installs the handler, then generates the software interrupt. When the interrupt returns, the program fetches the result from register **BX** and saves it in a normal variable, which it then evaluates to report the machine type. Before terminating, SOFTINT restores the vector to its original condition.

Program 23.3 Installing and Using a Software Interrupt

```
/* SOFTINT.C: Uses a software interrupt to identify the    */
/*      host computer type                                 */

#include <dos.h>
#include <conio.h>

#define A0   0xA0
void interrupt (*oldvec)();
```

Program 23.3 **(continued)**

```c
void interrupt a0isr (bp, di, si, ds, es, dx, cx,
                      bx, ax, ip, cs, flags)

   /* This software ISR returns the machine byte in
      in register BX */
{
  bx = peekb (0xF000, 0xFFFE);
} /* ----------------------- */

void main ()
{
unsigned char machine;

  oldvec = getvect (A0);      /* get the old vector for A0 */
  setvect (A0, a0isr);                      /* stuff vector */

  geninterrupt (A0);              /* do software interrupt */
  machine = _BX;                            /* save result */

  cputs ("The machine type is ");
  switch (machine) {
    case 0xFF: cputs ("standard PC"); break;
    case 0xFE: cputs ("XT"); break;
    case 0xFD: cputs ("PCjr"); break;
    case 0xFC: cputs ("286-based"); break;
    case 0xFA: cputs ("PS/2-30"); break;
    case 0xF9: cputs ("PC Convertible");
    case 0xF8: cputs ("PS/2-80"); break;
    default  : cputs ("unknown"); break;
  }

  setvect (A0, oldvec);       /* restore the old vector */
}
```

The register arguments to the interrupt handler propagate a scad of warning messages from the compiler, each advising that the variable is never used. Although annoying, they do no harm.

Now let's wrap up the book with a discussion of EMS.

CHAPTER 24

USING EXPANDED MEMORY IN TURBO C

Parkinson's Law states that work expands to fill the available time. A variant of that rule seems to apply to computers: software expands to fill available memory. When the present microcomputer era began with the IBM PC and MS-DOS, 640K seemed like an enormous amount of memory. After all, the previous generation of small machines had a maximum of 64K, and many large mainframes at that time ran with half a meg or even less. So although the 8088 chip that powered early PCs had a larger potential address space, the DOS limit of 640K seemed more than generous.

Within a couple of years, Parkinson's Law had taken effect and 640K was decried as woefully inadequate. No one had figured on the new generation of software with vast amounts of code to manage the user interface, nor had anyone foreseen that PCs would become workhorses largely replacing the mainframe.

The 640K barrier became an insurmountable wall, and users demanded a solution. Thus was born EMS, the Expanded Memory Specification, which Lotus announced in 1985. Intel and Microsoft quickly jumped on the bandwagon, seeing EMS as a way around the 640K barrier until a new operating system with a greater addressing range could be developed. That operating system is, of course, OS/2, which is now in use but will probably not become the standard PC operating system for several more years. Thus, EMS promises to remain with us for a while longer.

The basic premise of EMS is that a computer can be equipped with several megabytes of memory beyond the reach of DOS. A combination of dedicated hardware and firmware, coupled with some software, can manage this memory, shuttling data back and forth between expanded and conventional memory via a buffer. The net result is that EMS makes an enormous amount of memory available to a program.

Naturally, this data-shuttling doesn't happen by magic (although part of it seems to). It requires some special programming techniques. Those techniques, along with a discussion of how EMS works, are the subject of this chapter.

Extended Versus Expanded Memory, Compounded by EEMS

Let's begin by clearing up some confusing terminology. Extended memory is any memory that goes beyond 1MB (segment FFFFh, or absolute address 1,048,575). *Expanded* memory is a specific implementation of *extended* memory. We'll explain the implementation in a moment. Meanwhile, let's discuss some basics of extended memory addressing.

The address range controlled by DOS is segments 0 through 9FFFh (absolute addresses 0 through 655,359). A program can place code or data anywhere within this range, and DOS will be able to access it.

The PC has more active memory areas at or above segment A000h, but this is reserved for hardware use. For example, the video buffers are in this high region, as are the ROM BIOS code, the machine identification byte, and other hardware-related things that must occupy memory but needn't be managed by DOS. As we'll see shortly, EMS grabs an uncommitted piece of this high memory as a transfer buffer.

All PCs have memory above segment A000h regardless of the amount of main memory they possess. Say a machine has 512K of main memory. This memory occupies segments 0 through 7FFFh. The hardware memory still begins at A000h or above. In between—say segments 8000h through 9FFFh—is a gap.

Extended memory thus begins at or above segment 10000h (absolute address 1,048,576 or greater). This memory is not addressable by the machine's CPU, because segment addresses of more than four hex digits require a register wider than 16 bits. (Note: The 80286 and 80386 running in protected mode can directly address extended memory, but the hows and whys are beyond the scope of this book.)

In general, extended memory resides on one or more separate boards installed in the computer's card cage. Each board has its own microprocessor acting as an embedded controller and running under firmware to control the memory and communicate with the host system.

Some software packages such as Framework can utilize extended memory directly by communicating with the controller(s). This is highly advanced stuff, and we won't cover it here because there's an easier way to access extended memory. That's through the implementation known as *expanded* memory.

Expanded memory relies on a software unit called a *device driver*. A device driver is a special kind of interrupt handler that DOS installs in low memory during a cold start. There are a number of default device drivers built into DOS, for handling the printer, the serial ports, the keyboard, and other hardware units. Installable—that is, optional—device drivers are specified in the

CONFIG.SYS file, which is located in the root directory of the boot disk. The CONFIG.SYS entry is

DEVICE = drivername

During startup, DOS checks CONFIG.SYS and loads any such specified device drivers. The installation process includes hooking the driver into one or more interrupt vectors.

The usual name for the EMS device driver is EMM.SYS. The letters EMM stand for Expanded Memory Manager. The .SYS suffix is the customary extension for device drivers. EMM.SYS is not a guaranteed name, however; many board manufacturers ship a special EMS device driver with a different name. For convenience, we'll refer to it here as EMM, and if yours goes by a different name you can make the substitution. The CONFIG.SYS entry for installing this driver, then, is

DEVICE = EMM.SYS

So what does EMM do? In short, it allows programs to specify how the extended memory is allocated and managed, and it handles the transfer of information to and from the extended memory. Because this memory is under the control of a specific discipline imposed by EMM, it is called *expanded* memory or, more often, simply EMS.

EMM, then, is the device driver itself, and EMS is the expanded memory it controls. EMM behaves much like DOS Int 21h, the gateway to most of the DOS services. You place a function code and parameters in registers, then execute software interrupt 67h. EMM takes it from there. We'll talk much more about this shortly.

Confounding this alphabet soup is EEMS, a competing and similar standard put forth by a different set of vendors. EEMS stands for Enhanced Expanded Memory Specification. It hasn't gained the popularity of the LIM (Lotus/Intel/Microsoft) EMS version, and so we won't discuss it further.

There are several versions of EMS. The most recent as of this writing is LIM EMS 4.0, introduced late in 1987. All earlier versions have a major number of 3, with the minor number indicating tweaks in the revision level. LIM 4.0 supports all of the 3.n functions and significantly expands the number of operations, chiefly to support multiprocessing, to allow code to be executed from expanded RAM, and to allow for up to 32MB of EMS memory (LIM 3.n provides up to 8MB). To date, LIM 4.0 has not attracted as much enthusiasm as the earlier versions.

Because this chapter is an introduction to EMS, it concentrates on the 3.n functions. Once you've covered the material here, you'll have the concepts necessary to delve into the new 4.0 functions if you're so inclined.

Determining If EMM Is Present

Before you can use EMS, the EMM device driver must be present in the system. Your program should check for it. Here's how.

Every DOS device driver has a fixed-format header containing certain information about the driver and the nature of the device it controls. DOS places the start of the header at a segment boundary. Somewhere within that segment is the entry point that gains control when Int 67h fires. Therefore the vector for Int 67h contains the driver's segment and an offset that is beyond the header.

Commencing at offset 10 (decimal) within the header is the name of the driver. A valid EMS device driver, regardless of its filename on disk, contains the embedded driver name EMMXXXX0 (that's a zero character at the end, followed by a null terminator). This is a name guaranteed by convention and included by all vendors.

Therefore, to determine if an EMS device driver is alive and well in the system, do the following:

1. Fetch the vector for Int 67h.
2. Form a far pointer consisting of the fetched segment and offset 10 decimal.
3. Compare the eight characters indicated by the pointer with the literal string EMMXXXX0.

If they're the same, EMS is active; otherwise it's not.

Later in this chapter, Program 24.2 furnishes the function isEMS() to do this.

How EMS Works

Somewhere within the memory above the 640K mark, there is an uncommitted 64K segment. The exact whereabouts of this RAM depends on the hardware configuration, and EMM knows how to find it.

This 64K piece of memory serves as the EMS frame buffer, which is a two-way communications area between conventional and expanded RAM. Your program can find out where it is by issuing Int 67h, Function 41h; EMM returns the segment address in register DX (C functions for communicating with EMM are provided later in this chapter).

To save data in EMS, your program merely copies the data to the frame buffer. EMM watches the frame buffer and, whenever it's changed, automatically moves the new data into EMS. To read data from EMS, you issue an Int 67h function to tell EMM what you want to read, and EMM copies it into the frame buffer. Your program can then fetch the data from the frame buffer, copying it into normal variables or a heap node. Conceptually, then, the frame buffer is a window giving a view of some portion of the EMS memory space.

It's actually four windows, because EMM divides the frame buffer into four pages of 16K each. The EMS documentation generally refers to these as *physical pages*. Similarly, the entire EMS RAM is divided into 16K pieces, which are called *logical pages*. Any logical page can be associated with any physical page in the frame buffer, thus giving access to that portion of EMS memory. The association of a logical to a physical page is made via mapping, an important EMM function.

There are some parallels between EMS and disk files. Before you can use a file, you have to open it and acquire an identifier such as a handle. Similarly, it's first necessary to allocate some number of EMS logical pages and acquire a handle for them. Most EMS functions require passing the EMS handle, which identifies to EMM which set of pages you mean, just as a file handle specifies a particular file.

Mapping says, in effect, "Associate logical page L belonging to handle H with physical page P." Thereafter, until the next remapping, physical page P in the frame buffer will contain an image of handle H's logical page L.

Why handles? Well, you might have several disk files open at the same time, and similarly you might have several storage areas allocated in EMS simultaneously. A handle identifies which allocation group you're talking about. It's how EMM keeps track of files in EMS RAM.

Because there are four pages in the frame buffer, you can access up to four different EMS files simultaneously. You can also access four pages from the same file in any logical-to-physical mapping order. Or you can have a combination. For example, this might be the mapping:

PP	LP	Handle
0	3	C
1	0	A
2	1	A
3	7	B

Here three EMS files are mapped to four physical pages in the frame buffer. Physical pages 1 and 2 map to consecutive logical pages associated with handle A. Therefore, you could copy up to 32K bytes to or from physical page 1 at one time and be assured that you're working with truly consecutive data. In the other two pages, you can only safely deal with up to 16K at a time.

EMS is volatile memory; that is, when the power goes out, its contents are gone. Therefore, a program that uses EMS for data storage must retrieve anything valuable and store it to disk before terminating. A program can, however, pass an open EMS handle to a child process; consider using a command-line argument. This is an alternate and generally better way of passing along data than the environment.

When you have finished using a handle, close it using EMM function 45h. Closing releases the logical pages and makes the handle available for other uses.

Implementing the Basic EMS Functions

EMS 3.n furnishes 16 functions, of which seven are absolutely essential to working with expanded memory. These seven are furnished by the EMS.H library (Program 24.1) and its source listing (EMS.C in Program 24.2), plus an eighth that returns the EMM version number. If you want to know more, see Duncan, Hyman, or the EMS spec itself, which you can obtain from Intel, Lotus, or Microsoft.

Program 24.1 **Foundation Routines for EMS**

```
/* EMS.H: Basic functions for Expanded Memory (3.n) */

#define PP0 0              /* frame physical page offsets */
#define PP1 0x4000
#define PP2 0x8000
#define PP3 0xC000

int isEMS (void);
    /* Returns TRUE if EMS is installed, FALSE if not */

void EMSerror (int code);
     /* Print explanation of EMS error code */

int EMSstatus (void);     /* Returns EMS device status */

int EMSframe (unsigned *segment);
    /* Gets segment of 64K page frame used by EMS */
    /* Returns segment in argument */
    /* Returns success code directly */

int EMSpages (unsigned *totalPages, unsigned *freePages);
    /* Gets total EMS pages available, number of free */
    /*   pages (not already allocated), returns them  */
    /*   to the arguments (page is 16K)               */
    /* Returns success code directly.                 */

int EMSversion (unsigned *major, unsigned *minor);
    /* Returns the EMS version number via arguments */

int EMSopen (unsigned *handle, int npages);
    /* Allocates npages 16K pages to an EMS handle */
    /* Handle is returned via argument and must be */
    /*   used for all EMS I/O's                    */
```

Program 24.1 (continued)

```c
int EMSmap (unsigned handle, int lpage, unsigned ppage);
        /* Ties EMS logical page associated with handle  */
        /*    to physical (frame) page so that the logical */
        /*    page can be accessed by the caller          */

int EMSclose (unsigned handle);
        /* Releases space allocated to handle and frees */
        /*    the handle for reassignment               */
```

Program 24.2 EMS Source Library

```c
/* EMS.C: Basic functions for Expanded Memory (3.n) */

#include <dos.h>
#include <string.h>
#include <conio.h>
#include "ems.h"

union REGS inreg, outreg;

#define EMS 0x67
#define callEMS() int86 (EMS, &inreg, &outreg)
#ifndef TRUE
#define FALSE 0
#define TRUE  !FALSE
#endif
/* ------------------------------------------------------ */

int isEMS (void)

    /* Returns TRUE if EMS is installed, FALSE if not */
    /* Checks device driver name to find out */
{
char far *ident;
char id [8];

  ident = (char far*) getvect (EMS);   /* dev driver addr */
  ident = MK_FP (FP_SEG (ident), 10);     /* point to name */
  movedata (FP_SEG (ident), 10, _DS, (unsigned) id, 8);
  return ((strncmp (ident, "EMMXXXX0", 8) == 0)
          ? TRUE : FALSE);
} /* ----------------------------- */

void EMSerror (int code)

    /* Print explanation of EMS error code */
{
  cputs ("\r\n\nEMS error: ");
  switch (code) {
    case  0: cputs ("None"); break;
```

Program 24.2 **(continued)**

```
      case 128: cputs ("Software malfunction"); break;
      case 129: cputs ("Hardware malfunction"); break;
      case 131: cputs ("Invalid handle"); break;
      case 143:
      case 132: cputs ("Invalid function call"); break;
      case 133: cputs ("No handles left"); break;
      case 134: cputs ("Page mapping error"); break;
      case 135:
      case 136: cputs ("Not enough pages"); break;
      case 137: cputs ("Can't allocate 0 pages"); break;
      case 138: cputs ("Too many pages requested"); break;
      case 139: cputs ("Invalid page"); break;
      case 140: cputs ("Device driver out of memory"); break;
      case 141: cputs ("Duplicate handle"); break;
      case 142: cputs ("Used unopened handle"); break;
   }
   cputs ("\r\n\n");
} /* ---------------------- */

int EMSstatus (void)

      /* Returns EMS device status */
{
   inreg.h.ah = 0x40;                       /* EMS function */
   callEMS ();                              /* call driver */
   return (outreg.h.ah);                    /* return status */
} /* ---------------------- */

int EMSframe (unsigned *segment)

      /* Gets segment of 64K page frame used by EMS */
      /* Returns segment in argument */
      /* Returns success code directly */
{
   inreg.h.ah = 0x41;
   callEMS ();
   *segment = outreg.x.bx;                  /* segment is in BX */
   return (outreg.h.ah);                    /* return success */
} /* ---------------------- */

int EMSpages (unsigned *totalPages, unsigned *freePages)

      /* Gets total EMS pages available, number of free */
      /*   pages (not already allocated), returns them  */
      /*   to the arguments (page is 16K)               */
      /* Returns success code directly.                 */
{
   inreg.h.ah = 0x42;
   callEMS ();
   *freePages  = outreg.x.bx;
   *totalPages = outreg.x.dx;
   return (outreg.h.ah);
} /* ---------------------- */
```

Program 24.2 **(conthued)**

```c
int EMSversion (unsigned *major, unsigned *minor)

      /* Returns the EMS version number via arguments */
{
  inreg.h.ah = 0x46;
  callEMS ();
  *major = outreg.h.al >> 4;        /* break out components */
  *minor = outreg.h.al & 0x0F;
  return (outreg.h.ah);
} /* ------------------ HANDLE FUNCTIONS --------------- */

int EMSopen (unsigned *handle, int npages)

      /* Allocates npages 16K pages to an EMS handle */
      /* Handle is returned via argument and must be */
      /*    used for all EMS I/O's                   */
{
  inreg.h.ah = 0x43;
  inreg.x.bx = npages;
  callEMS ();
  *handle = outreg.x.dx;
  return (outreg.h.ah);
} /* ----------------------- */

int EMSmap (unsigned handle, int lpage, unsigned ppage)

      /* Ties EMS logical page associated with handle   */
      /*    to physical (frame) page so that the logical */
      /*    page can be accessed by the caller          */
{
  inreg.h.ah = 0x44;
  inreg.h.al = (unsigned) ppage / PP1;      /* digit 0-3 */
  inreg.x.bx = lpage;
  inreg.x.dx = handle;
  callEMS ();
  return (outreg.h.ah);
} /* ----------------------- */

int EMSclose (unsigned handle)

      /* Releases space allocated to handle and frees */
      /*    the handle for reassignment               */
{
  inreg.h.ah = 0x45;
  inreg.x.dx = handle;
  callEMS ();
  return (outreg.h.ah);
} /* ----------------------- */
```

Now let's examine the library source file. The REGS objects are registers used in calling the device driver via the EMS interrupt, and the callEMS() macro is shorthand for the actual call. PP0 through PP3 define the offsets for the four physical pages within the frame buffer. The remaining definitions ensure the existence of Boolean values. As for the functions:

- isEMS() checks to see if EMM or an equivalent is present in the system and hooked into Int 67h. It returns **TRUE** if so and **FALSE** otherwise. Always call this function first, before you begin issuing EMS calls.

- EMSerror() doesn't deal with EMM itself, but instead translates EMM error codes into English statements displayed on the screen. Call this function whenever EMM returns a non-zero result. You might wish to modify EMSerror() in some way to prevent it from corrupting the display.

- EMSstatus() checks the status of the EMM driver, returning **0** when the device driver is functioning properly and one of the codes shown in EMSerror() when there's a problem. It's advisable to call this function immediately after isEMS() to make sure that the driver is not only installed, but operational.

- EMSframe() gets the segment address of the 64K frame buffer used by EMM. The function loads the segment into the unsigned variable indicated by the pointer passed as an argument, and returns a success code directly. You must call this function in order to determine where the frame buffer is; afterwards, use the returned segment to build far pointers to the physical pages.

- EMSpages() tells the total number of 16K logical pages in the EMS address space, and how many are free for allocation. It loads the results into the variables pointed to by the arguments, and returns a success code directly. This function is handy for finding out in advance if there will be enough pages to satisfy an EMS allocation request.

- EMSversion() reports the EMM major and minor version numbers. The main reason for calling it is to find out if LIM 4.0 services are available, in the event that you want to use them.

- EMSopen() allocates the indicated number of 16K logical pages in the EMS address space, and assigns an EMS handle to that hunk of EMS memory. Via the parametric pointer, it passes back the handle, which is required for all operations affecting the allocated space. This is analogous to creating a disk file, except that the amount of space is fixed.

- EMSmap() maps one of the logical pages associated with the given handle into one of the four physical pages in the frame buffer. In other words, it makes the physical page a window into the logical page. Note that EMM expects the physical page to be identified by a digit 0–3, but the Turbo C function's **ppage** argument is the page's frame buffer offset. This is a deliberate effort to make the function call more intuitive by using the constants PP0 through PP3. For example,

    EMSmap (handle, 3, PP2);

maps logical page 3 to physical page 2. Because PP1 is not only an offset but also the size of one page, the expression that loads register AL resolves the page offset down to a digit 0–3. A call to **EMSmap()** is necessary each time you want to move the window to a new EMS logical page.

- **EMSclose()** deallocates the EMS logical pages associated with the handle, and returns both the EMS memory space and the handle itself to the available pool. This is analogous to closing a disk file, but with one important difference: If you forget to close a disk file, the normal termination of a program will close it for you.

That's not so with EMS. The EMM driver has no way of knowing when your program has ended, so if you've neglected to call **EMSclose()**, the space remains unavailable, the data within it are unchanged, and the handle is still active. This is useful when spawning a child process, but potentially catastrophic if you've simply ended the program without calling **EMSclose()**. Therefore, you must *always* call **EMSclose()** when you have no further use for the EMS space allocated to the handle.

A Demonstration

The EMSTEST.C program in Program 24.3 checks the EMS subsystem, and also puts each of the functions in the EMS library to work. It reports what it's doing at each step, and whether the test was successful.

After reporting the general status of EMS, the version number, and so on, the program allocates one logical page to a handle and maps that page to physical page 0 in the frame buffer. It then copies a 16K array of integers into the physical page, which stores the array in EMS. Having done that, it remaps logical page 0 to physical page 2. Thus, PP2 becomes a window into EMS, and it should contain the same data copied earlier to PP0.

To prove this, the program copies from PP2 into a different array, then compares the arrays. If they're the same, the test succeeds: otherwise it fails.

Regardless of the outcome, if EMM is alive and healthy, space will have been allocated to a handle, so the program calls **EMSclose()** to release it, then quits.

If your system doesn't have EMS, the program simply reports **EMS not detected** and ends. Otherwise, it produces a full screen of information derived from the test.

The comments in the program explain what each step does. You can refer to it as a model for interfacing to EMS.

Program 24.3 **An EMS Test Program**

```c
/* EMSTEST.C: Tests EMS routines */

#include <dos.h>
#include <string.h>
#include <conio.h>
#include <process.h>
#include "ems.h"

#define PAGESIZE 16384
#define NELEM    PAGESIZE / sizeof (int)

void main ()
{
unsigned a1, a2, status, frameSeg, handle;
int  n, y [NELEM], z [NELEM], far *frame;

  clrscr ();

  /* Find out if the EMS is installed and alive */
  cputs ("Checking EMS board:");
  if (!(status = isEMS ()))
    cputs ("\r\n  EMS not detected");
  else {
    cputs ("\r\n  EMS is active");
    status = EMSstatus ();
    cprintf ("\r\n  Initial status is %d", status);
    if (status)
      EMSerror (status);
    else
      cputs (" (No error)");

    /* Get the EMS version number */
    if ((status = EMSversion (&a1, &a2)) == 0)
      cprintf ("\r\n  Version number is %d.%02d", a1, a2);
    else EMSerror (status);

    /* Find out where the communications frame is */
    if ((status = EMSframe (&frameSeg)) == 0)
      cprintf ("\r\n  Frame is at segment %04X", frameSeg);
    else EMSerror (status);

    /* Determine the number of logical 16K pages */
    if ((status = EMSpages (&a1, &a2)) == 0) {
      cprintf ("\r\n Pages: total = %u", a1);
      cprintf ("\r\n          free  = %u", a2);
    }
    else EMSerror (status);

    /* NOW GET READY TO TEST THE EMS I/O */
```

```
cputs ("\r\n\nEMS write/read test:");

/* First get one page and assign to a handle */
cputs ("\r\n  Opening a handle");
if ((status = EMSopen (&handle, 1)) != 0) {
  EMSerror (status);
  exit (1);
}

/* Map the handle's page to physical frame 0 */
cprintf ("\r\n  Mapping handle %X to frame page 0",
         handle);
if ((status = EMSmap (handle, 0, PP0)) != 0) {
  EMSerror (status);
  exit (1);
}
EMSpages (&a1, &a2);
cprintf ("\r\n  Free pages now = %d", a2);

/* Initialize an array to be stored in the EMS */
for (n = 0; n < NELEM; n++)
  y [n] = n;

/* Now store it in EMS */
frame = MK_FP (frameSeg, PP0); /* destination pointer */
for (n = 0; n < NELEM; n++)      /* copy array to dest */
  frame [n] = y [n];

/* Remap handle to frame page 2 */
cprintf ("\r\n  Remapping handle %X to frame page 2",
         handle);
if ((status = EMSmap (handle, 0, PP2)) != 0) {
  EMSerror (status);
  exit (1);
}

/* Copy the saved data back to a different array (z) */
frame  = MK_FP (frameSeg, PP2);
for (n = 0; n < NELEM; n++) /* copy array from source */
  z [n] = frame [n];

/* Check to make sure both arrays are the same */
if (strncmp ((char*) y, (char*) z, PAGESIZE) == 0)
  cputs ("\r\n\n  ** Test passed **");
else
  cputs ("\r\n\n  ** Test failed **");

/* Regardless of outcome, close the EMS handle */
cprintf ("\r\n\nClosing handle %X", handle);
if ((status = EMSclose (handle)) != 0)
  EMSerror (status);
EMSpages (&a1, &a2);
```

Program 24.3 **(continued)**

```
    cprintf ("\r\nFree pages now = %d", a2);
    cputs ("\r\n\nTest completed");
  }
}
```

A Graphics Application Using EMS

If it's fair to regard EMS as a sort of high-speed file store, it's just as reasonable to consider it an alternative to the heap. You can save and retrieve any sort of data there, including screen images. So let's consider an application in which EMS helps to achieve graphics animation.

The image we'll develop is a fairly simple one: a hoop rotating about its vertical axis. The real-world analogy is a radio direction finder's antenna. This is a loop of wire that turns, locking in on radio signals and reporting the direction to the transmitters. Navigators on ships and airplanes use such a device to find the bearings to two transmitters at known locations. They can then draw the bearings on a chart; where the lines cross is the location of the craft. What we'll see is the antenna itself, rotating continuously through 360 degrees.

Rotation of a circle about a vertical axis results in a series of ellipses. When the hoop is perpendicular to the viewing axis, it forms a full circle, and when parallel to the viewing axis, a vertical line. In between these extremes are ellipses whose Y dimension is invariant, but whose X dimension varies.

When viewed from above, the rate of rotation is constant. Seen edge-on, however, it is not if we're to simulate realistic rotation. The changes are relatively slow when the hoop is fairly perpendicular to the viewing axis and become increasingly faster as the circle approaches the parallel perpective. Using trigonometry, the aspect of each ellipse is given by

X radius = R cos theta

where R is the radius of the circle and theta is the angle of rotation (where the angle is measured in radians for the Turbo C **cos()** function).

The conversion from degrees to radians is straightforward. A circle is 360 degrees or 2*pi radians. Therefore a half-circle is 180 degrees or pi radians, so one degree equals pi/180 radians. It's more intuitive for people—i.e. programmers—to work in degrees, so we can apply this as a factor in converting degrees to radians.

If we consider the problem, we can see that it's only necessary to represent a circle through one-quarter of its full rotation. If played forward and then backward, the image will appear to move through a 180-degree turn about its axis. Two repetitions will simulate a complete rotation.

Suppose we select an image size that is between 2K and 4K. We can then store four images in one 16K EMS page. To achieve relatively smooth motion from one angle to the next, the granularity of angles has to be fairly close together. Given four images per page through a 90-degree rotation, if we select 32 images, the requirement is eight EMS pages to contain them.

The EMS frame buffer maps to four pages maximum. Therefore, if the 32 images are saved in consecutive pages, we can map 16 at a time into the frame buffer and use **putimge()** to store them and **getimage()** to fetch them. The exercise becomes one of calculating a pointer offset from the start of the frame buffer for each image.

Say we call the first 16 images "low EMS" and the second 16 "high EMS." Then to save the 32 consecutive images we do the following for a 180-degree rotation:

```
allocate 8 pages to an EMS handle;
set step to 90 degrees / 32 images;
map low EMS;
for image = 1 to 32 {
   convert image angle to radians;
   find cosine;
   draw ellipse at angle;
   if image == 16
      map high EMS;
   calculate pointer offset into frame buffer;
   save image;
}
```

Having done this, we can fetch the images back for a 180-degree rotation with

```
map low EMS;
for image = 1 to 32 {
   if image == 16
      map high EMS;
   calculate frame pointer for image;
   copy to display;
}
for image = 32 to 1 {
   if image == 15
      map low EMS;
   calculate frame pointer for image;
   copy to display;
}
```

This discussion provides an overview of the Program 24.4, HOOP.C. The program first draws and saves 32 ellipse images in EMS, then plays them back 10 times. Given all that this book has developed, the details should become apparent by examining the listing and running the program.

Program 24.4 Graphics Animation Using EMS

```c
/* HOOP.C: Uses 8 pages of EMS to simulate animation */

#include <dos.h>
#include <graphics.h>
#include <math.h>
#include <conio.h>
#include <process.h>
#include <stdlib.h>
#include "ems.h"

/* DEFINES */
#define IMAGES    32                    /* number of images */
#define RADPERDEG M_PI / 180.0          /* radians per degree */
#define STEPSIZE  90.0 / (IMAGES-1)     /* step size in deg */
#define STEP      STEPSIZE * RADPERDEG  /* and in radians */
#define YRADIUS   55                    /* y radius of ellipse */
#define XRADIUS   60                    /* and max x radius */
#define CX        160                   /* center X of ellipse */
#define CY        100                     /* and center Y */
#define LEFT      CX - XRADIUS          /* image area extremes */
#define TOP       CY - YRADIUS
#define RITE      CX + XRADIUS
#define BOTTOM    CY + YRADIUS
#define NODESIZE  4096                  /* size of an image node */
#define LPAGES    8                        /* EMS pages */
#define NTIMES    10                    /* number of playback times */

/* GLOBAL VARIABLES */
unsigned handle;                        /* EMS file handle */
unsigned frame;                 /* pointer to EMS frame buffer */
unsigned picsize;                     /* size of screen area */

/* Local functions */
void eoj (void);
void initEMS (void);
void saveImages (void);
void playback (int);
void mapLowEMS (void);
void mapHighEMS (void);
void far *frameaddr (int);

/* ------------------------------------------------------ */

void main ()
```

Program 24.4 **(continued)**

```c
{
int   driver = CGA, mode = CGAC0, status;

    /* Set up to run */
    initEMS ();                               /* prepare EMS */
    initgraph (&driver, &mode, "");           /* and graphics */
    if (graphresult () != grOk) {
      cputs ("Cannot run this program without graphics");
      exit (1);
    }

    /* Ready to run. Get actual image size and EMS space */
    picsize = imagesize (LEFT, TOP, RITE, BOTTOM);
    status = EMSopen (&handle, LPAGES);
    if (status != 0) {
      eoj ();
      EMSerror (status);
      exit (1);
    }
    atexit (eoj);                       /* register exit procedure */

    saveImages ();                /* build images and store in EMS */

    playback (NTIMES);        /* play back the rotating hoop */
} /* ----------------------- */

void initEMS (void)

        /* Initialize EMS */
{
unsigned n, freepages;
int      status;

    if (!isEMS()) {                     /* if EMS not present... */
      cputs ("Cannot run this program without EMS");
      exit (1);
    } else {
      status = EMSstatus ();            /* check EMS status */
      if (status != 0) {                /* if not OK... */
        EMSerror (status);              /* show problem */
        exit (1);                       /* and quit */
      } else {
        EMSpages (&n, &freepages);      /* get free pages */
        if (freepages < LPAGES) {       /* if not enough... */
          cputs ("Not enough EMS pages available to run");
          exit (1);
        }
      }
    }
    EMSframe (&frame);              /* get frame buffer address */
} /* ----------------------- */

void eoj (void)
```

Program 24.4 **(continued)**

```
      /* Exit processing for program */
{
  EMSclose (handle);
  closegraph ();
} /* ----------------------- */

void saveImages (void)

      /* Build 32 hoop images and save in EMS */
{
unsigned n, xrad;
double    angle;
void far *frameloc;

  mapLowEMS ();                       /* map Lpages 0-3 to frame */
  for (n = 0; n < IMAGES; n++) {
    cleardevice ();                            /* fresh screen */
    setcolor (2);
    line (CX, TOP, CX, BOTTOM);
    setcolor (3);
    angle = STEP * n;                        /* angle in radians */
    xrad = cos (angle) * XRADIUS;  /* X radius of ellipse */
    ellipse (CX, CY, 0, 360, xrad, YRADIUS-5);

    /* save image in EMS frame buffer */
    if (n == IMAGES / 2)            /* if frame is full... */
      mapHighEMS ();                     /* remap to high EMS */
    frameloc = frameaddr (n);          /* get frame location */
    getimage (LEFT, TOP, RITE, BOTTOM, frameloc); /* copy */
  }
} /* ----------------------- */

void playback (int times)

      /* Play back the saved images */
{
int     t, n;
void far *frameloc;

  for (t = 0; t < times; t++) {
    mapLowEMS ();                     /* start with low images */
    for (n = 0; n < IMAGES; n++) {          /* play forward */
      if (n == (IMAGES / 2))        /* if frame used up... */
        mapHighEMS ();                     /* remap to high EMS */
      frameloc = frameaddr (n);        /* get frame location */
      putimage (LEFT, TOP, frameloc, COPY_PUT);   /* copy */
    }
    for (n = (IMAGES - 1); n >= 0; n--) {  /* play backwd */
      if (n == ((IMAGES / 2) - 1))
        mapLowEMS ();
      frameloc = frameaddr (n);
      putimage (LEFT, TOP, frameloc, COPY_PUT);
```

Program 24.4 **(continued)**

```
      }
  }
} /* ----------------------- */

void far *frameaddr (int image)

      /* Compute frame address for image */
{
void far *addr;
unsigned offset;

  if (image < (IMAGES / 2))
    offset = NODESIZE * image;
  else
    offset = NODESIZE * (image - (IMAGES / 2));
  addr = MK_FP (frame, offset);
  return (addr);
} /* ----------------------- */

void mapLowEMS (void)

      /* Map low logical pages to frame buffer */
{
  EMSmap (handle, 0, PP0);
  EMSmap (handle, 1, PP1);
  EMSmap (handle, 2, PP2);
  EMSmap (handle, 3, PP3);
} /* ----------------------- */

void mapHighEMS (void)

      /* Map high logical pages to frame buffer */
{
  EMSmap (handle, 4, PP0);
  EMSmap (handle, 5, PP1);
  EMSmap (handle, 6, PP2);
  EMSmap (handle, 7, PP3);
} /* ----------------------- */
```

Farewell

Turbo C provides an extremely powerful and flexible tool for developing highly advanced applications for the IBM PC and related machines. This book has exploited many of its potentials and developed numerous tools that you can adapt to meet you needs. Along the way, we hope you have picked up some useful techniques and become a more sophisticated C programmer, for teaching has been our intent as much as tool-building.

No single book can tell you everything you ever need to know about anything, least of all about programming a thing as complex as a computer, which is the most pliable, challenging machine ever devised. Programmers are like lawyers: Given any problem, either will come up with at least seven solutions, all of which are workable and passionately defensible. Therefore some—perhaps including you—will differ with the approach we've taken to specific problems in these pages. And that's fine, because it proves the point that there's no one right way to do anything.

If this book furnishes one workable solution to each of the problems it presents, it accomplishes a goal. And if it teaches you how to solve a difficult problem and makes you a better programmer in the process, then it succeeds.

Obviously, we hope this book succeeds, and that it helps you succeed as a programmer, for that is its only purpose.

Happy programming.

HEADER FILES INCLUDED WITH TURBO C

Turbo C comes with some two dozen header (.H) files, which the manual recommends that you install in the \TURBOC\INCLUDE subdirectory. Once you have set up the environment under the Options pulldown on Turbo C's main menu, the compiler will look in this subdirectory for the header files. An important part of programming in Turbo C is knowing which header files to include.

Header files are your friends because they save a lot of research, typing, and grief. They predefine constants, system structures such as File Control Blocks and the like, and external function calls. The latter is particularly important because it's easy to forget that you have to declare as variables those functions that return other than an int; cos(), for example, which returns a double. Failure to do so results in the program interpreting the returned value as an integer, thus causing much hair-tearing over why the program doesn't work as expected. Inclusion of the appropriate header file(s) can thus prevent premature baldness in C programmers.

This appendix summarizes what is in each of the .H files bundled with Turbo C. These files are extremely comprehensive (though not exhaustive) in defining system-level data structures and constants such as error codes, as well as all the functions built into Turbo C's libraries.

A common-sense rule applies to the use of .H files. Before you go to the trouble of defining some system data structure, look in the header file that seems to deal with the kind of problem you're wrestling with. It's probably already there, and you can use it with the simple directive

```
#include <whatever.h>
```

You might still have to consult other documentation to figure out what the fields are or the codes mean, but at least you won't have to write the definitions.

In some cases, the issue might spill into more than one .H file. For example, a certain commonality exists among the character, string, allocation, and memory-manipulation categories, which are covered by CTYPE, STRING, ALLOC, and MEM, respectively. In that event, err on the side of overzealousness in including the .H files. There is nothing in a .H file that makes your resulting .EXE program bigger, since the compiler does not generate code for unused constants and function declarations. A cautious programmer might write an **#include** file that includes all the .H files: This is effective, but guaranteed to slow down the compiler, and you'd still have to open the relevant .H file to find out what's there and how to refer to it. What's better is to include all the .H files that you *think* are pertinent.

So here is a brief summary of what each .H file deals with. For more specific information, look at the file itself.

.H file	*Contents*
ALLOC	Memory allocation functions such as **free()**, **calloc()**, **realloc()**, and so on. See also MEM.
ASSERT	The debugging macro **assert()**, which prints out whether an expected condition is true or not.
BIOS	Declares calls to ROM BIOS and defines structures.
CONIO	Direct (low-level) console I/O routines via DOS. See also IO.H.
CTYPE	Character test and manipulation routines, including a number of useful macros.
DIR	Directory/path inquiries and structures. Overlaps with DOS.H to some extent.
DOS	File attributes, FCB and error-reporting structures, the FAT, register names, DOS calls.
ERRNO	System error codes defined as constants.
FCNTL	File control values. Commonality with the preceding three files.
FLOAT	Limits on floating-point values, matters related to the 80×87 math coprocessor and emulation package. See also MATH.
GRAPHICS	Constants, definitions, and function prototypes for the Turbo C graphics programming subsystem.
IO	Low-level I/O functions (**creat()**, **eof()**, and so on, as well as structures. See also CONIO.
LIMITS	Implementation-specific limits on values. Not particularly useful unless you're importing C programs from other environments (UNIX or whatever).
MATH	Declares floating-point functions. Also a number of very useful constants such as pi, e, and so forth, carried out to an excruciating level of precision. Some overlap with FLOAT.

.H file	*Contents*
MEM	Functions for memory manipulation (**movedata()**, **setmem()**, and so on). See also ALLOC.
PROCESS	Constants and functions for spawning parent/child processes under the DOS EXEC facility.
SETJMP	Structures and functions for **setjmp()/longjmp()** functions.
SHARE	Constants for file-sharing among concurrent applications.
SIGNAL	Defines software signals for such matters as floating point trap, memory violation, abort, and so forth.
STDARG	Definitions for accessing parameters in functions that accept a variable number of arguments.
STDDEF	An assortment of common macros and constants (for example, **NULL**), as well as such type modifiers as **unsigned**.
STDIO	Obligatory for virtually all C programs. But look at it; it contains more than you probably realize.
STDLIB	Declarations of most of the "standard library" routines.
STRING	Functions for string manipulation, as well as some memory management functions overlapping with MEM. and ALLOC.
TIME	Structures and functions dealing with times and dates.

TURBO C
FILE FUNCTIONS

Turbo C provides a rich set of file-manipulation functions. Part III and especially Chapter 5 discussed them in general, and this appendix lists them comprehensively.

The order is alphabetic by function name. Each entry contains a synopsis of the function's purpose, its prototype, the header (.H) file containing its prototype, and the kind of function it is (utility, handle, stream).

Not included here are direct disk-access functions such as **absread()** and **biosdisk()**, which are only marginally related to file operations.

Name: **access**
Purpose: Determine file access (existence, read, write, execute).
Prototype: **int access (char *filname, int request);**
Include: IO.H
Type: Utility

Name: **chdir**
Purpose: Change working directory; equivalent to the DOS command.
Prototype: **int chdir (char *path);**
Include: DIR.H
Type: Utility

Name: **__chmod/chmod**
Purpose: Change file access mode.
Prototypes: **int chmod (char *filename, int permission);**
int __chmod(char *filename, int func[,int attrib]);
Include: IO.H
Type: Utility

Name: **clearerr**
Purpose: Clear error condition on stream.

Prototype: void clearerr (FILE *stream);
Include: STDIO.H
Type: Stream

Name: __close/close
Purpose: Close a file.
Prototypes: int __close (int handle);
int close (int handle);
Include: IO.H
Type: Handle

Name: creat/creat
Purpose: Create new file or rewrite one that exists.
Prototypes: int __creat (char *filename, int attrib);
int creat (char *filename, int permission);
Include: IO.H
Type: Handle

Name: creatnew
Purpose: Create new file.
Prototype: int creatnew (char *filename, int attrib);
Include: IO.H
Type: Handle

Name: creattemp
Purpose: Create temporary file.
Prototype: int creattemp (char *path, int attrib);
Include: IO.H
Type: Handle

Name: dup/dup2
Purpose: Duplicate a file handle.
Prototypes: int dup (int oldhandle, int newhandle);
int dup2 (int oldhandle, int newhandle);
Include: IO.H
Type: Handle

Name: eof
Purpose: Signal end-of-file.
Prototype: int eof (int *handle);
Include: IO.H
Type: Handle

Name: **fclose**
Purpose: Close a stream.
Prototype: **int fclose (FILE *stream);**
Include: STDIO.H
Type: Stream

Name: **fcloseall**
Purpose: Close all streams except *stdin* and *stdout*.
Prototype: **int fcloseall (void);**
Include: STDIO.H
Type: Stream

Name: **fdopen**
Purpose: Associate handle with a stream file.
Prototype: **FILE *fdopen (int handle, char *type);**
Include: STDIO.H
Type: Stream, handle (bridge function)

Name: **feof**
Purpose: Signal stream end-of-file.
Prototype: **int feof (FILE *stream);**
Include: STDIO.H
Type: Stream

Name: **ferror**
Purpose: Detect stream error.
Prototype: **int ferror (FILE *stream);**
Include: STDIO.H
Type: Stream

Name: **fflush**
Purpose: Flush buffer for a stream.
Prototype: **int fflush (FILE *stream);**
Include: STDIO.H
Type: Stream

Name: **fgetc**
Purpose: Get character from input stream.
Prototype: **int fgetc (FILE *stream);**
Include: STDIO.H
Type: Stream

Name: **fgets**
Purpose: Get string from input stream.
Prototype: **char *fgets (char *string, int n, FILE *stream);**
Include: STDIO.H
Type: Stream

Name: **filelength**
Purpose: Get size of disk file in bytes.
Prototype: **long filelength (int handle);**
Include: IO.H
Type: Handle

Name: **fileno**
Purpose: Get file handle associated with stream.
Prototype: **int fileno (FILE *stream);**
Include: STDIO.H
Type: Stream, handle (bridge function)

Name: **findfirst**
Purpose: Finds first occurrence of filename pattern in specified path.
Prototype: **int findfirst (char *path, struct ffblk *blk, int attrib);**
Include: DIR.H
Type: Utility

Name: **findnext**
Purpose: Find subsequent occurrences of filename pattern set with **findfirst**.
Prototype: **int findnext (struct ffblk *blk);**
Include: DIR.H
Type: Utility

Name: **flushall**
Purpose: Clear all open stream buffers.
Prototype: **int flushall (void);**
Include: STDIO.H
Type: Stream

Name: **fnmerge**
Purpose: Merge text strings to form path and filename.
Prototype: **void fnmerge (char *path, char *drive, char *dir, char *name, char *ext);**
Include: DIR.H
Type: Utility

Name: fnsplit
Purpose: Explode pathname into its components.
Prototype: int fnsplit (char *path, char *drive, char *dir, char *name, char *ext);
Include: DIR.H
Type: Utility

Name: fopen
Purpose: Open a stream.
Prototype: FILE *fopen (char *filename, char *operation);
Include: STDIO.H
Type: Stream

Name: fprintf
Purpose: Write formatted output to stream.
Prototype: int fprintf (FILE *stream, char *format[, arg..]);
Include: STDIO.H
Type: Stream

Name: fputc
Purpose: Write character to stream.
Prototype: int fputc (int ch, FILE *stream);
Include: STDIO.H
Type: Stream

Name: fputs
Purpose: Write string to stream.
Prototype: int fputs (char *string, FILE *stream);
Include: STDIO.H
Type: Stream

Name: fread
Purpose: Read data (usually binary) from a stream.
Prototype: int fread (void *ptr, int size, int nitems, FILE *stream);
Include: STDIO.H
Type: Stream

Name: freopen
Purpose: Replace one open stream with another.
Prototype: FILE *freopen (char *filename, char *type, FILE *stream);
Include: STDIO.H
Type: Stream

Name: **fscanf**
Purpose: Read formatted (usually text) input from stream.
Prototype: **int fscanf(FILE *stream, char *format[, arg,..]);**
Include: STDIO.H
Type: Stream

Name: **fseek**
Purpose: Reposition stream file pointer (disk files only).
Prototype: **int fseek (FILE *stream, long offset, int origin);**
Include: STDIO.H
Type: Stream

Name: **fstat**
Purpose: Get information about an open file.
Prototype: **int fstat (char *handle, struct stat *buffer);**
Include: SYS/STAT.H
Type: Handle

Name: **ftell**
Purpose: Return current position in open file.
Prototype: **long ftell (FILE *stream);**
Include: STDIO.H
Type: Stream

Name: **fwrite**
Purpose: Write data (usually binary) to a stream.
Prototype: **int fwrite (void *ptr, int size, int nitems, FILE *stream);**
Include: STDIO.H
Type: Stream

Name: **getc**
Purpose: Get character from input stream.
Prototype: **int getc (FILE *stream);**
Include: STDIO.H
Type: Stream

Name: **getcurdir**
Purpose: Get current directory on a specified drive.
Prototype: **int getcurdir (int drive, char *directory);**
Include: DIR.H
Type: Utility

Name: **getcwd**
Purpose: Get current directory on default drive.

Prototype: char *getcwd (char *buffer, int buffLen);
Include: DIR.H
Type: Utility

Name: **getftime**
Purpose: Get date and time for open file.
Prototype: **int getftime (int handle, struct ftime *ftime);**
Include: DOS.H
Note: struct ftime is defined in IO.H
Type: Handle

Name: **getverify**
Purpose: Get status of file verification.
Prototype: **int getverify (void);**
Include: DOS.H
Type: Utility

Name: **getw**
Purpose: Get word (integer) from stream.
Prototype: **int getw (FILE *stream);**
Include: STDIO.H
Type: Stream

Name: **isatty**
Purpose: Determine if handle represents physical I/O device.
Prototype: **int isatty (int handle);**
Include: IO.H
Type: Handle

Name: **lock**
Purpose: Lock shared file region.
Prototype: int lock (int handle, long offset, long length);
Include: IO.H
Type: Handle

Name: **lseek**
Purpose: Reposition file read/write pointer.
Prototype: **long lseek (int handle, long offset, int origin);**
Include: IO.H
Type: Handle

Name: **mkdir**
Purpose: Create subdirectory; equivalent to DOS command.
Prototype: **int mkdir (char *path);**

Include: DIR.H
Type: Utility

Name: **mktemp**
Purpose: Generate unique temporary filename.
Prototype: **char *mktemp (char *mask);**
Include: DIR.H
Type: Utility

Name: **__open/open**
Purpose: Open file for I/O.
Prototype: **int __open (char *path, int access);**
          int open (char *path, int access[, int permiss]);
Include: IO.H
Note: Access flags are defined in FCNTL.H
Type: Handle

Name: **parsfnm**
Purpose: Parse filename, place components into FCB.
Prototype: **char *parsfnm (char *cmd, struct fcb *fcb, int alRegOption);**
Include: DOS.H
Type: FCB

Name: **putc**
Purpose: Write character to output stream.
Prototype: **int putc (int ch, FILE *stream);**
Include: STDIO.H
Type: Stream

Name: **putw**
Purpose: Write word (integer or character) to output stream.
Prototype: **int putw (int w, FILE *stream);**
Include: STDIO.H
Type: Stream

Name: **randbrd**
Purpose: Read random data block (usually binary) from file.
Prototype: **int randbrd (struct fcb *fcb, int nrecs);**
Include: DOS.H
Type: FCB

Name: **randbwr**
Purpose: Write random data block (usually binary) to file.

    Prototype: int randbwr (struct fcb *fcb, int nrecs);
      Include: DOS.H
         Type: FCB

         Name: __read/read
      Purpose: Read from file.
   Prototypes: int __read (int handle, void *buffer, int nbytes);
               int read (int handle, void *buffer, int nbytes);
      Include: IO.H
         Type: Handle

         Name: rename
      Purpose: Rename a file.
    Prototype: int rename (char *oldname, char *newname);
      Include: STDIO.H
         Type: Utility

         Name: rewind
      Purpose: Move file pointer to start of file.
    Prototype: int rewind (FILE *stream);
      Include: STDIO.H
         Type: Stream

         Name: rmdir.
      Purpose: Remove directory; equivalent to DOS command.
    Prototype: int rmdir (char *path);
      Include: DIR.H
         Type: Utility

         Name: searchpath
      Purpose: Search DOS path for a given filename.
    Prototype: char *searchpath (char *filename);
      Include: DIR.H
         Type: Utility

         Name: setbuf
      Purpose: Assign buffering to stream.
    Prototype: void setbuf (FILE *stream, char *buffer);
      Include: STDIO.H
         Type: Stream

         Name: setftime
      Purpose: Override DOS to set file date and time.

Prototype: **int setftime (int handle, struct ftime *ftime);**
Include: IO.H
Type: Handle

Name: **setmode**
Purpose: Set mode of open file.
Prototype: **int setmode (int handle, unsigned mode);**
Include: IO.H
Type: Handle

Name: **setvbuf**
Purpose: Assign buffering to stream.
Prototype: **int setvbuf (FILE *stream, char *buffer, int type, unsigned *size);**
Include: STDIO.H
Type: Stream

Name: **setverify**
Purpose: Set file writing verification.
Prototype: **void setverify (int state);**
Include: DOS.H
Type: Utility

Name: **stat**
Purpose: Get information about an open file.
Prototype: **int stat (char *pathname, struct stat *statbuff);**
Include: SYS/STAT.H
Type: Utility

Name: **tell**
Purpose: Get current position of file pointer.
Prototype: **long tell (int handle);**
Include: IO.H
Type: Handle

Name: **ungetc**
Purpose: Push most recently fetched character back into input stream.
Prototype: **int ungetc (char ch, FILE *stream);**
Include: STDIO.H
Type: Stream

Name: **unlink**
Purpose: Delete a disk file.

Prototype: int unlink (char *filename);
Include: DOS.H
Type: Utility

Name: unlock
Purpose: Release lock on shared file region.
Prototype: int unlock (int handle, long offset, long length);
Include: DOS.H
Type: Handle

Name: vfprintf
Purpose: Write formatted output to stream.
Prototype: int vfprintf (FILE *stream, char *format, va__list parameters);
Include: STDIO.H, STDARG.H
Type: Stream

Name: vfscanf
Purpose: Read formatted input from a stream.
Prototype: vfscanf (FILE *stream, char *format, valist parameters);
Include: STDIO.H
Type: Stream

Name: __write/write
Purpose: Write data to a file.
Prototypes: int __write (int handle, void *buffer, int nbytes);
int write (int handle, void *buffer, int nbytes);
Include: IO.H
Type: Handle

APPENDIX C

SOFTWARE TOOLS FURNISHED BY THIS BOOK

This book has developed eight libraries that extend Turbo C and provide you with powerful new tools for software development. These libraries and their associated header (.H) files are scattered all over the book. Consequently, we bring them together here to serve as a convenient reference.

The files are as follows:

BIOSDATA.H*

TEXTBOX.H

CURSOR.H

POPUP.H

MOUSE.H

VCOORDS.H

BEZIER.H

PSP.H*

EMS.H

* Not a library.

You should place these header files into a directory where Turbo C looks for source files. This is not necessarily the INCLUDE subdirectory recommended for standard Turbo C header files. By convention, the bracketed notation

```
#include <stdfile.h>
```

tells the C compiler to look only in the standard INCLUDE directory, while the quoted notation

#include "userfile.h"

tells the compiler to follow its predefined directory search path until it finds user-defined .H files. These forms of notation are customary, and the programs in this book adhere to them.

Because these files are explained in detail elsewhere, and are accompanied there by the corresponding source (.C) files, this appendix merely provides a brief description of each one and shows the chapter where you can find out more.

Here they are, in order of appearance in the book.

BIOSAREA.H: Chapter 7

Provides access to the low-level information contained in the ROM BIOS work area. Your program must initialize a far pointer to the BIOSDATA structure in order to gain access to the structure contents. This is declared as follows:

far BIOSDATA *bios = MK__FP (0×0040, 0×0000);

```
/* biosarea.h: ROM BIOS data area at 0x0040:0 in memory */

#ifndef   byte
#define   byte    unsigned char                /* define byte as a type */
#endif

/* BIT FIELDS USED IN ROM BIOS DATA AREA */
typedef struct {
   unsigned  hasFloppies : 1,        /* 1 = system has floppy drives */
             nu1 : 1,                                   /* not used */
             mbRAM : 2,                         /* motherboard RAM size */
             initVideo : 2,                      /* initial video mode */
             nDisks : 2,                        /* nbr of floppy drives */
             nu8 : 1,                                   /* not used */
             nSerialPorts : 3,       /* nbr of serial ports attached */
             gamePort : 1,               /* 1 = game port attached */
             nu13 : 1,                                  /* not used */
             nLPT : 2;                       /* number of printers */
} EQFLAGS;                  /* this is the equipment flags structure */

typedef struct {
   unsigned  riteShiftDown : 1,       /* 1 = right shift key is down */
```

```
                    leftShiftDown : 1,        /* 1 = left shift key is down */
                    ctrlShiftDown : 1,        /* 1 = ctrl-shift combo is down */
                    altShiftDown : 1,         /* 1 = alt-shift combo is down */
                    scrollLockOn : 1,         /* 1 = scroll lock mode is on */
                    numLockOn : 1,            /* 1 = num lock mode is on */
                    capsLockOn : 1,           /* 1 = caps lock mode is on */
                    insOn : 1,                /* 1 = ins mode is on */
                    unused : 3,               /* spare bits */
                    ctrlNumLockOn : 1,        /* 1 = ctrl-NumLock mode on */
                    scrollLockDown : 1,       /* 1 = scroll lock key is down */
                    numLockDown : 1,          /* 1 = num lock key is down */
                    capsLockDown : 1,         /* 1 = caps lock key is down */
                    insDown : 1;              /* 1 = ins key is down */
} KBDFLAGS;                         /* this is the keyboard flags structure */

typedef struct {
    unsigned    serialPortAddr[4];
    unsigned    parallelPortAddr[4];
    EQFLAGS     eqptFlags;
    byte        mfgrTestFlags;
    unsigned    mainMem;
    unsigned    expRAM;
    KBDFLAGS    kbdStat;
    byte        keypad;
    unsigned    kbdBuffHead;
    unsigned    kbdBuffTail;
    char        kbdBuff[32];
    byte        seekStat;
    byte        motorStat;
    byte        motorCnt;
    byte        diskErr;
    byte        NECStatus[7];
    byte        videoMode;
    unsigned    scrnWidth;
    unsigned    vidBuffSz;
    unsigned    vidBuffOfs;
    byte        cursPos[8][2];
    byte        cursBottom;
    byte        cursTop;
    byte        activeDispPage;
    unsigned    activeDispPort;
    byte        CRTModeReg;
    byte        palette;
    unsigned    dataEdgeTimeCount;
    unsigned    CRCReg;
    char        lastInputValue;
    unsigned    tick;
    int         hour;
    byte        timerOverflow;
    byte        brkStat;
    unsigned    resetFlag;
    long        hardDiskStat;
```

```
    byte        parallelTimeout[4];
    byte        serialTimeout[4];
    unsigned    kbdBuffOfs;
    unsigned    kbdBuffEnd;
} BIOSDATA;
```

TEXTBOX.H: Chapter 8

Draws single- or double-scored boxes in text mode.

```
/* textbox.h: Prototype for textbox.obj module */

void textbox (int left, int top, int right,
              int bottom, int style);
```

CURSOR.H: Chapter 8

Routines to control the appearance of the text cursor.

```
/* CURSOR.H: Prototypes for cursor appearance functions */

void cursoff (void);            /* turn hardware cursor off */
void curson (void);             /* turn hardware cursor on */
void cursShape (int top, int bottom);    /* change shape */
```

POPUP.H: Chapter 9

Routines and structures for creating and controlling pop-up windows, pull-down menus, dialog boxes, and menu bars.

```
/* POPUP.H: Prototype and typedef for POPUP.C library */

extern struct text_info;

typedef struct {
    int  left, top, right, bottom,     /* border location */
         style,                        /* border style */
```

```
          normal, hilite,              /* text attributes */
          normback, hiback, border;
  char *text;                     /* fixed text contents */
  void *save;                     /* pointer to save buffer */
  struct text_info  prev;         /* previous video state */
} POPUP;

typedef struct {
  int  row,                       /* row where bar appears */
       interval,                  /* cols between first chars */
       fore, back;                /* foreground/background colors */
  char *choice;                   /* pointer to text contents */
} MENUBAR;

void popShow (POPUP *pop);        /* display popup window */

void popErase (POPUP *pop);
        /* Erase popup window, restoring overlaid image */

void popCenter (POPUP *win, char *string);
                          /* Center string in window */

void popRewrite (POPUP *win, int row, char attrib);
        /* Rewrite pop-up row with new character attribute */

void popHilite (POPUP *win, int row);
                          /* Hilight text in popup row */

void popNormal (POPUP *win, int row);
             /* Set text in popup row to normal attribs */

void menubar (MENUBAR *spec);
             /* Write the menu bar described by spec */
```

VCOORDS.H: Chapter 11

Initialization and conversion routines for mapping an arbitrary system of
virtual coordinates used for representing graphics objects to the physical
coordinates of the display device.

```
/* VCOORDS.C: Header for implementing 800 x 600 virtual
             display area in Turbo C graphics */

#define VH 600              /* height */
#define VW 800              /* width  */

/* GLOBALS DEFINED IN LIBRARY, EXTERNALLY VISIBLE */
extern int   px, py;              /* physical x and y width */
```

```
extern double xf, yf;        /* x and y translation factors */

void setFactors (void);      /* compute translation factors */
int dx (int vx);             /* translate virt X to device X */
int dy (int vy);             /* translate virt Y to device Y */
```

BEZIER.H: Chapter 14_____

Routines for drawing Bezier curves in two dimensions.

```
/* BEZIER.H: Prototypes for drawing Bezier curves in 2D */

/* Return coordinates for current 'u' */
void bezierFcn (double *x, double *y, double u,
              double  coeff[], int n, int p[][2]);

/* Draw a Bezier curve */
void drawBezier (int p[][2], int npts, int segments);
```

PSP.H: Chapter 20_____

A data structure for accessing fields within the .EXE file's Program Segment
Prefix.

```
/* PSP.H: Defines the program segment prefix structure */

typedef struct {
  unsigned  int20h,              /* pgm term call (no value) */
            topofmem;            /* segment of top of memory */
  char      res1,                      /* reserved by DOS */
            int21h [5];              /* no value in Turbo C */
  long      oldtermvec,     /* old int 22h interrupt vector */
            oldcbvec,          /* old Ctrl-Break int vector */
            oldcritvec;    /* old critical error int vector */
  char      res2 [22];                 /* reserved area */
  unsigned  envblock;       /* segment of environment block */
  char      res3 [46],                 /* reserved area */
            avail [36],          /* FCB's: open memory */
            cmdtaillen,          /* length of command tail */
            cmdtail [127];         /* command tail text */
} PSPSTRUC;
```

EMS.H: Chapter 24

Eight basic functions for interfacing with EMM, the device driver for the
Lotus/Intel/Microsoft Expanded Memory Specification (EMS), Version 3.2
and higher.

```
/* EMS.H: Basic functions for Expanded Memory (3.n) */

#define PP0 0                    /* frame physical page offsets */
#define PP1 0x4000
#define PP2 0x8000
#define PP3 0xC000

int isEMS (void);
     /* Returns TRUE if EMS is installed, FALSE if not */

void EMSerror (int code);
      /* Print explanation of EMS error code */

int EMSstatus (void);      /* Returns EMS device status */

int EMSframe (unsigned *segment);
      /* Gets segment of 64K page frame used by EMS */
      /* Returns segment in argument */
      /* Returns success code directly */

int EMSpages (unsigned *totalPages, unsigned *freePages);
      /* Gets total EMS pages available, number of free */
      /*    pages (not already allocated), returns them  */
      /*    to the arguments (page is 16K)               */
      /* Returns success code directly.                  */

int EMSversion (unsigned *major, unsigned *minor);
      /* Returns the EMS version number via arguments */

int EMSopen (unsigned *handle, int npages);
      /* Allocates npages 16K pages to an EMS handle */
      /* Handle is returned via argument and must be */
      /*    used for all EMS I/O's                   */

int EMSmap (unsigned handle, int lpage, unsigned ppage);
      /* Ties EMS logical page associated with handle  */
      /*    to physical (frame) page so that the logical */
      /*    page can be accessed by the caller          */

int EMSclose (unsigned handle);
      /* Releases space allocated to handle and frees */
      /*    the handle for reassignment               */
```

APPENDIX D

SUGGESTED REFERENCES

A programmer's reference shelf can never be too full. Studying programming is like studying the Bible; the more sources and opinions, the better. They might all be wrong or inadequate or obtusely worded, but at least they direct you, as well as furnishing the factual background and the point of departure for your own incursions into the infinitely complex, fascinating underworld of software development.

Here are the works I found useful in writing this book, in approximate order of importance. All are cited within the text at some point or another.

C Language

Turbo C 2.0 Documentation, by Borland International, which accompanies the Turbo C product. The present book is not a surrogate manual for those who have pirated Turbo C, but rather it interacts with the official documentation. If you have obtained a "backup copy" of Turbo C from a friend, you are not only in violation of the law, but you have deprived yourself of an invaluable resource.

Note particularly the ANSI/ISO extensions, which are used in the present book and are available as a draft document either from AT&T or the involved standards organizations but not discussed in the following two references.

The C Programming Language, by Brian W. Kernighan and Dennis M. Ritchie (Englewood Cliffs, NJ: Prentice-Hall, 1978). This is the seminal work on C as a language. No C programmer's library is complete without this book. Often referred to in the literature as "K&R," it furnishes the standard by which all C implementations are measured.

The C Programming Tutor, by Leon A. Wortman and Thomas O. Sidebottom (Bowie, MD: Brady/Prentice-Hall, 1984). This book provides many workaday examples of C programming constructs. In effect, it translates the somewhat difficult language of K&R into everyday situations that C programmers need.

DOS and Related Topics: _____

Advanced MS-DOS, by Ray Duncan (Redmond, WA: Microsoft Press, 1986). Duncan is perhaps the leading writer on DOS and related topics, and his *Advanced MS-DOS* is a distillation of several other books published by Microsoft and his columns in *Dr. Dobbs' Journal, PC Magazine,* the Microsoft magazine, and other sources. If you can afford only one DOS book, get this one.

Programmer's Problem Solver for the IBM PC, XT, & AT, by Robert Jourdain (New York: Brady/Prentice Hall, 1986). Jourdain's book furnishes machine-specific, problem-oriented solutions to a number of programming issues that are not found anywhere else. Especially valuable are his insights into hardware features of the IBM-class machines and software mechanisms for accessing them.

The IBM PC-DOS Handbook, by Richard Allen King (Berkeley, CA: Sybex, Inc, 1983, updated 1987). This book fills in some gaps left by Duncan, and provides some further details.

Memory Resident Utilities, Interrupts, and Disk Management with MS & PC DOS, by Michael Hyman (Portland, OR: Management Information Source, Inc., 1987). Hyman offers short, succint, and highly practical chapters that deal with difficult programming issues.

Technical Reference (DOS and the target machine), published either by IBM, Microsoft, or the machine's vendor. These are terse manuals sold at added cost with a machine or separately by the vendor. They furnish no-frills, machine-specific information about supported DOS commands, options, and (in the machine manual) a listing of the ROM BIOS.

Inside the IBM PC, by Peter Norton (New York: Brady Books, 1986). The leading expert on the IBM PC architecture offers a lucid discourse on a variety of topics interesting to programmers in the PC environment. An essential background work for enhancing one's understandings of the machine's inner workings.

INDEX

ABOUT THE AUTHOR

Stretching **Turbo C** is Kent Porter's seventeenth book. All but one of these books deal with computers and software. In addition to books, Porter writes the monthly Structured Programming column for *Dr. Dobbs' Journal* and the Micro Connections column for *Database Programming and Design*, plus feature articles and product reviews for these and other leading computer magazines. He has also lectured and led seminars on software development both in the United States and overseas. In 1988, he was a guest lecturer at the Computer Science Department of a German engineering school.

Porter lives and works in Silicon Valley, where he is the Senior Technical Editor for the renowned *Dr. Dobb's Journal*, the magazine that made C the language of choice for microcomputer systems software.

A Californian, Porter holds a B.S. in Information Systems from the University of San Francisco.